Recast is the magical adventure story of a boy,

JD, who wants to be the Master of Magicians

in a world full of magical particles, BOXES.

JD is chased by assassins and monsters

because of his latent abilities, which had been secret.

God sends enemies against JD and just watches.

Will JD become the Master of Magicians?

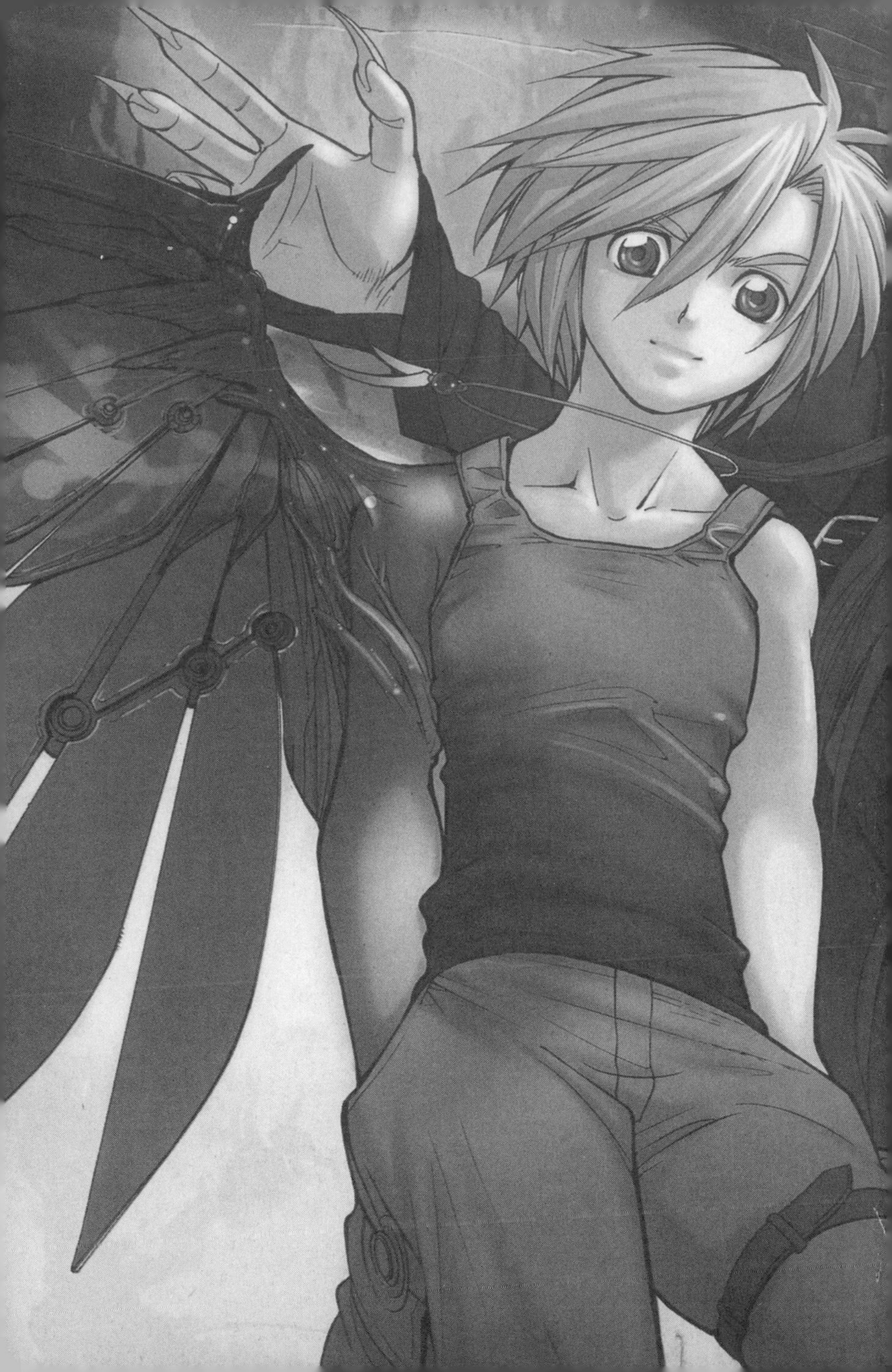

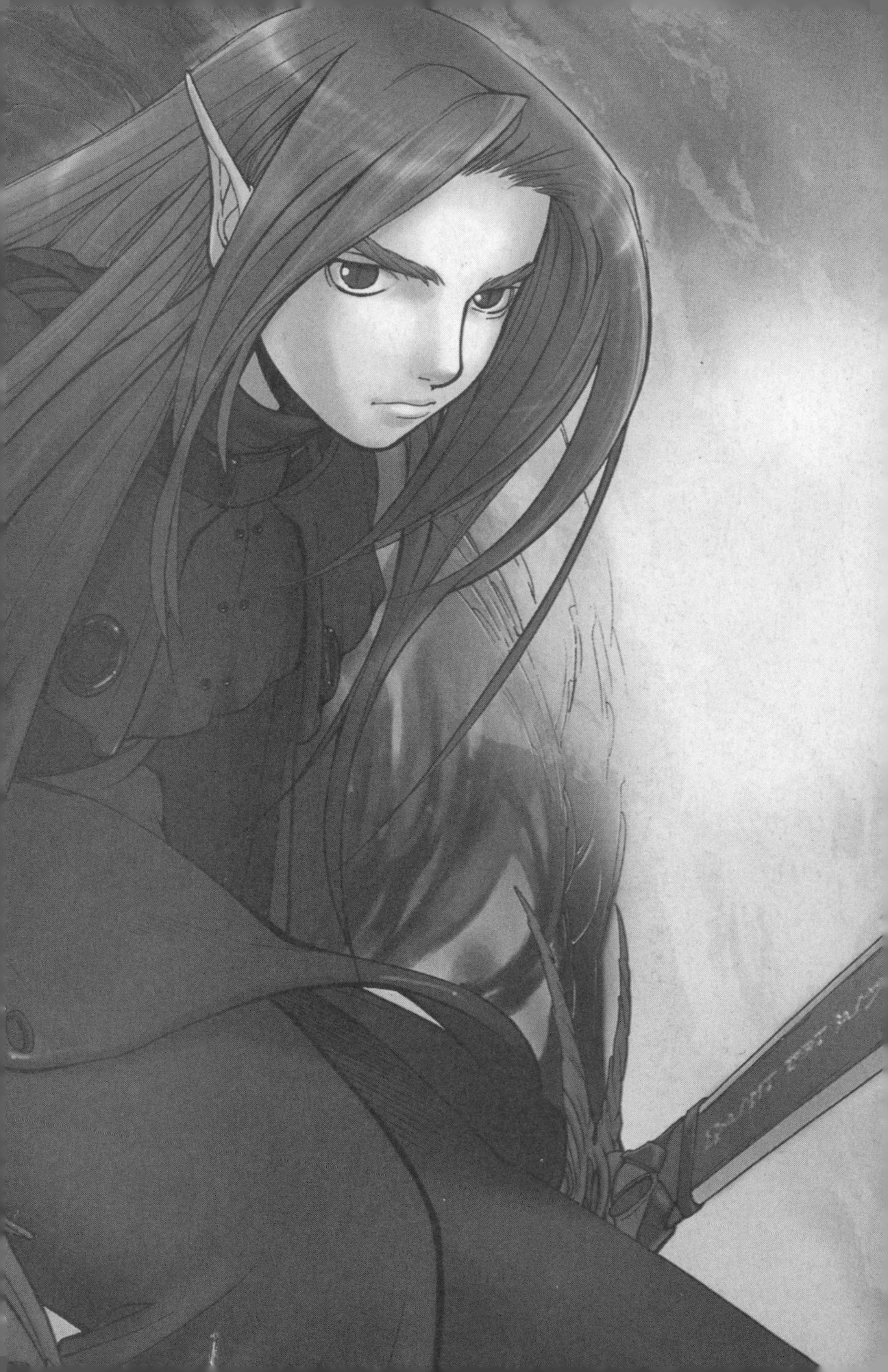

Recast Vol. 2
Created by Seung-Hui Kye

Translation - Woo Sok Park
Retouch and Lettering - Star Print Brokers
Production Artist - Michael Paolilli
Graphic Designer - James Lee

Editor - Hope Donovan
Digital Imaging Manager - Chris Buford
Pre-Production Supervisor - Erika Terriquez
Art Director - Anne Marie Horne
Production Manager - Elisabeth Brizzi
Managing Editor - Vy Nguyen
VP of Production - Ron Klamert
Editor-in-Chief - Rob Tokar
Publisher - Mike Kiley
President and C.O.O. - John Parker
C.E.O. and Chief Creative Officer - Stuart Levy

A **TOKYOPOP**® Manga

TOKYOPOP and 🐱 are trademarks or registered trademarks of TOKYOPOP Inc.

TOKYOPOP Inc.
5900 Wilshire Blvd. Suite 2000
Los Angeles, CA 90036

E-mail: info@TOKYOPOP.com
Come visit us online at www.TOKYOPOP.com

ISBN: 978-1-59816-665-1

First TOKYOPOP printing: March 2007
10 9 8 7 6 5 4 3 2 1
Printed in the USA

VOLUME 2

by
Seung-Hui Kye

HAMBURG // LONDON // LOS ANGELES // TOKYO

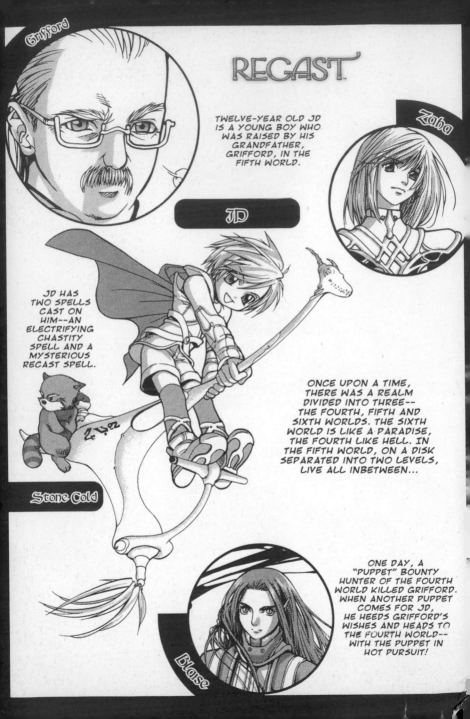

REGAST

Grifford

JD

Zaha

Stone Cold

Blaze

TWELVE-YEAR OLD JD IS A YOUNG BOY WHO WAS RAISED BY HIS GRANDFATHER, GRIFFORD, IN THE FIFTH WORLD.

JD HAS TWO SPELLS CAST ON HIM--AN ELECTRIFYING CHASTITY SPELL AND A MYSTERIOUS RECAST SPELL.

ONCE UPON A TIME, THERE WAS A REALM DIVIDED INTO THREE-- THE FOURTH, FIFTH AND SIXTH WORLDS. THE SIXTH WORLD IS LIKE A PARADISE, THE FOURTH LIKE HELL. IN THE FIFTH WORLD, ON A DISK SEPARATED INTO TWO LEVELS, LIVE ALL INBETWEEN...

ONE DAY, A "PUPPET" BOUNTY HUNTER OF THE FOURTH WORLD KILLED GRIFFORD. WHEN ANOTHER PUPPET COMES FOR JD, HE HEEDS GRIFFORD'S WISHES AND HEADS TO THE FOURTH WORLD-- WITH THE PUPPET IN HOT PURSUIT!

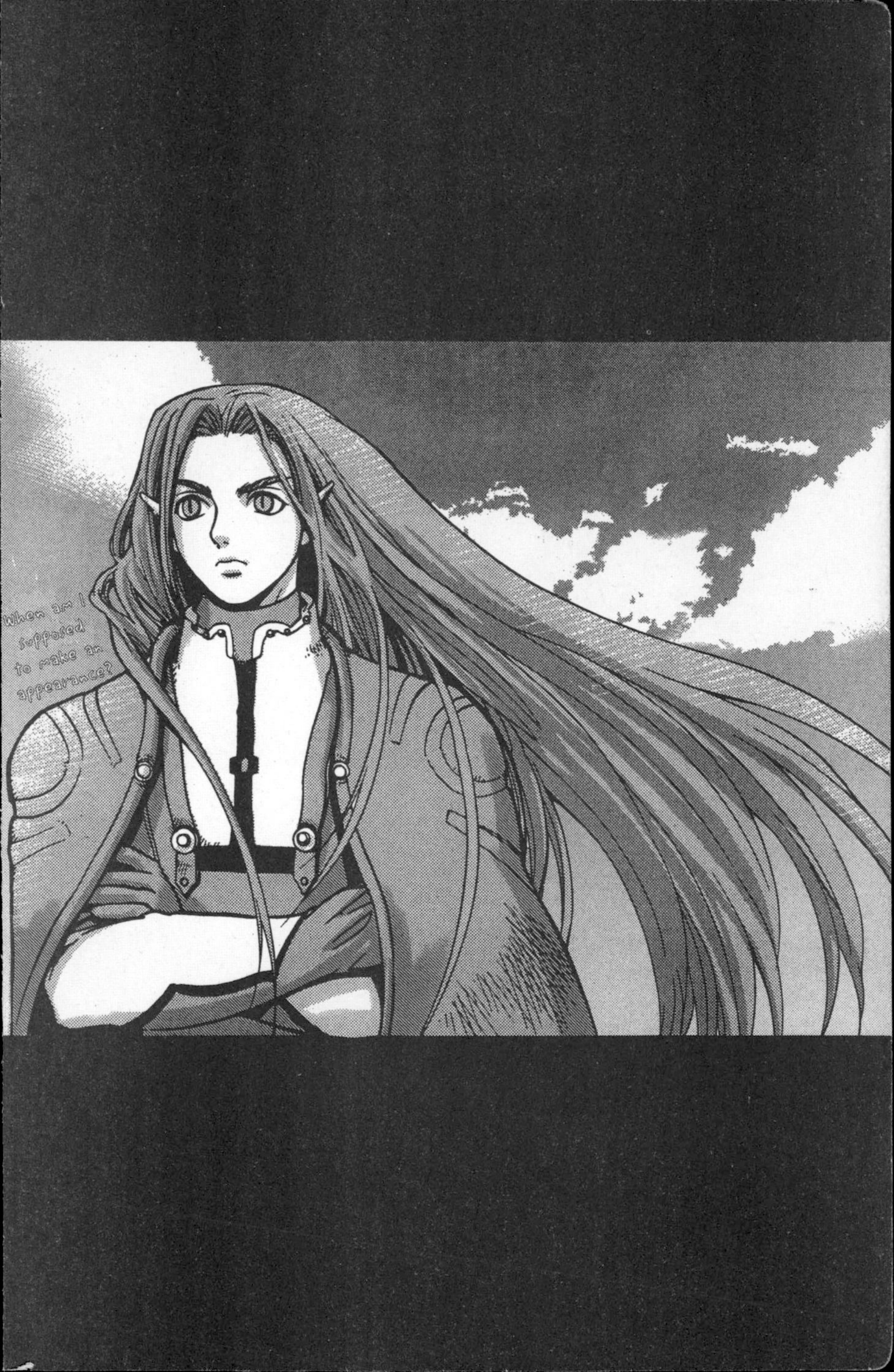
When am I supposed to make an appearance?

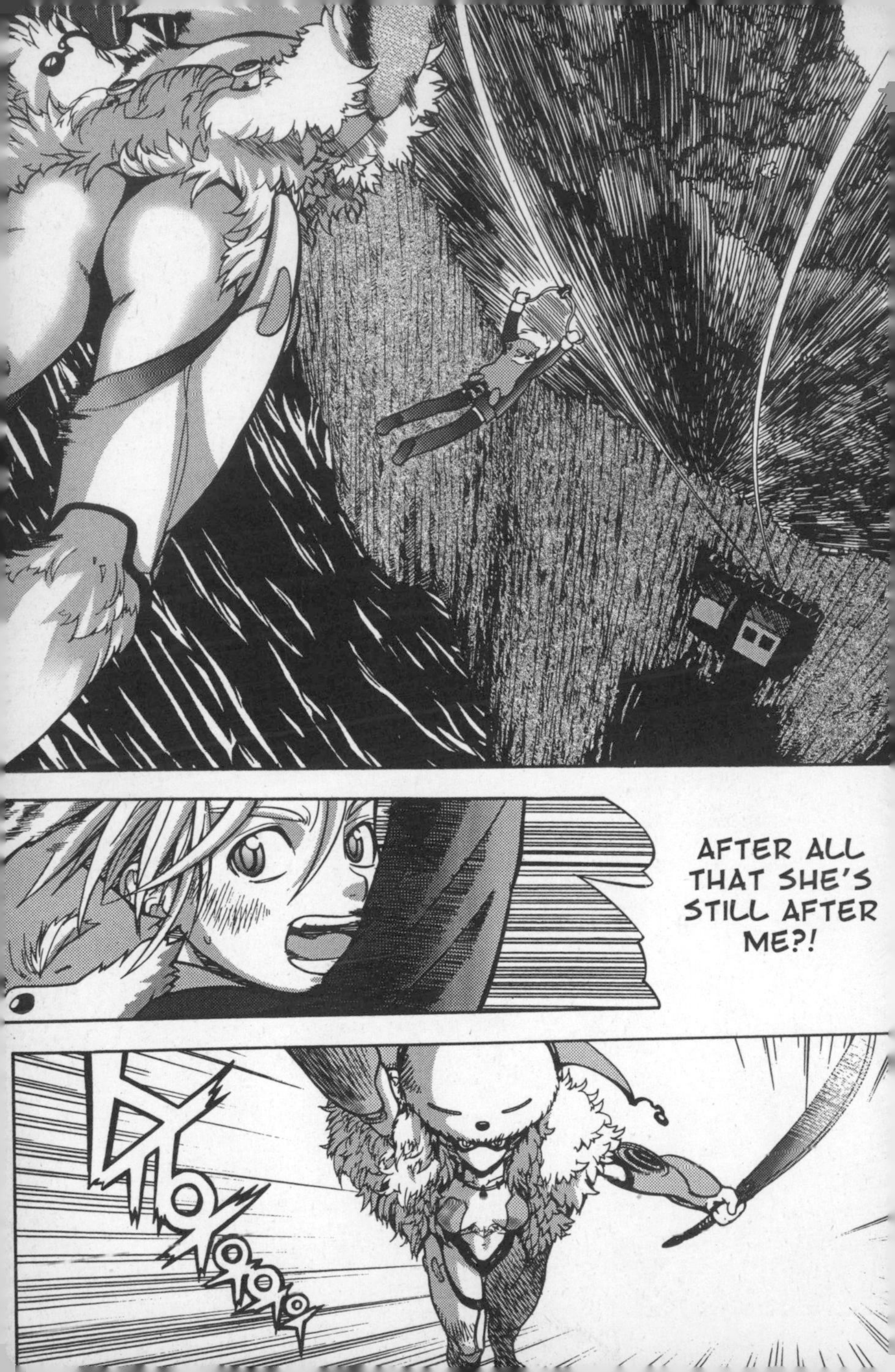
AFTER ALL THAT SHE'S STILL AFTER ME?!

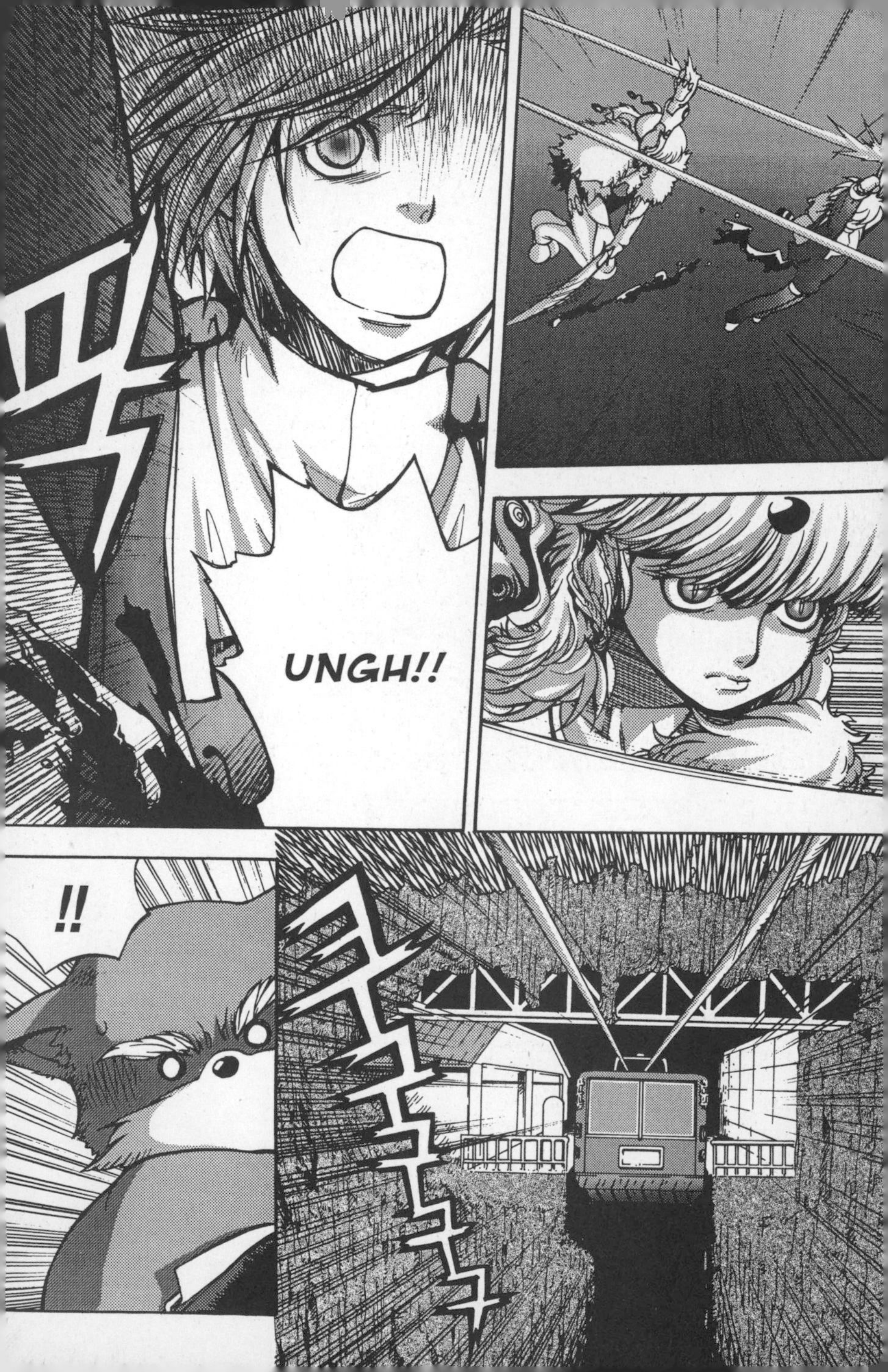
UNGH!!
!!

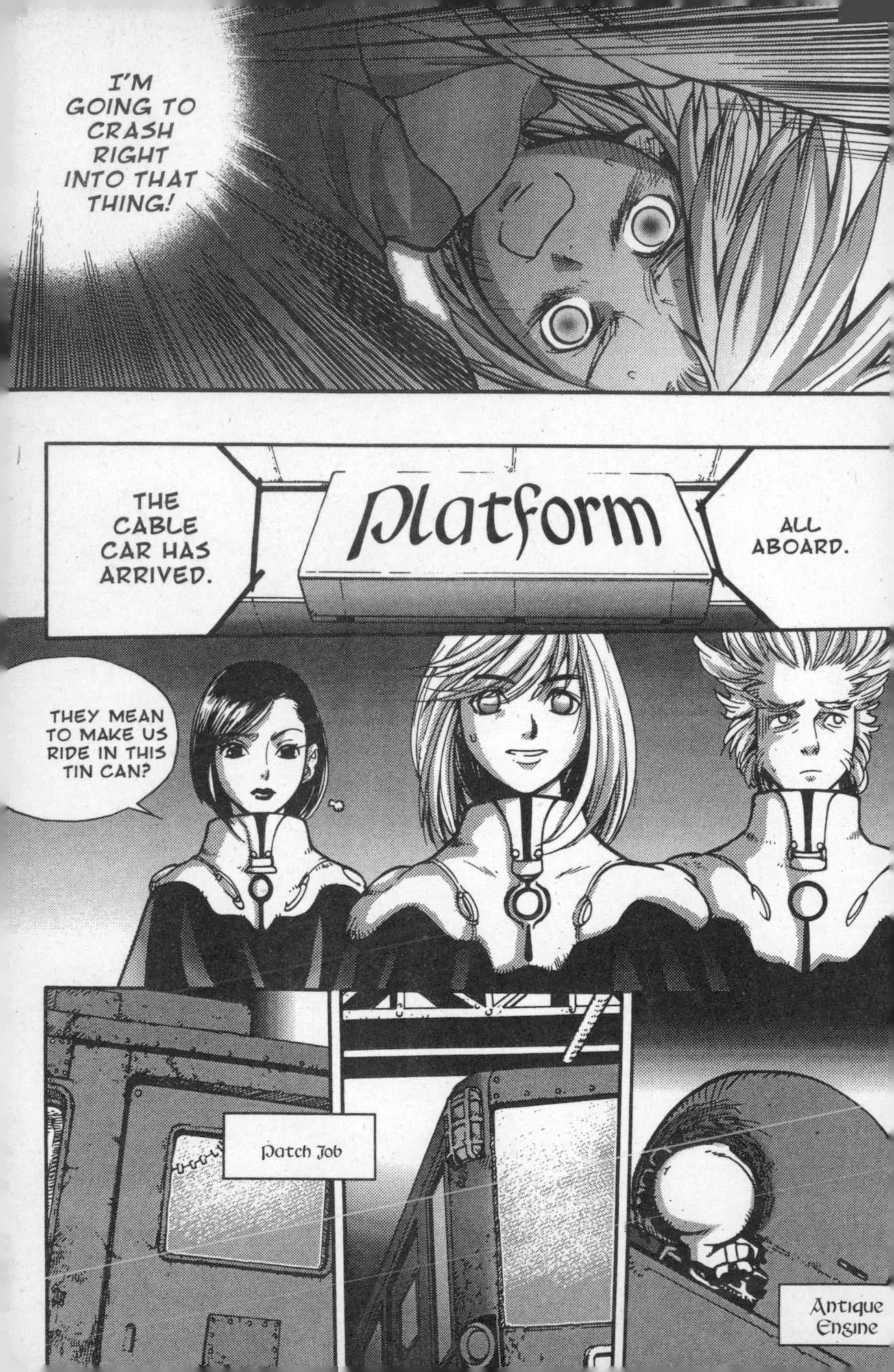
I'M GOING TO CRASH RIGHT INTO THAT THING!
THE CABLE CAR HAS ARRIVED.
Platform
ALL ABOARD.
THEY MEAN TO MAKE US RIDE IN THIS TIN CAN?
Patch Job
Antique Engine

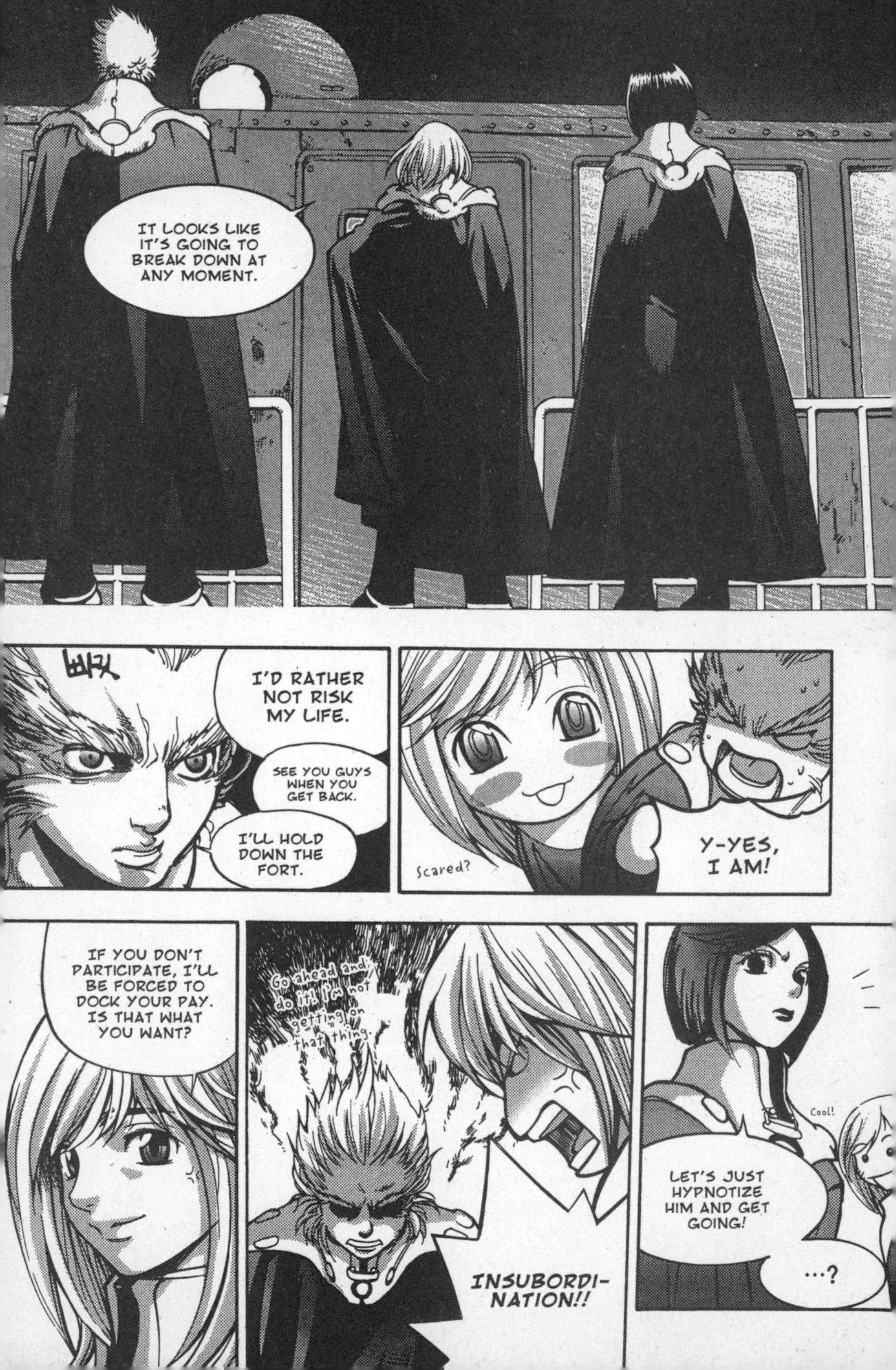
IT LOOKS LIKE IT'S GOING TO BREAK DOWN AT ANY MOMENT.
I'D RATHER NOT RISK MY LIFE.
SEE YOU GUYS WHEN YOU GET BACK.
I'LL HOLD DOWN THE FORT.
Scared?
Y-YES, I AM!
IF YOU DON'T PARTICIPATE, I'LL BE FORCED TO DOCK YOUR PAY. IS THAT WHAT YOU WANT?
Go ahead and do it! I'm not getting on that thing.
INSUBORDI-NATION!!
Cool!
LET'S JUST HYPNOTIZE HIM AND GET GOING!
...?

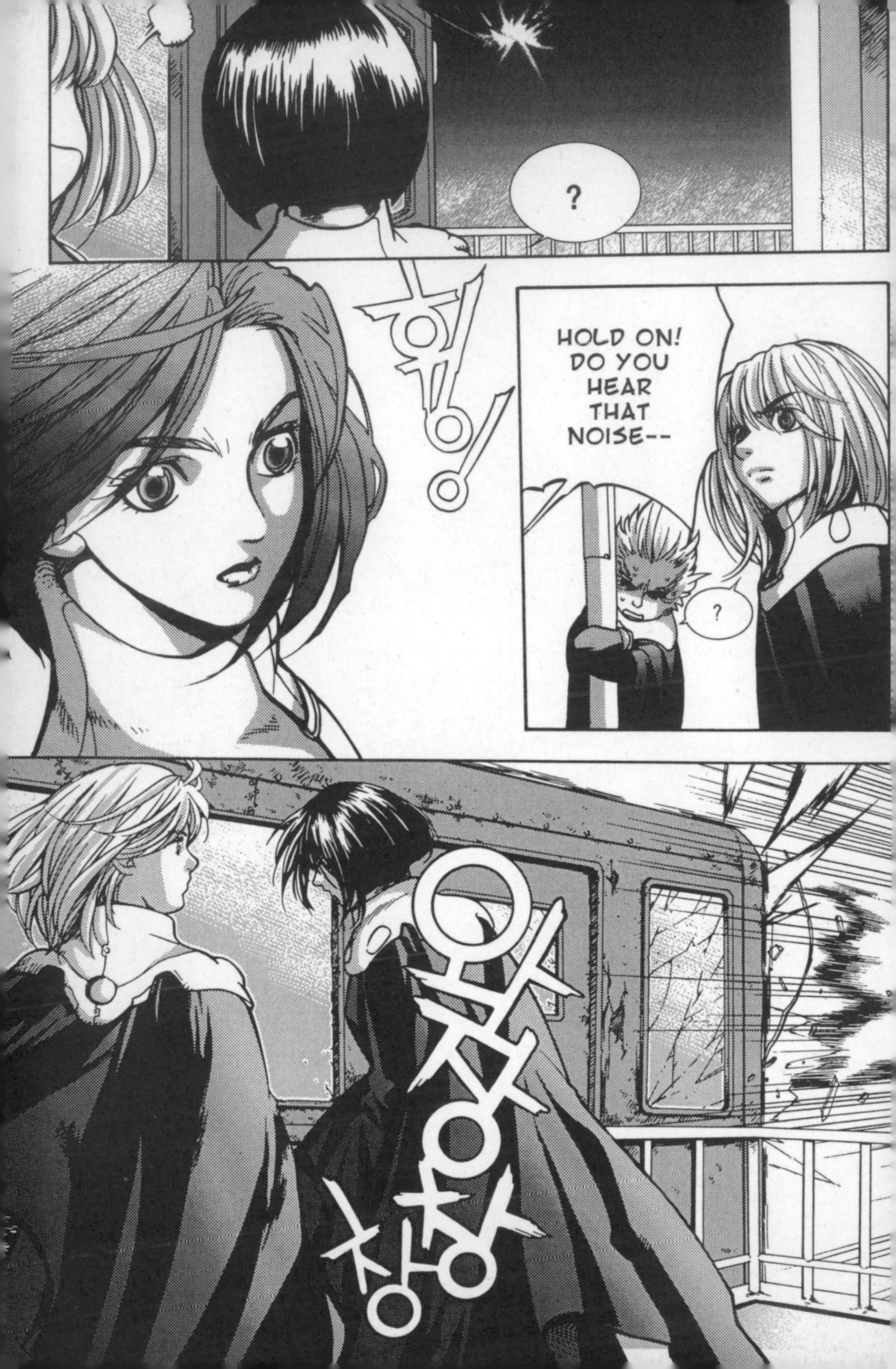
?
HOLD ON! DO YOU HEAR THAT NOISE--
?

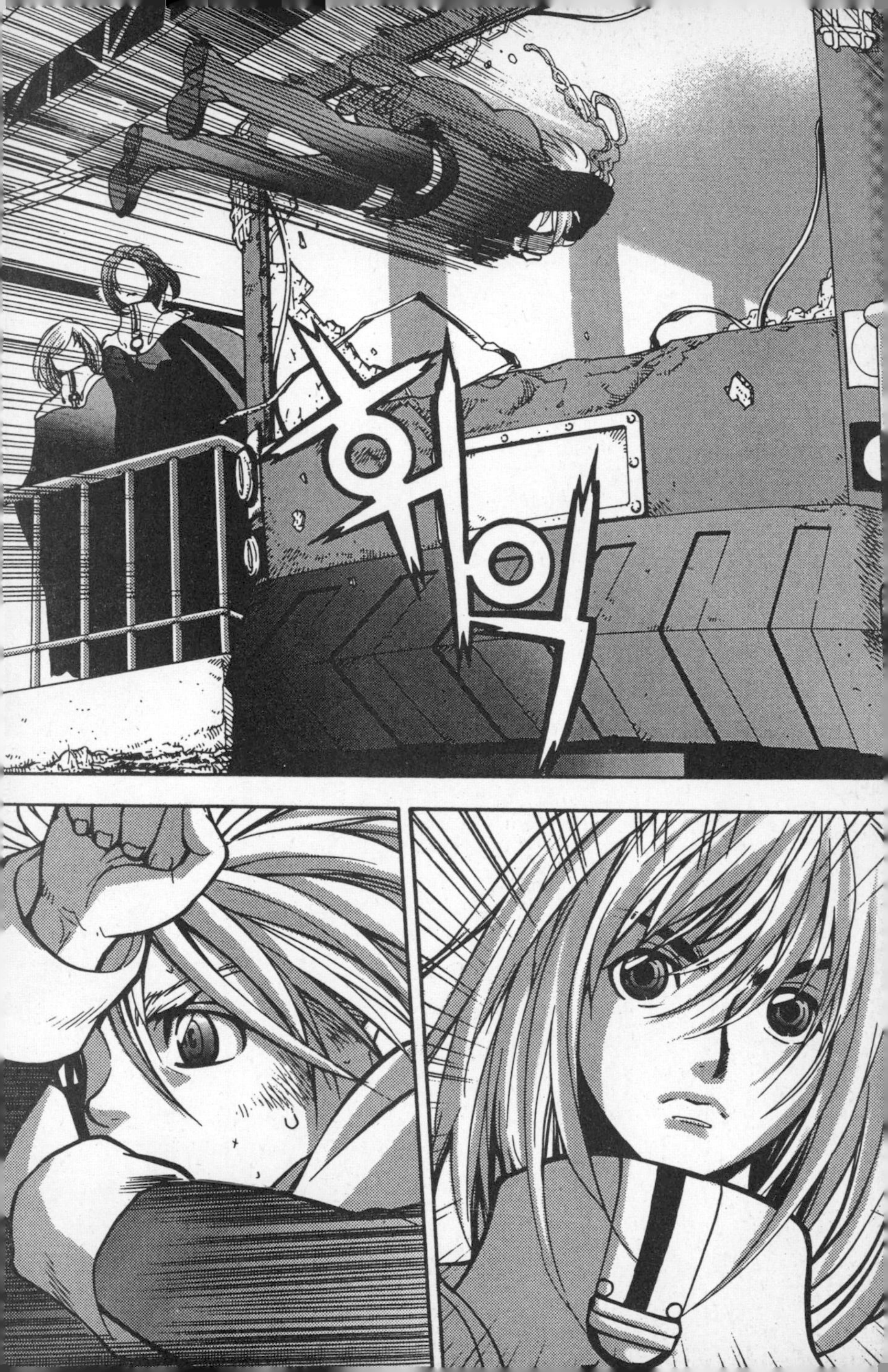

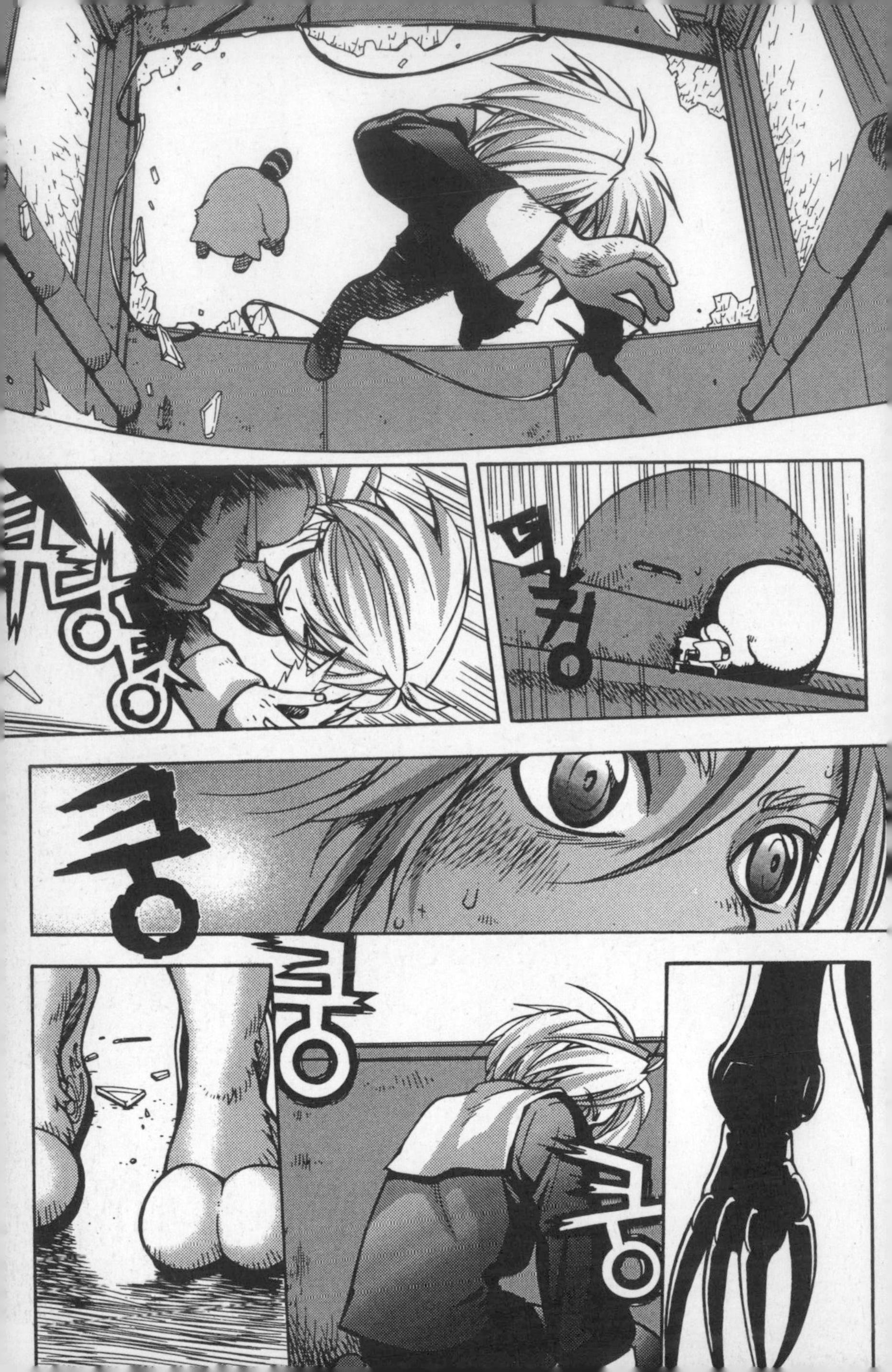

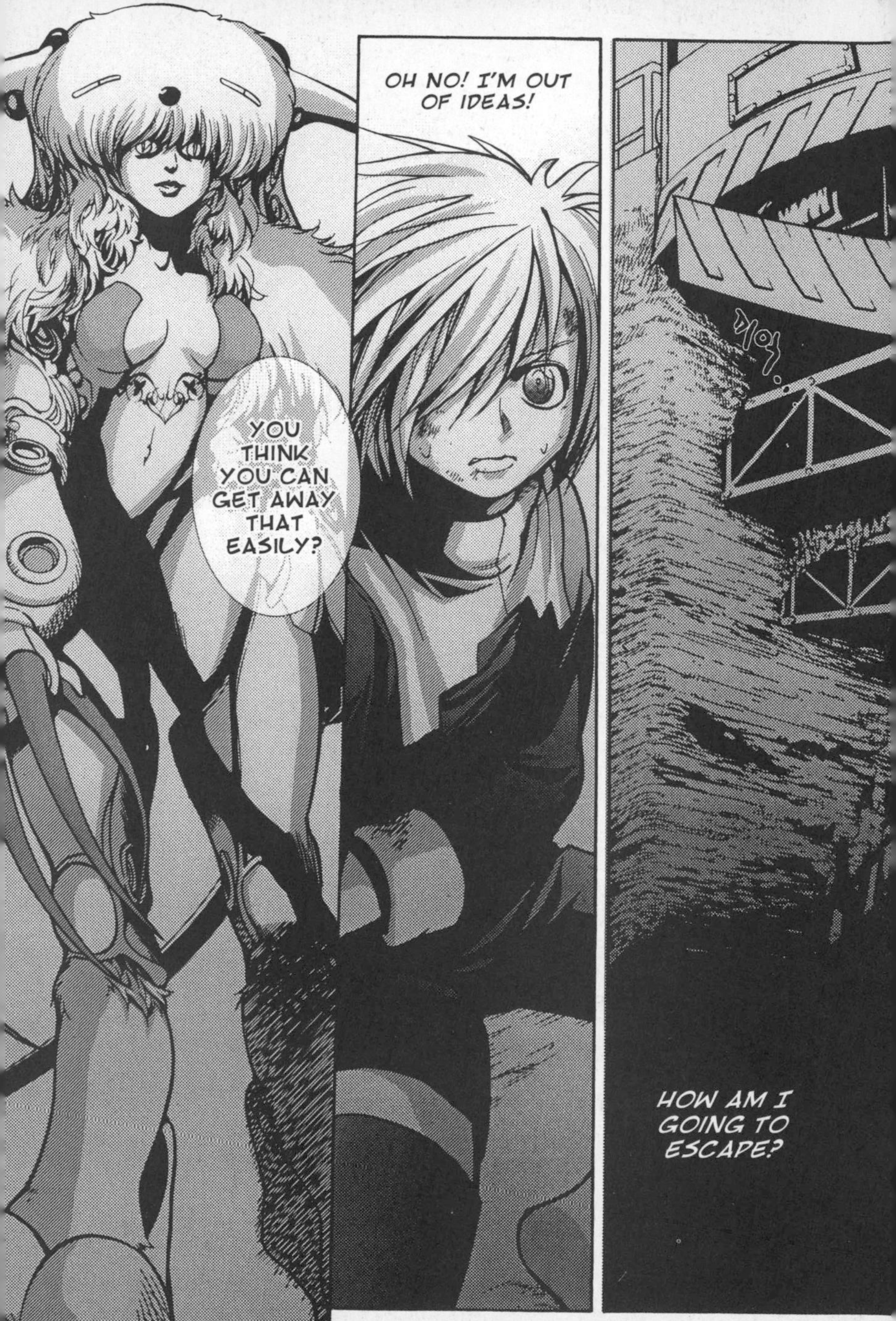
YOU THINK YOU CAN GET AWAY THAT EASILY?
OH NO! I'M OUT OF IDEAS!
HOW AM I GOING TO ESCAPE?

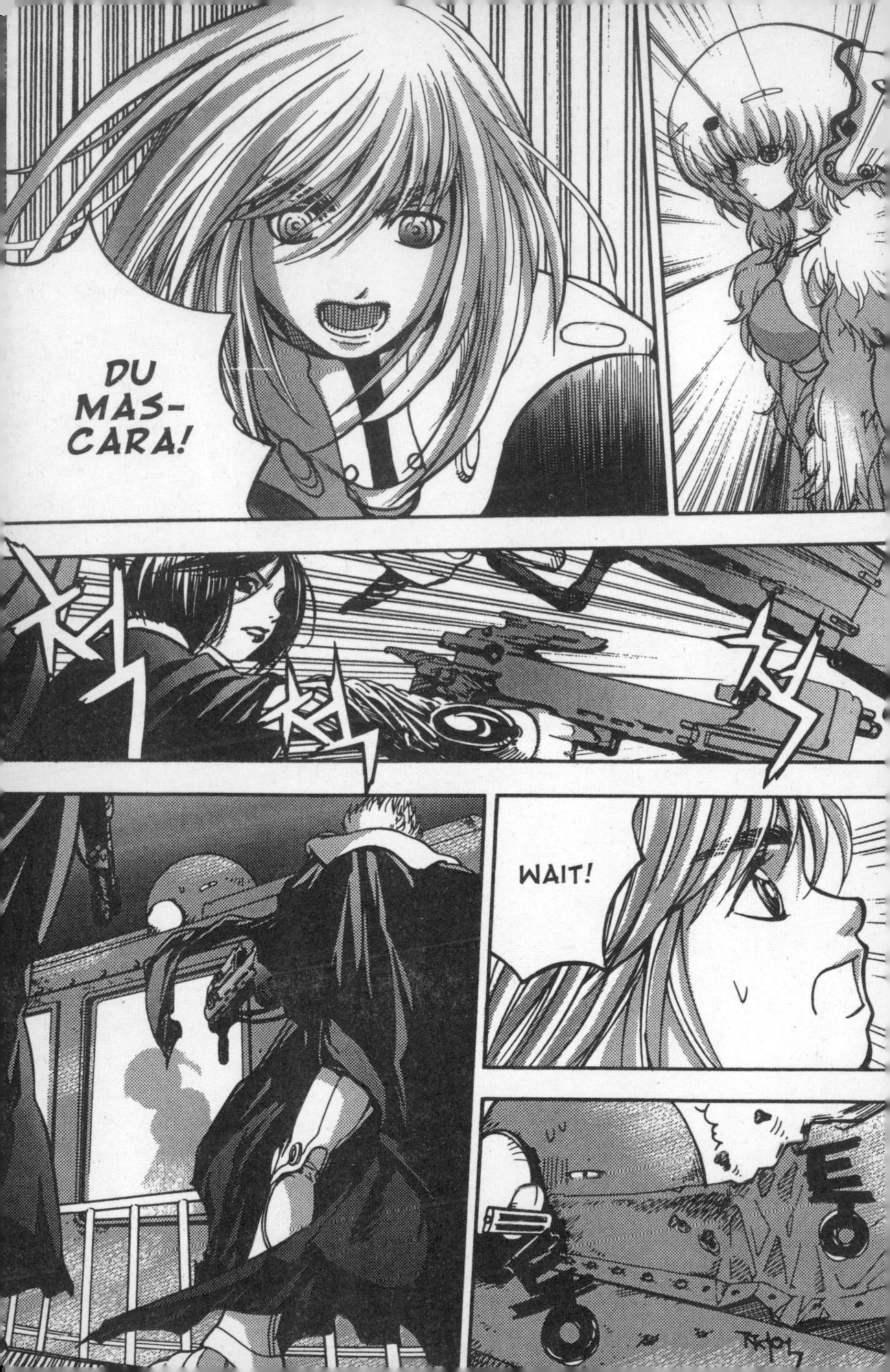
DU MAS-CARA!
WAIT!

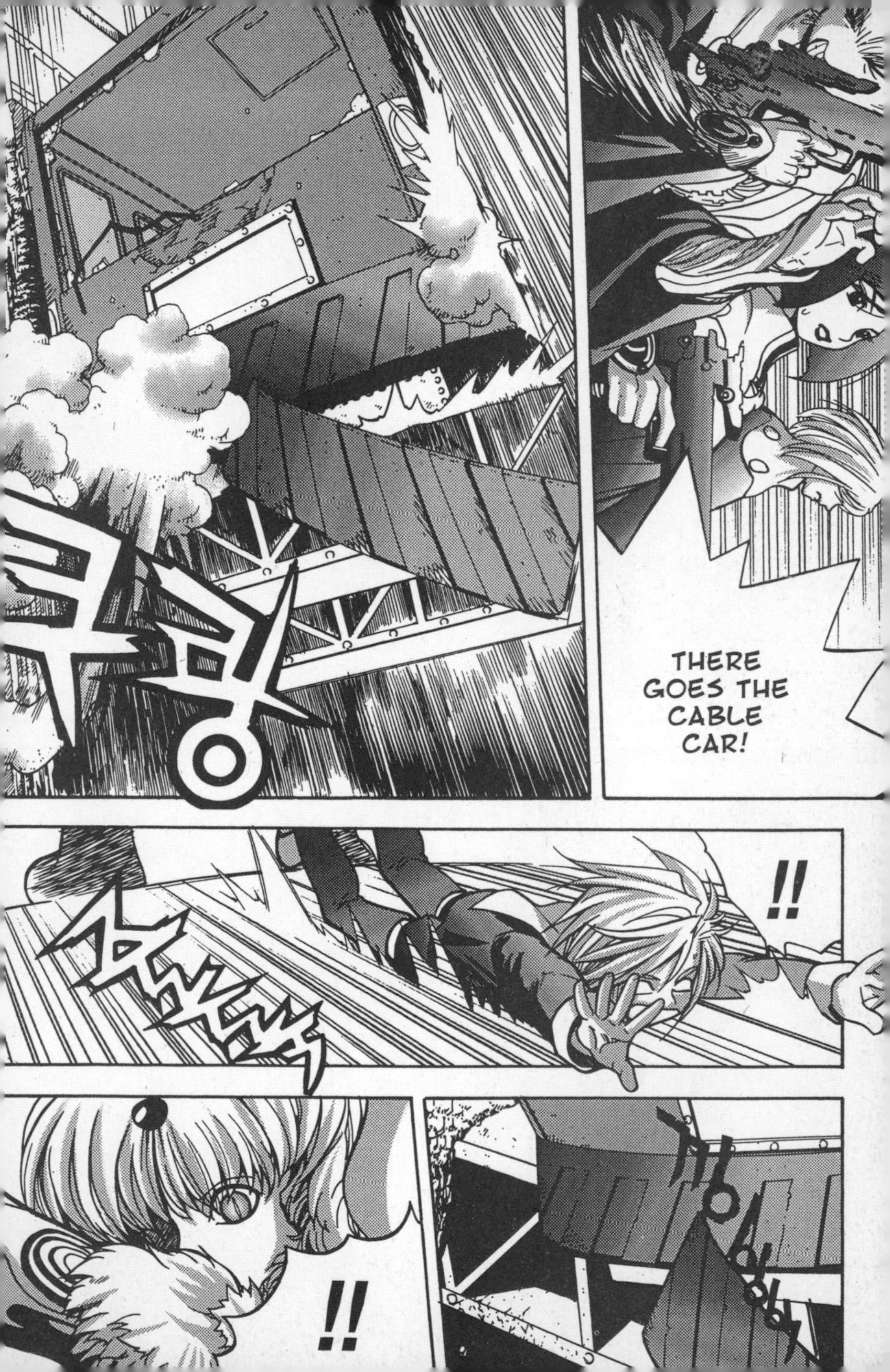
THERE GOES THE CABLE CAR!
!!
!!

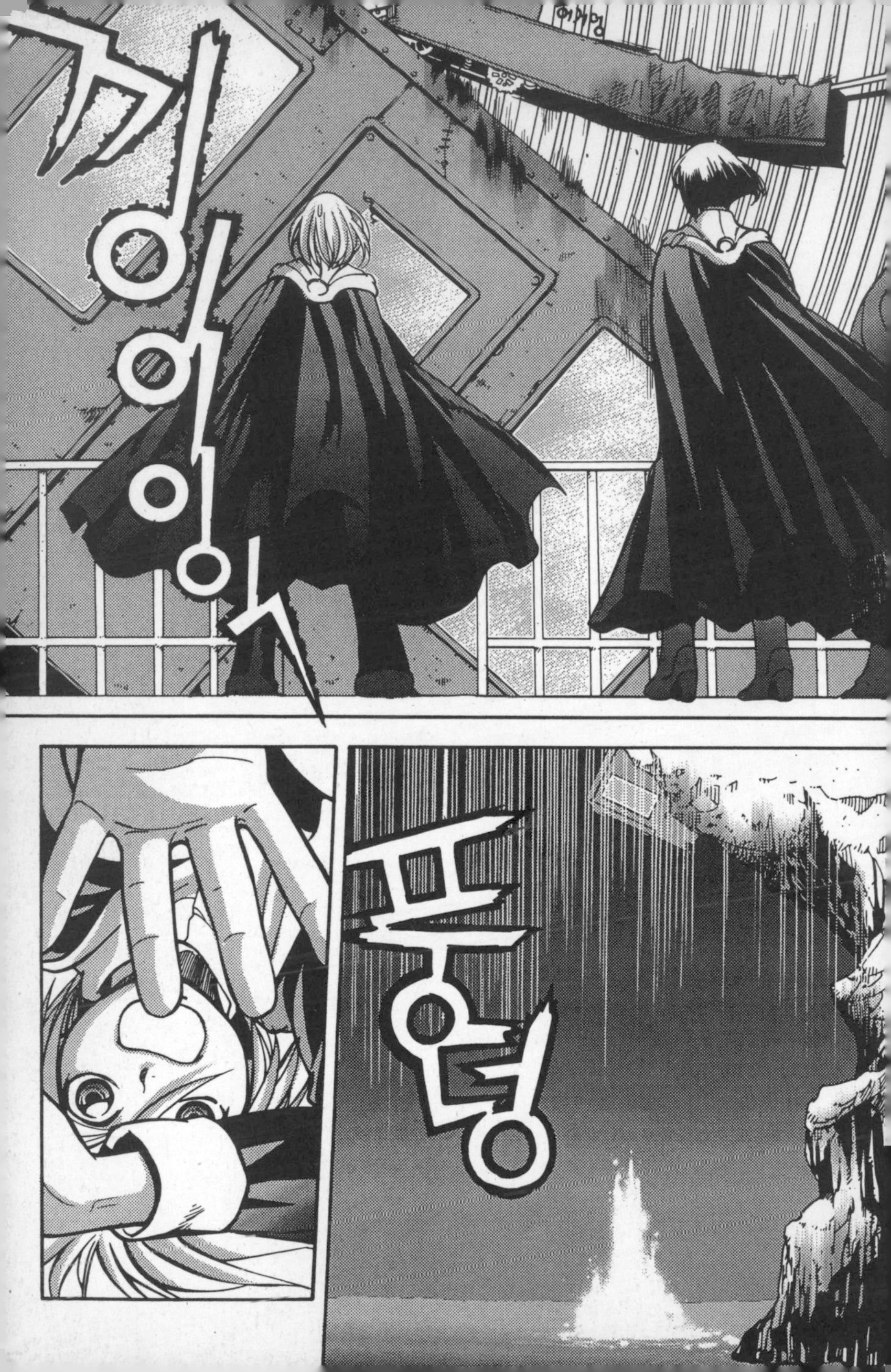
까아아앙
풍덩

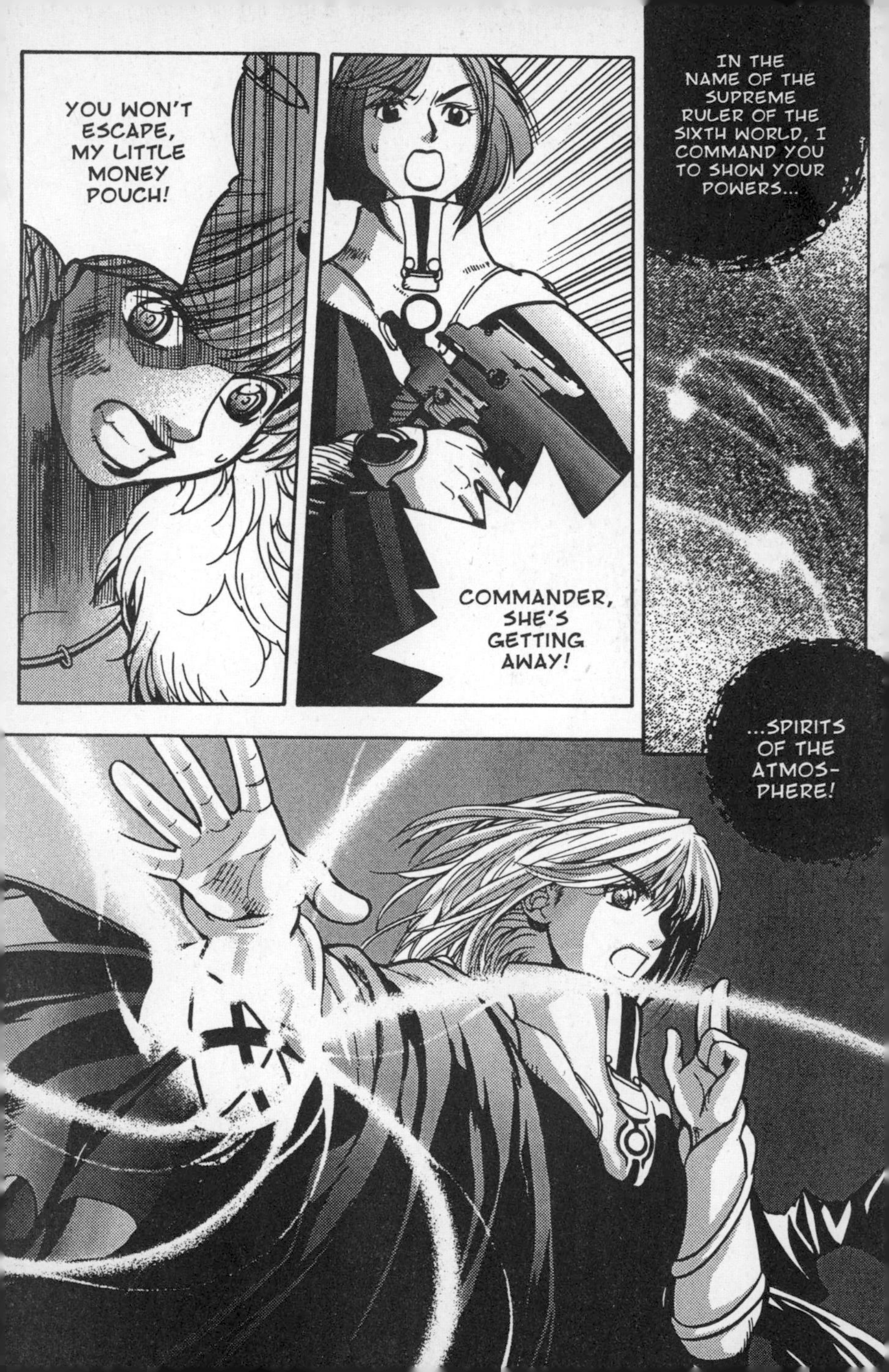
YOU WON'T ESCAPE, MY LITTLE MONEY POUCH!
COMMANDER, SHE'S GETTING AWAY!
IN THE NAME OF THE SUPREME RULER OF THE SIXTH WORLD, I COMMAND YOU TO SHOW YOUR POWERS...
...SPIRITS OF THE ATMOS-PHERE!

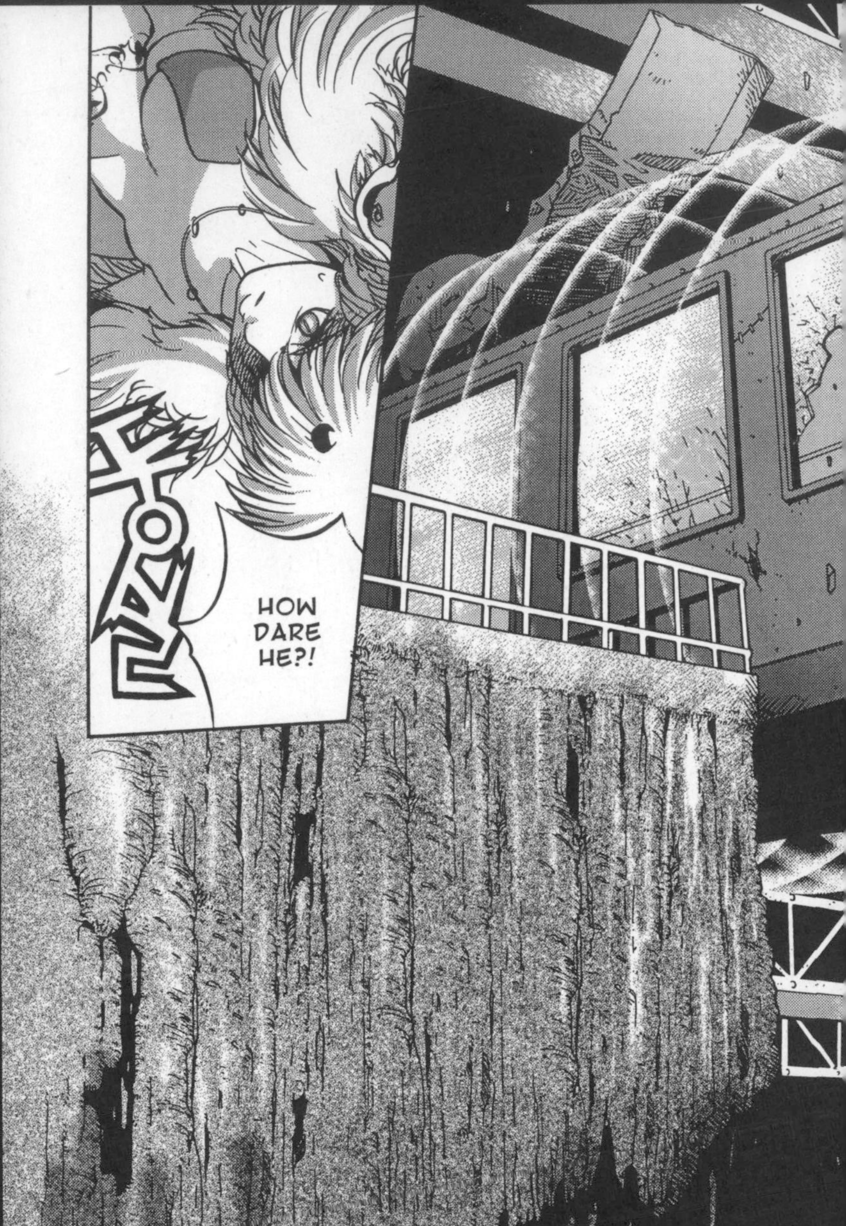
HOW DARE HE?!

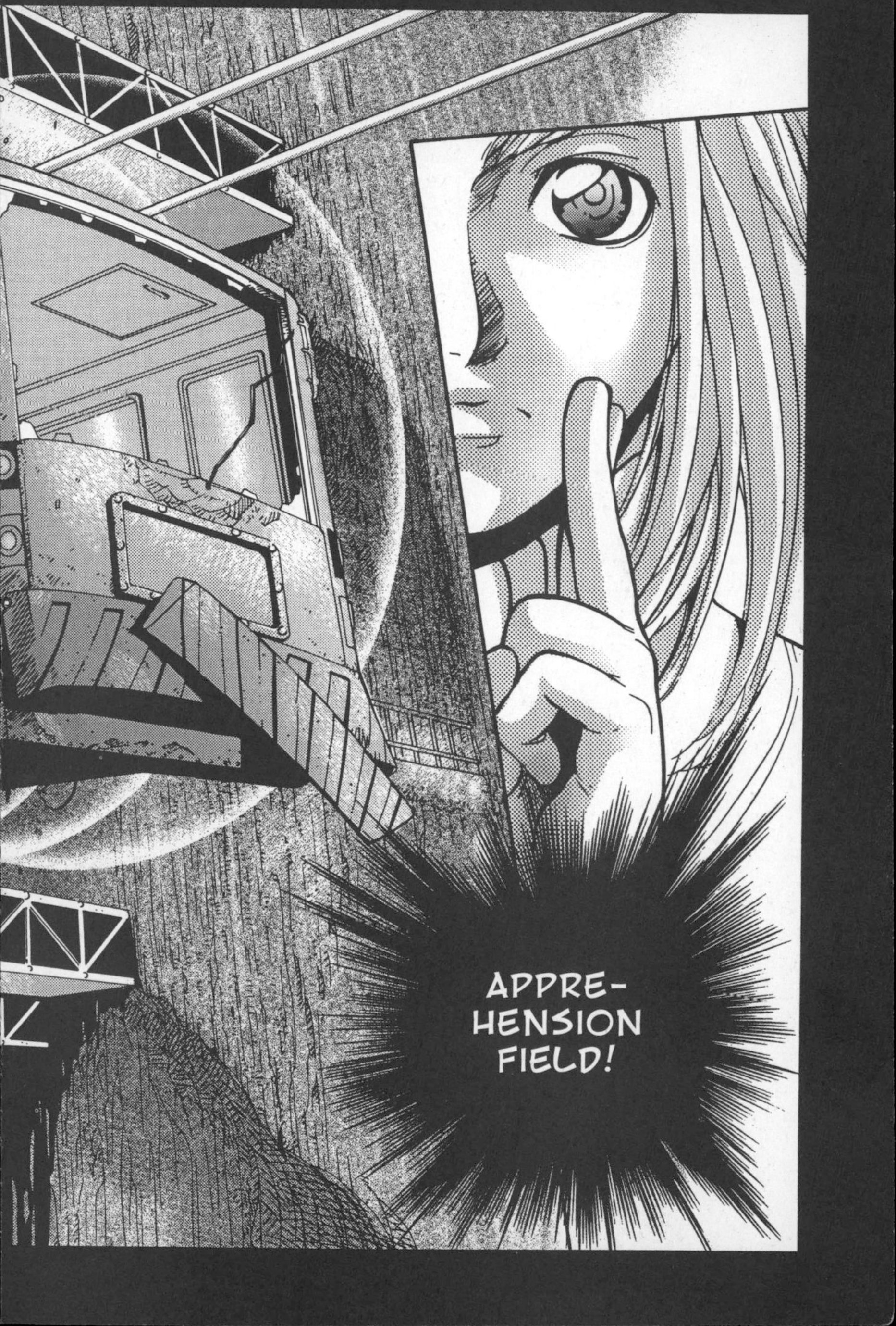
APPRE-
HENSION
FIELD!

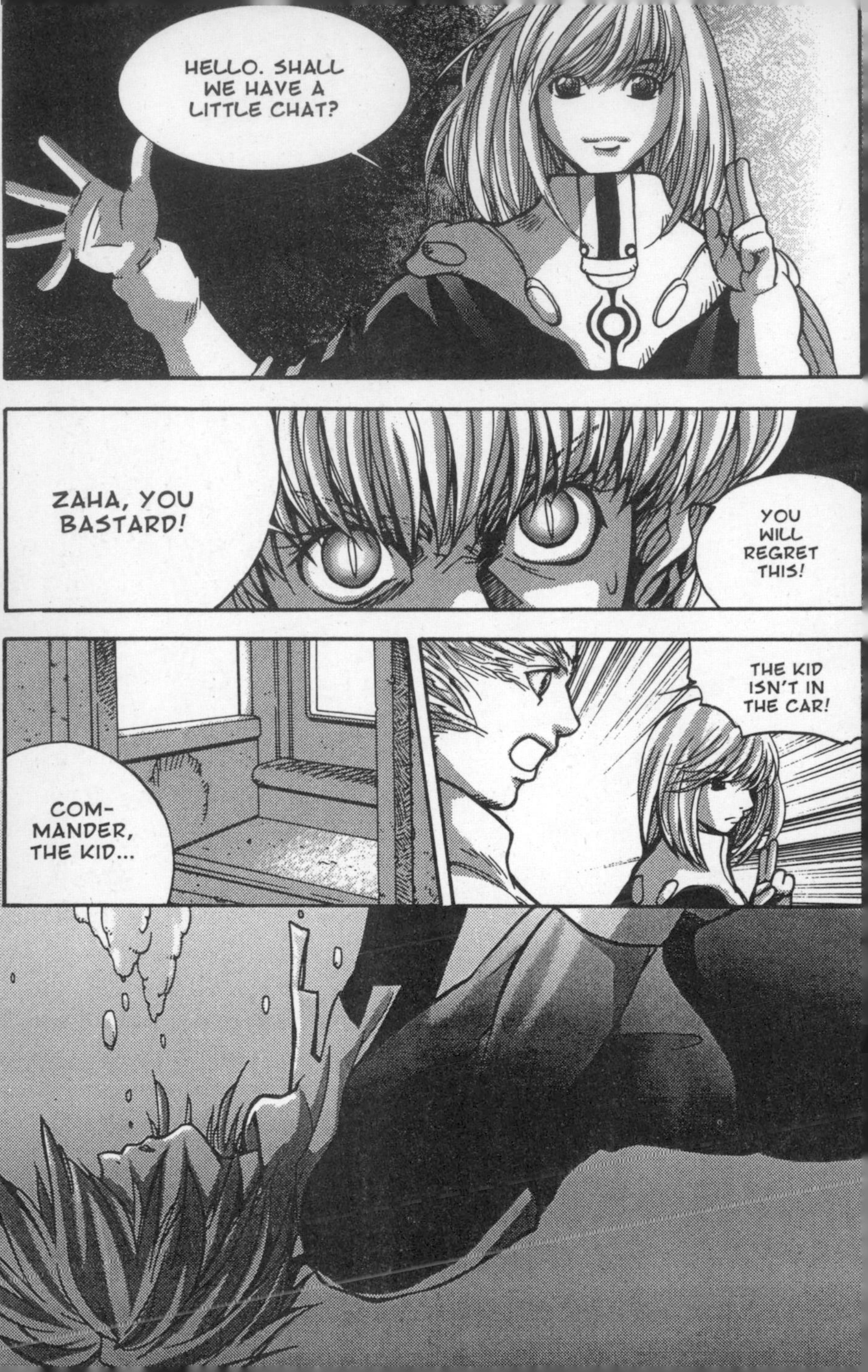
HELLO. SHALL WE HAVE A LITTLE CHAT?
ZAHA, YOU BASTARD!
YOU WILL REGRET THIS!
COM-MANDER, THE KID...
THE KID ISN'T IN THE CAR!

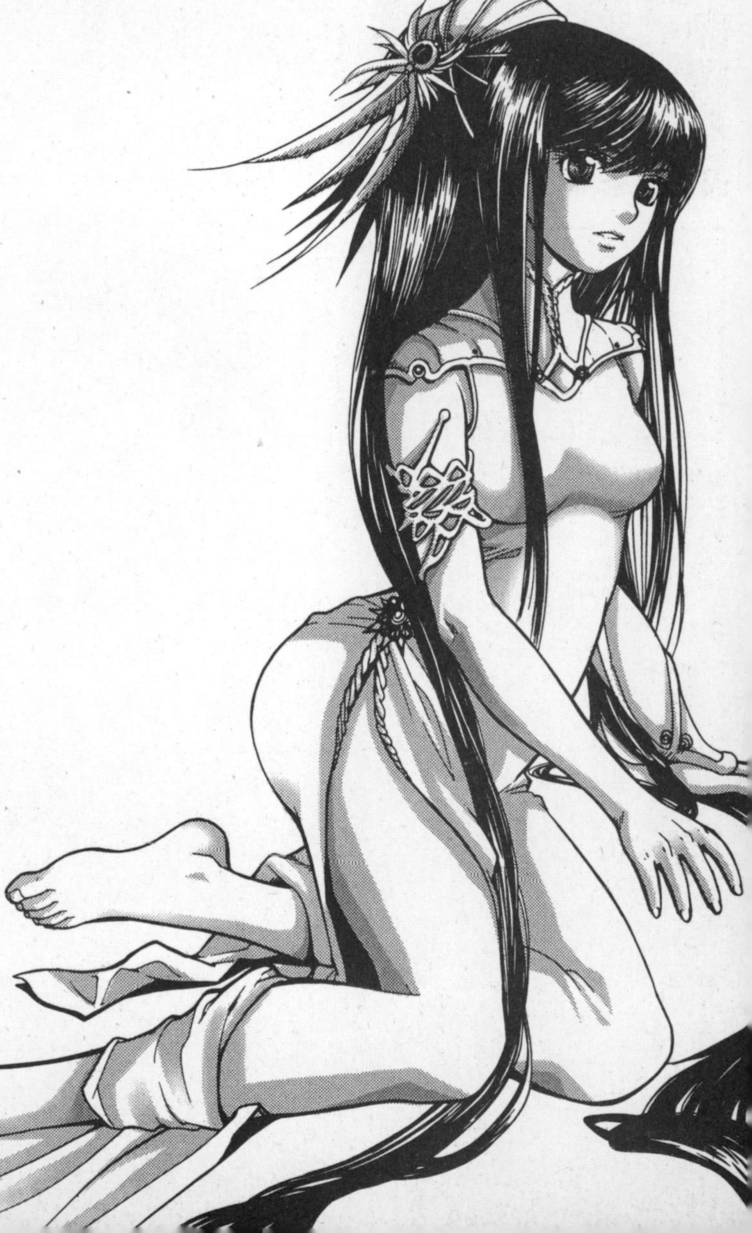

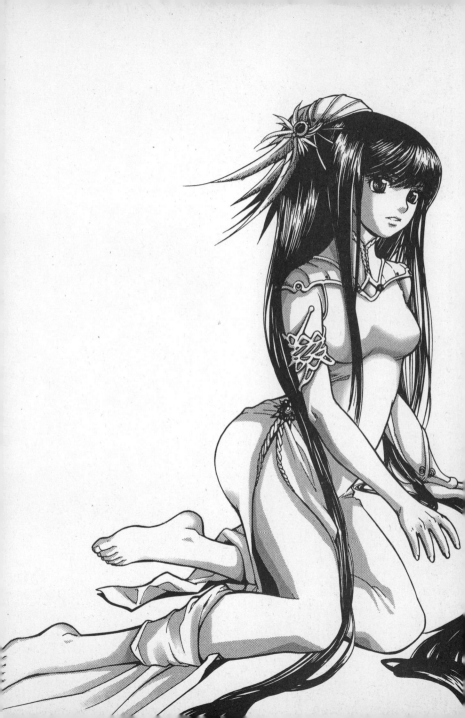

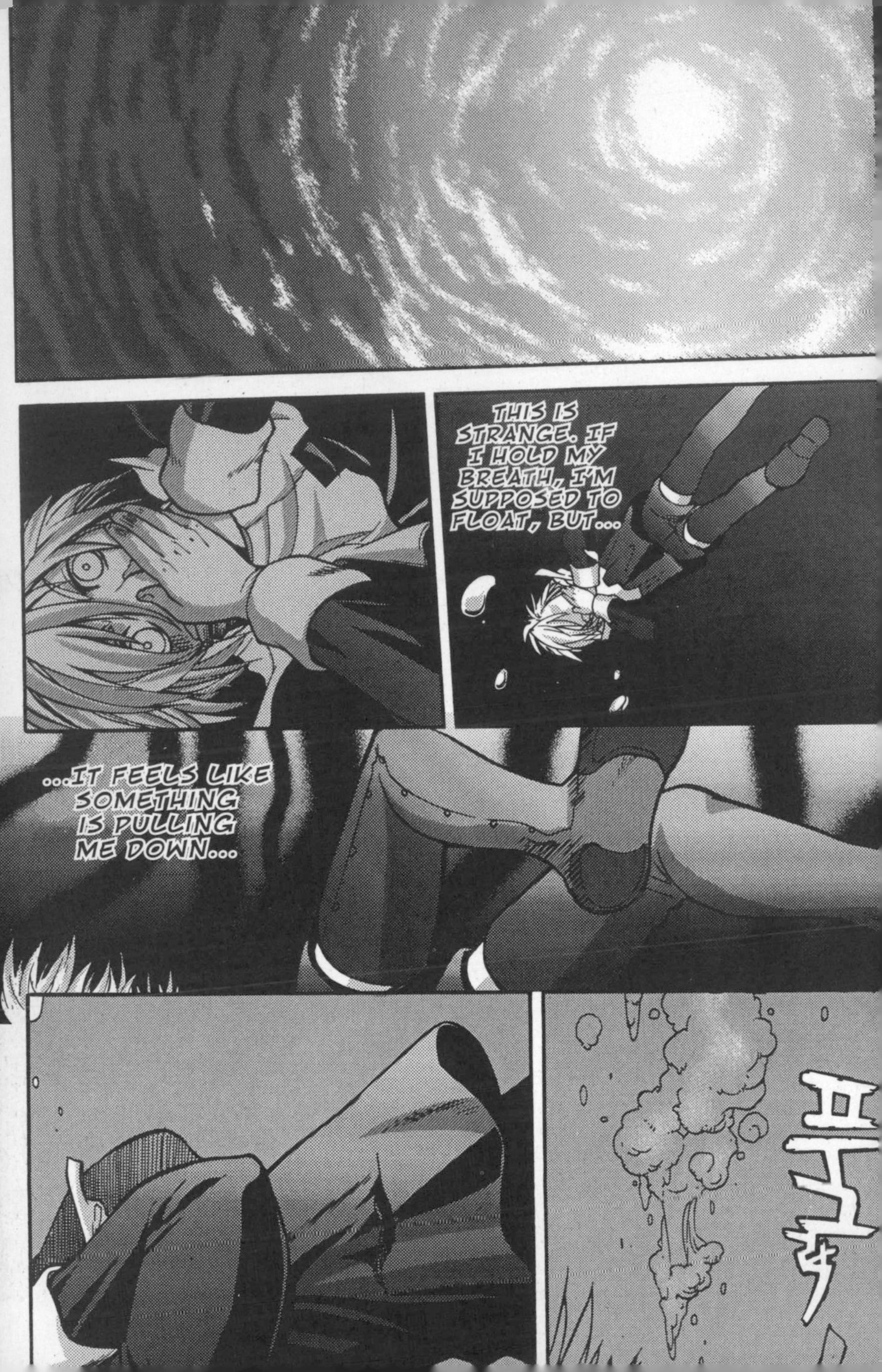
THIS IS STRANGE. IF I HOLD MY BREATH, I'M SUPPOSED TO FLOAT, BUT...
...IT FEELS LIKE SOMETHING IS PULLING ME DOWN...

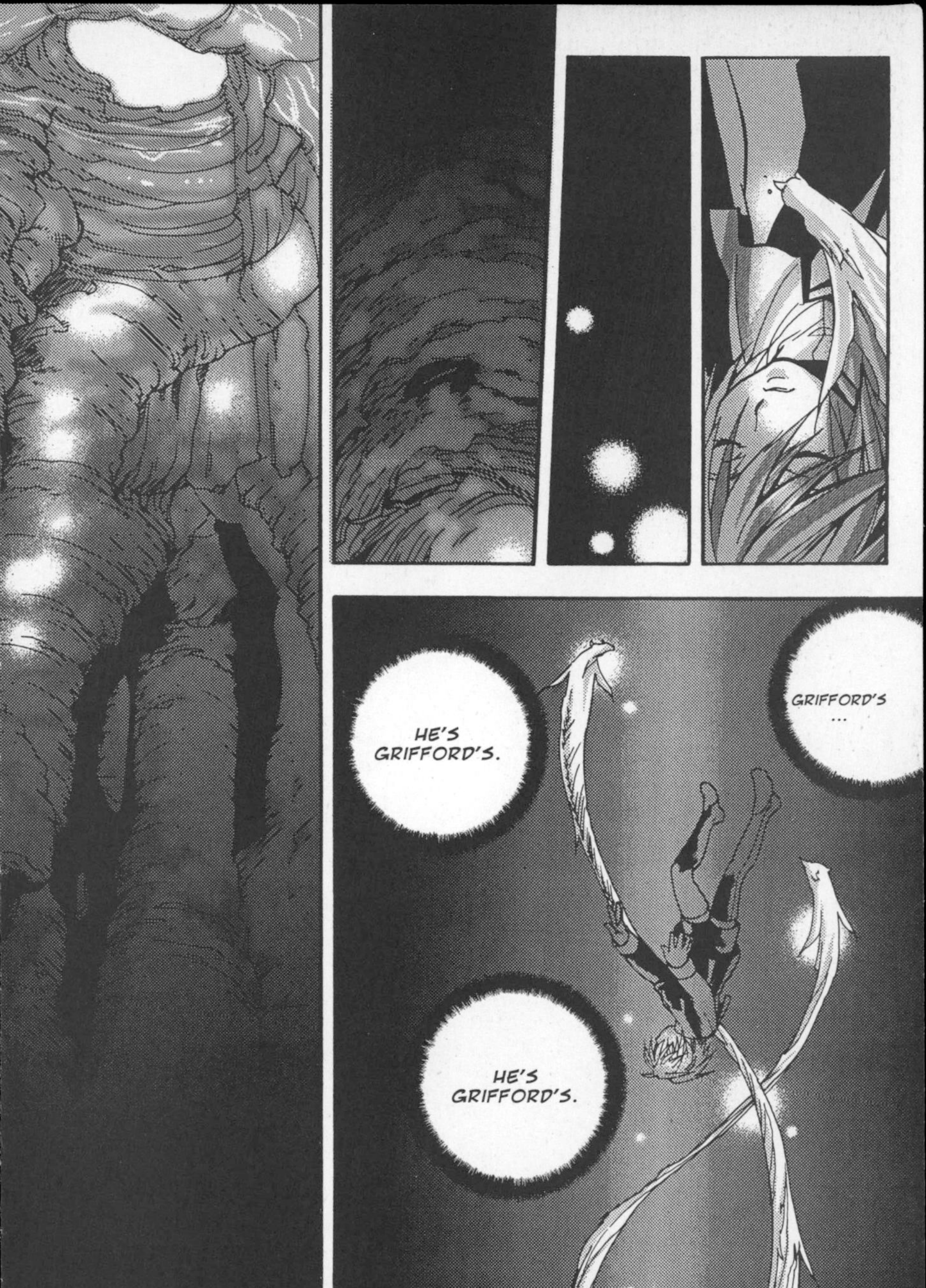
HE'S GRIFFORD'S.
GRIFFORD'S ...
HE'S GRIFFORD'S.

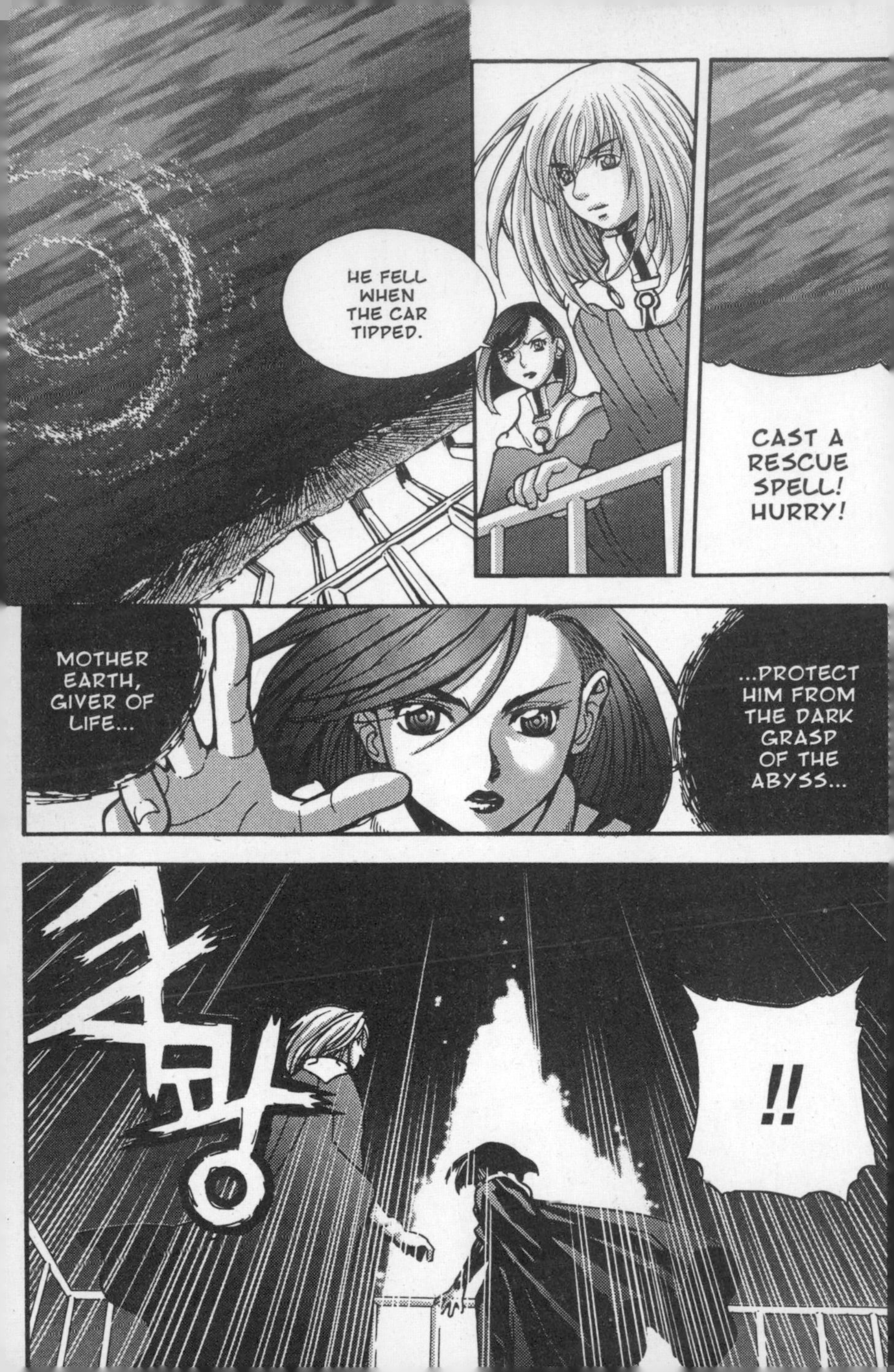
HE FELL WHEN THE CAR TIPPED.
CAST A RESCUE SPELL! HURRY!
MOTHER EARTH, GIVER OF LIFE...
...PROTECT HIM FROM THE DARK GRASP OF THE ABYSS...
!!

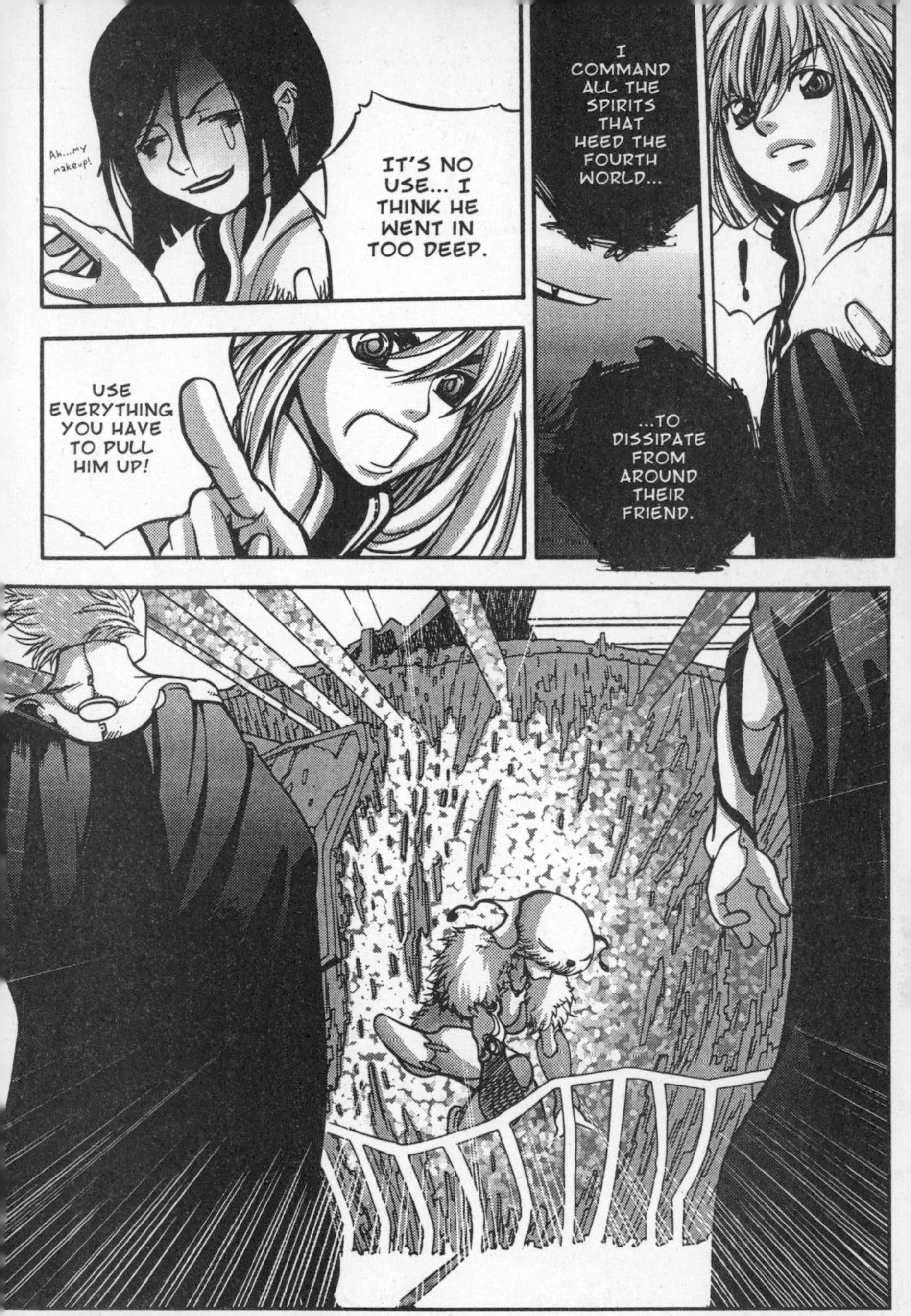
Ah...my makeup!
IT'S NO USE... I THINK HE WENT IN TOO DEEP.
USE EVERYTHING YOU HAVE TO PULL HIM UP!
I COMMAND ALL THE SPIRITS THAT HEED THE FOURTH WORLD...
!
...TO DISSIPATE FROM AROUND THEIR FRIEND.

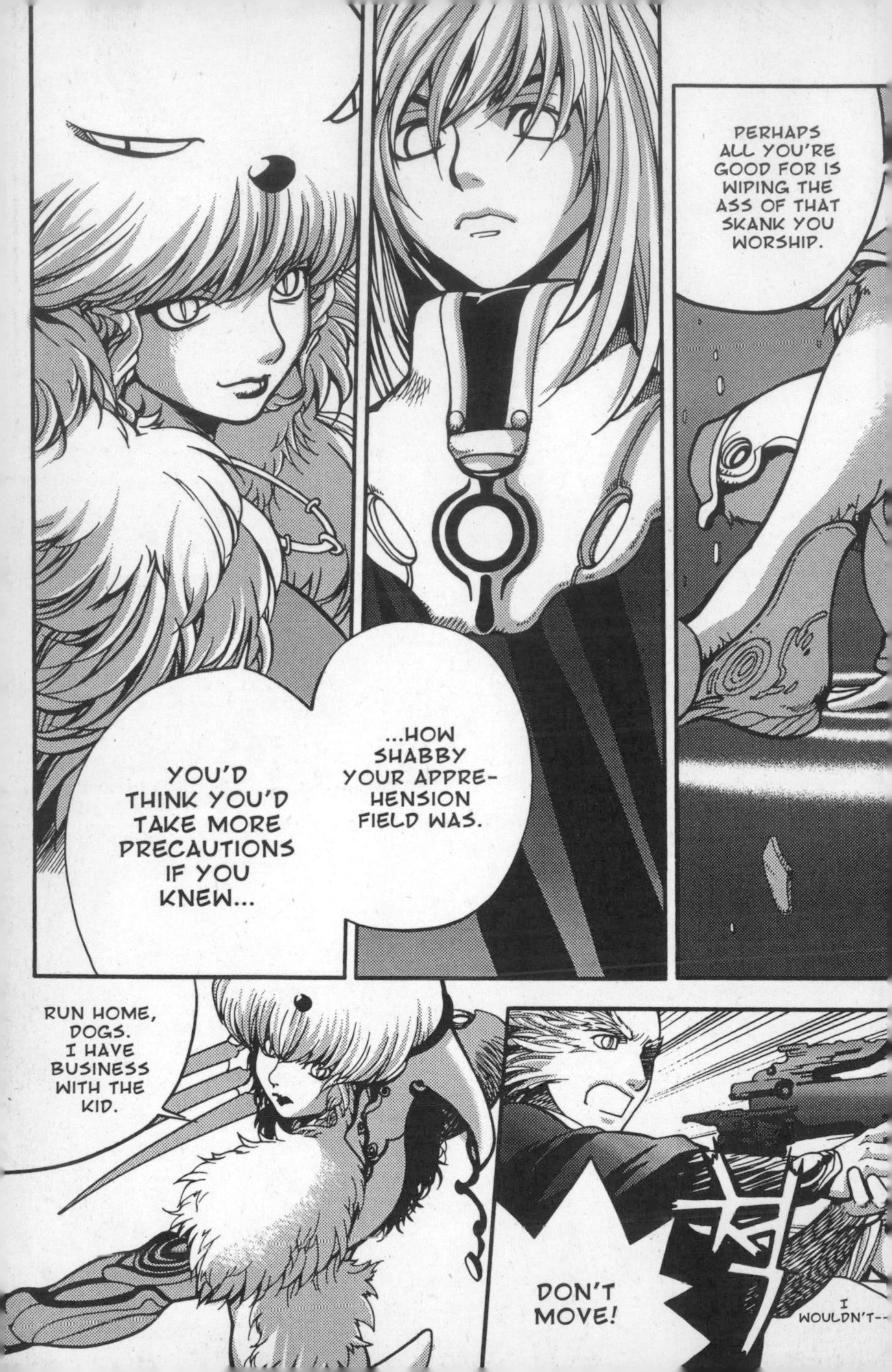
YOU'D THINK YOU'D TAKE MORE PRECAUTIONS IF YOU KNEW...
...HOW SHABBY YOUR APPRE-HENSION FIELD WAS.
PERHAPS ALL YOU'RE GOOD FOR IS WIPING THE ASS OF THAT SKANK YOU WORSHIP.
RUN HOME, DOGS. I HAVE BUSINESS WITH THE KID.
DON'T MOVE!
I WOULDN'T--

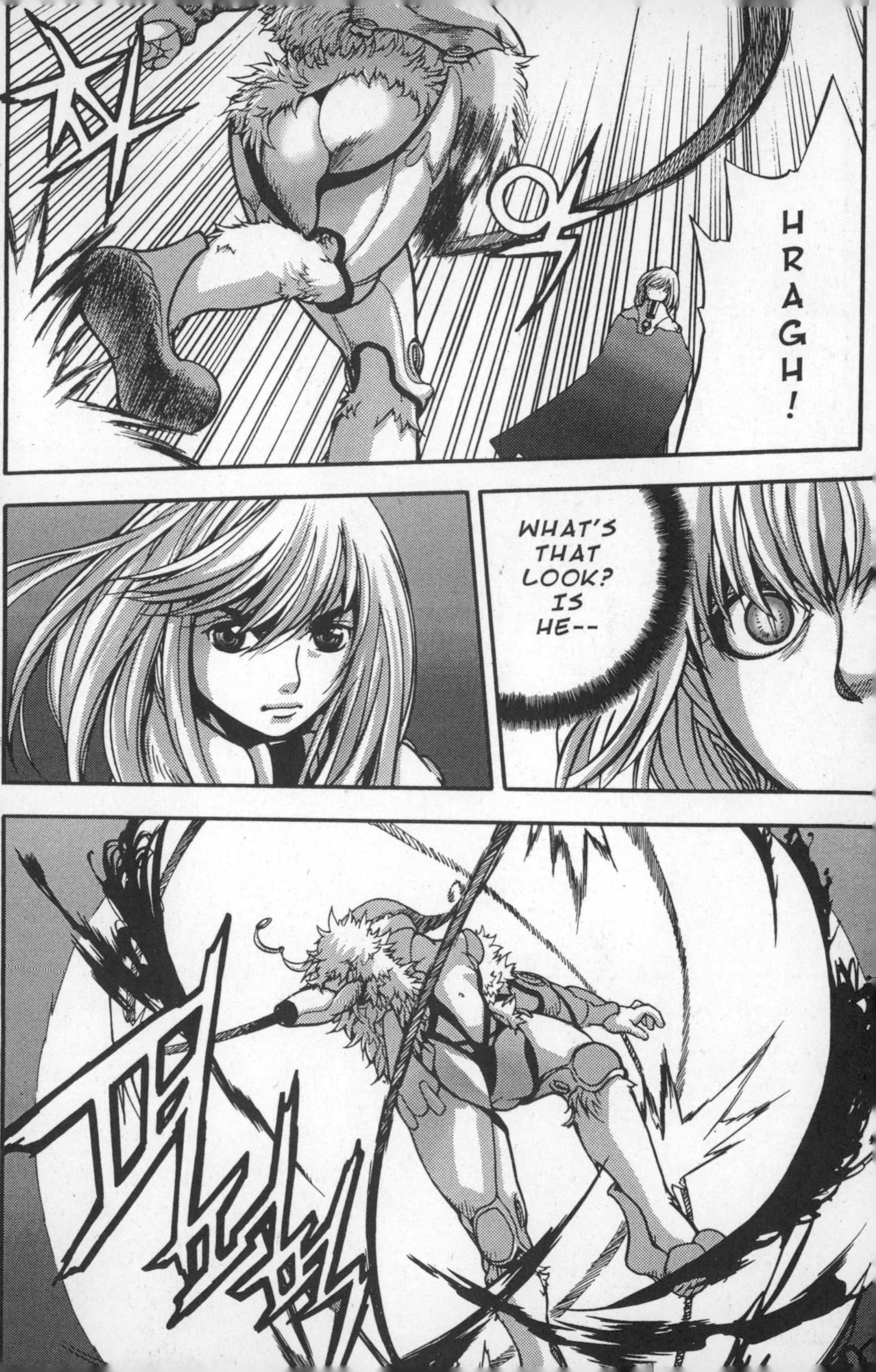
HRAGH!
WHAT'S THAT LOOK? IS HE--

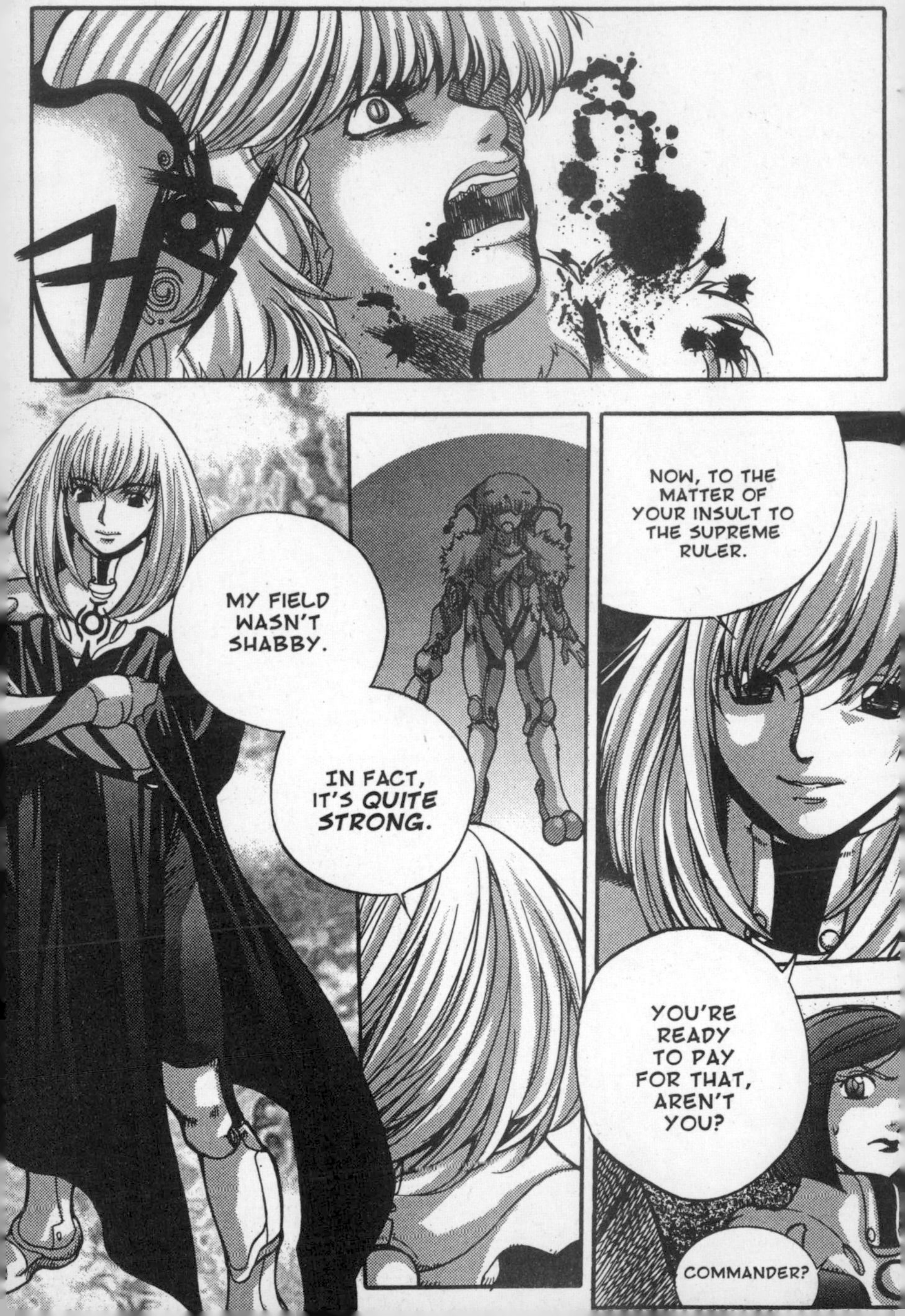
MY FIELD WASN'T SHABBY.
IN FACT, IT'S QUITE STRONG.
NOW, TO THE MATTER OF YOUR INSULT TO THE SUPREME RULER.
YOU'RE READY TO PAY FOR THAT, AREN'T YOU?
COMMANDER?

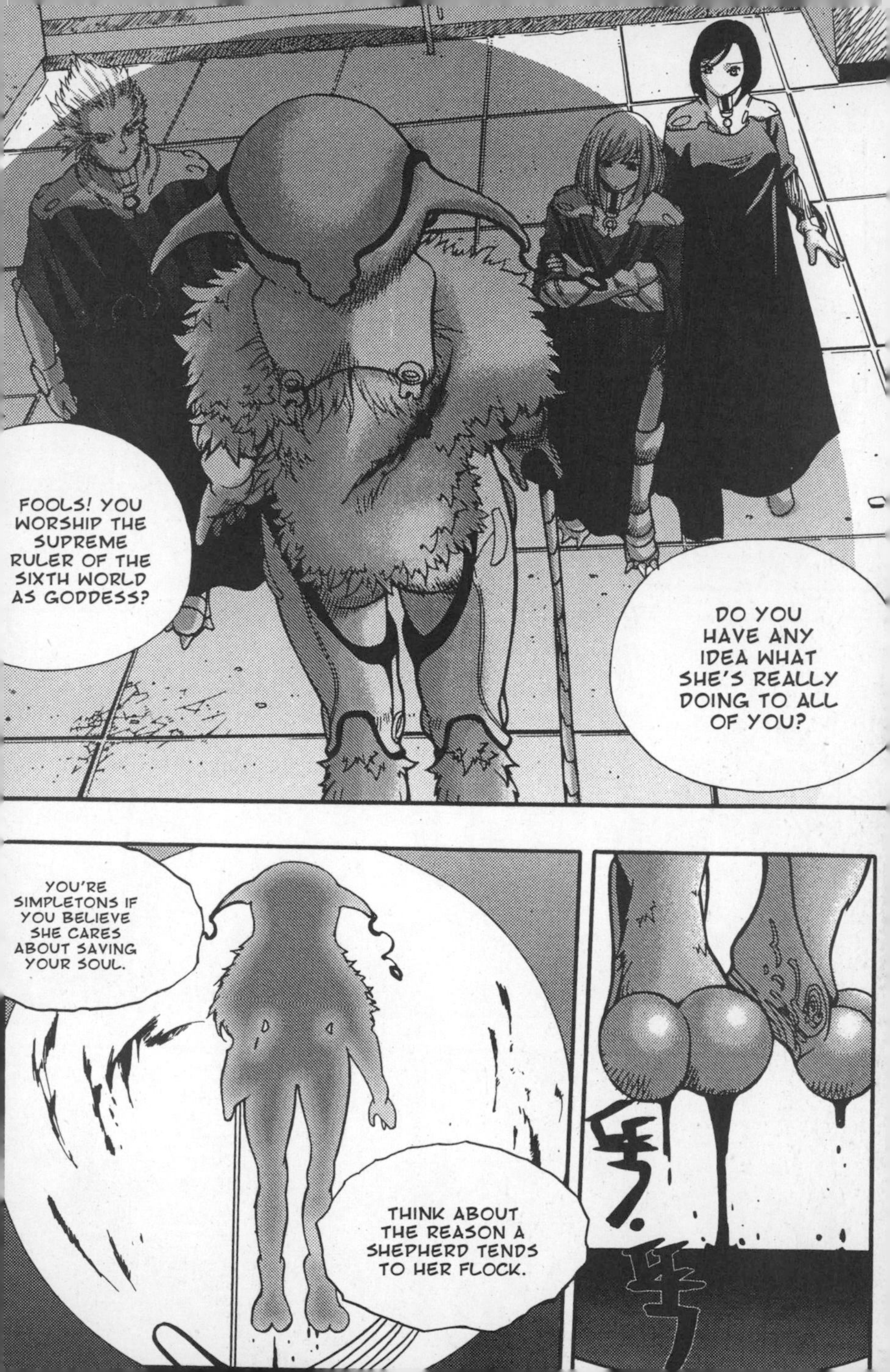
FOOLS! YOU WORSHIP THE SUPREME RULER OF THE SIXTH WORLD AS GODDESS?
DO YOU HAVE ANY IDEA WHAT SHE'S REALLY DOING TO ALL OF YOU?
YOU'RE SIMPLETONS IF YOU BELIEVE SHE CARES ABOUT SAVING YOUR SOUL.
THINK ABOUT THE REASON A SHEPHERD TENDS TO HER FLOCK.

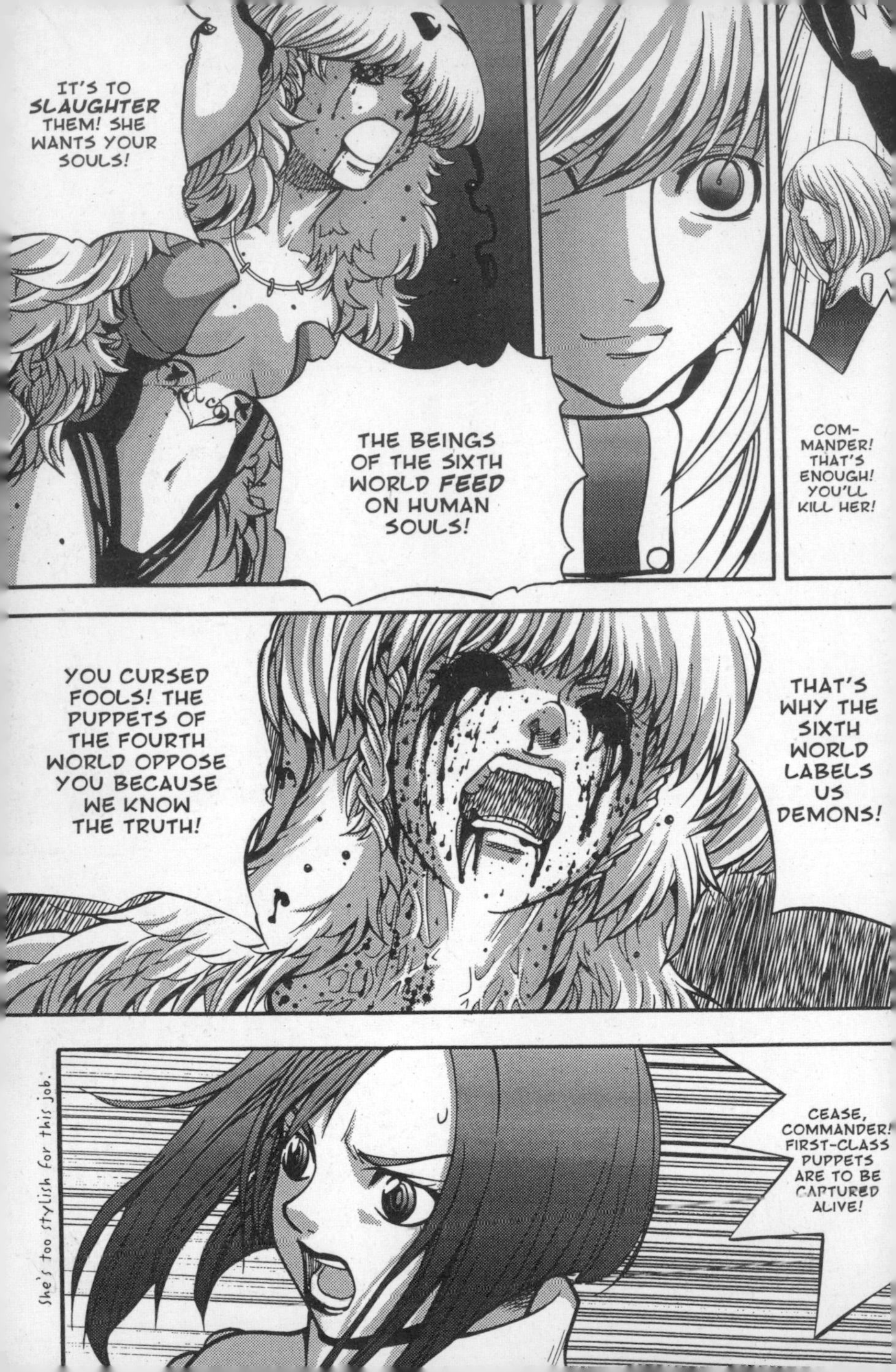
IT'S TO SLAUGHTER THEM! SHE WANTS YOUR SOULS!
THE BEINGS OF THE SIXTH WORLD FEED ON HUMAN SOULS!
COM-MANDER! THAT'S ENOUGH! YOU'LL KILL HER!
YOU CURSED FOOLS! THE PUPPETS OF THE FOURTH WORLD OPPOSE YOU BECAUSE WE KNOW THE TRUTH!
THAT'S WHY THE SIXTH WORLD LABELS US DEMONS!
She's too stylish for this job.
CEASE, COMMANDER! FIRST-CLASS PUPPETS ARE TO BE CAPTURED ALIVE!

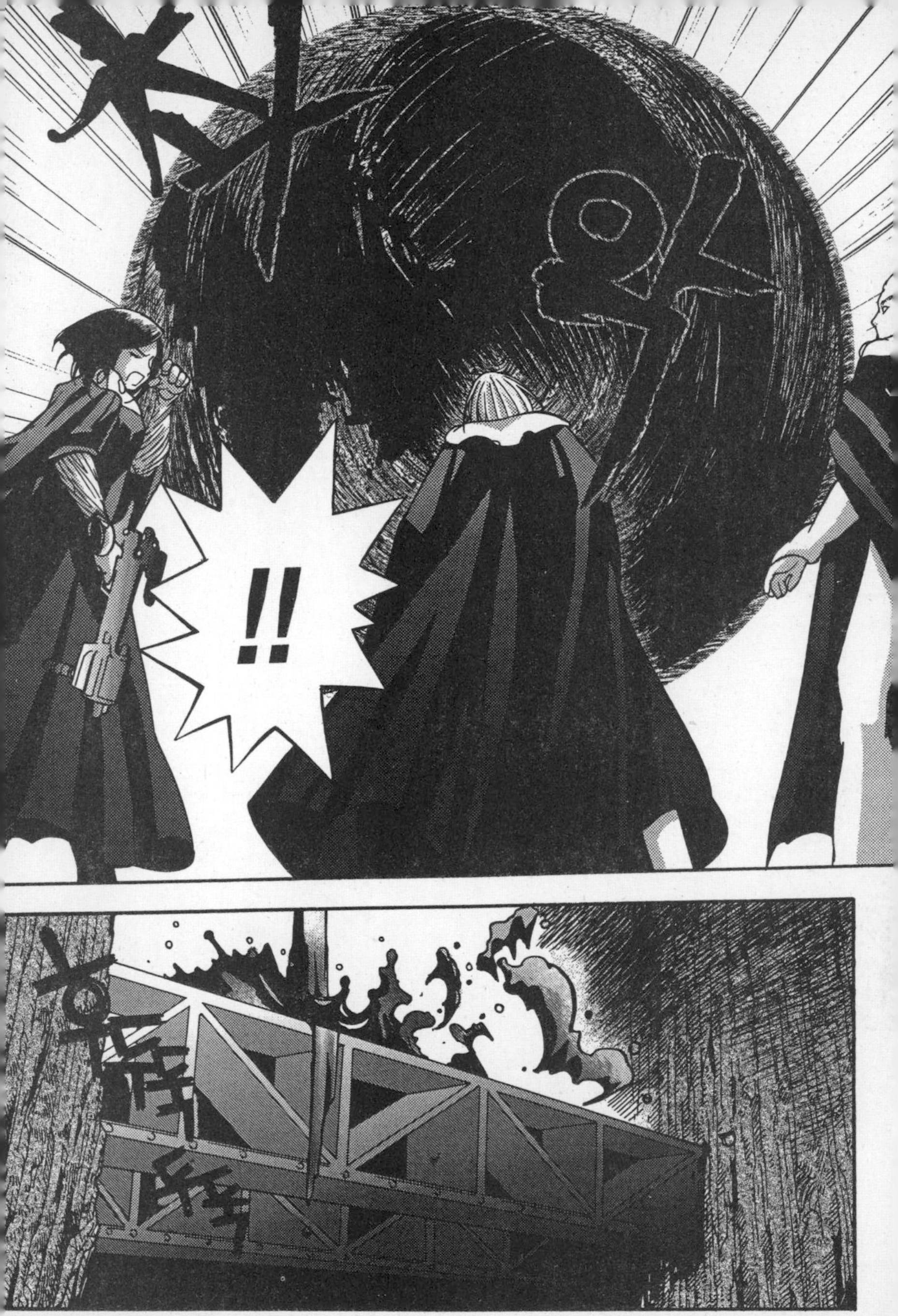
!!

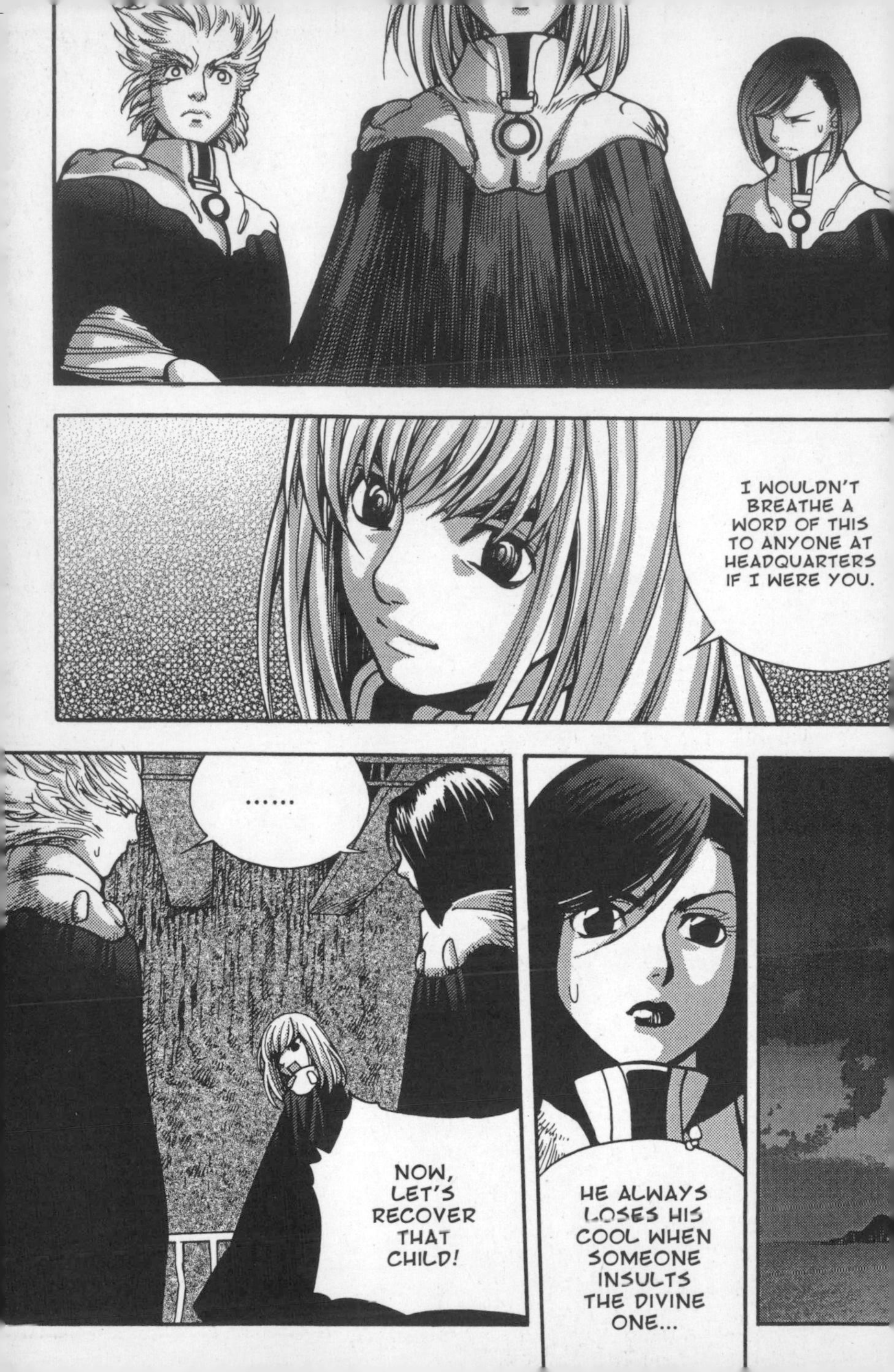

I WOULDN'T BREATHE A WORD OF THIS TO ANYONE AT HEADQUARTERS IF I WERE YOU.
......
NOW, LET'S RECOVER THAT CHILD!
HE ALWAYS LOSES HIS COOL WHEN SOMEONE INSULTS THE DIVINE ONE...

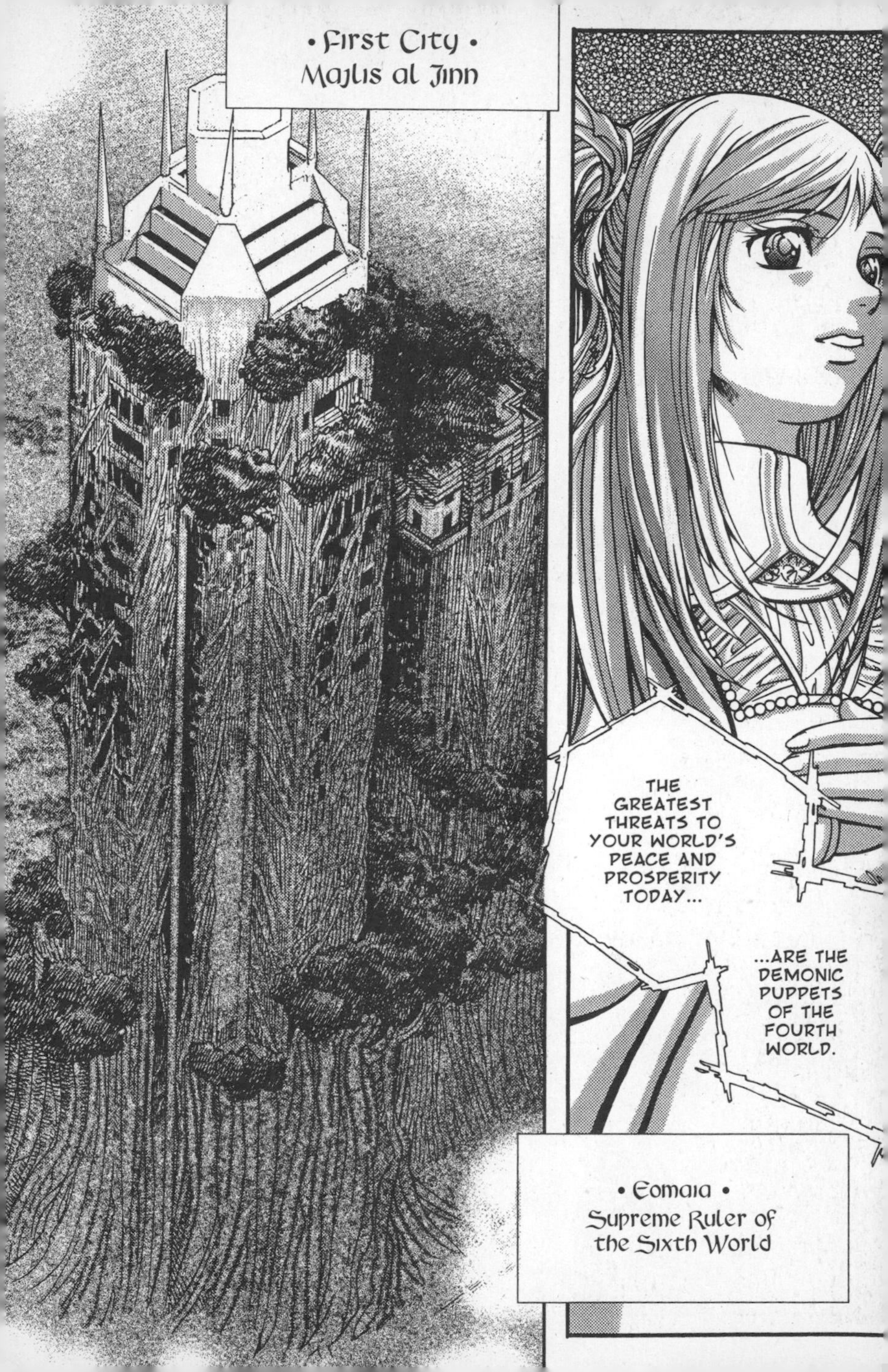
• First City •
Majlis al Jinn
THE GREATEST THREATS TO YOUR WORLD'S PEACE AND PROSPERITY TODAY...
...ARE THE DEMONIC PUPPETS OF THE FOURTH WORLD.
• Eomaia •
Supreme Ruler of the Sixth World

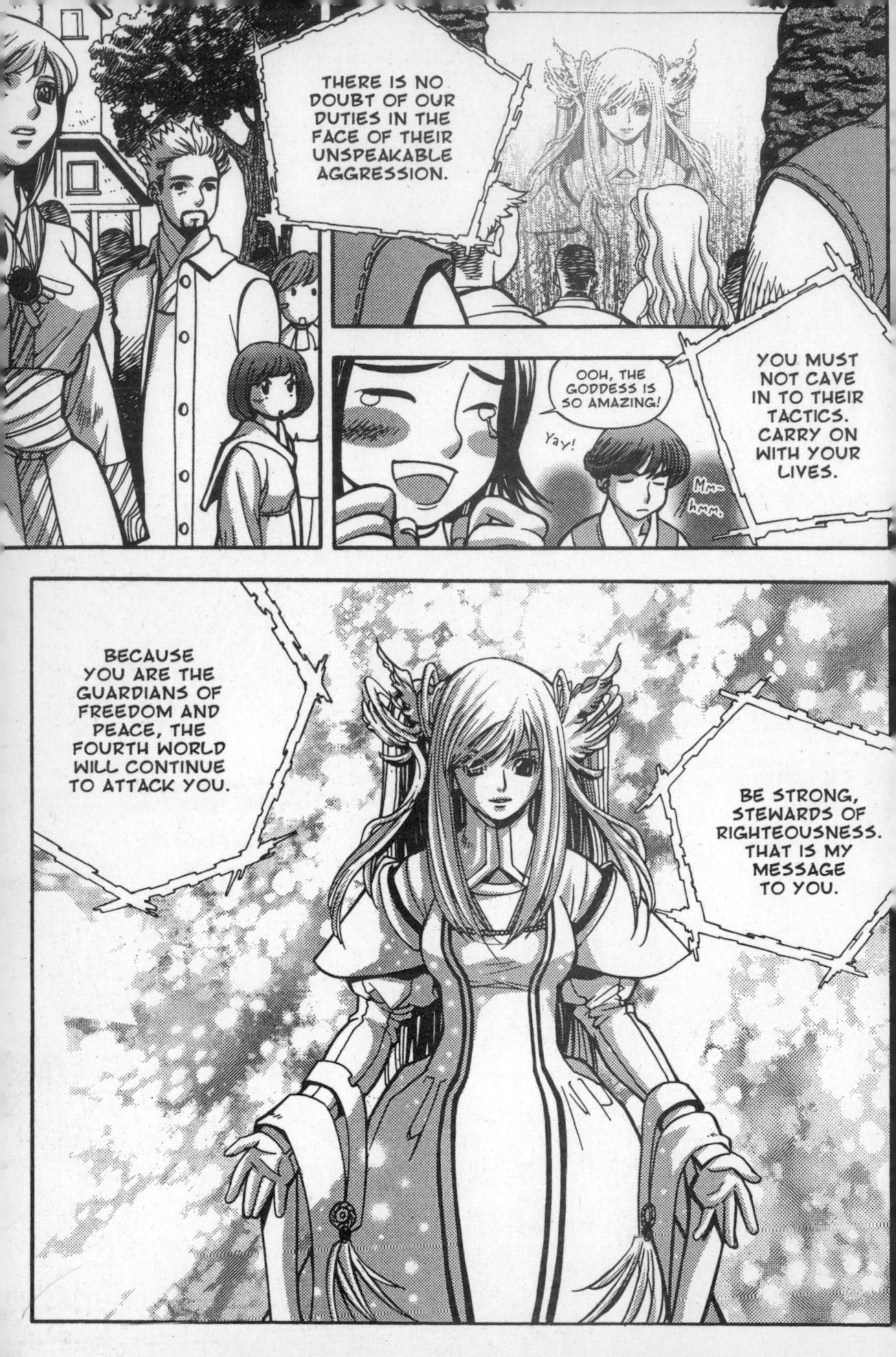
THERE IS NO DOUBT OF OUR DUTIES IN THE FACE OF THEIR UNSPEAKABLE AGGRESSION.
OOH, THE GODDESS IS SO AMAZING!
Yay!
Mm-hmm.
YOU MUST NOT CAVE IN TO THEIR TACTICS. CARRY ON WITH YOUR LIVES.
BECAUSE YOU ARE THE GUARDIANS OF FREEDOM AND PEACE, THE FOURTH WORLD WILL CONTINUE TO ATTACK YOU.
BE STRONG, STEWARDS OF RIGHTEOUSNESS. THAT IS MY MESSAGE TO YOU.

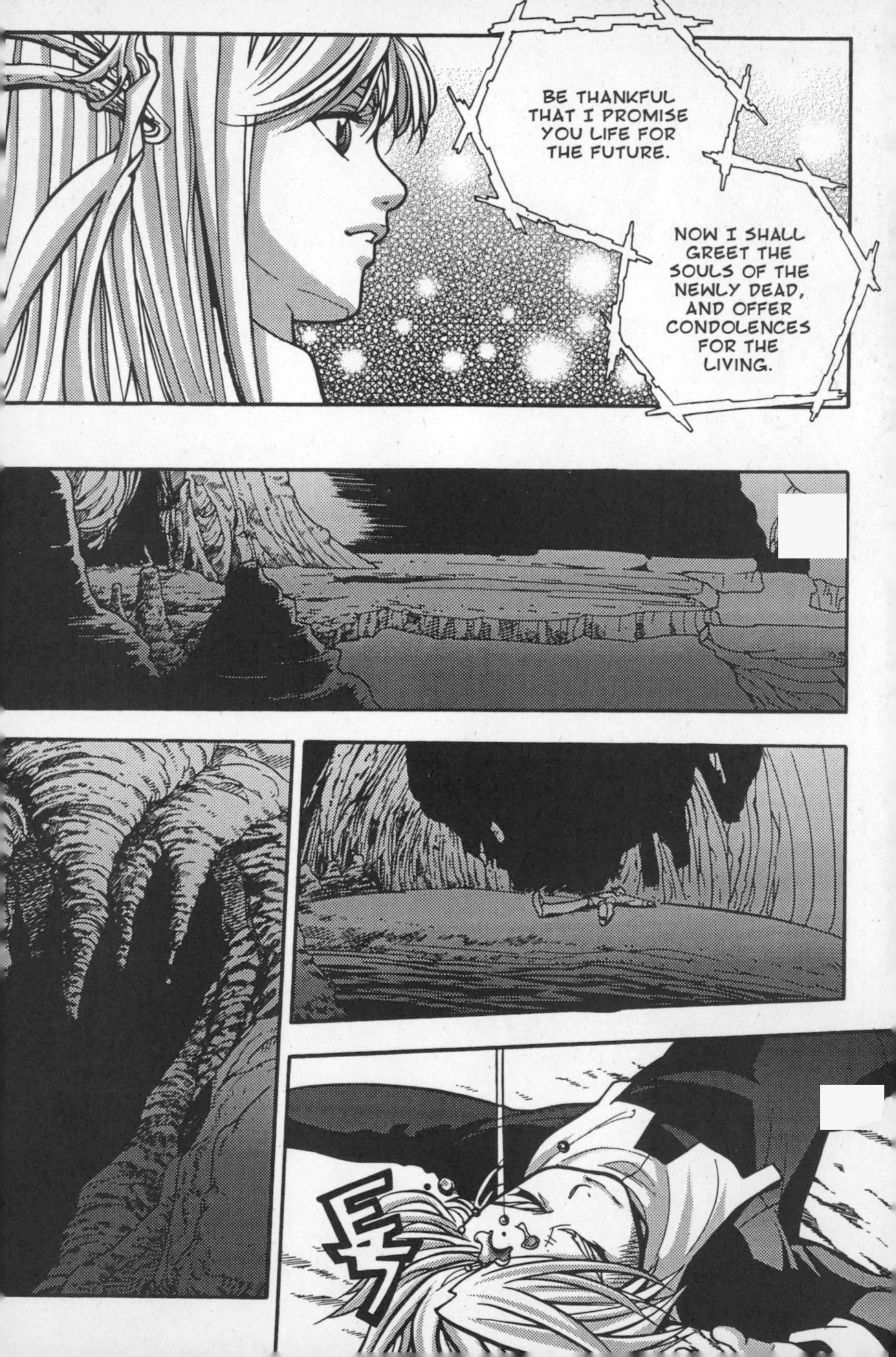
BE THANKFUL THAT I PROMISE YOU LIFE FOR THE FUTURE.
NOW I SHALL GREET THE SOULS OF THE NEWLY DEAD, AND OFFER CONDOLENCES FOR THE LIVING.

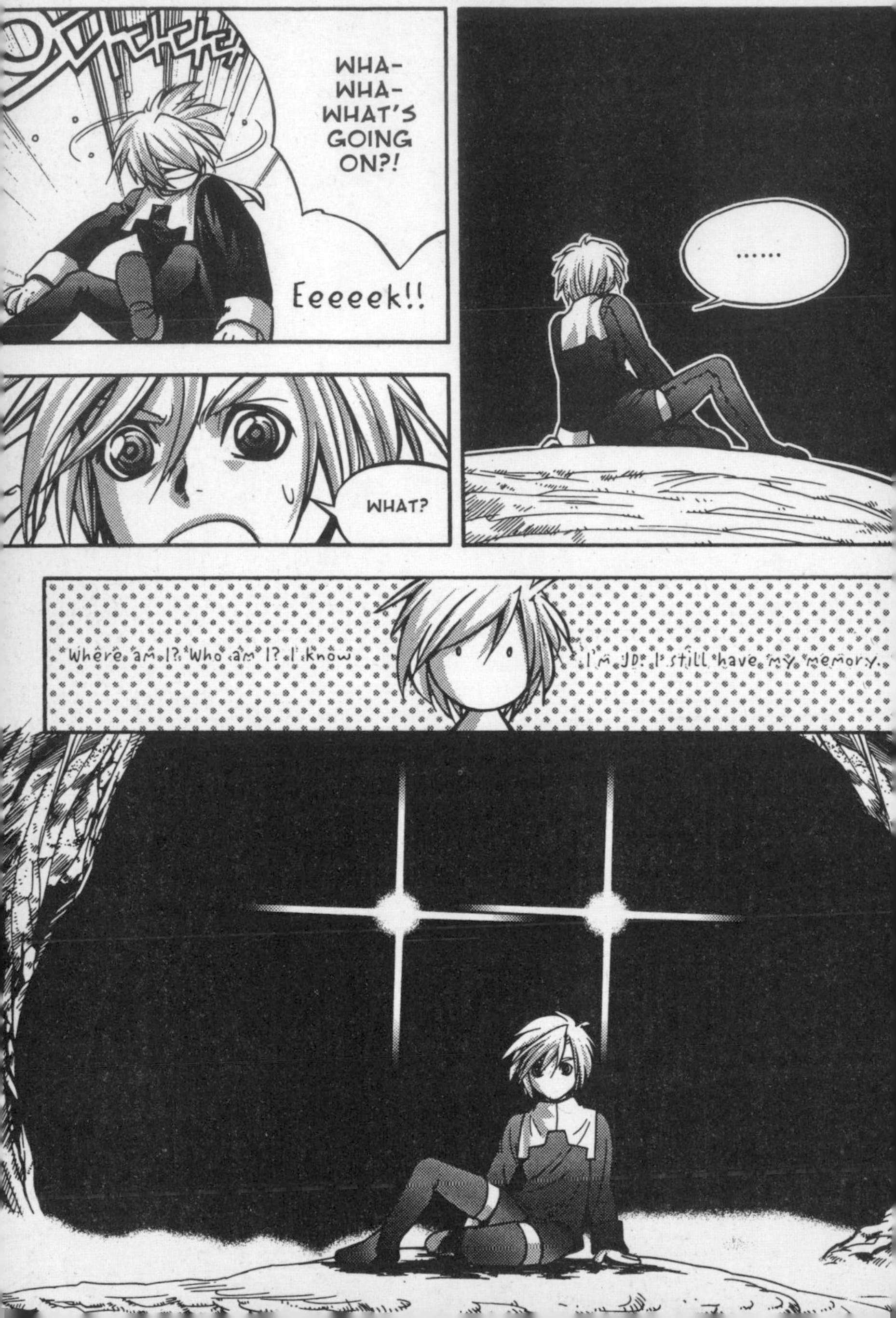
WHA-
WHA-
WHAT'S
GOING
ON?!
Eeeeek!!
......
WHAT?
Where am I? Who am I? I know
I'm JD. I still have my memory.

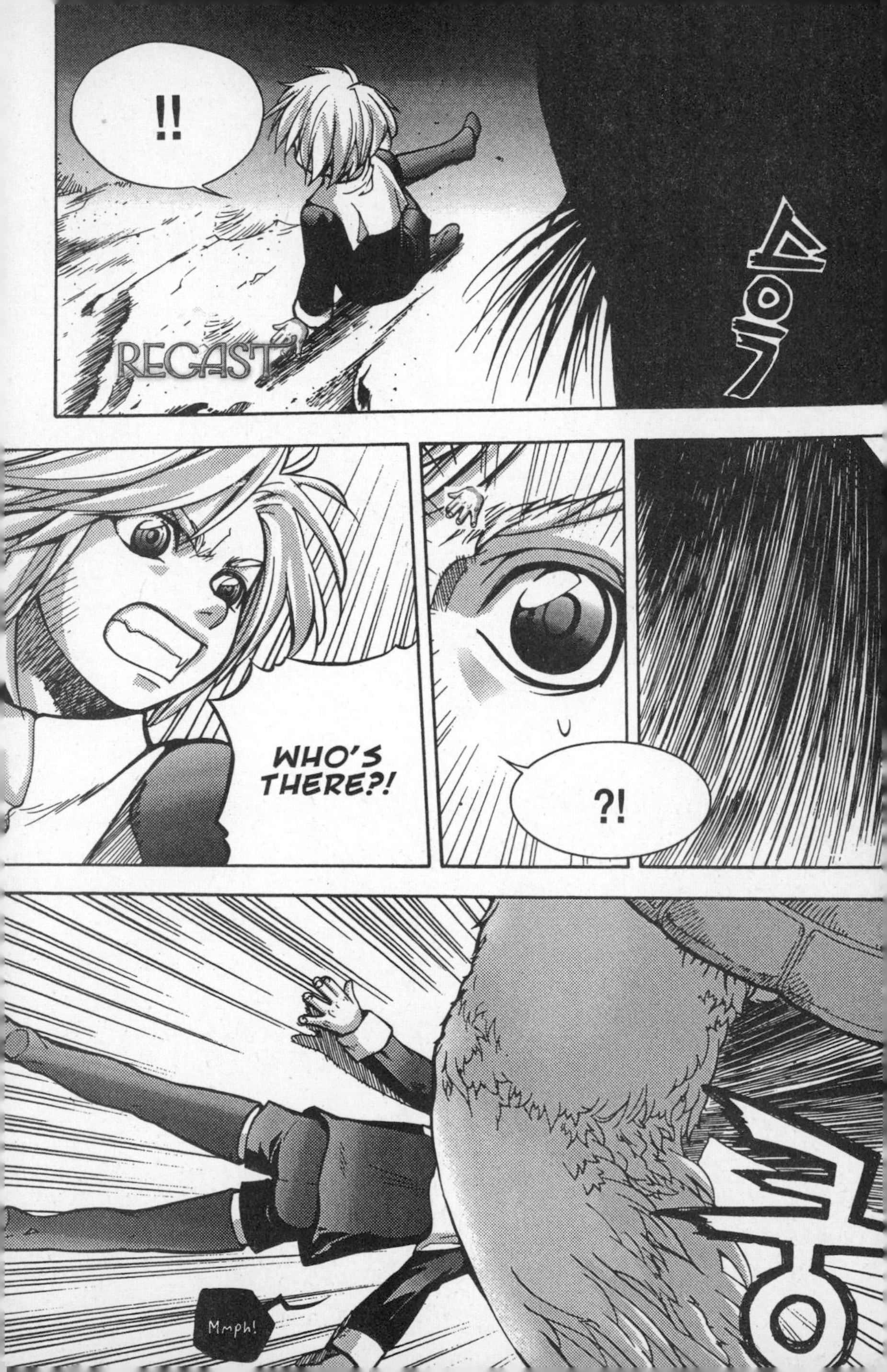
!!
REGAST
WHO'S THERE?!
?!
Mmph!

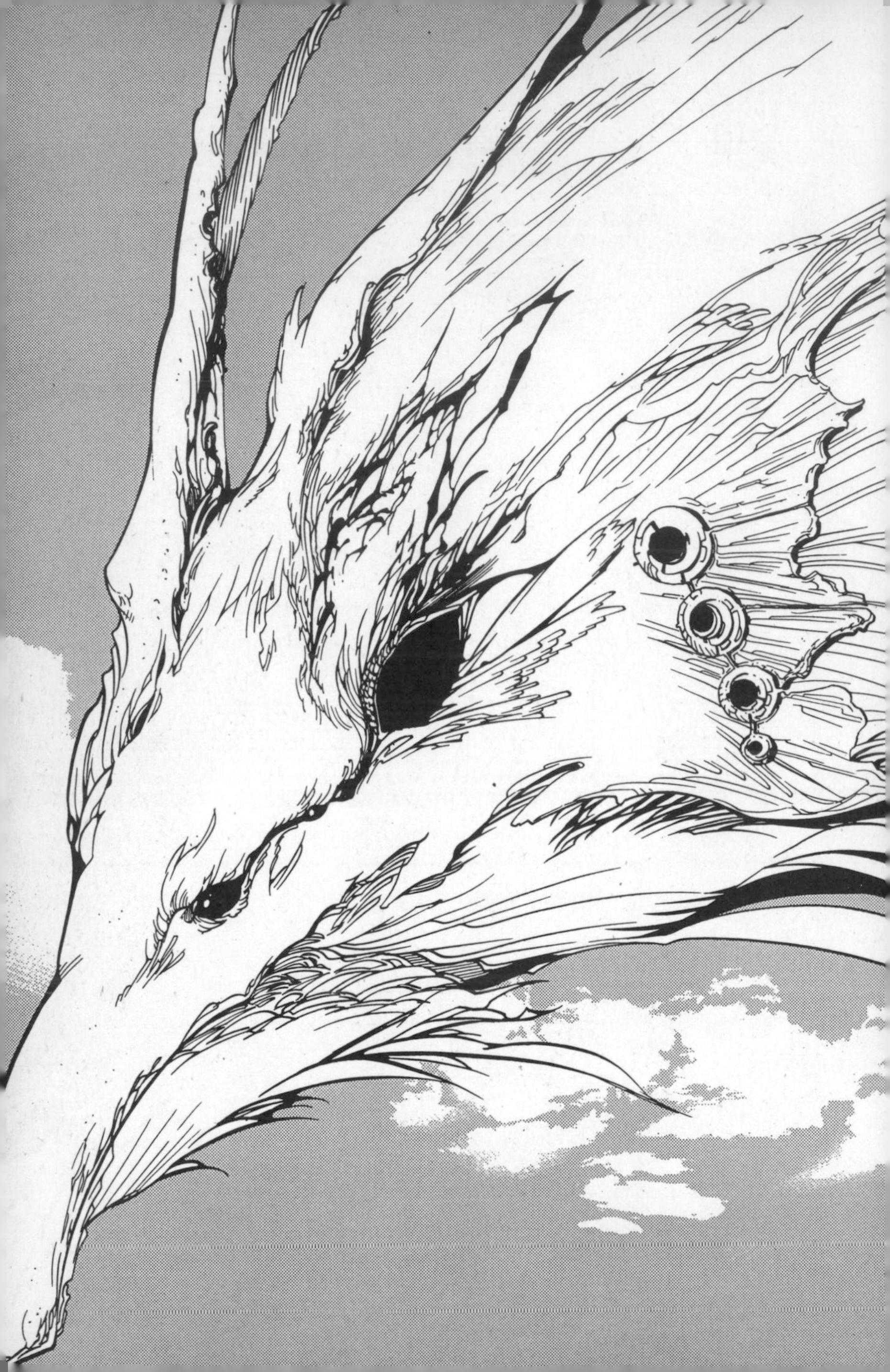

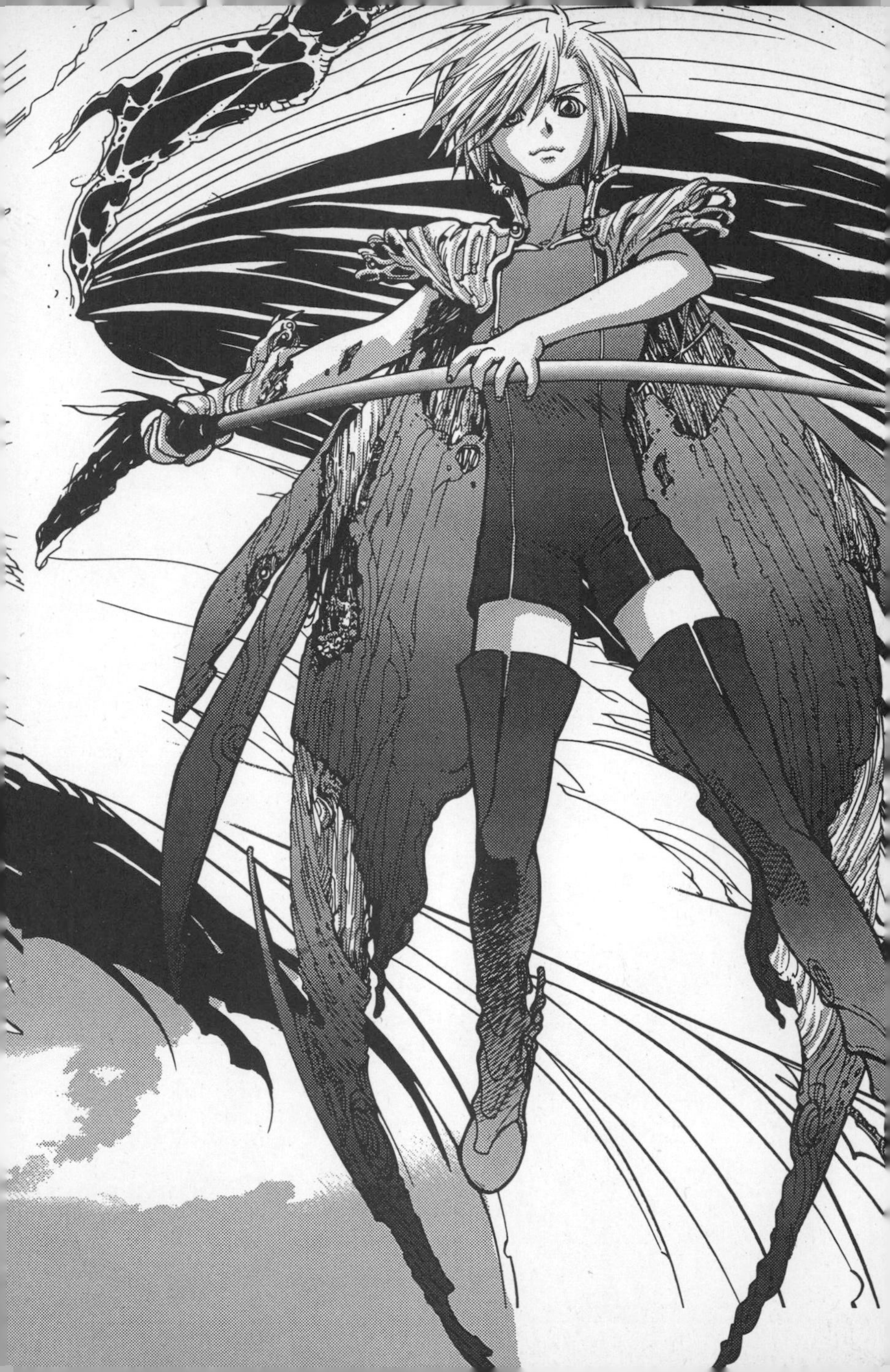

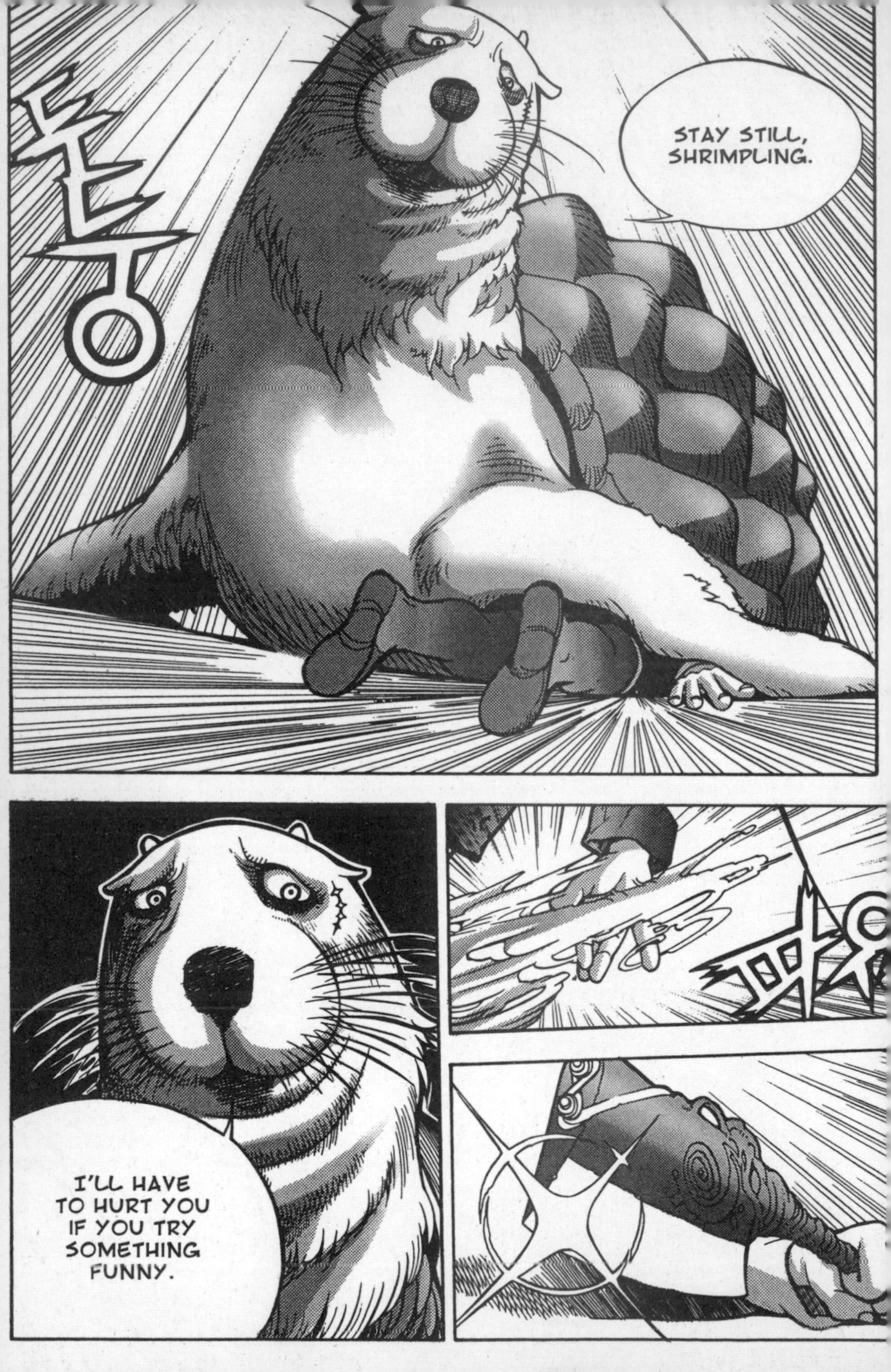
STAY STILL, SHRIMPLING.
I'LL HAVE TO HURT YOU IF YOU TRY SOMETHING FUNNY.

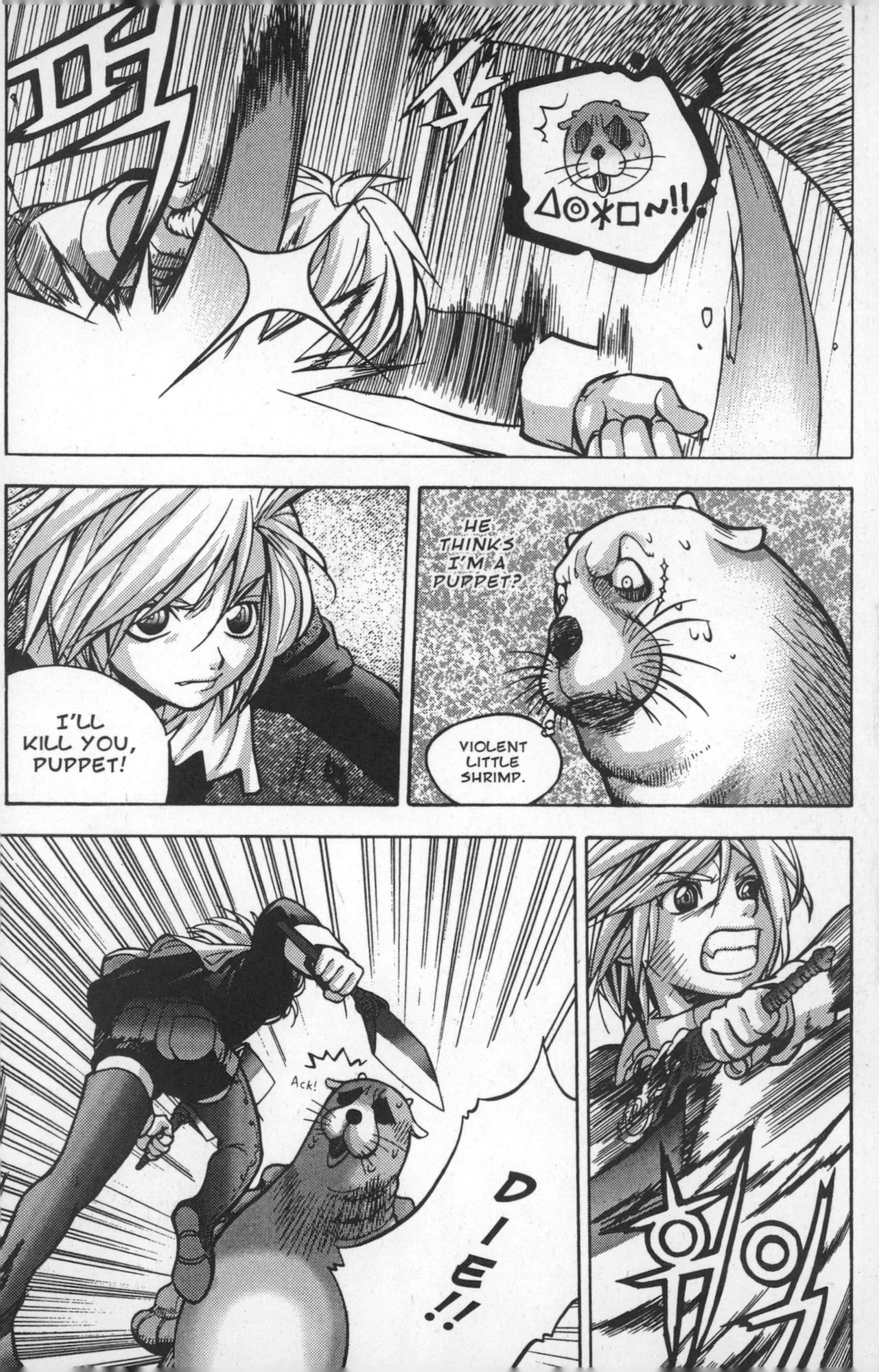
△◎✻□~!!
I'LL KILL YOU, PUPPET!
HE THINKS I'M A PUPPET?
VIOLENT LITTLE SHRIMP.
Ack!
DIE!!

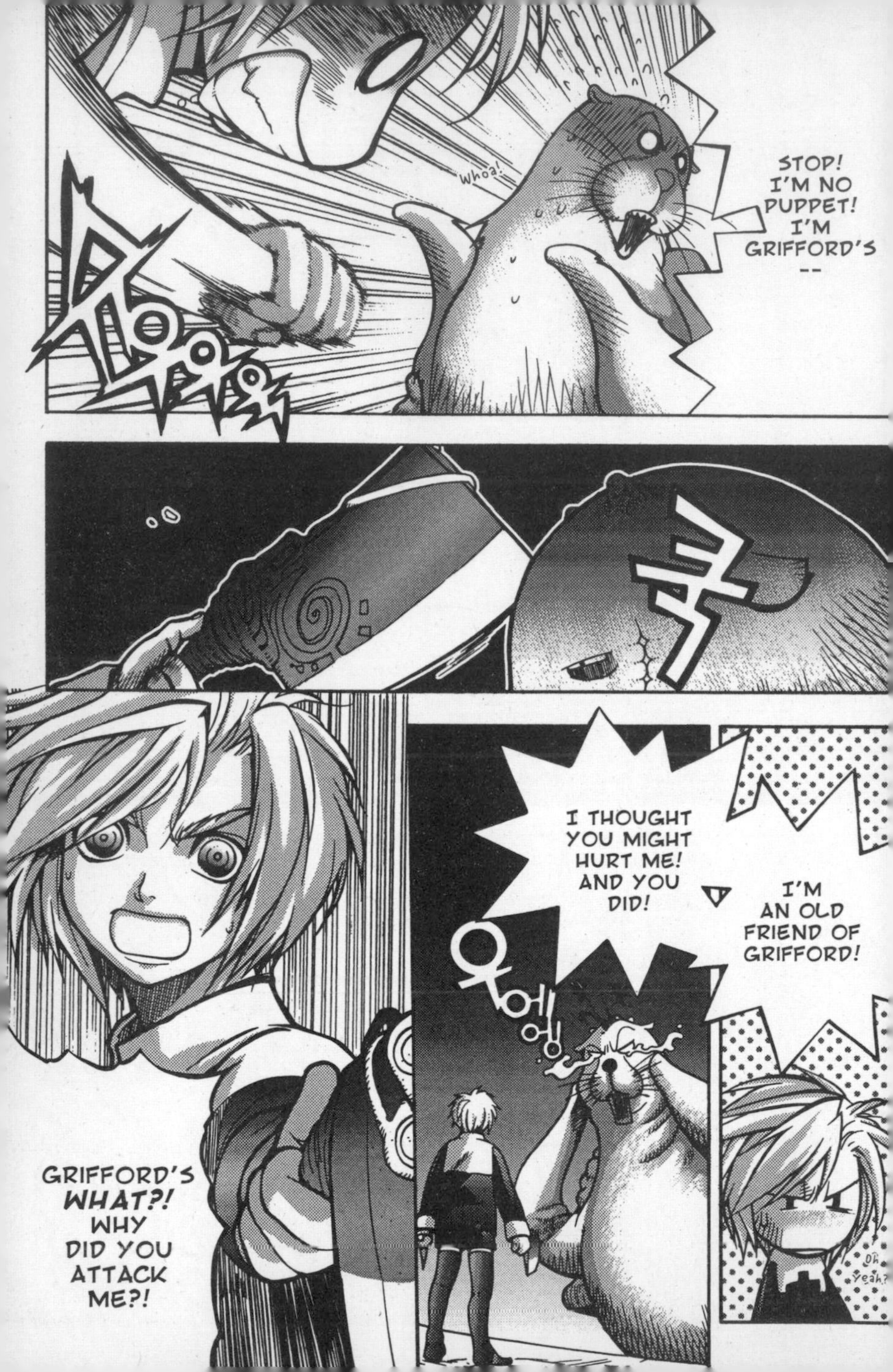
Whoa!
STOP! I'M NO PUPPET! I'M GRIFFORD'S --
GRIFFORD'S WHAT?! WHY DID YOU ATTACK ME?!
I THOUGHT YOU MIGHT HURT ME! AND YOU DID!
I'M AN OLD FRIEND OF GRIFFORD!
Oh yeah?

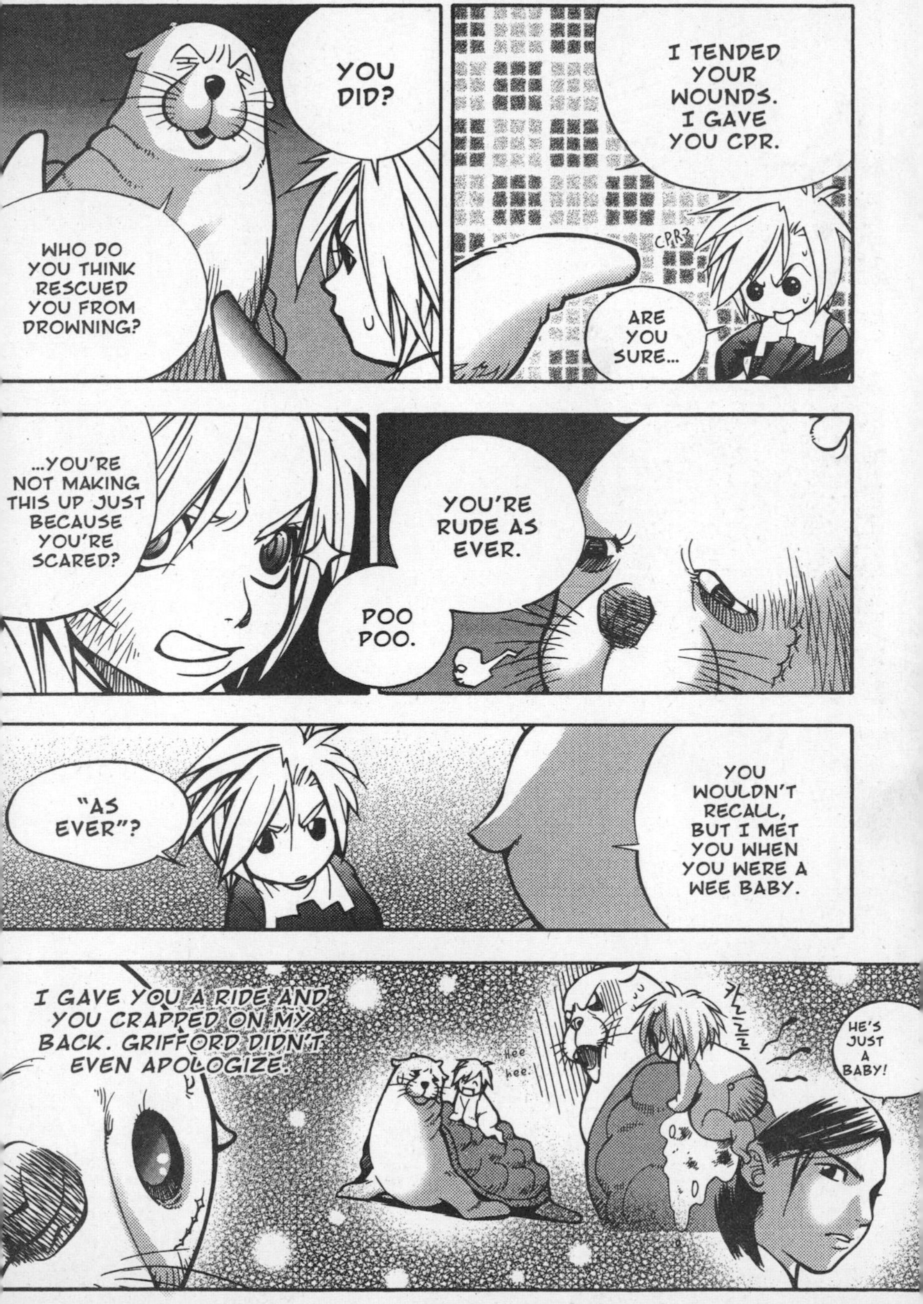
WHO DO YOU THINK RESCUED YOU FROM DROWNING?
YOU DID?
I TENDED YOUR WOUNDS. I GAVE YOU CPR.
CPR?
ARE YOU SURE...
...YOU'RE NOT MAKING THIS UP JUST BECAUSE YOU'RE SCARED?
YOU'RE RUDE AS EVER.
POO POO.
"AS EVER"?
YOU WOULDN'T RECALL, BUT I MET YOU WHEN YOU WERE A WEE BABY.
I GAVE YOU A RIDE AND YOU CRAPPED ON MY BACK. GRIFFORD DIDN'T EVEN APOLOGIZE.
Hee hee.
HE'S JUST A BABY!

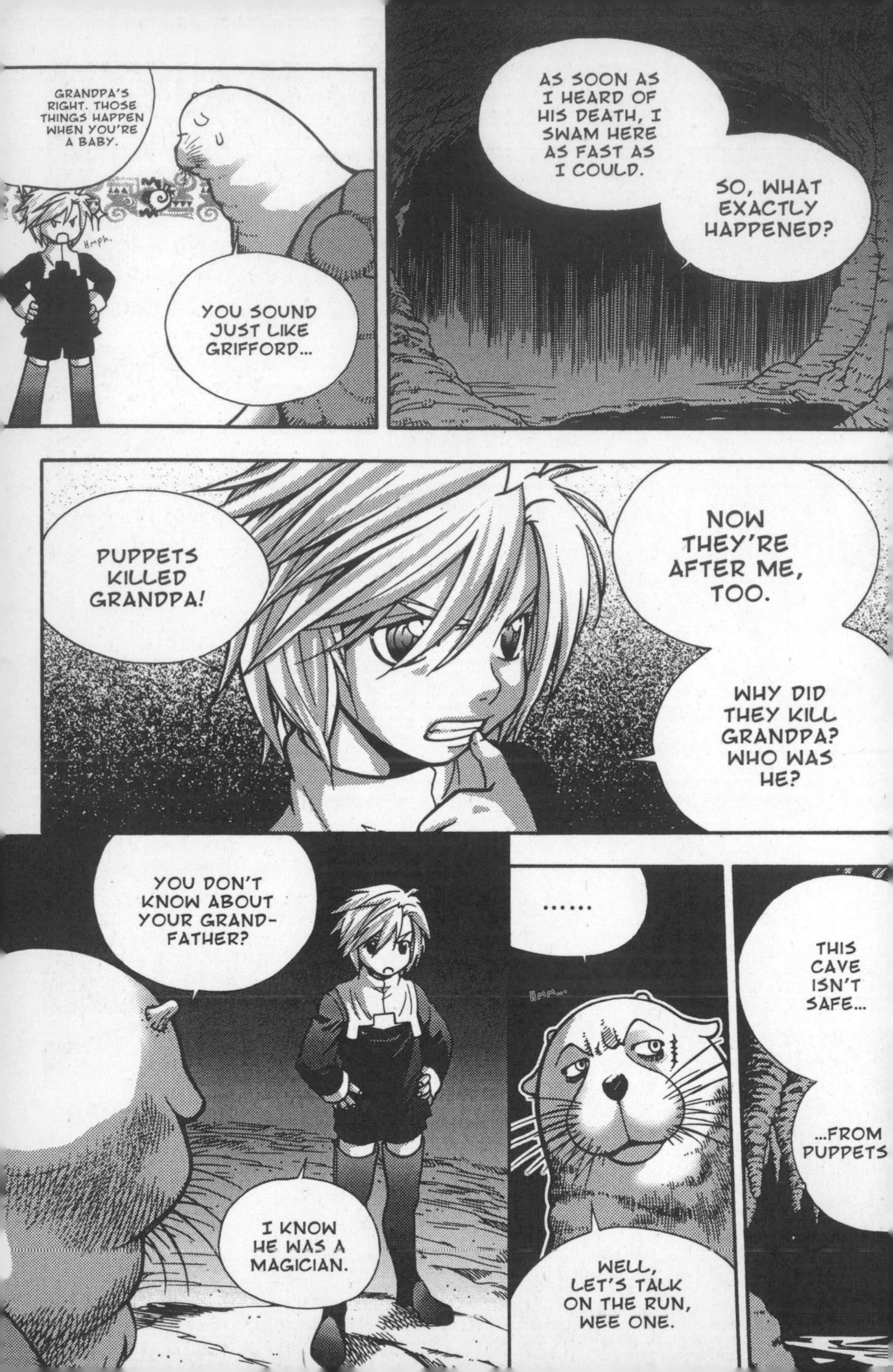
GRANDPA'S RIGHT. THOSE THINGS HAPPEN WHEN YOU'RE A BABY.
Hmph.
YOU SOUND JUST LIKE GRIFFORD...
AS SOON AS I HEARD OF HIS DEATH, I SWAM HERE AS FAST AS I COULD.
SO, WHAT EXACTLY HAPPENED?
PUPPETS KILLED GRANDPA!
NOW THEY'RE AFTER ME, TOO.
WHY DID THEY KILL GRANDPA? WHO WAS HE?
YOU DON'T KNOW ABOUT YOUR GRAND-FATHER?
I KNOW HE WAS A MAGICIAN.
......
Hmm...
WELL, LET'S TALK ON THE RUN, WEE ONE.
THIS CAVE ISN'T SAFE...
...FROM PUPPETS

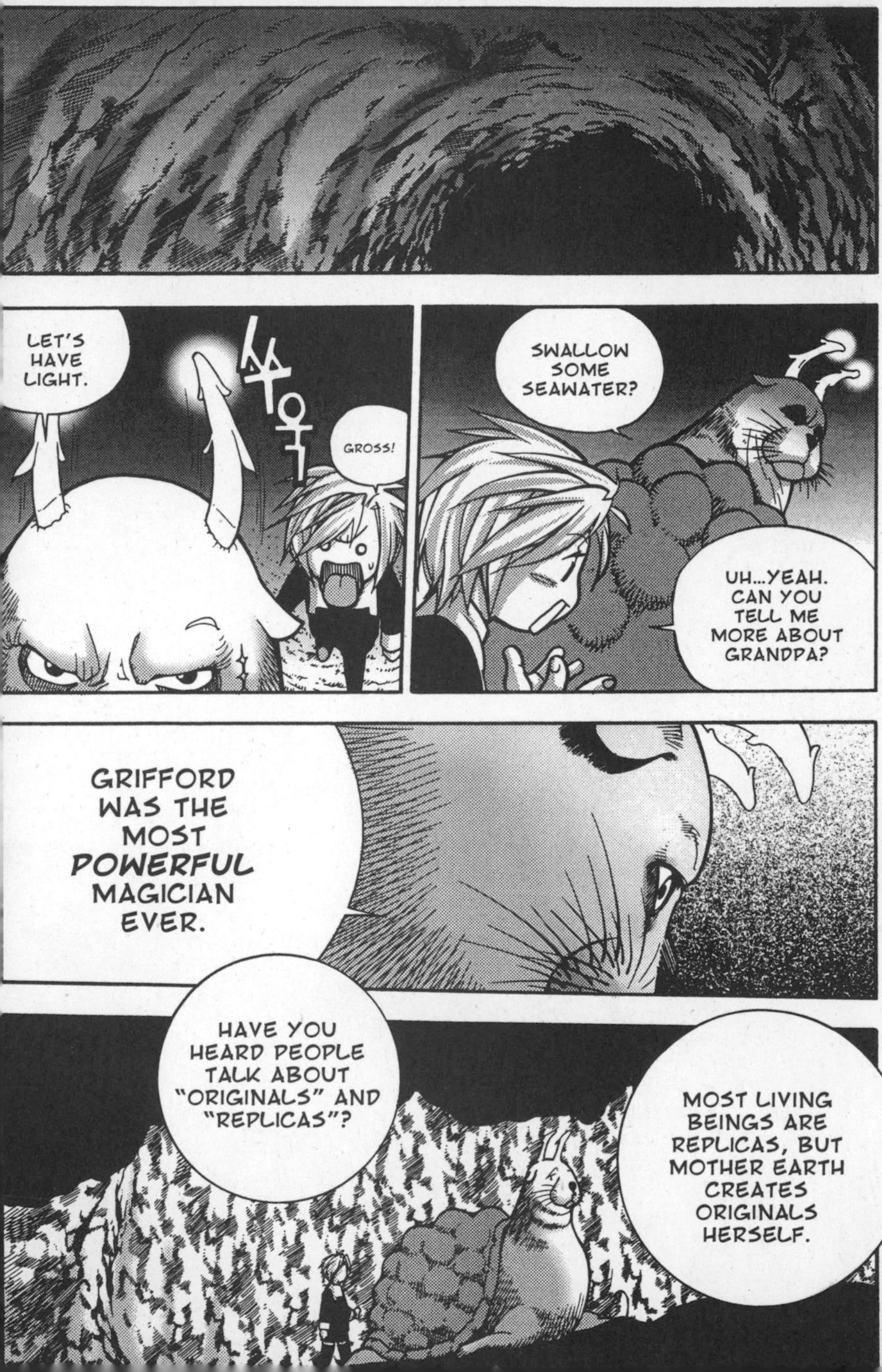
LET'S HAVE LIGHT.
GROSS!
SWALLOW SOME SEAWATER?
UH...YEAH. CAN YOU TELL ME MORE ABOUT GRANDPA?
GRIFFORD WAS THE MOST *POWERFUL* MAGICIAN EVER.
HAVE YOU HEARD PEOPLE TALK ABOUT "ORIGINALS" AND "REPLICAS"?
MOST LIVING BEINGS ARE REPLICAS, BUT MOTHER EARTH CREATES ORIGINALS HERSELF.

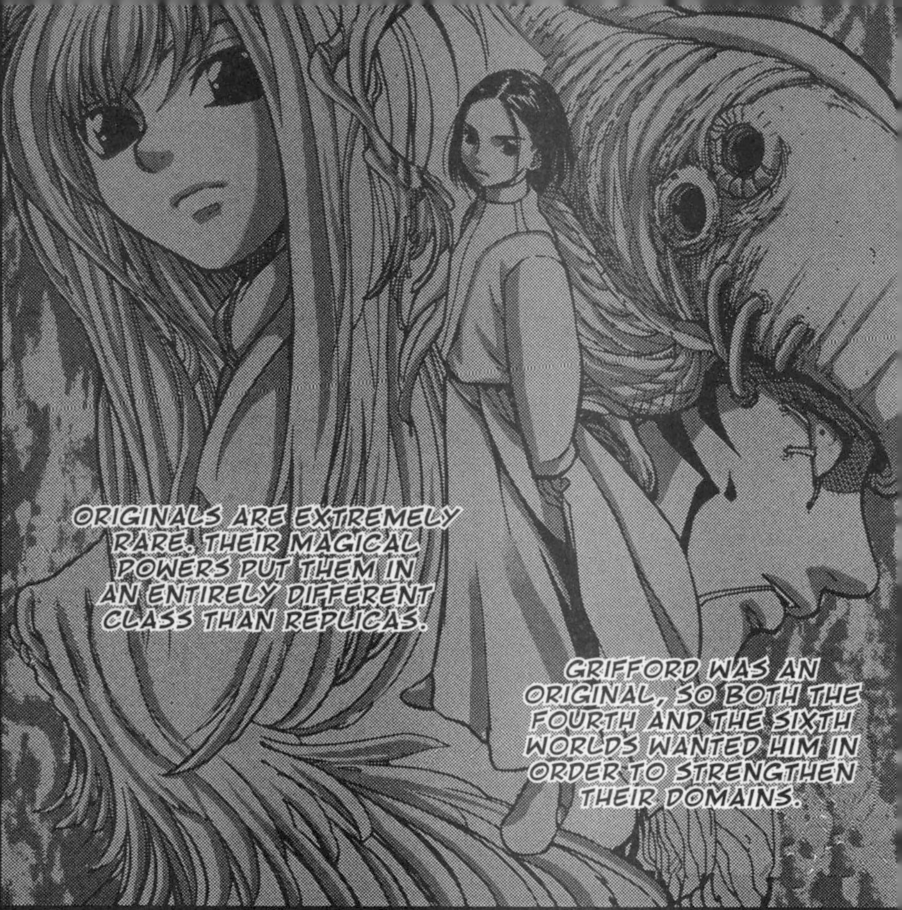
ORIGINALS ARE EXTREMELY RARE. THEIR MAGICAL POWERS PUT THEM IN AN ENTIRELY DIFFERENT CLASS THAN REPLICAS.
GRIFFORD WAS AN ORIGINAL, SO BOTH THE FOURTH AND THE SIXTH WORLDS WANTED HIM IN ORDER TO STRENGTHEN THEIR DOMAINS.
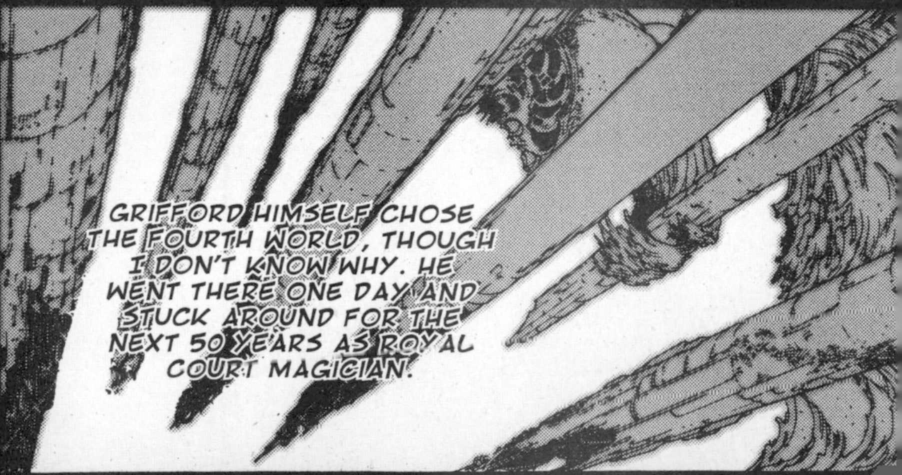
GRIFFORD HIMSELF CHOSE THE FOURTH WORLD, THOUGH I DON'T KNOW WHY. HE WENT THERE ONE DAY AND STUCK AROUND FOR THE NEXT 50 YEARS AS ROYAL COURT MAGICIAN.

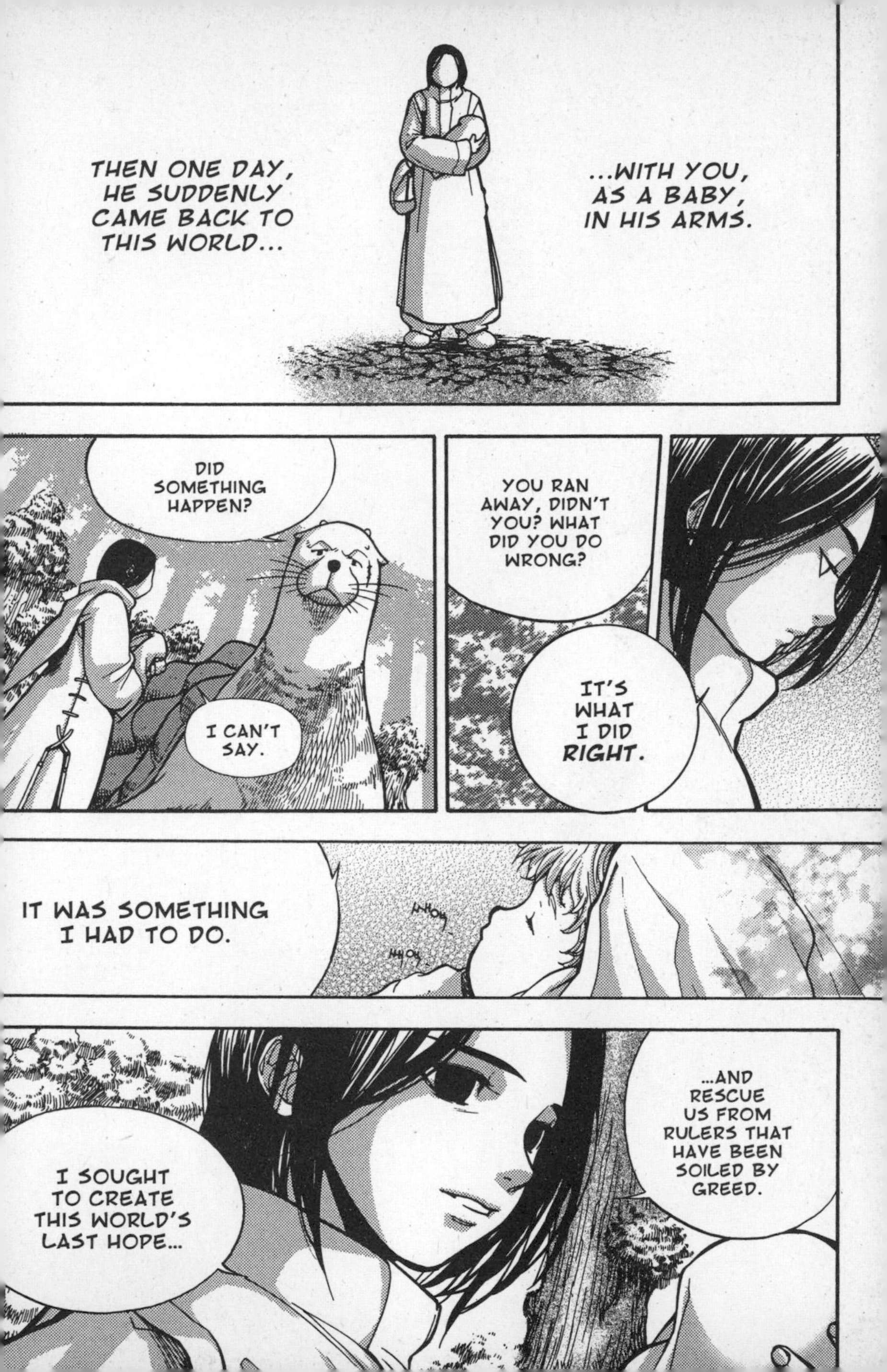
THEN ONE DAY, HE SUDDENLY CAME BACK TO THIS WORLD...
...WITH YOU, AS A BABY, IN HIS ARMS.
DID SOMETHING HAPPEN?
I CAN'T SAY.
YOU RAN AWAY, DIDN'T YOU? WHAT DID YOU DO WRONG?
IT'S WHAT I DID RIGHT.
IT WAS SOMETHING I HAD TO DO.
I SOUGHT TO CREATE THIS WORLD'S LAST HOPE...
...AND RESCUE US FROM RULERS THAT HAVE BEEN SOILED BY GREED.

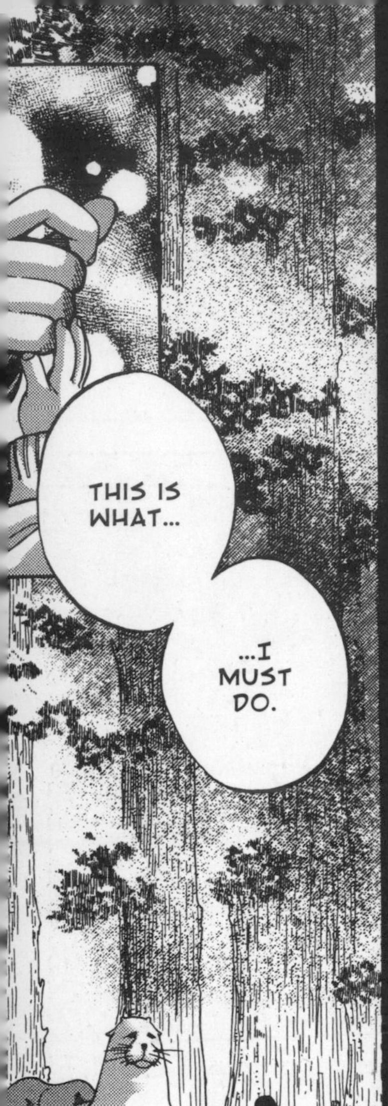
THIS IS WHAT...
...I MUST DO.

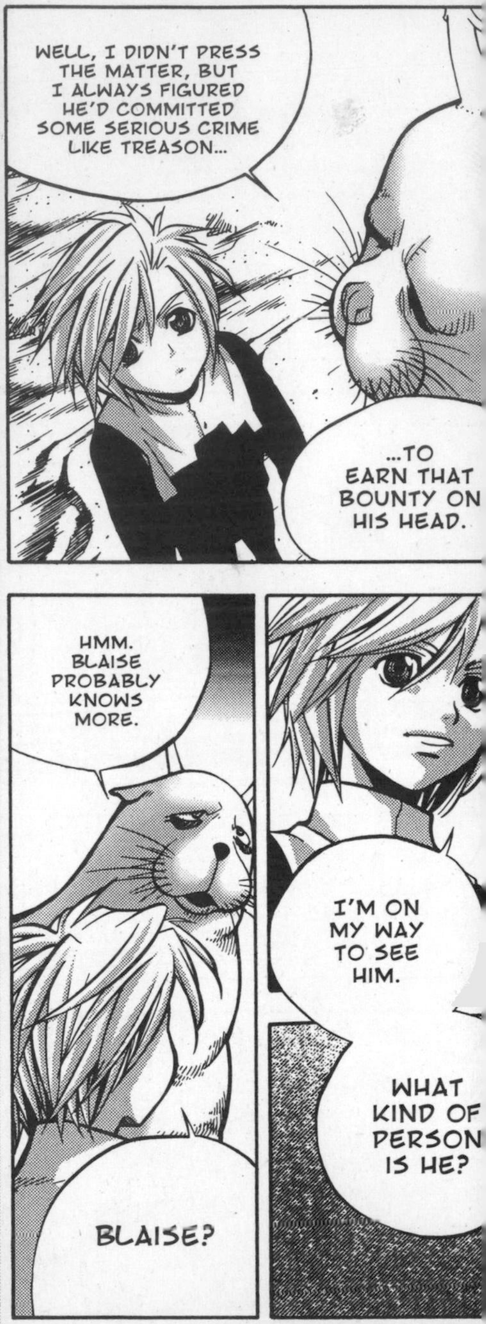
WELL, I DIDN'T PRESS THE MATTER, BUT I ALWAYS FIGURED HE'D COMMITTED SOME SERIOUS CRIME LIKE TREASON...
...TO EARN THAT BOUNTY ON HIS HEAD.
HMM. BLAISE PROBABLY KNOWS MORE.
BLAISE?
I'M ON MY WAY TO SEE HIM.
WHAT KIND OF PERSON IS HE?

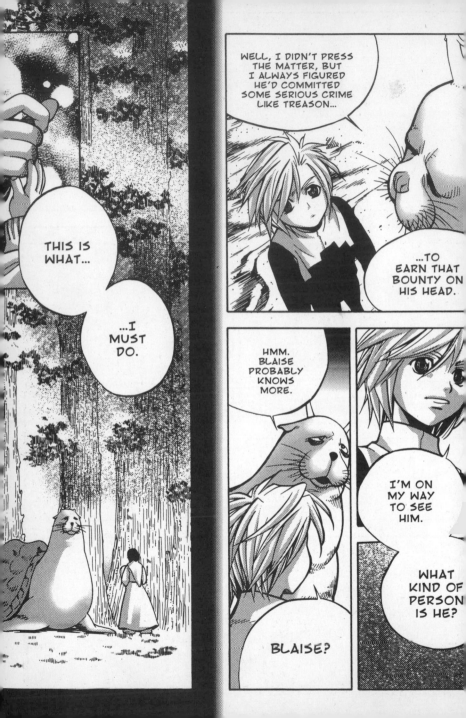

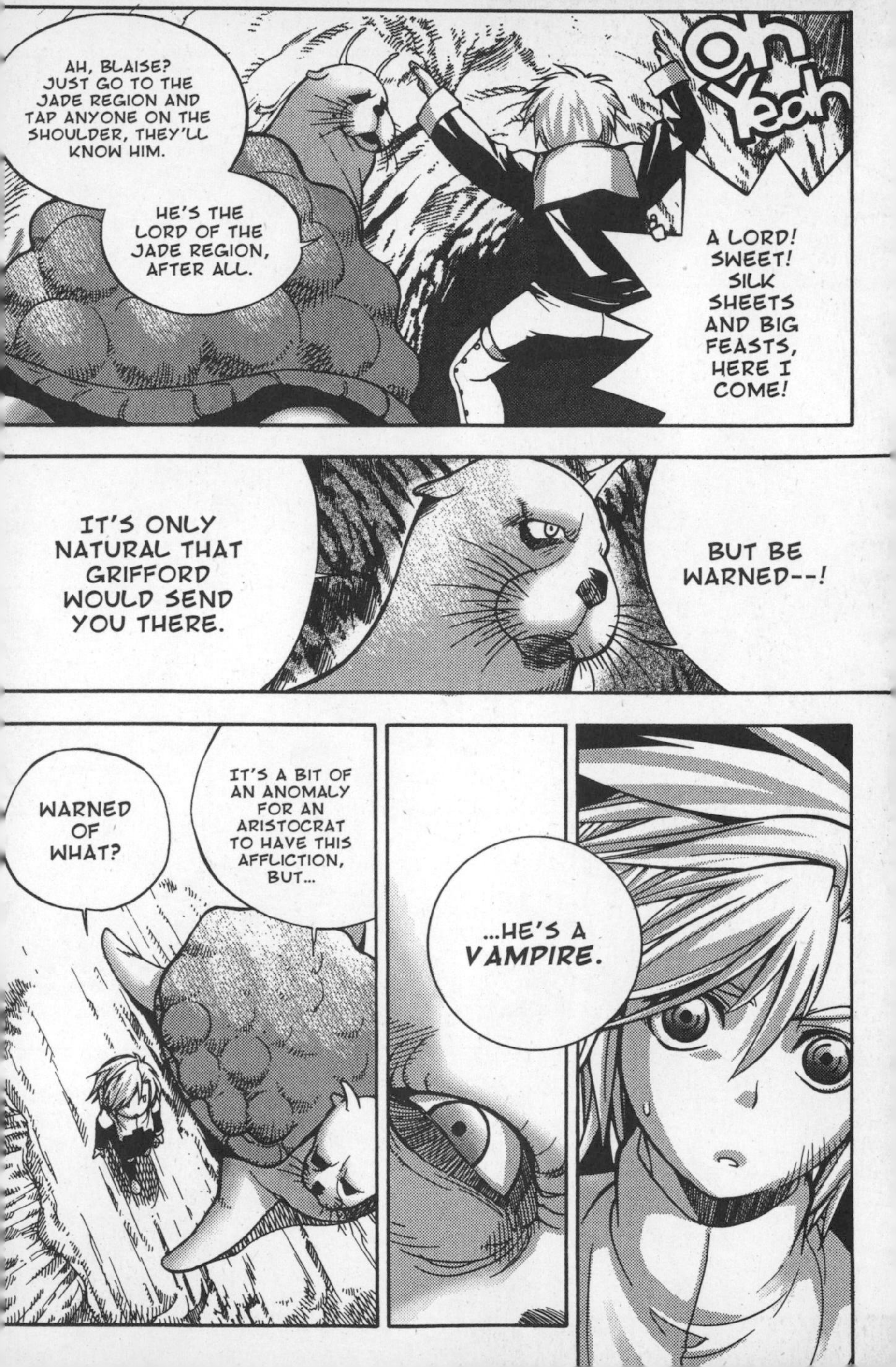
AH, BLAISE? JUST GO TO THE JADE REGION AND TAP ANYONE ON THE SHOULDER, THEY'LL KNOW HIM.
HE'S THE LORD OF THE JADE REGION, AFTER ALL.
Oh Yeah
A LORD! SWEET! SILK SHEETS AND BIG FEASTS, HERE I COME!
IT'S ONLY NATURAL THAT GRIFFORD WOULD SEND YOU THERE.
BUT BE WARNED--!
WARNED OF WHAT?
IT'S A BIT OF AN ANOMALY FOR AN ARISTOCRAT TO HAVE THIS AFFLICTION, BUT...
...HE'S A VAMPIRE.

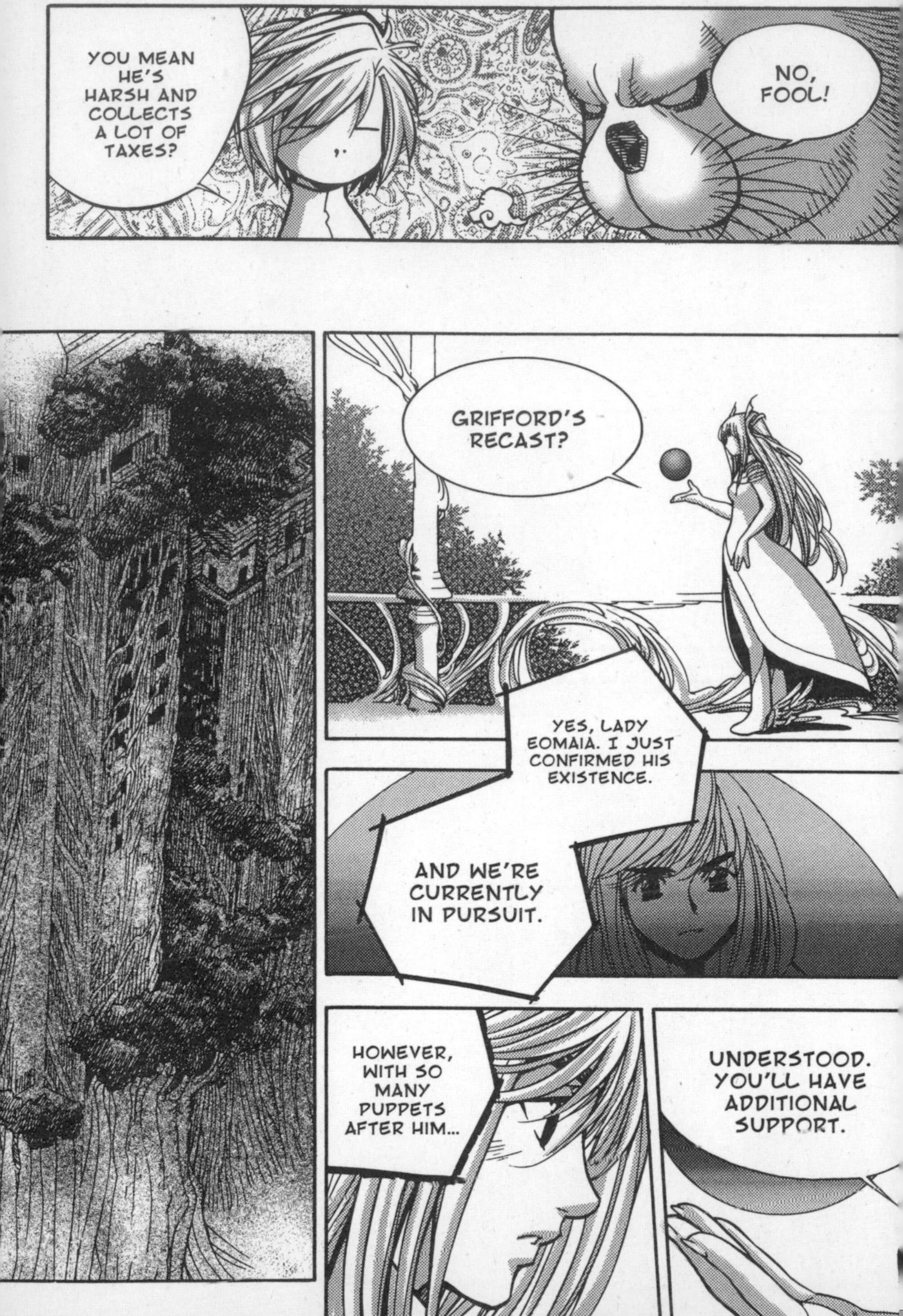
YOU MEAN HE'S HARSH AND COLLECTS A LOT OF TAXES?
NO, FOOL!
GRIFFORD'S RECAST?
YES, LADY EOMAIA. I JUST CONFIRMED HIS EXISTENCE.
AND WE'RE CURRENTLY IN PURSUIT.
HOWEVER, WITH SO MANY PUPPETS AFTER HIM...
UNDERSTOOD. YOU'LL HAVE ADDITIONAL SUPPORT.

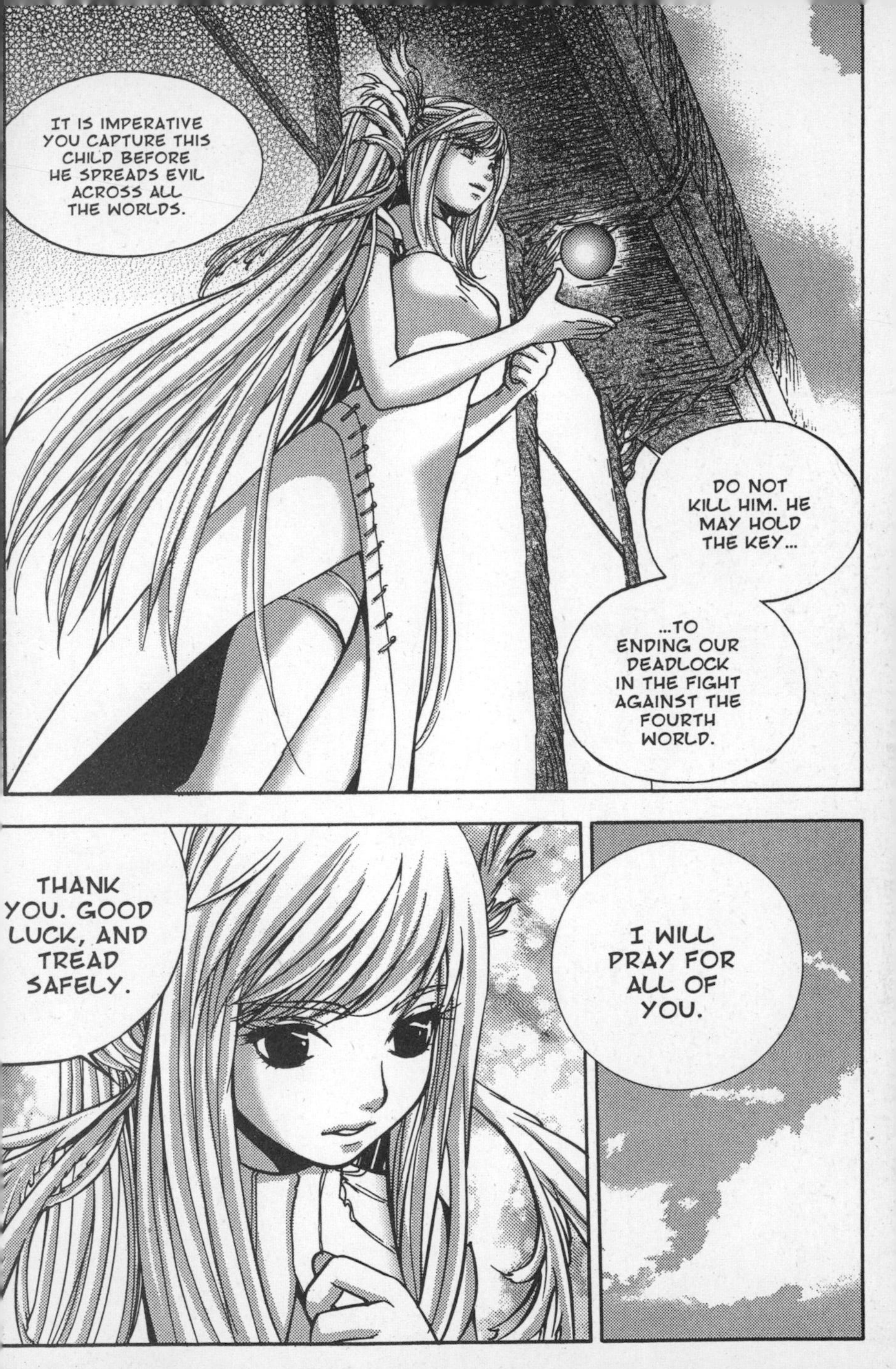
IT IS IMPERATIVE YOU CAPTURE THIS CHILD BEFORE HE SPREADS EVIL ACROSS ALL THE WORLDS.
DO NOT KILL HIM. HE MAY HOLD THE KEY...
...TO ENDING OUR DEADLOCK IN THE FIGHT AGAINST THE FOURTH WORLD.
THANK YOU. GOOD LUCK, AND TREAD SAFELY.
I WILL PRAY FOR ALL OF YOU.

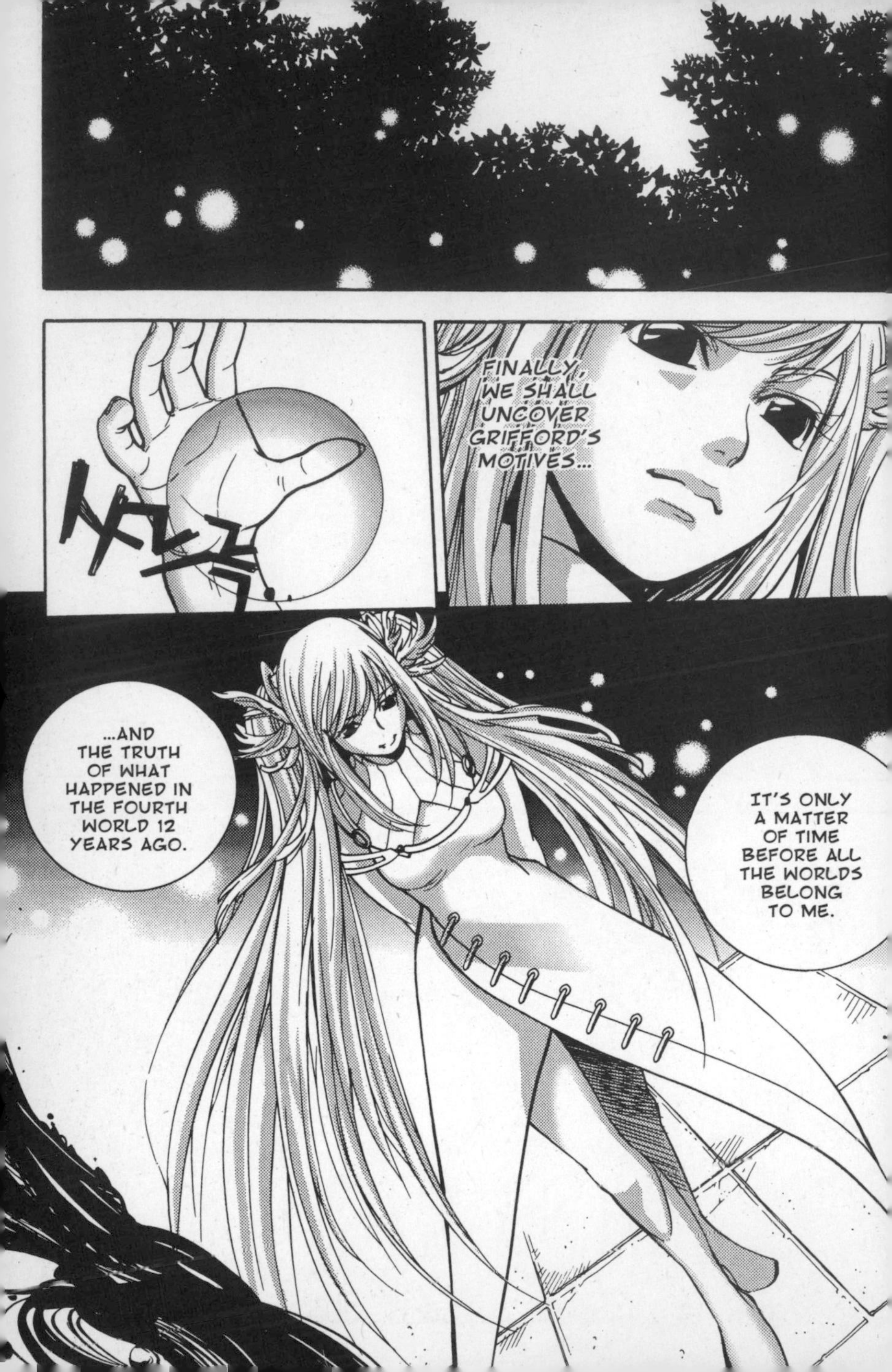
FINALLY, WE SHALL UNCOVER GRIFFORD'S MOTIVES...
...AND THE TRUTH OF WHAT HAPPENED IN THE FOURTH WORLD 12 YEARS AGO.
IT'S ONLY A MATTER OF TIME BEFORE ALL THE WORLDS BELONG TO ME.

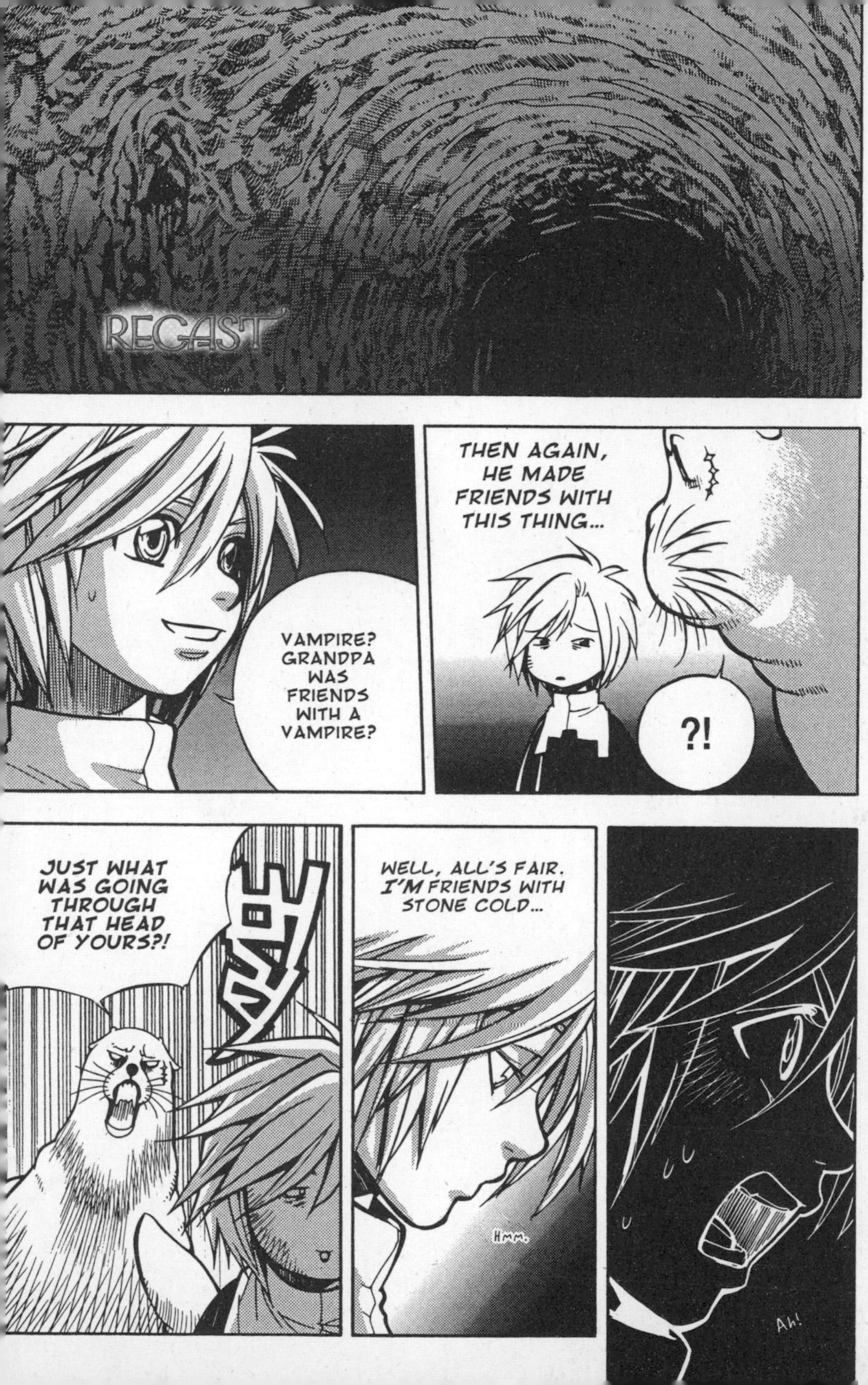
REGAST
VAMPIRE? GRANDPA WAS FRIENDS WITH A VAMPIRE?
THEN AGAIN, HE MADE FRIENDS WITH THIS THING...
?!
JUST WHAT WAS GOING THROUGH THAT HEAD OF YOURS?!
WELL, ALL'S FAIR. *I'M* FRIENDS WITH STONE COLD...
Hmm.
Ah!

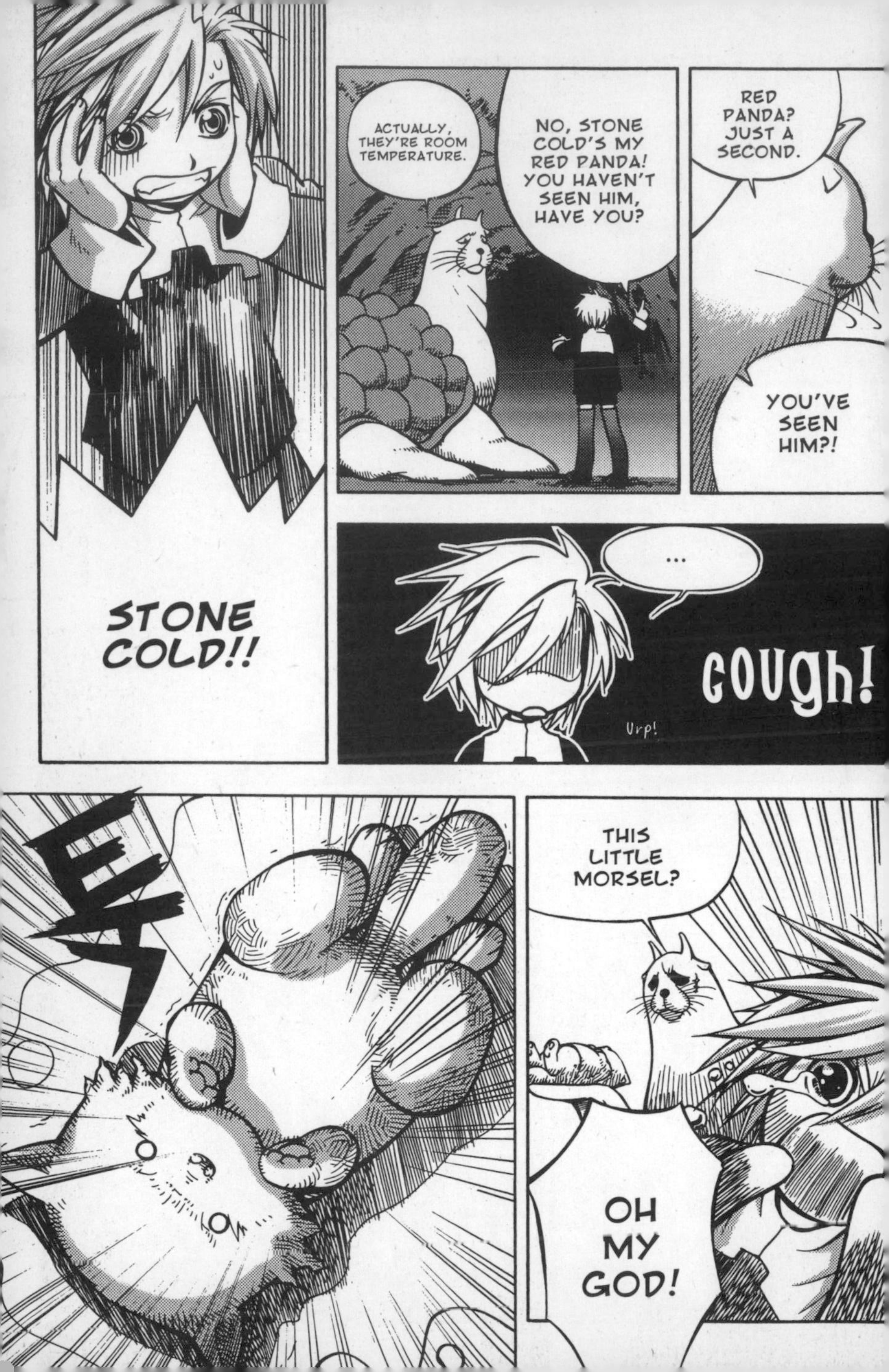
STONE COLD!!
ACTUALLY, THEY'RE ROOM TEMPERATURE.
NO, STONE COLD'S MY RED PANDA! YOU HAVEN'T SEEN HIM, HAVE YOU?
RED PANDA? JUST A SECOND.
YOU'VE SEEN HIM?!
...
COUGH!
Urp!
THIS LITTLE MORSEL?
OH MY GOD!

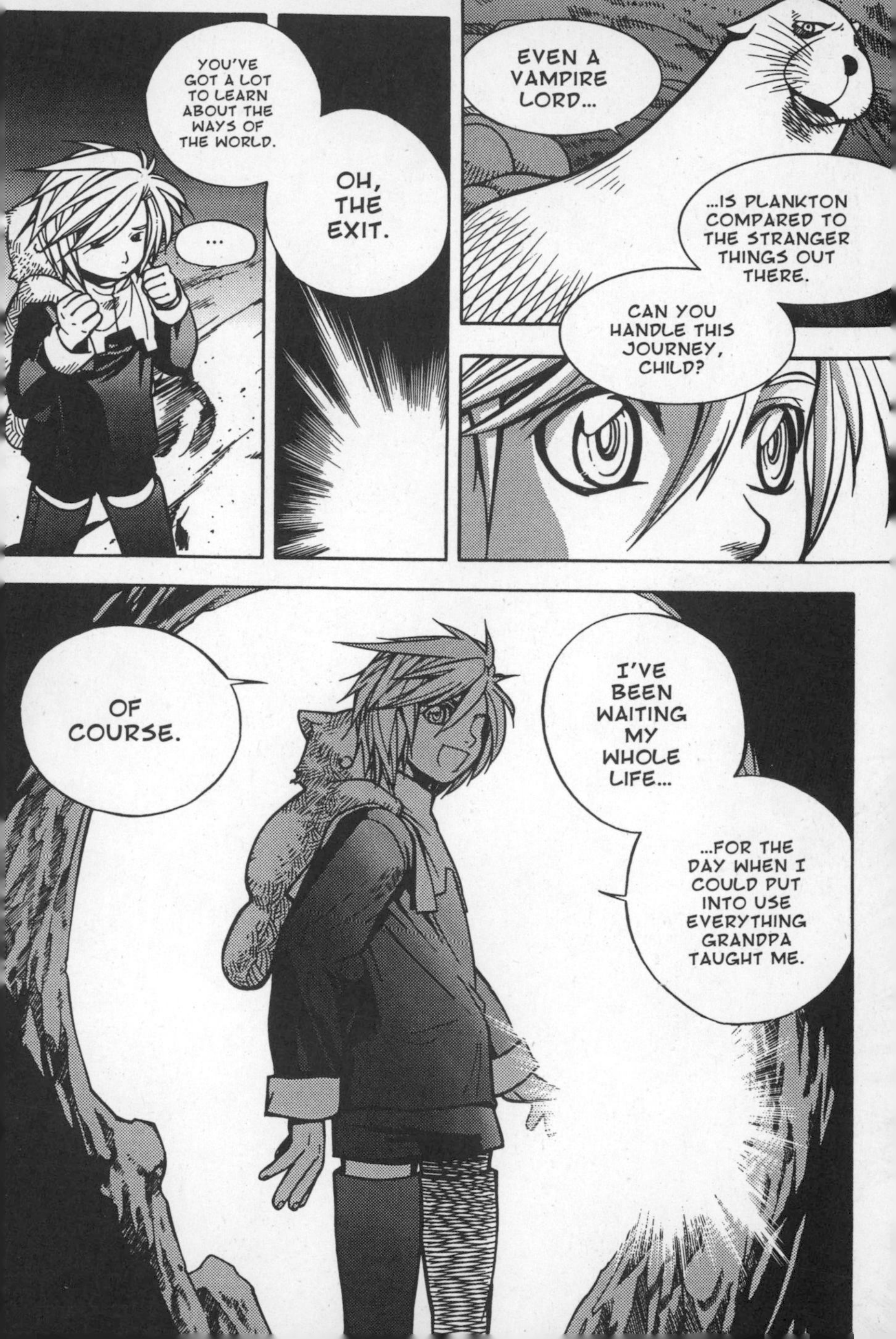
YOU'VE GOT A LOT TO LEARN ABOUT THE WAYS OF THE WORLD.
...
OH, THE EXIT.
EVEN A VAMPIRE LORD...
...IS PLANKTON COMPARED TO THE STRANGER THINGS OUT THERE.
CAN YOU HANDLE THIS JOURNEY, CHILD?
OF COURSE.
I'VE BEEN WAITING MY WHOLE LIFE...
...FOR THE DAY WHEN I COULD PUT INTO USE EVERYTHING GRANDPA TAUGHT ME.

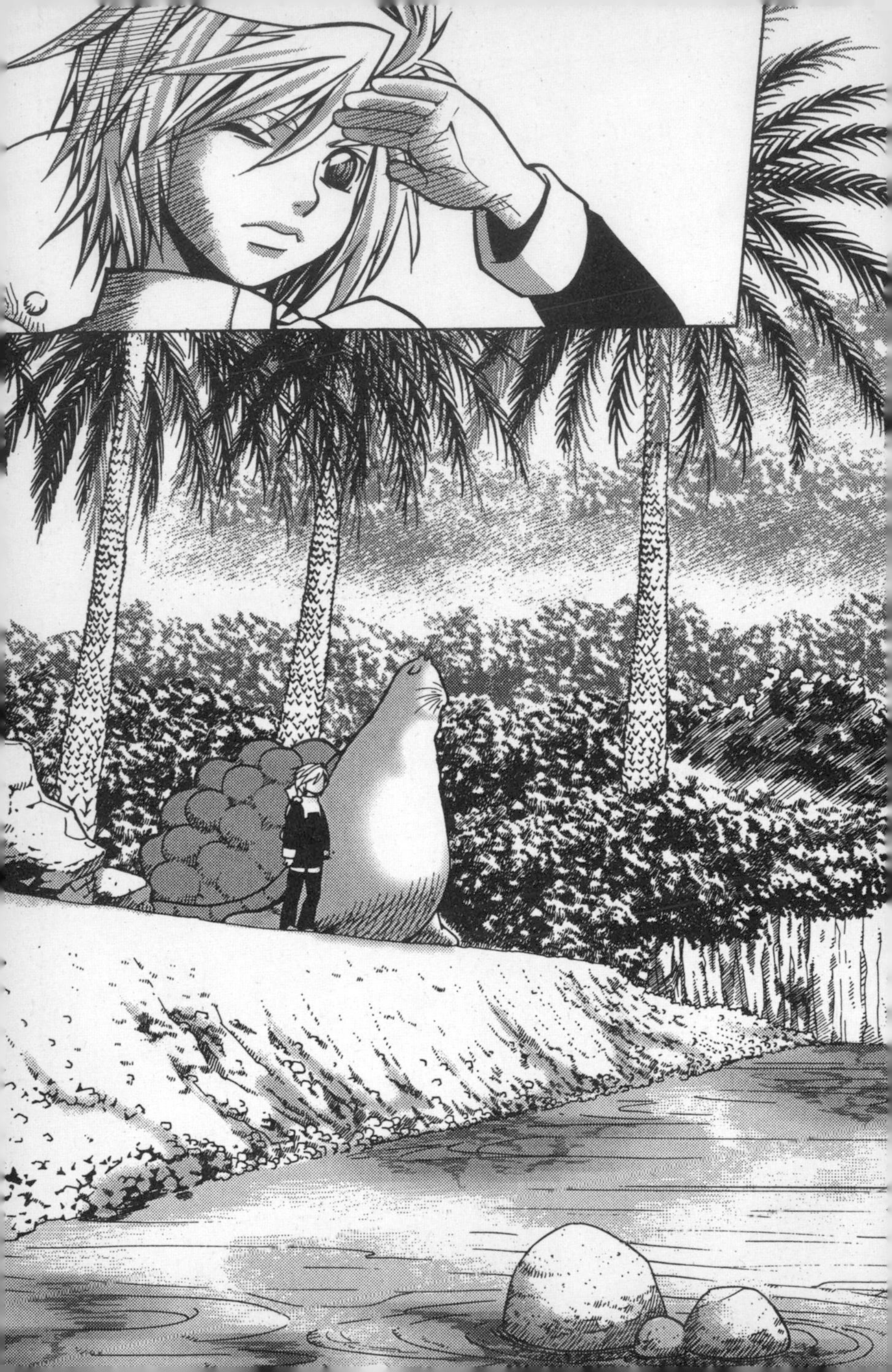

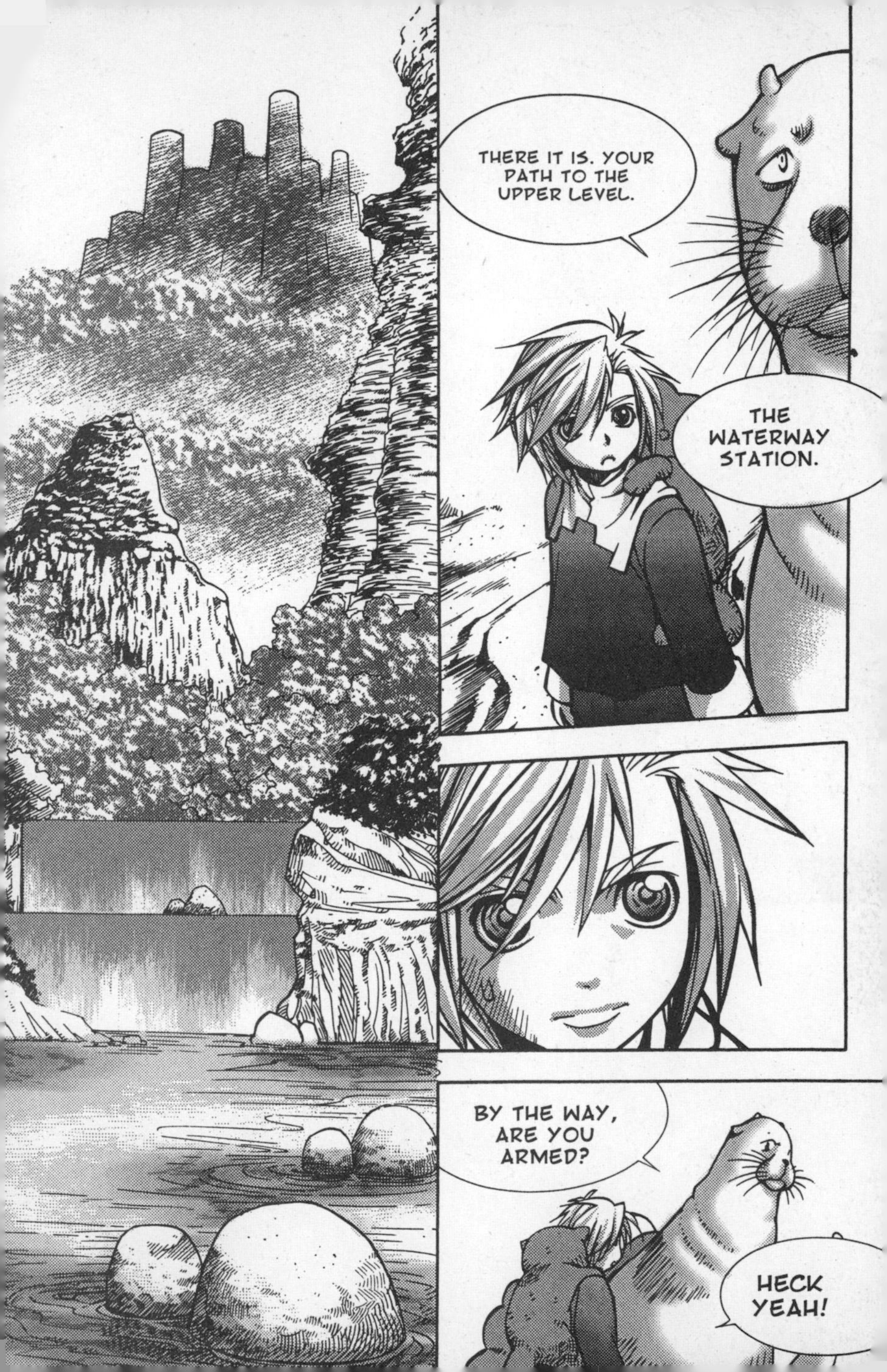
THERE IT IS. YOUR PATH TO THE UPPER LEVEL.
THE WATERWAY STATION.
BY THE WAY, ARE YOU ARMED?
HECK YEAH!

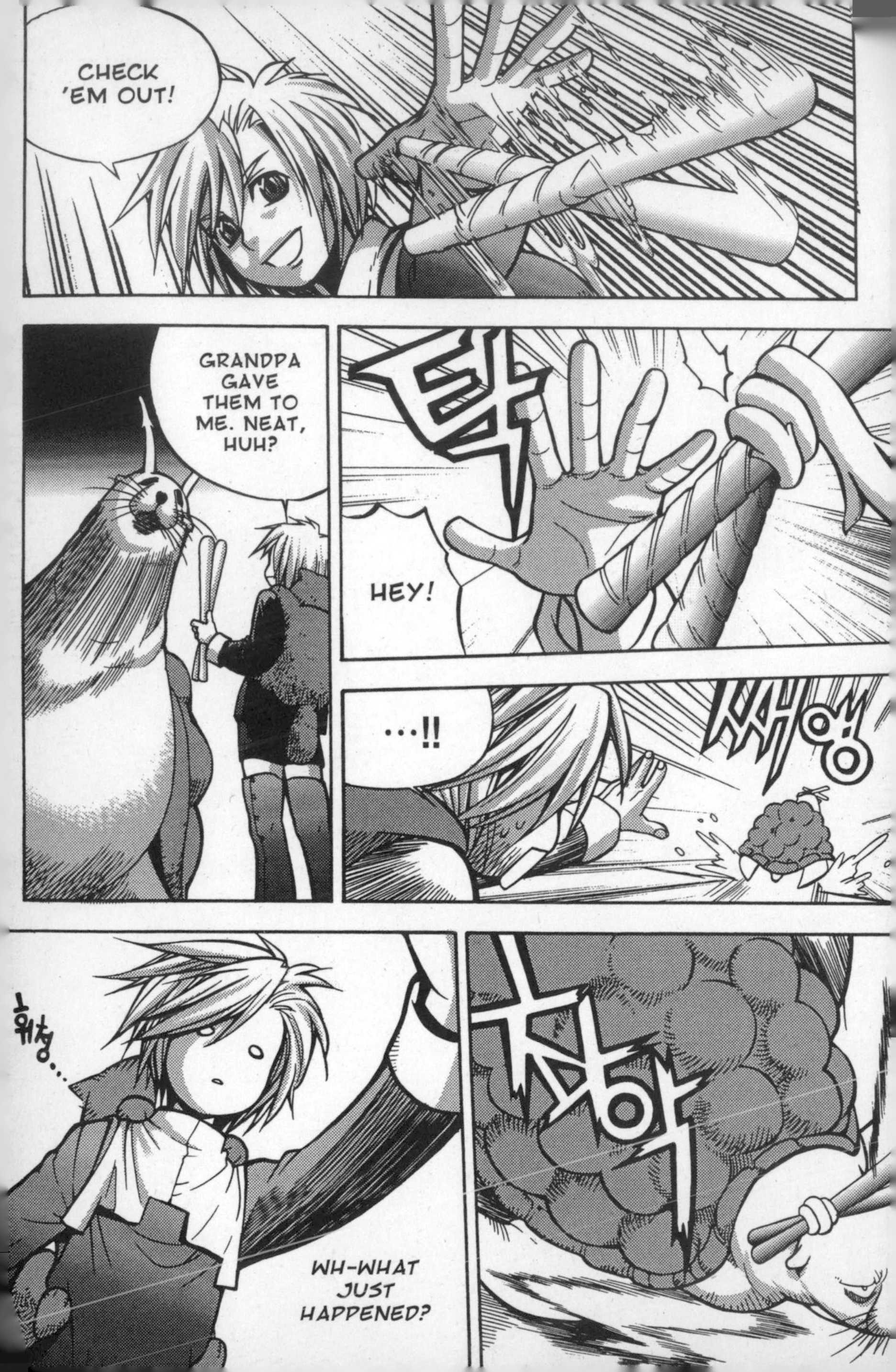
CHECK 'EM OUT!
GRANDPA GAVE THEM TO ME. NEAT, HUH?
HEY!
...!!
휘청...
WH-WHAT JUST HAPPENED?

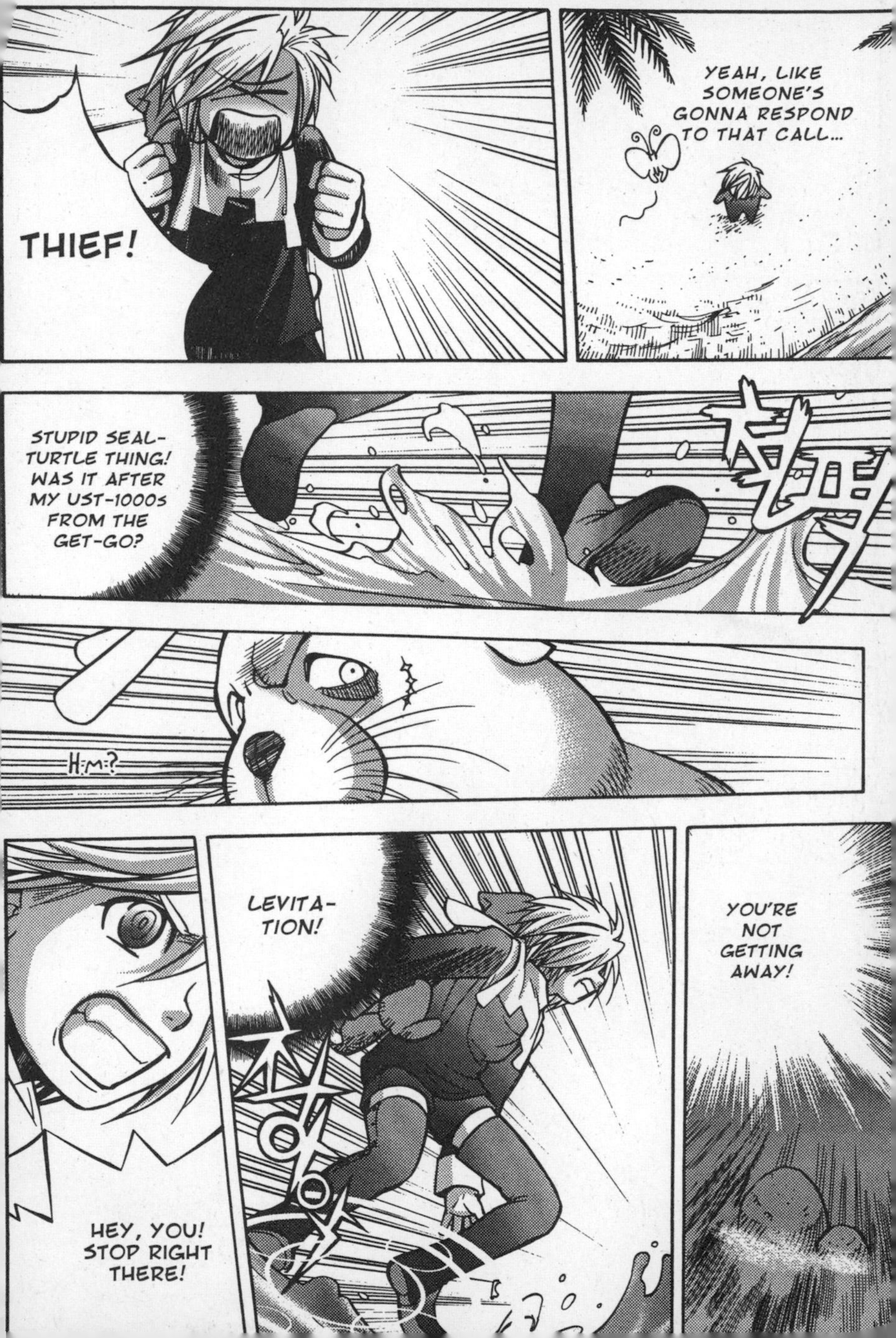
THIEF!
YEAH, LIKE SOMEONE'S GONNA RESPOND TO THAT CALL...
STUPID SEAL-TURTLE THING! WAS IT AFTER MY UST-1000S FROM THE GET-GO?
H-M?
HEY, YOU! STOP RIGHT THERE!
LEVITA-TION!
YOU'RE NOT GETTING AWAY!

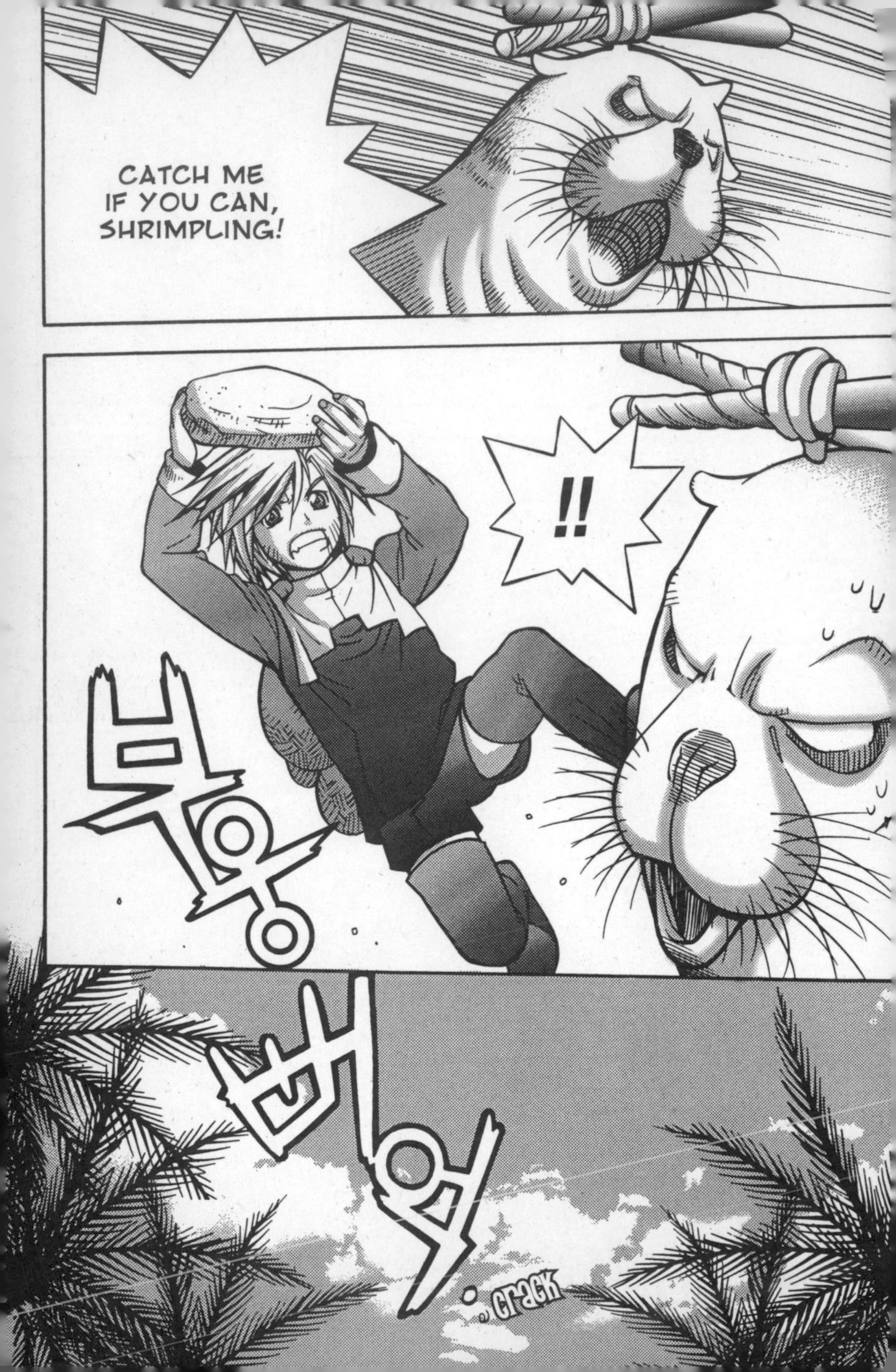
CATCH ME
IF YOU CAN,
SHRIMPLING!
!!
crack

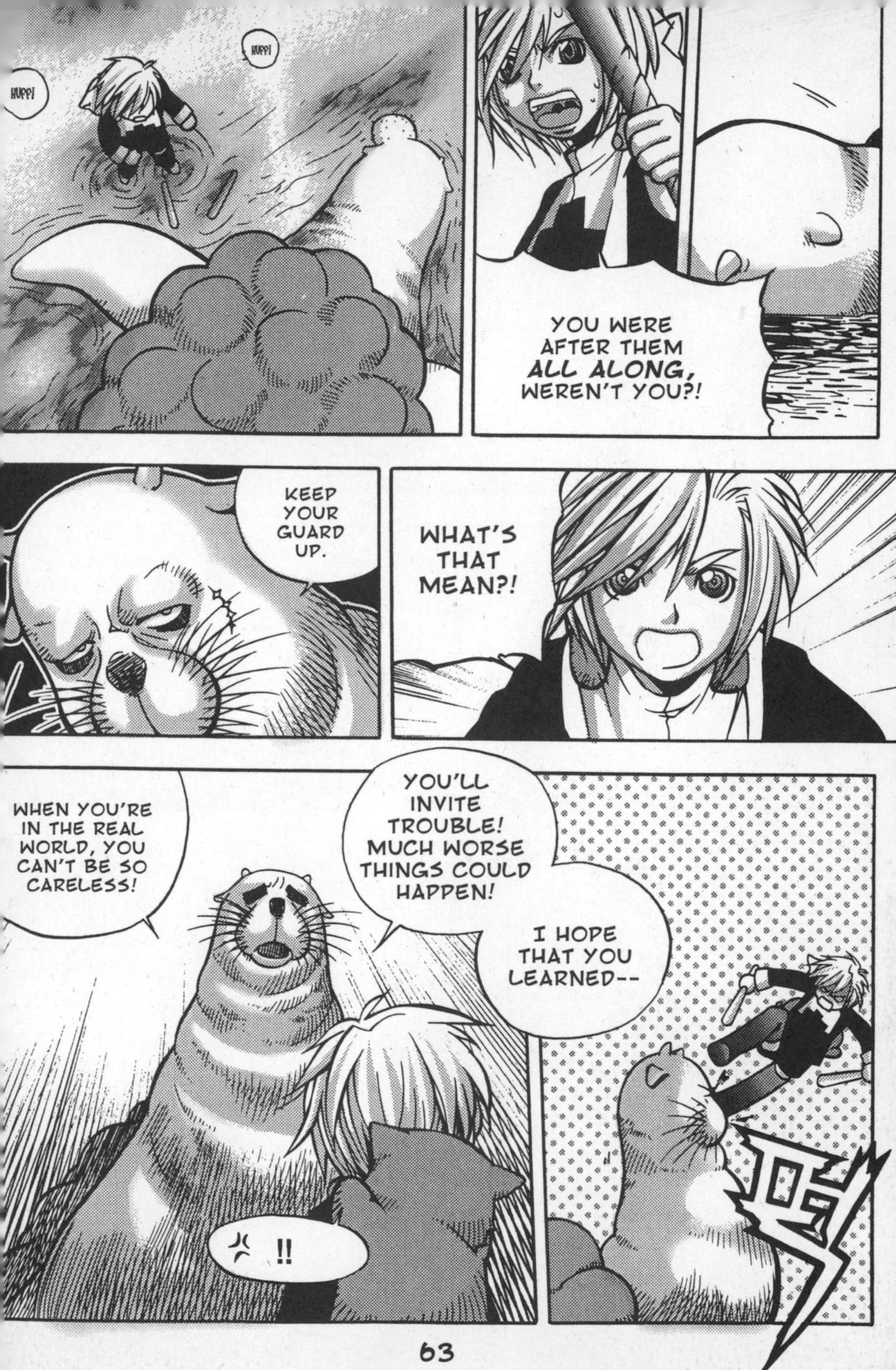
HUFF!
HUFF!
YOU WERE AFTER THEM **ALL ALONG,** WEREN'T YOU?!
KEEP YOUR GUARD UP.
WHAT'S THAT MEAN?!
WHEN YOU'RE IN THE REAL WORLD, YOU CAN'T BE SO CARELESS!
YOU'LL INVITE TROUBLE! MUCH WORSE THINGS COULD HAPPEN!
!!
I HOPE THAT YOU LEARNED--

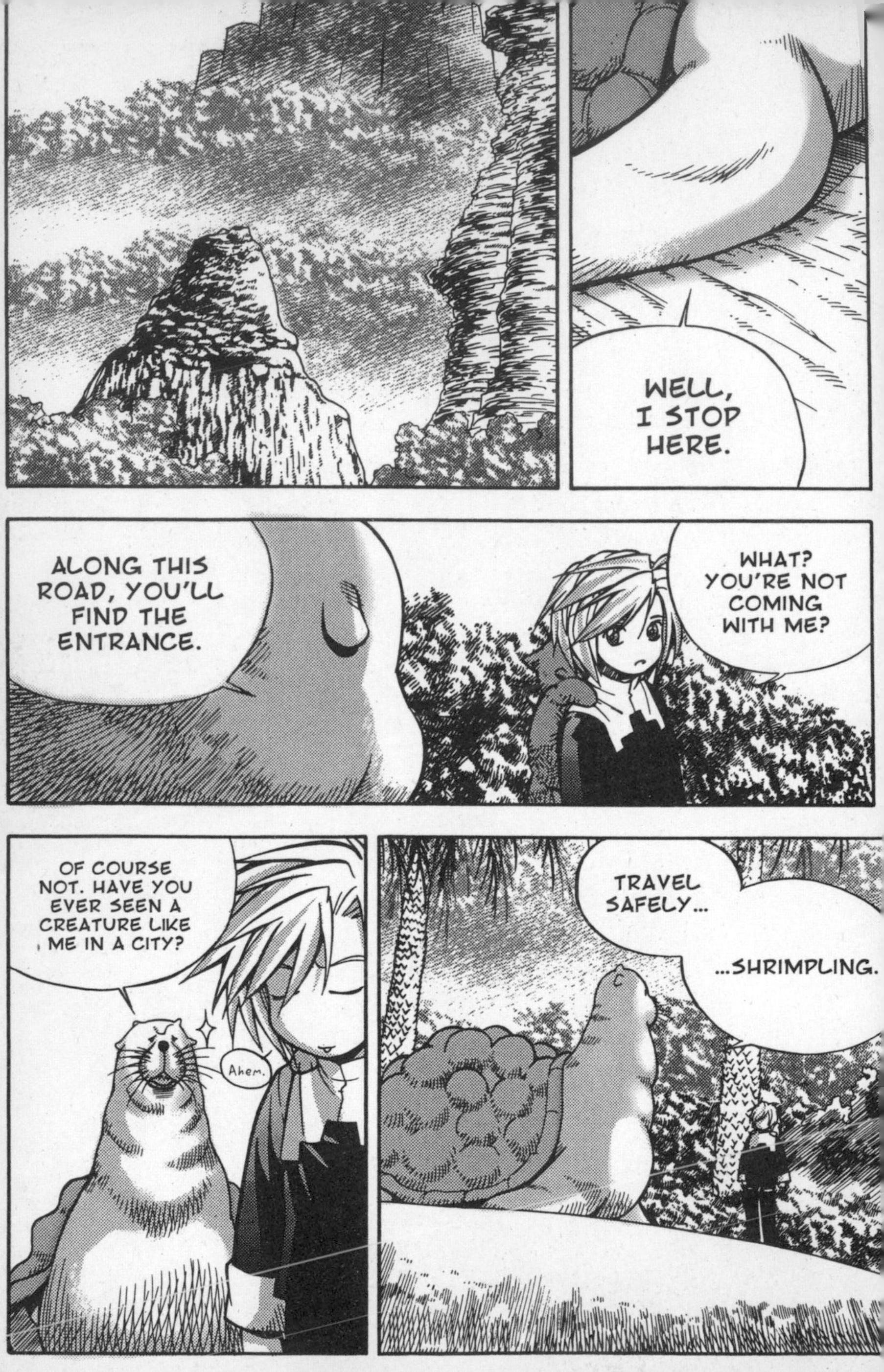
WELL, I STOP HERE.
ALONG THIS ROAD, YOU'LL FIND THE ENTRANCE.
WHAT? YOU'RE NOT COMING WITH ME?
OF COURSE NOT. HAVE YOU EVER SEEN A CREATURE LIKE ME IN A CITY?
Ahem.
TRAVEL SAFELY...
...SHRIMPLING.

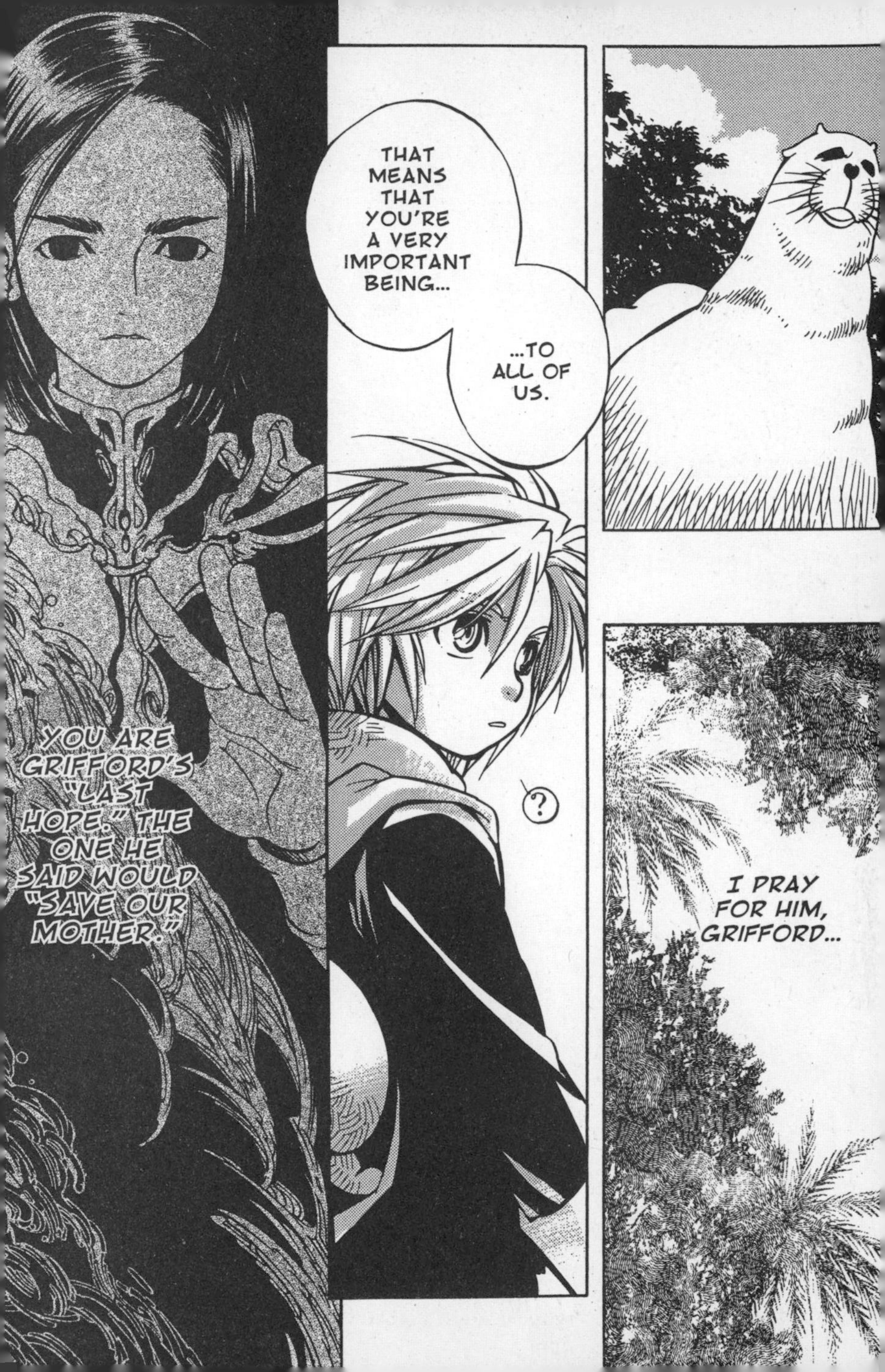
YOU ARE GRIFFORD'S "LAST HOPE." THE ONE HE SAID WOULD "SAVE OUR MOTHER."
THAT MEANS THAT YOU'RE A VERY IMPORTANT BEING...
...TO ALL OF US.
?
I PRAY FOR HIM, GRIFFORD...

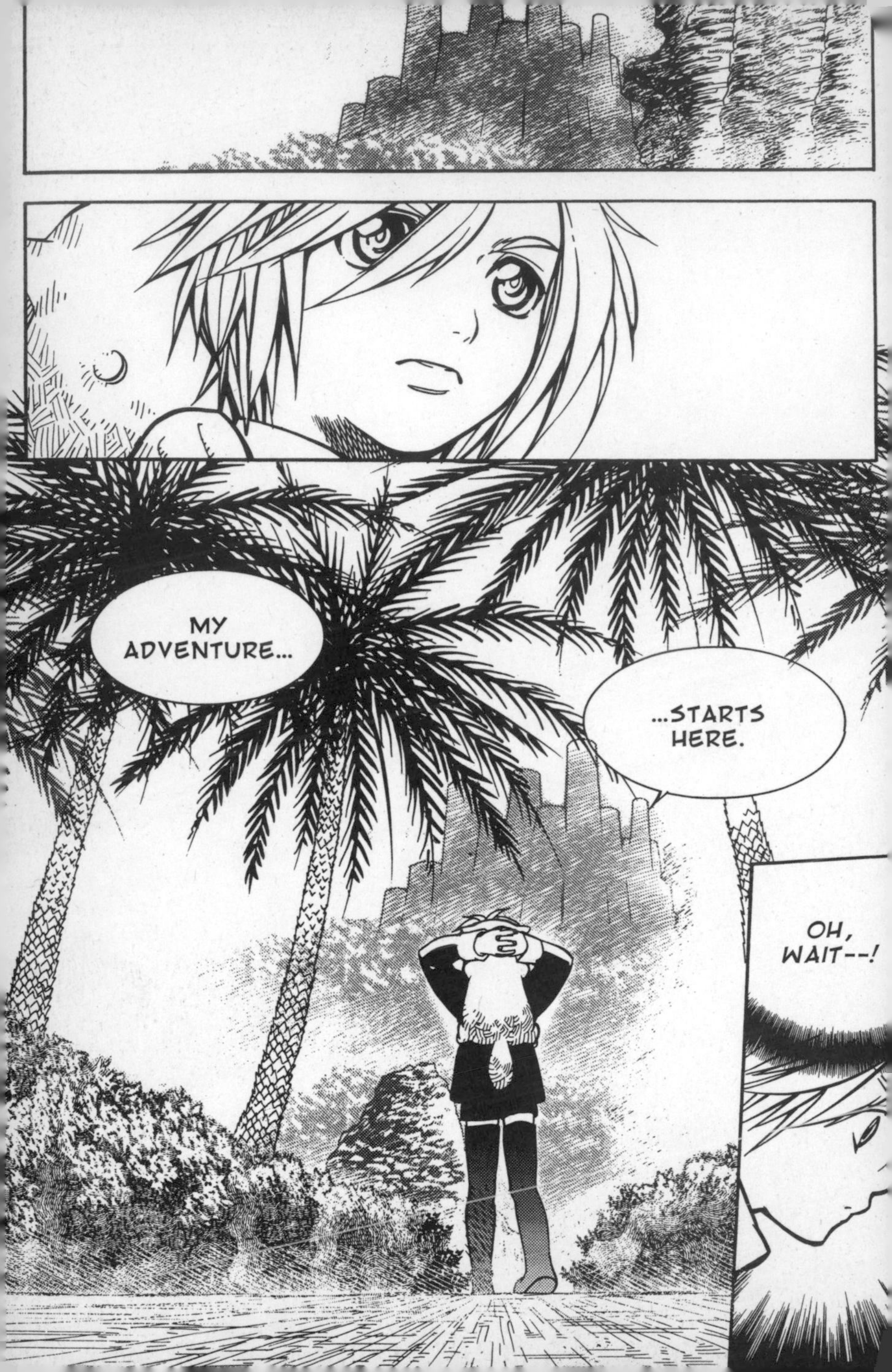
MY ADVENTURE...
...STARTS HERE.
OH, WAIT--!

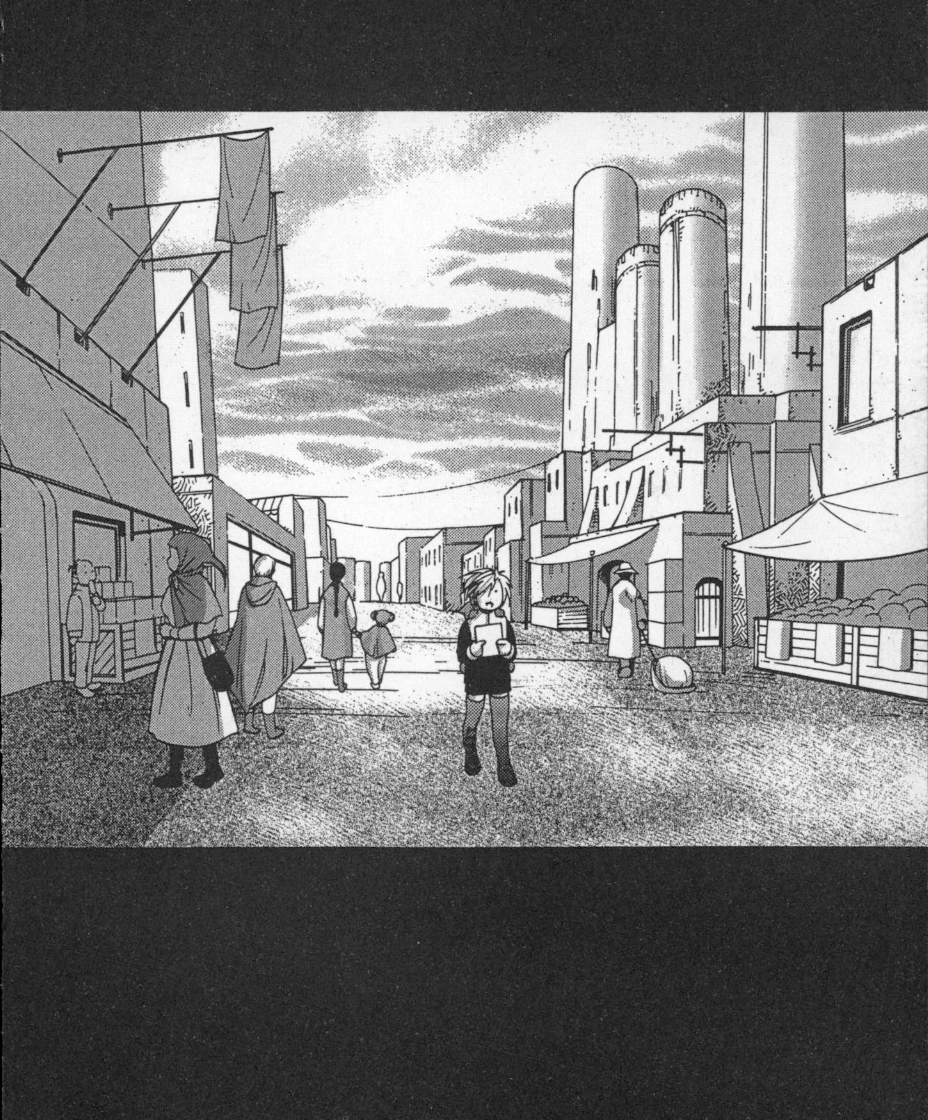

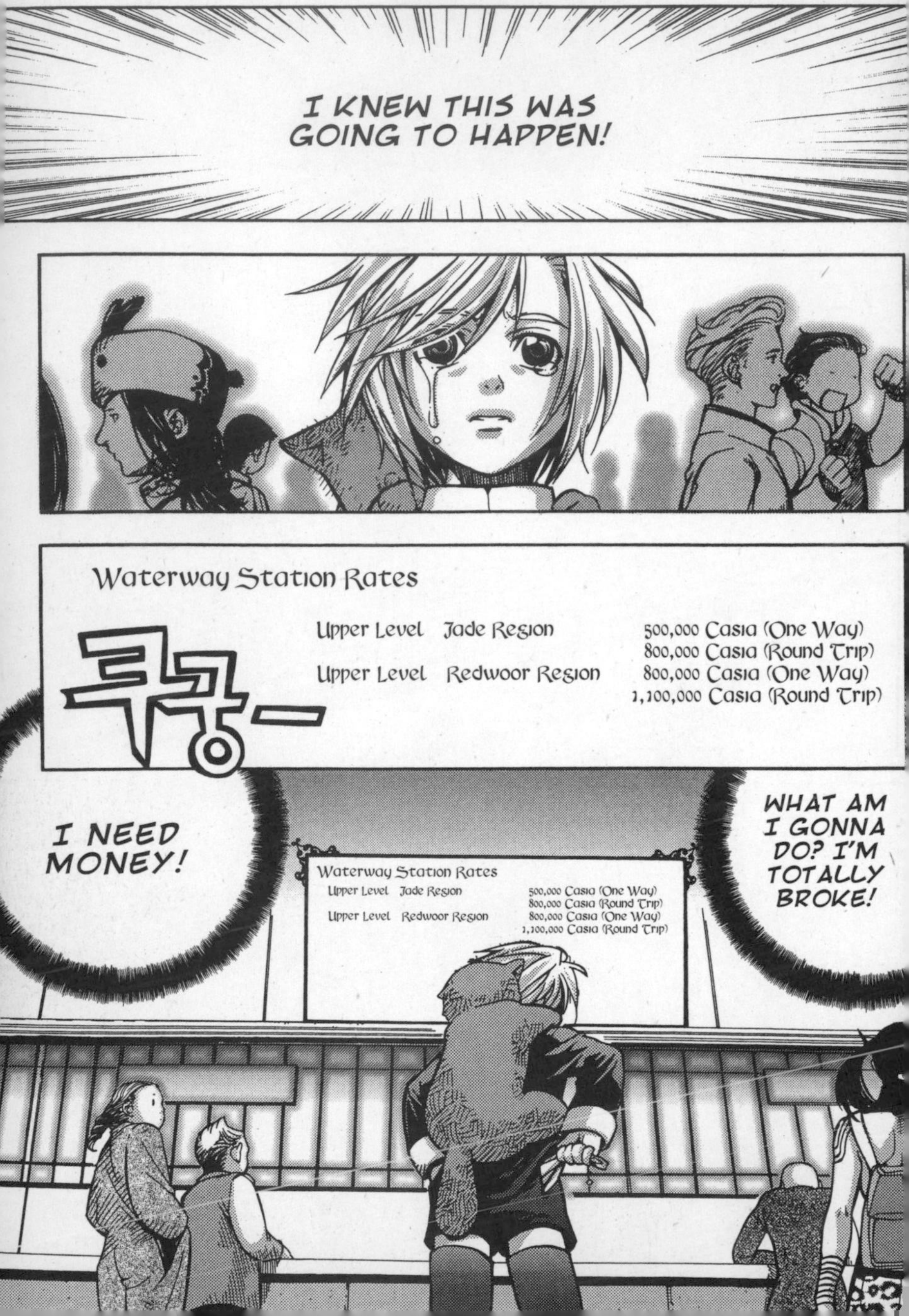
I KNEW THIS WAS GOING TO HAPPEN!
Waterway Station Rates
Upper Level Jade Region 500,000 Casia (One Way)
800,000 Casia (Round Trip)
Upper Level Redwoor Region 800,000 Casia (One Way)
1,100,000 Casia (Round Trip)
쿠궁-
I NEED MONEY!
Waterway Station Rates
Upper Level Jade Region 500,000 Casia (One Way)
800,000 Casia (Round Trip)
Upper Level Redwoor Region 800,000 Casia (One Way)
1,100,000 Casia (Round Trip)
WHAT AM I GONNA DO? I'M TOTALLY BROKE!

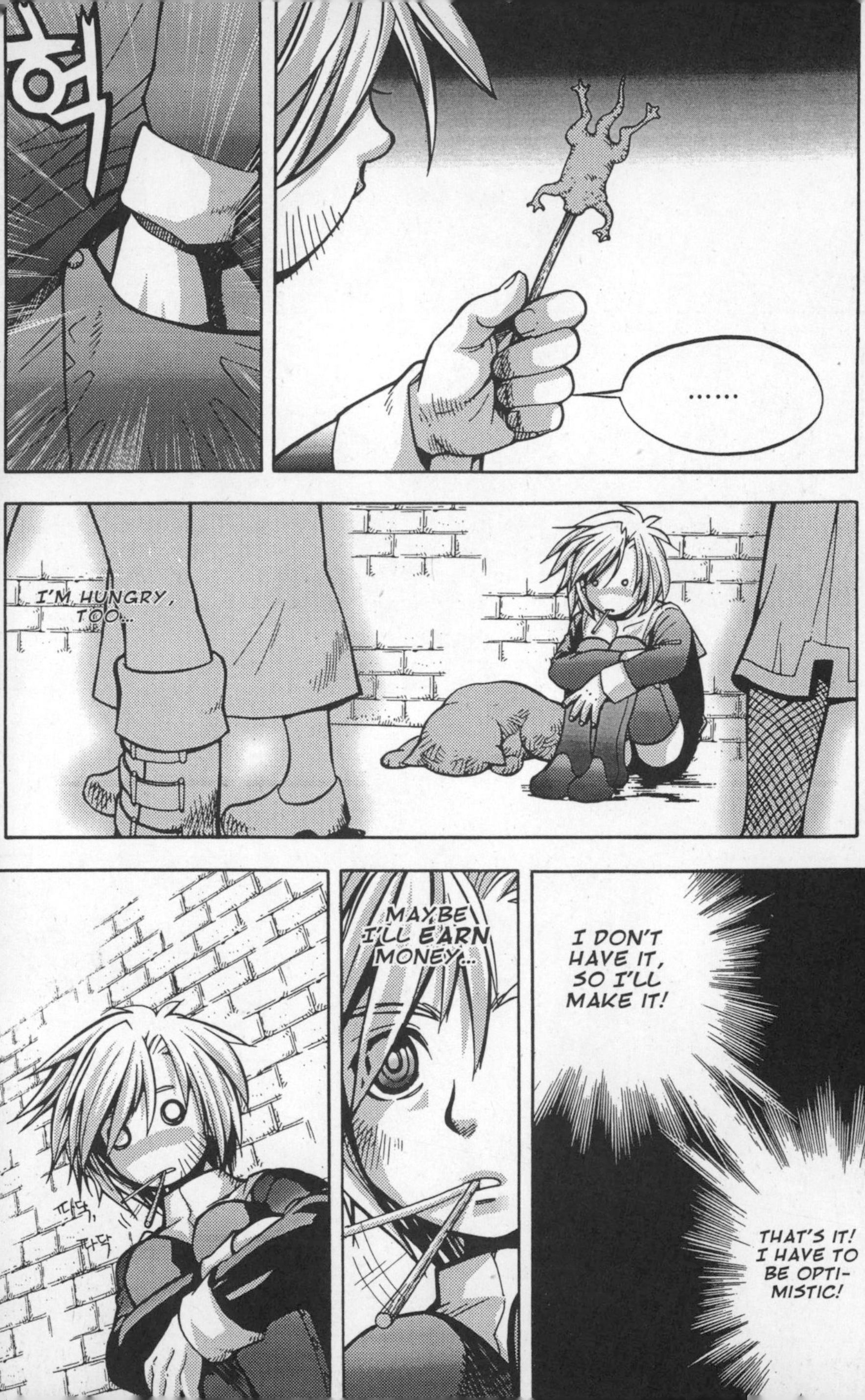
헉
......
I'M HUNGRY, TOO...
따닥,
따닥
MAYBE I'LL EARN MONEY...
I DON'T HAVE IT, SO I'LL MAKE IT!
THAT'S IT! I HAVE TO BE OPTI-MISTIC!

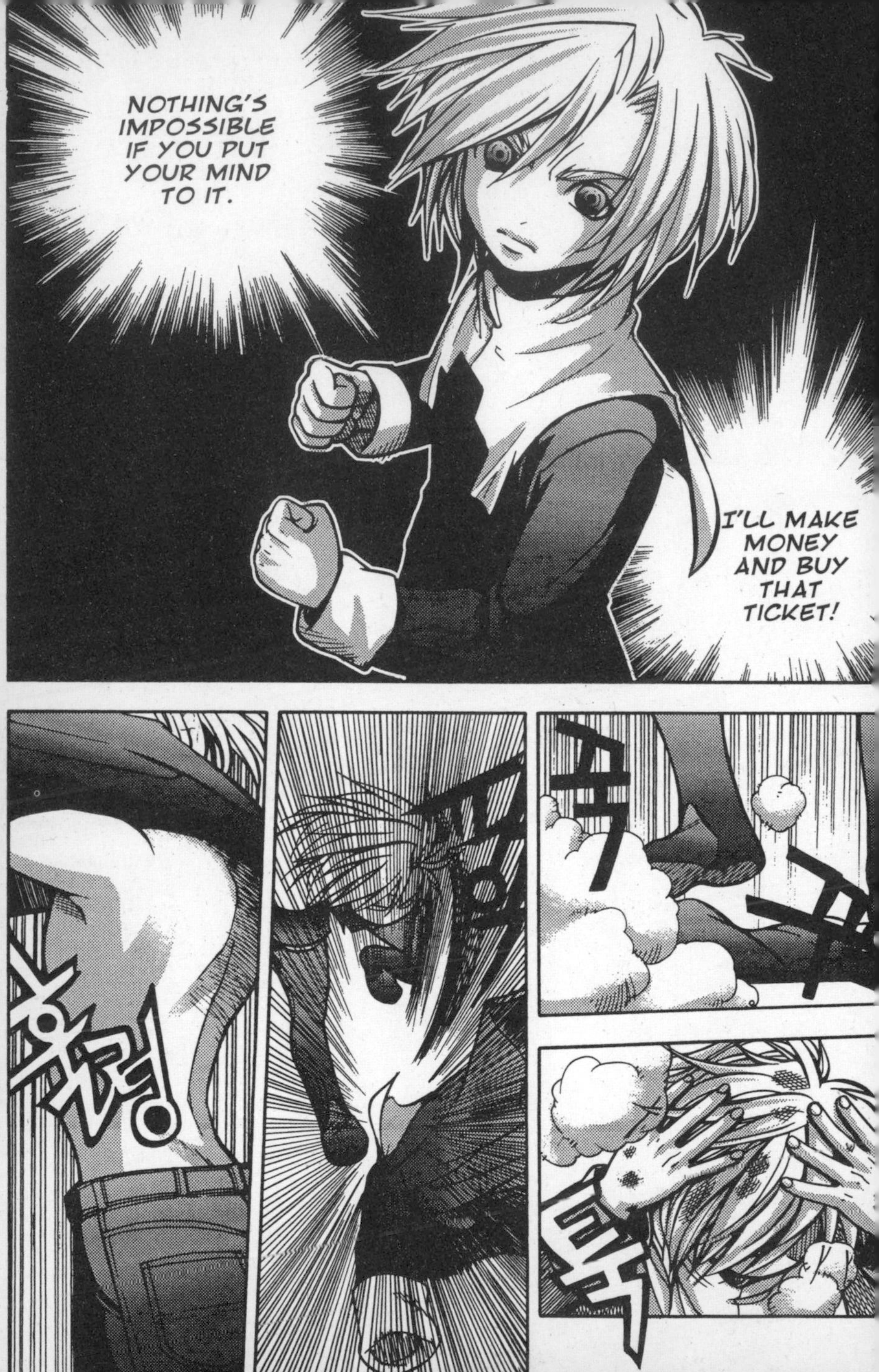
NOTHING'S IMPOSSIBLE IF YOU PUT YOUR MIND TO IT.
I'LL MAKE MONEY AND BUY THAT TICKET!

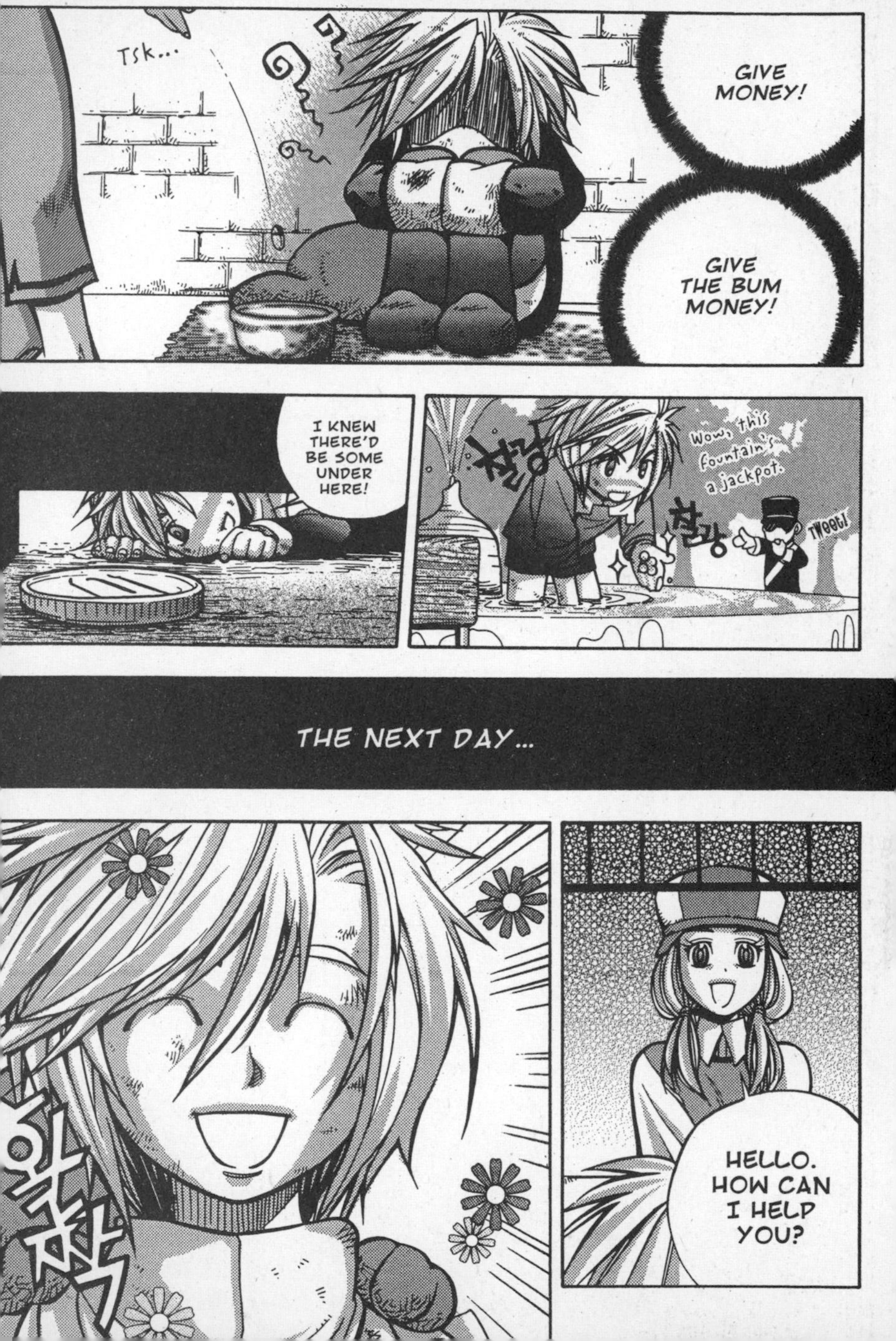
Tsk...
GIVE MONEY!
GIVE THE BUM MONEY!
I KNEW THERE'D BE SOME UNDER HERE!
Wow, this fountain's a jackpot.
TWEET!
THE NEXT DAY...
HELLO. HOW CAN I HELP YOU?

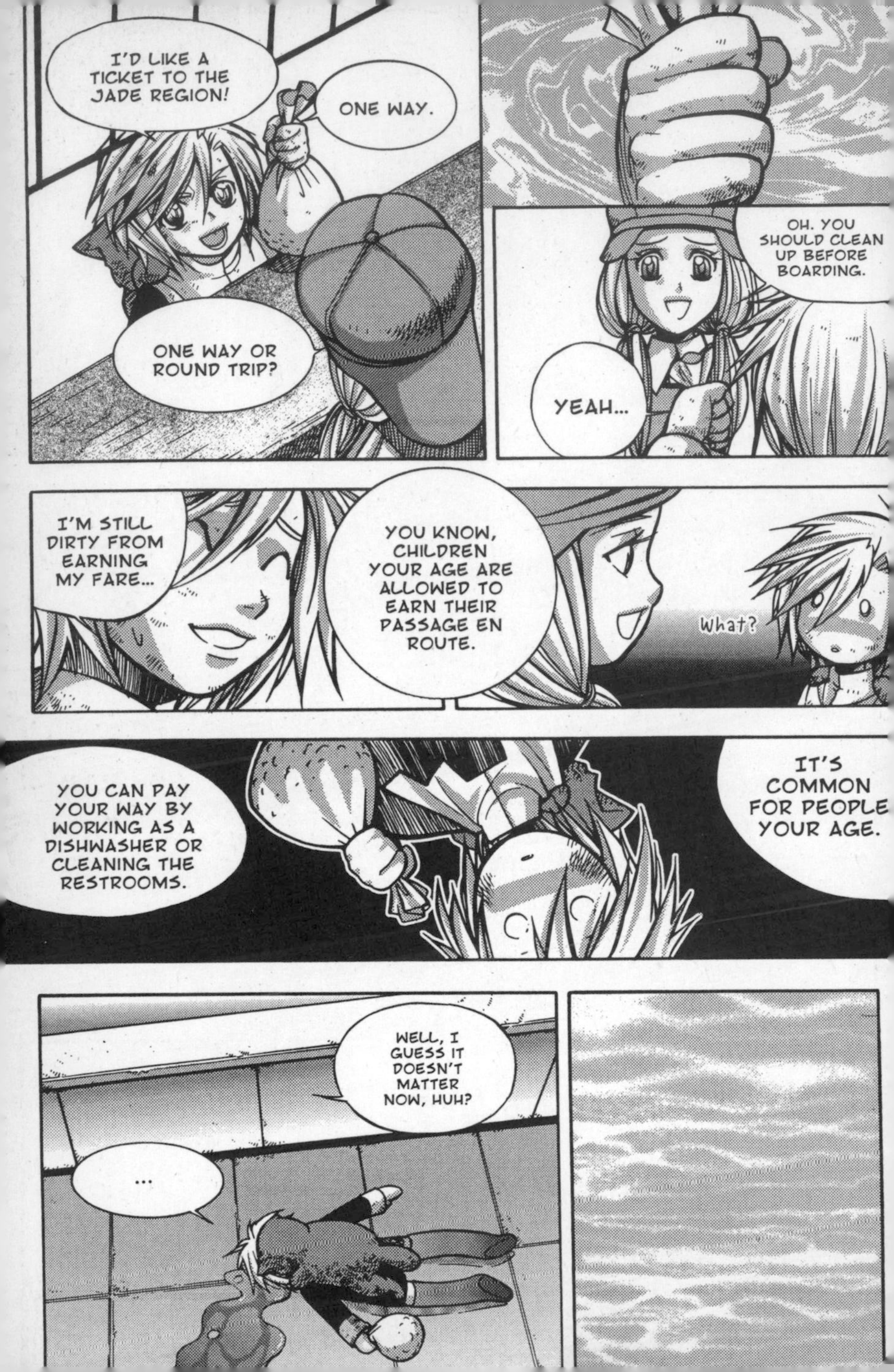
I'D LIKE A TICKET TO THE JADE REGION!
ONE WAY OR ROUND TRIP?
ONE WAY.
OH. YOU SHOULD CLEAN UP BEFORE BOARDING.
YEAH...
I'M STILL DIRTY FROM EARNING MY FARE...
YOU KNOW, CHILDREN YOUR AGE ARE ALLOWED TO EARN THEIR PASSAGE EN ROUTE.
What?
YOU CAN PAY YOUR WAY BY WORKING AS A DISHWASHER OR CLEANING THE RESTROOMS.
IT'S COMMON FOR PEOPLE YOUR AGE.
WELL, I GUESS IT DOESN'T MATTER NOW, HUH?
...

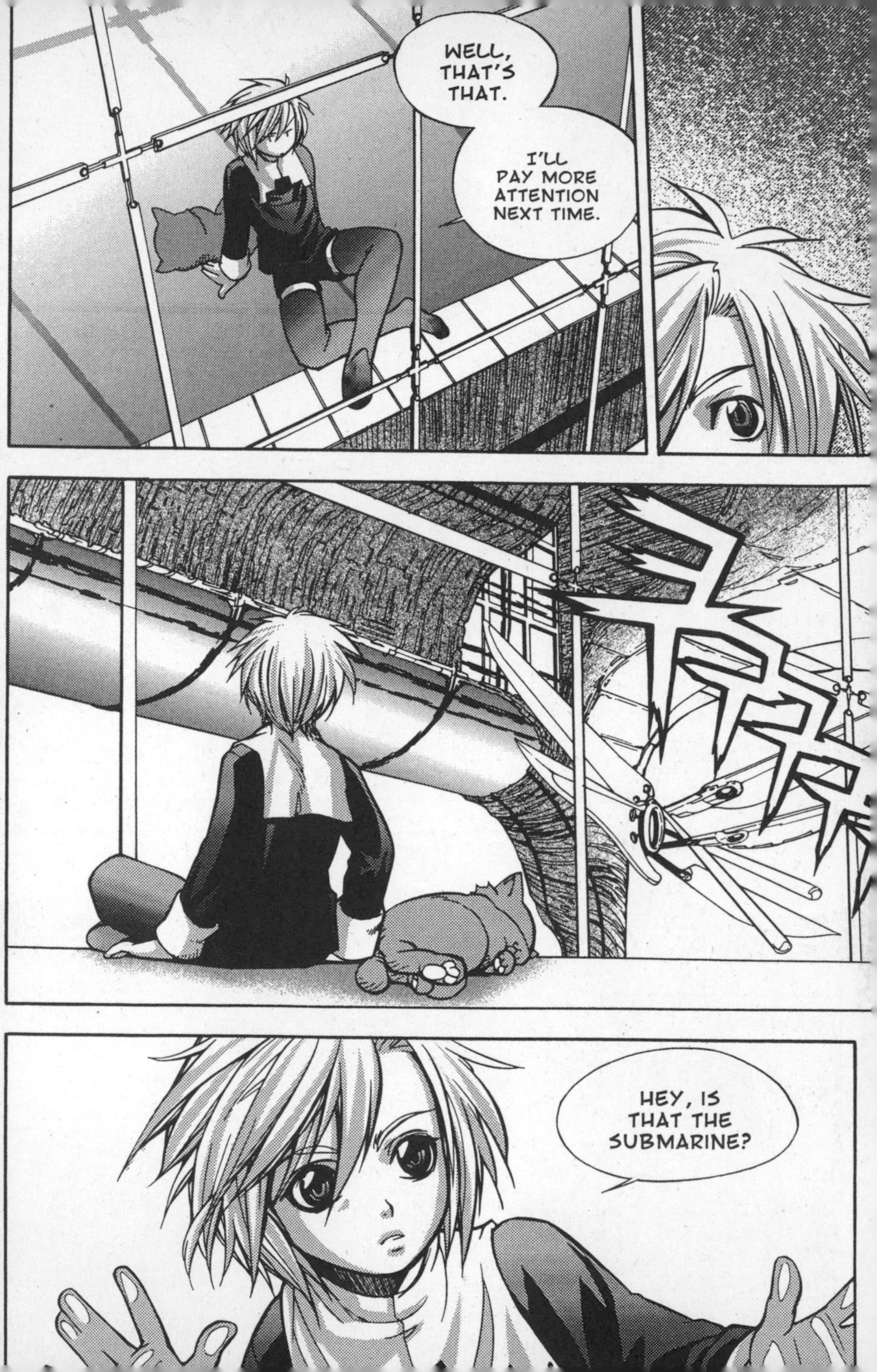
WELL, THAT'S THAT.
I'LL PAY MORE ATTENTION NEXT TIME.
HEY, IS THAT THE SUBMARINE?

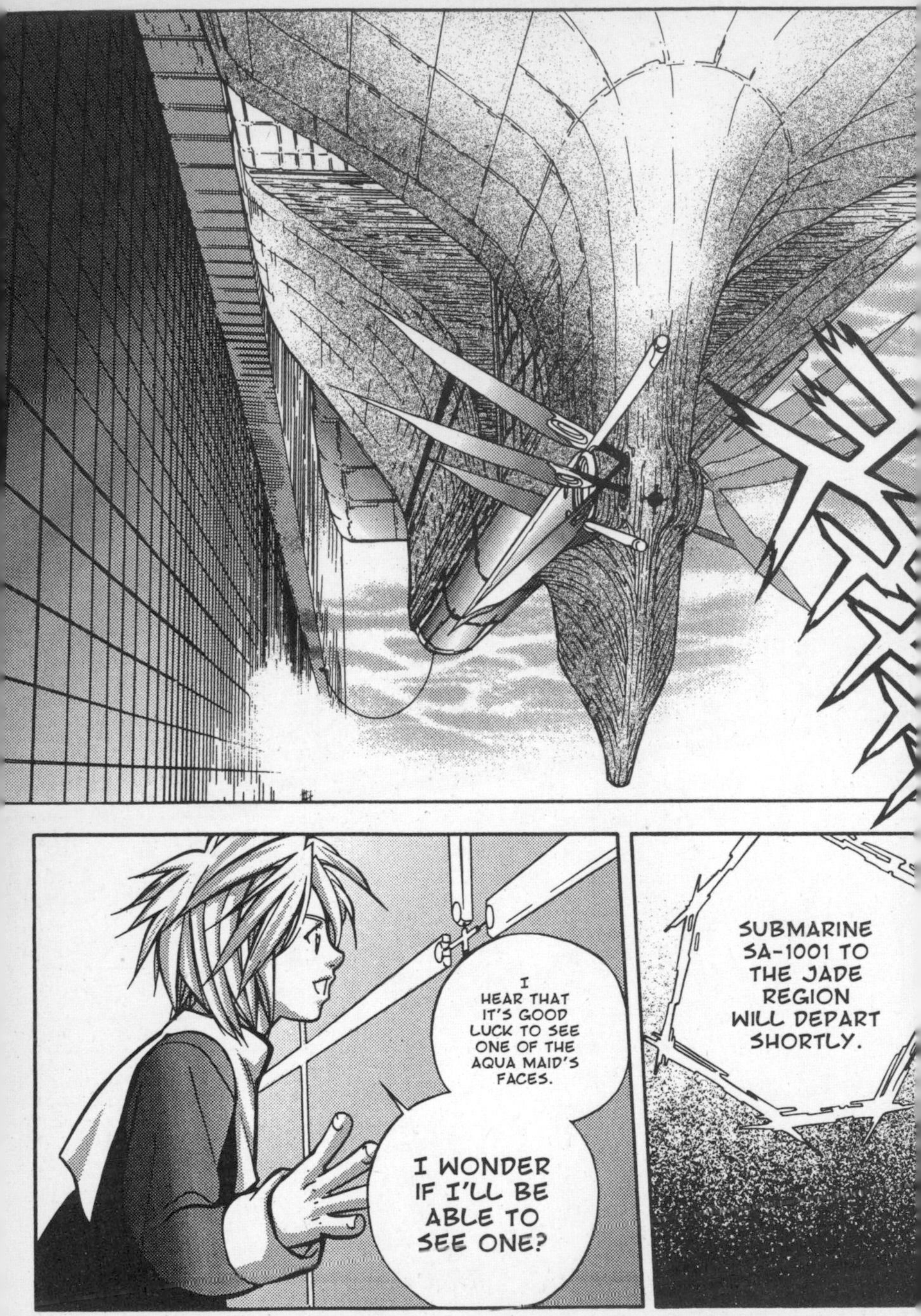
I HEAR THAT IT'S GOOD LUCK TO SEE ONE OF THE AQUA MAID'S FACES.
I WONDER IF I'LL BE ABLE TO SEE ONE?
SUBMARINE SA-1001 TO THE JADE REGION WILL DEPART SHORTLY.

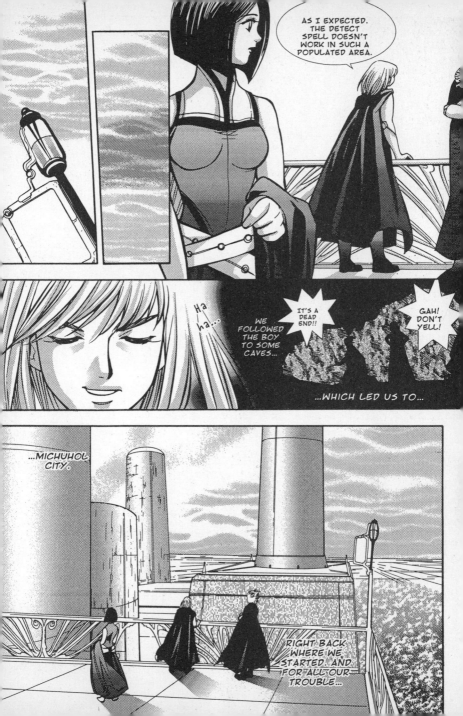

AS I EXPECTED. THE DETECT SPELL DOESN'T WORK IN SUCH A POPULATED AREA.

Ha ha...

WE FOLLOWED THE BOY TO SOME CAVES...

IT'S A DEAD END!!

GAH! DON'T YELL!

...WHICH LED US TO...

...MICHUHOL CITY.

RIGHT BACK WHERE WE STARTED. AND FOR ALL OUR TROUBLE...

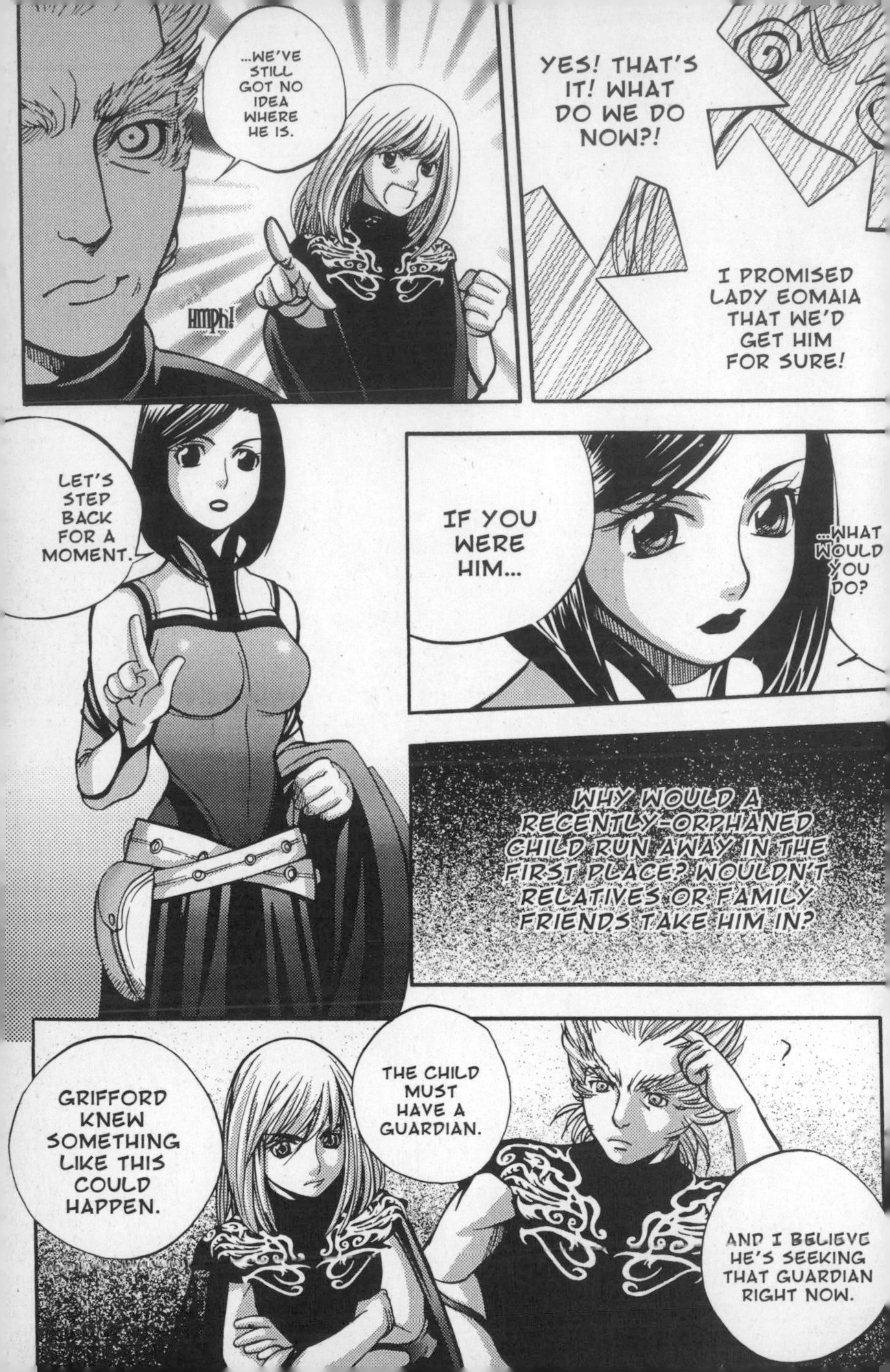
...WE'VE STILL GOT NO IDEA WHERE HE IS.
HMPH!
YES! THAT'S IT! WHAT DO WE DO NOW?!
I PROMISED LADY EOMAIA THAT WE'D GET HIM FOR SURE!
LET'S STEP BACK FOR A MOMENT.
IF YOU WERE HIM...
...WHAT WOULD YOU DO?
WHY WOULD A RECENTLY-ORPHANED CHILD RUN AWAY IN THE FIRST PLACE? WOULDN'T RELATIVES OR FAMILY FRIENDS TAKE HIM IN?
GRIFFORD KNEW SOMETHING LIKE THIS COULD HAPPEN.
THE CHILD MUST HAVE A GUARDIAN.
AND I BELIEVE HE'S SEEKING THAT GUARDIAN RIGHT NOW.

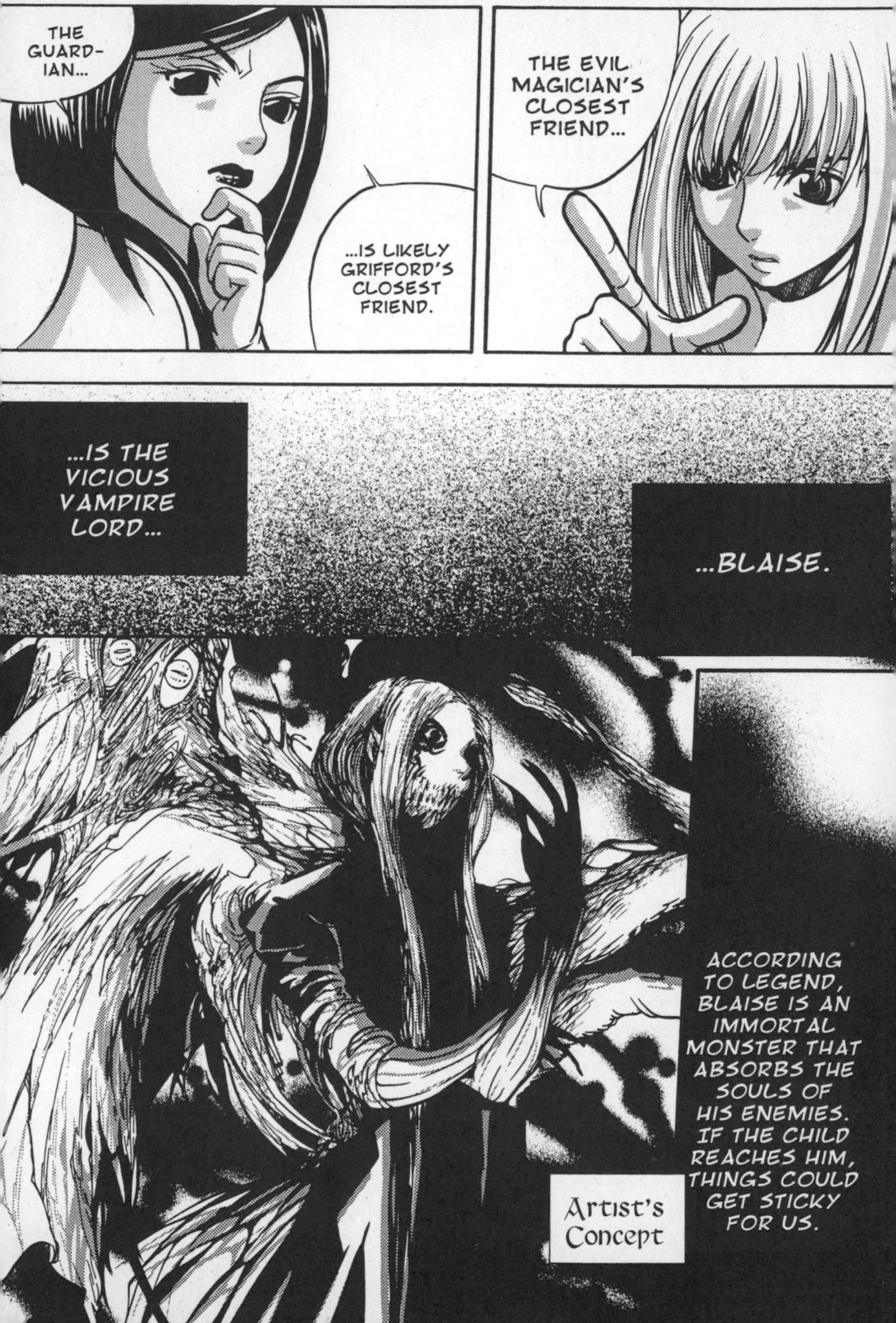
THE GUARDIAN...
...IS LIKELY GRIFFORD'S CLOSEST FRIEND.
THE EVIL MAGICIAN'S CLOSEST FRIEND...
...IS THE VICIOUS VAMPIRE LORD...
...BLAISE.
ACCORDING TO LEGEND, BLAISE IS AN IMMORTAL MONSTER THAT ABSORBS THE SOULS OF HIS ENEMIES. IF THE CHILD REACHES HIM, THINGS COULD GET STICKY FOR US.
Artist's Concept

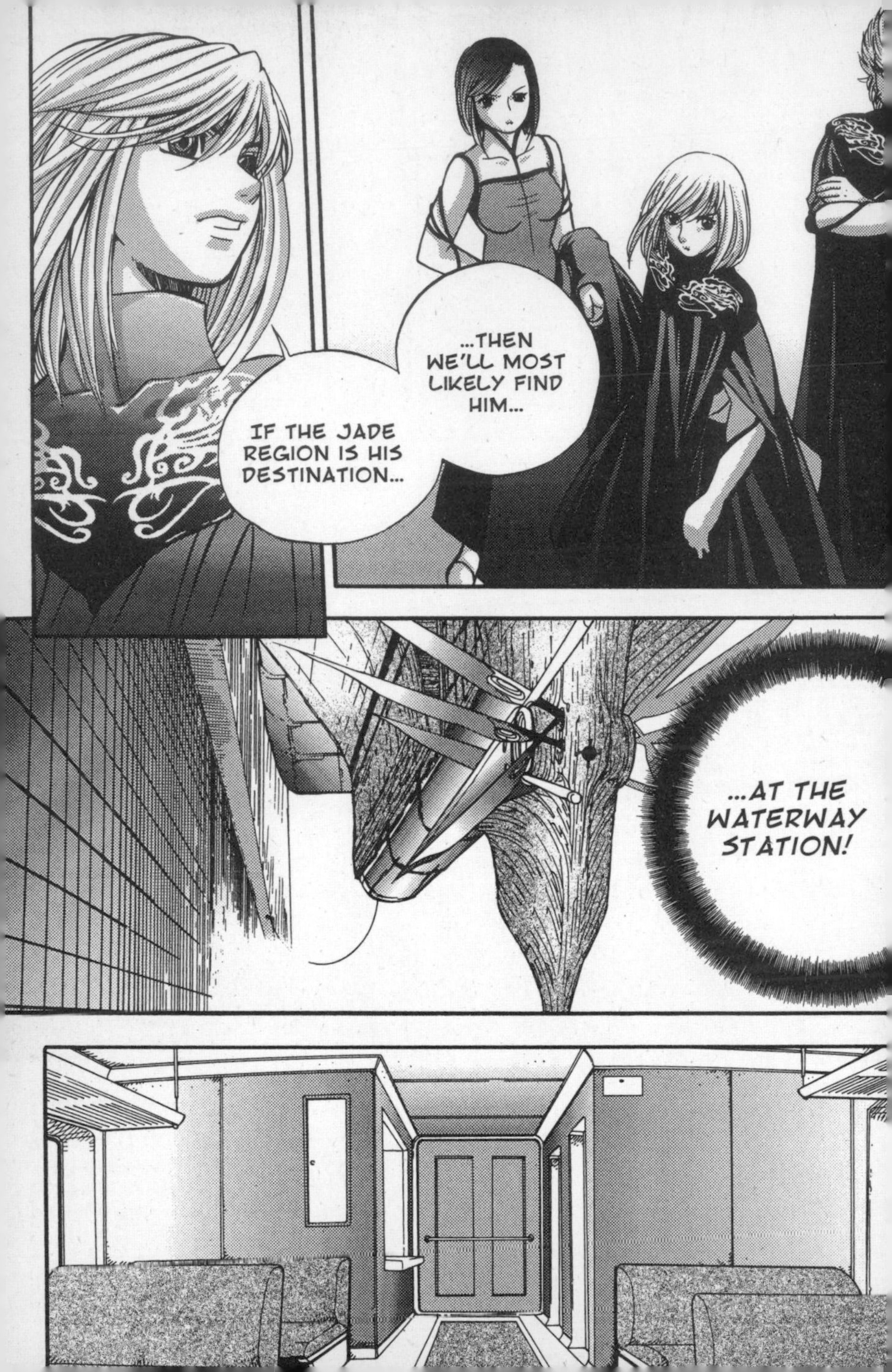
IF THE JADE REGION IS HIS DESTINATION...
...THEN WE'LL MOST LIKELY FIND HIM...
...AT THE WATERWAY STATION!

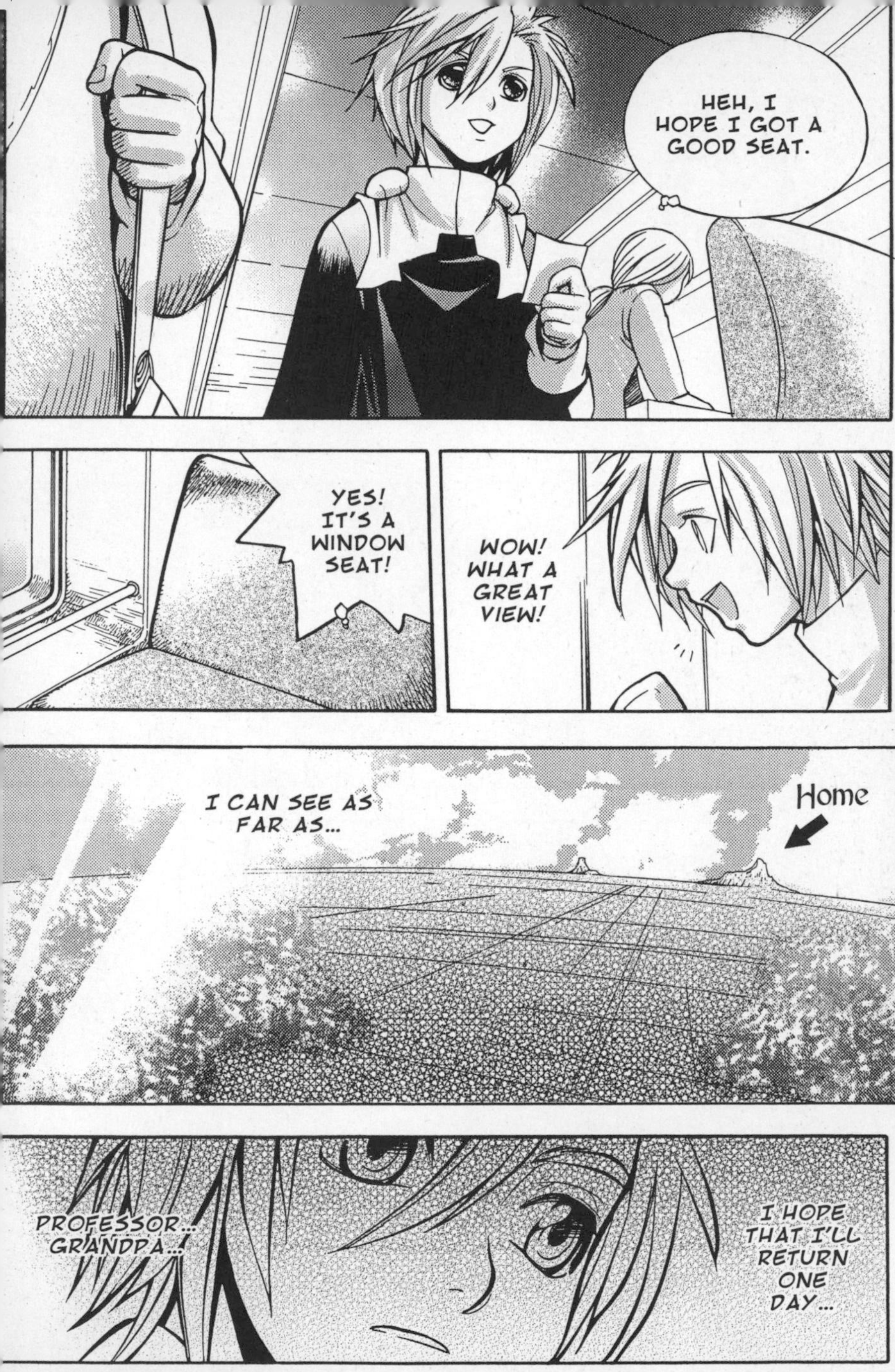
HEH, I HOPE I GOT A GOOD SEAT.
YES! IT'S A WINDOW SEAT!
WOW! WHAT A GREAT VIEW!
I CAN SEE AS FAR AS...
Home
PROFESSOR... GRANDPA...
I HOPE THAT I'LL RETURN ONE DAY...

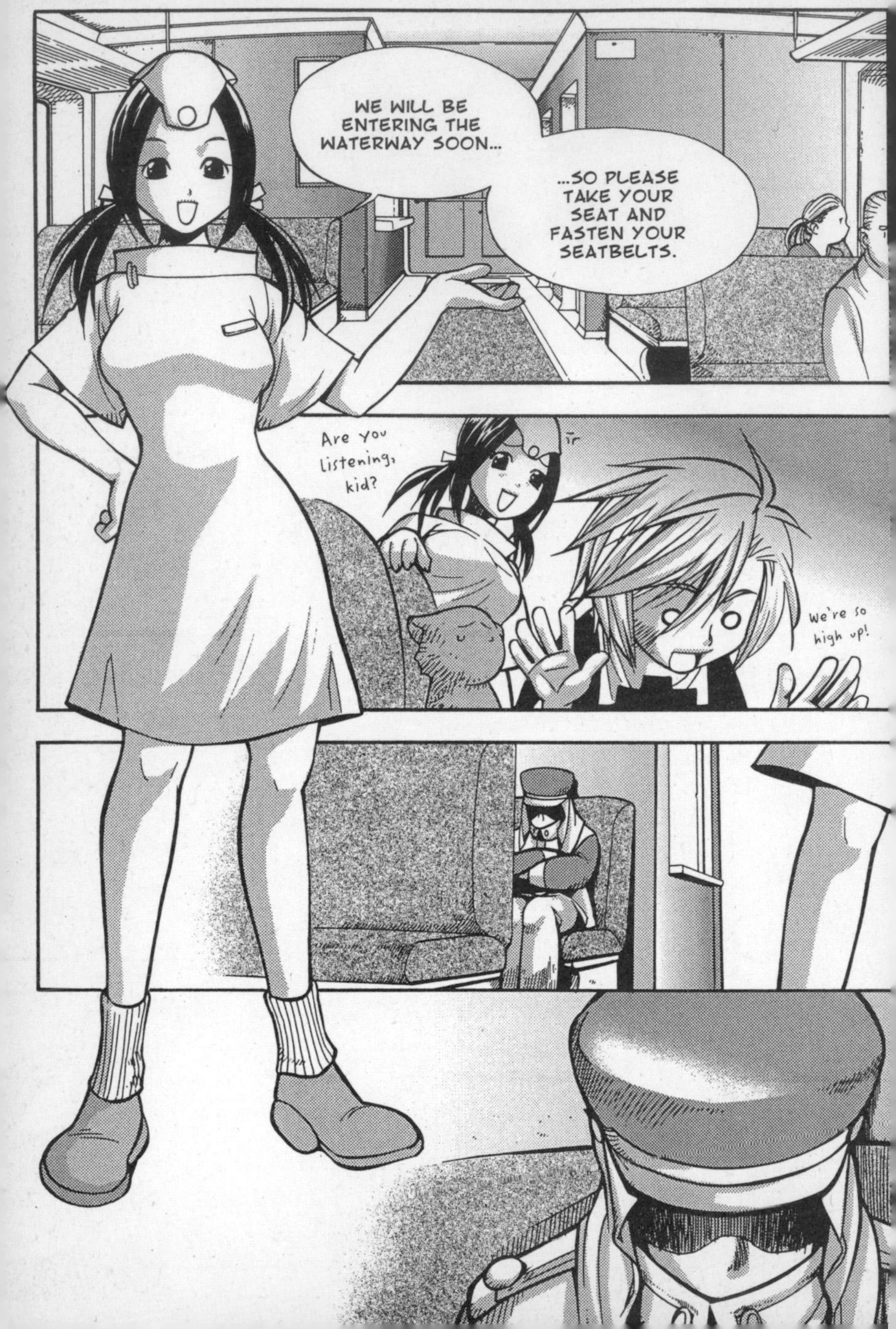
WE WILL BE ENTERING THE WATERWAY SOON...
...SO PLEASE TAKE YOUR SEAT AND FASTEN YOUR SEATBELTS.
Are you listening, kid?
We're so high up!

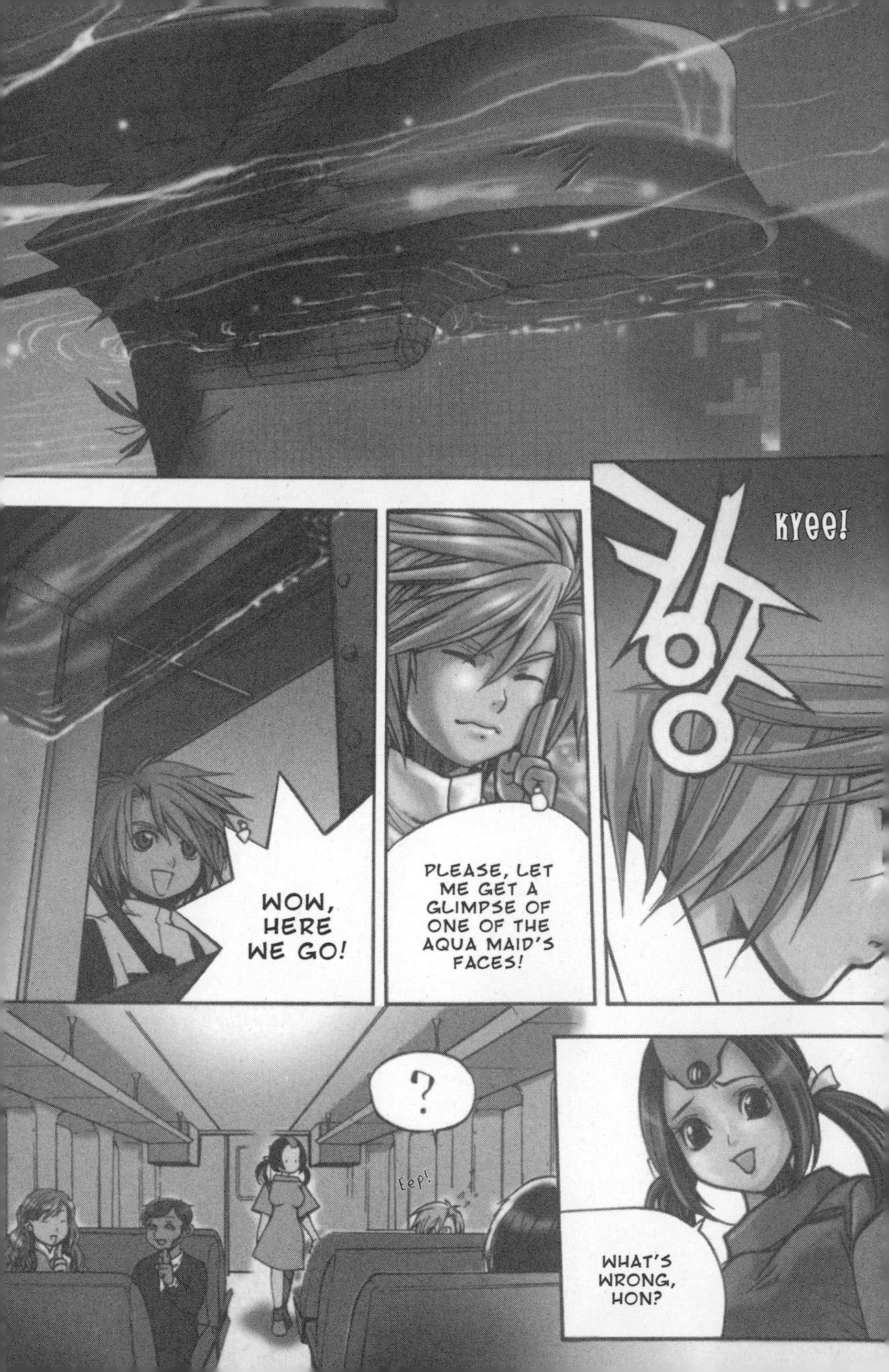
WOW, HERE WE GO!
PLEASE, LET ME GET A GLIMPSE OF ONE OF THE AQUA MAID'S FACES!
KYEE!
?
Eep!
WHAT'S WRONG, HON?

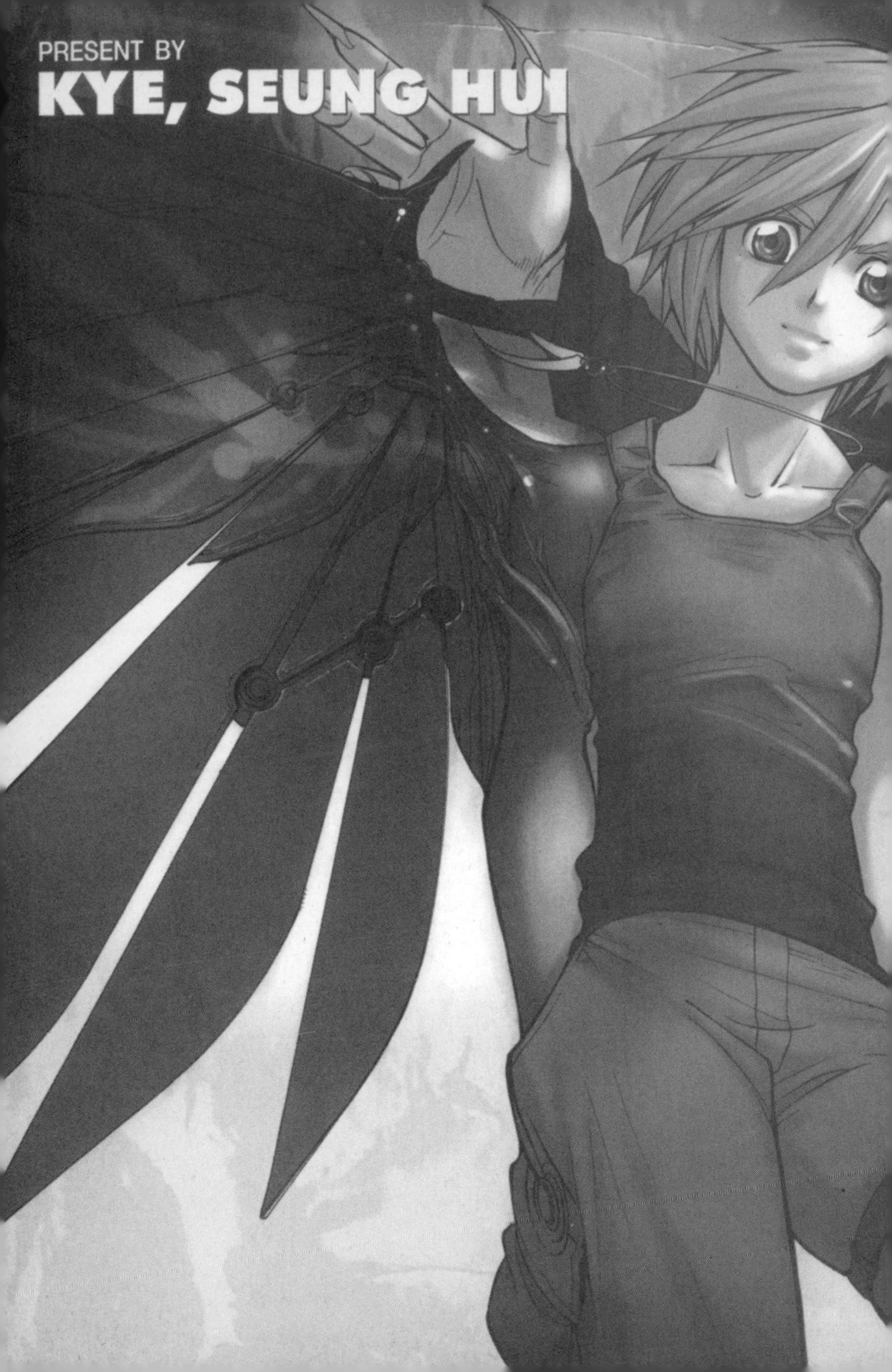
PRESENT BY
KYE, SEUNG HUI

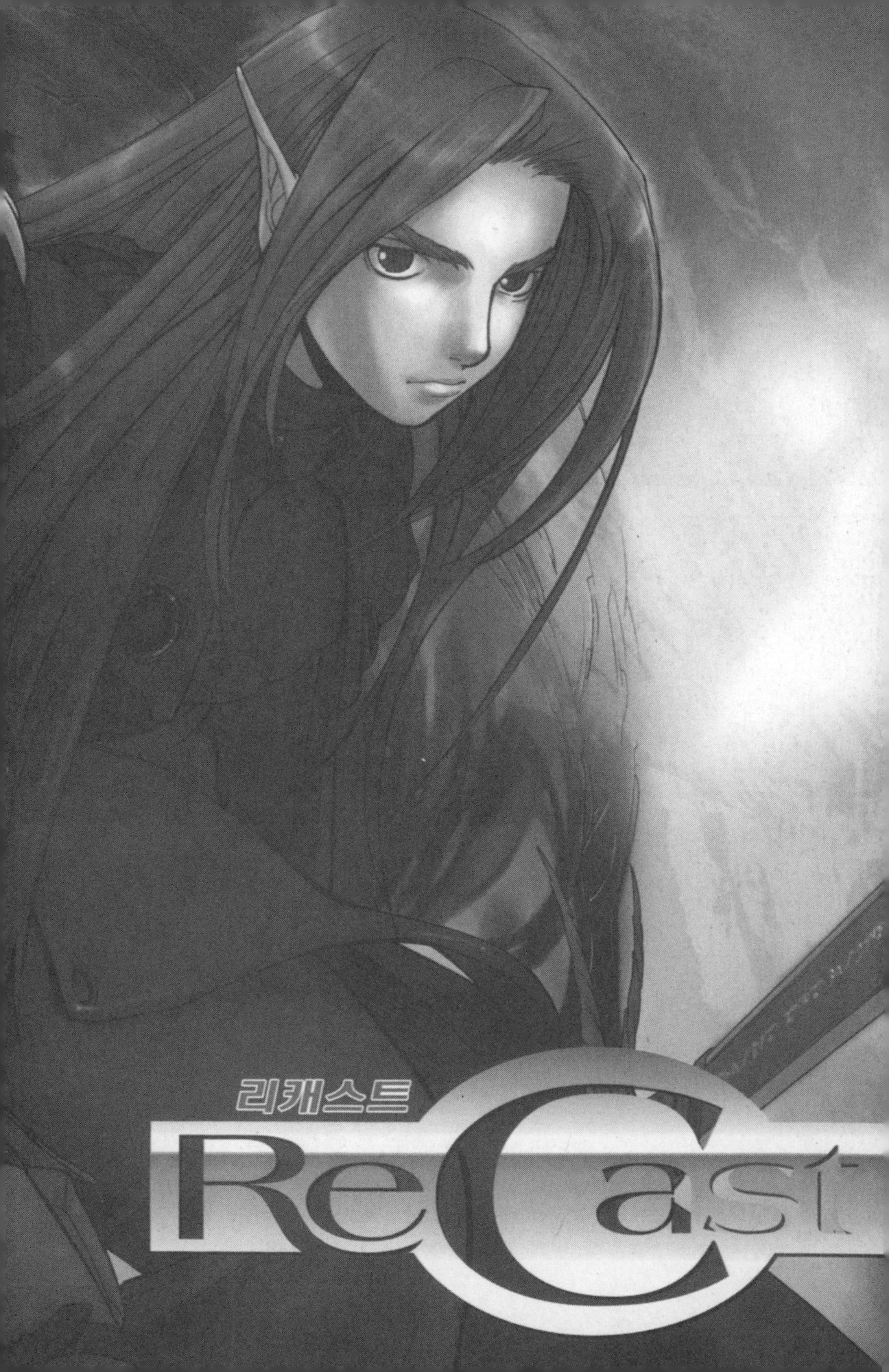

리캐스트
ReCast

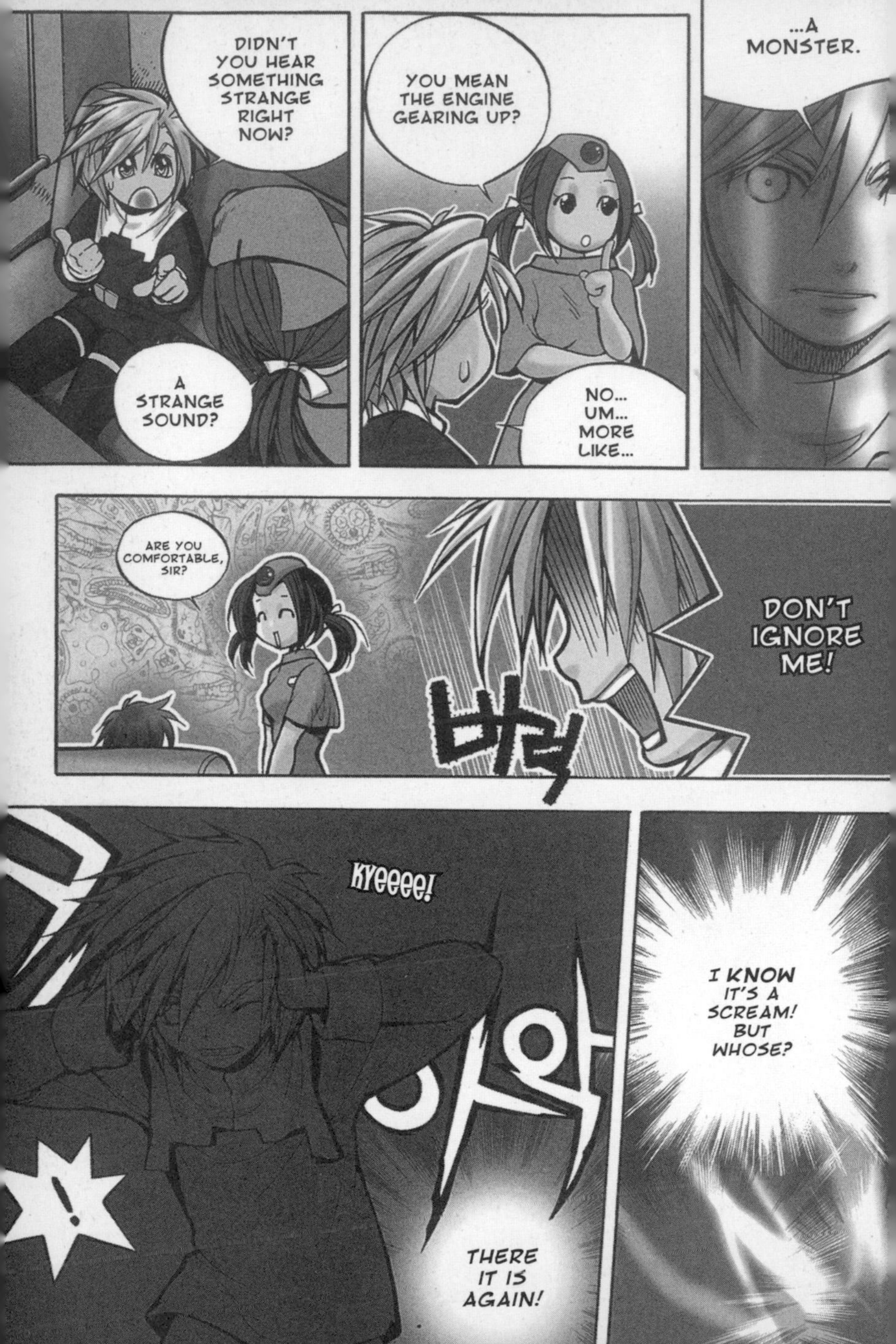

DIDN'T YOU HEAR SOMETHING STRANGE RIGHT NOW?
A STRANGE SOUND?
YOU MEAN THE ENGINE GEARING UP?
NO... UM... MORE LIKE...
...A MONSTER.
ARE YOU COMFORTABLE, SIR?
DON'T IGNORE ME!
Kyeeee!
!
THERE IT IS AGAIN!
I KNOW IT'S A SCREAM! BUT WHOSE?

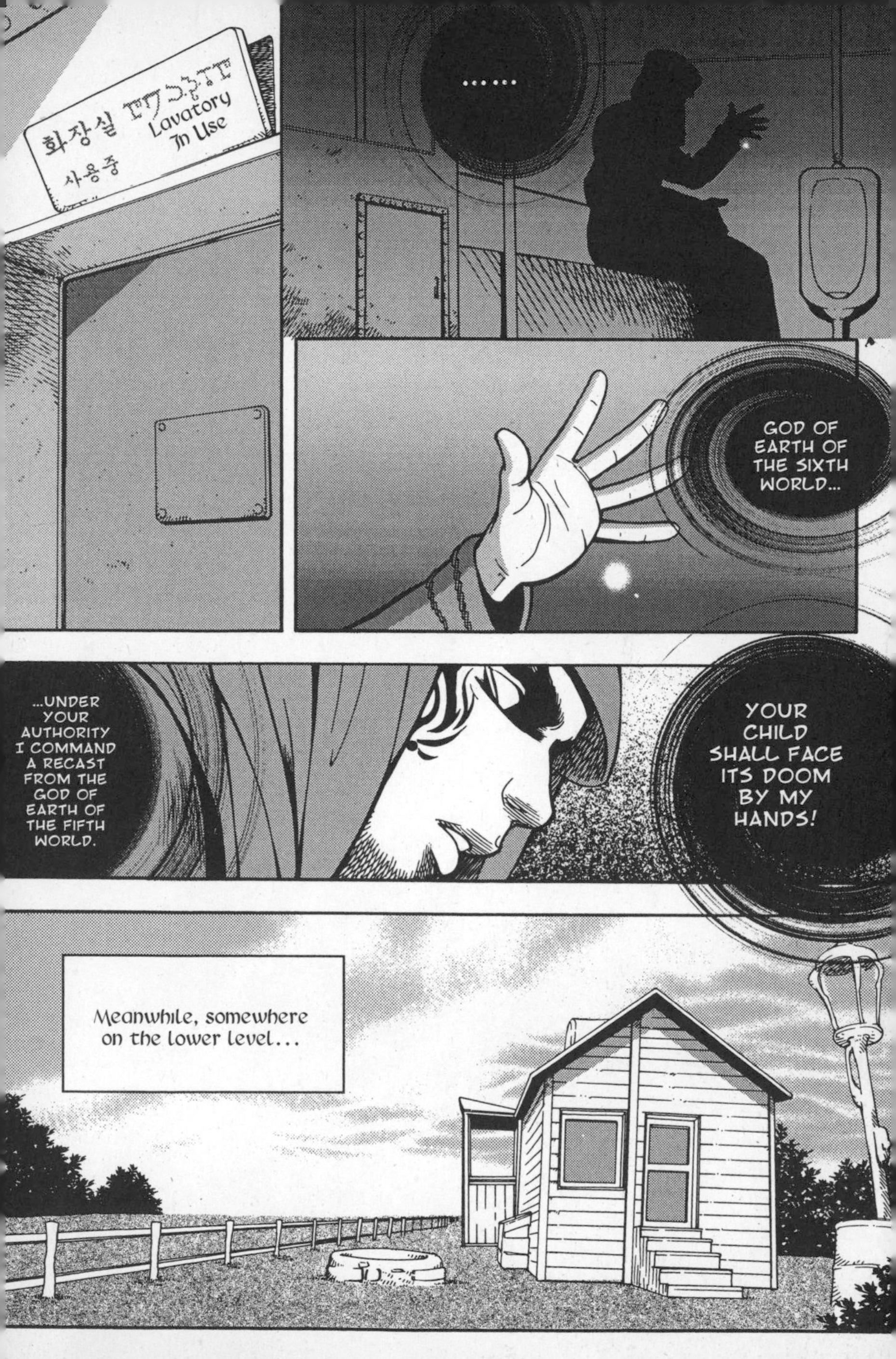

화장실
Lavatory
In Use
사용중
......
GOD OF EARTH OF THE SIXTH WORLD...
...UNDER YOUR AUTHORITY I COMMAND A RECAST FROM THE GOD OF EARTH OF THE FIFTH WORLD.
YOUR CHILD SHALL FACE ITS DOOM BY MY HANDS!
Meanwhile, somewhere on the lower level...

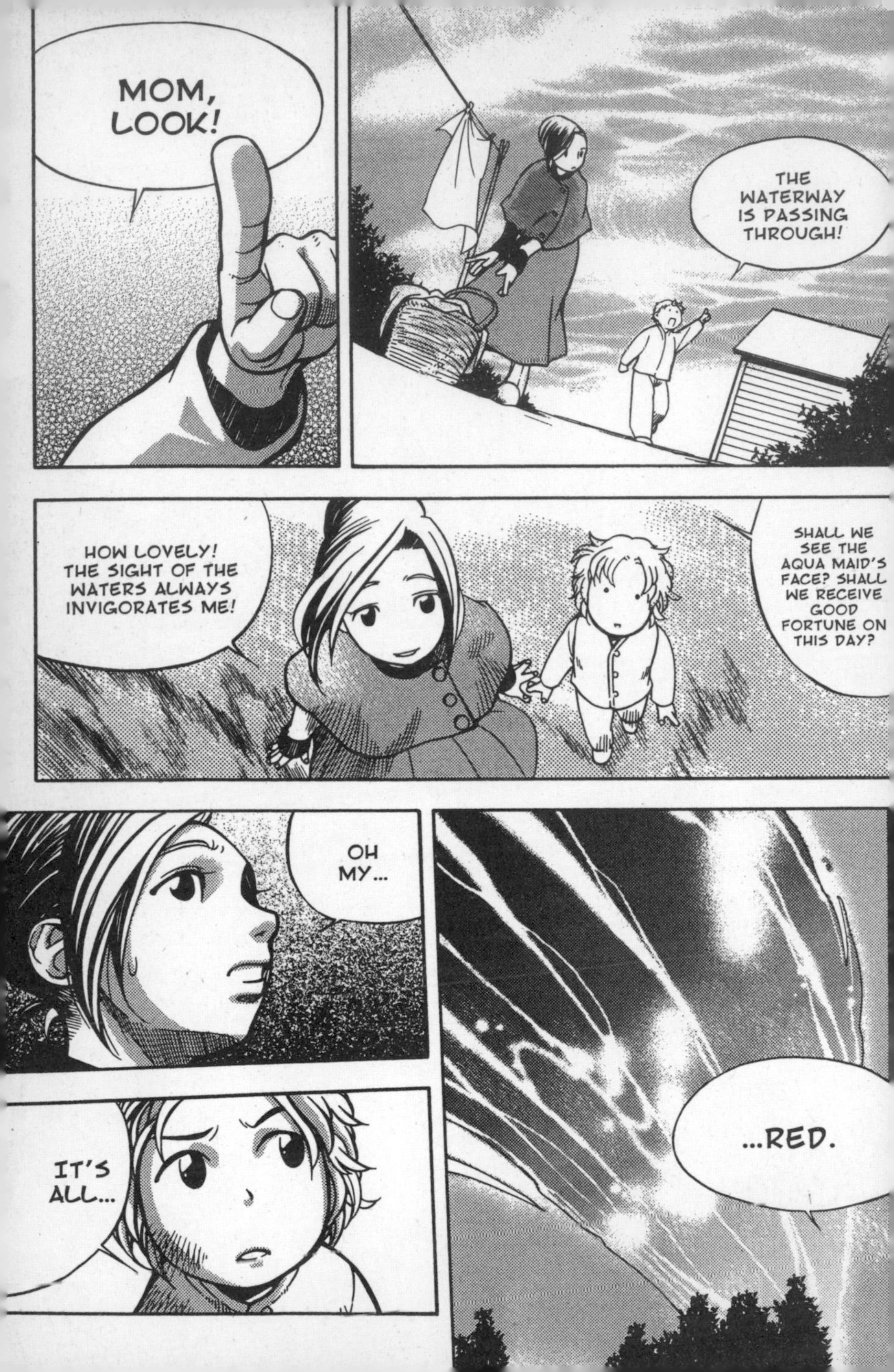
MOM, LOOK!
THE WATERWAY IS PASSING THROUGH!
HOW LOVELY! THE SIGHT OF THE WATERS ALWAYS INVIGORATES ME!
SHALL WE SEE THE AQUA MAID'S FACE? SHALL WE RECEIVE GOOD FORTUNE ON THIS DAY?
OH MY...
IT'S ALL...
...RED.

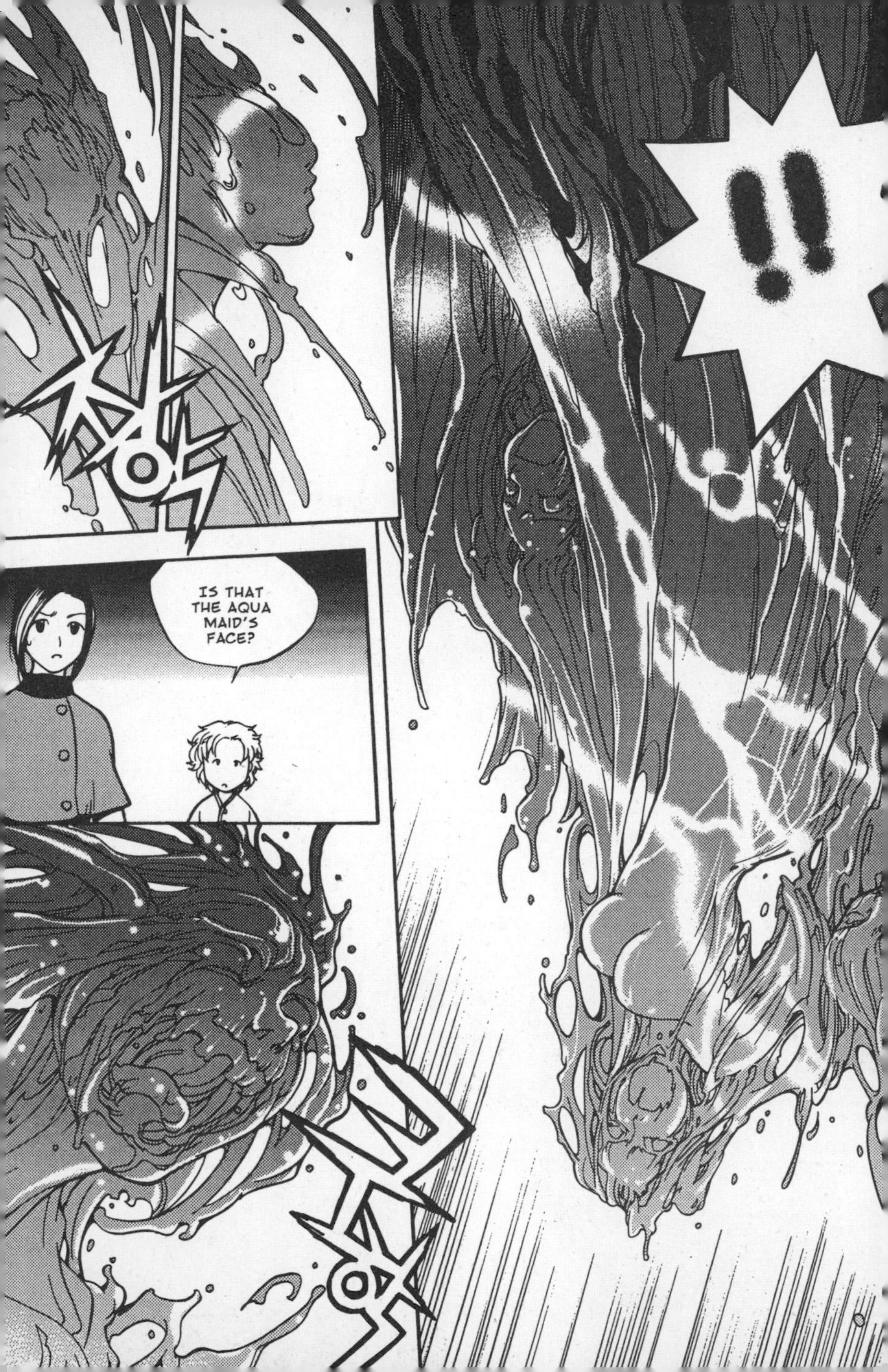
IS THAT THE AQUA MAID'S FACE?
!!

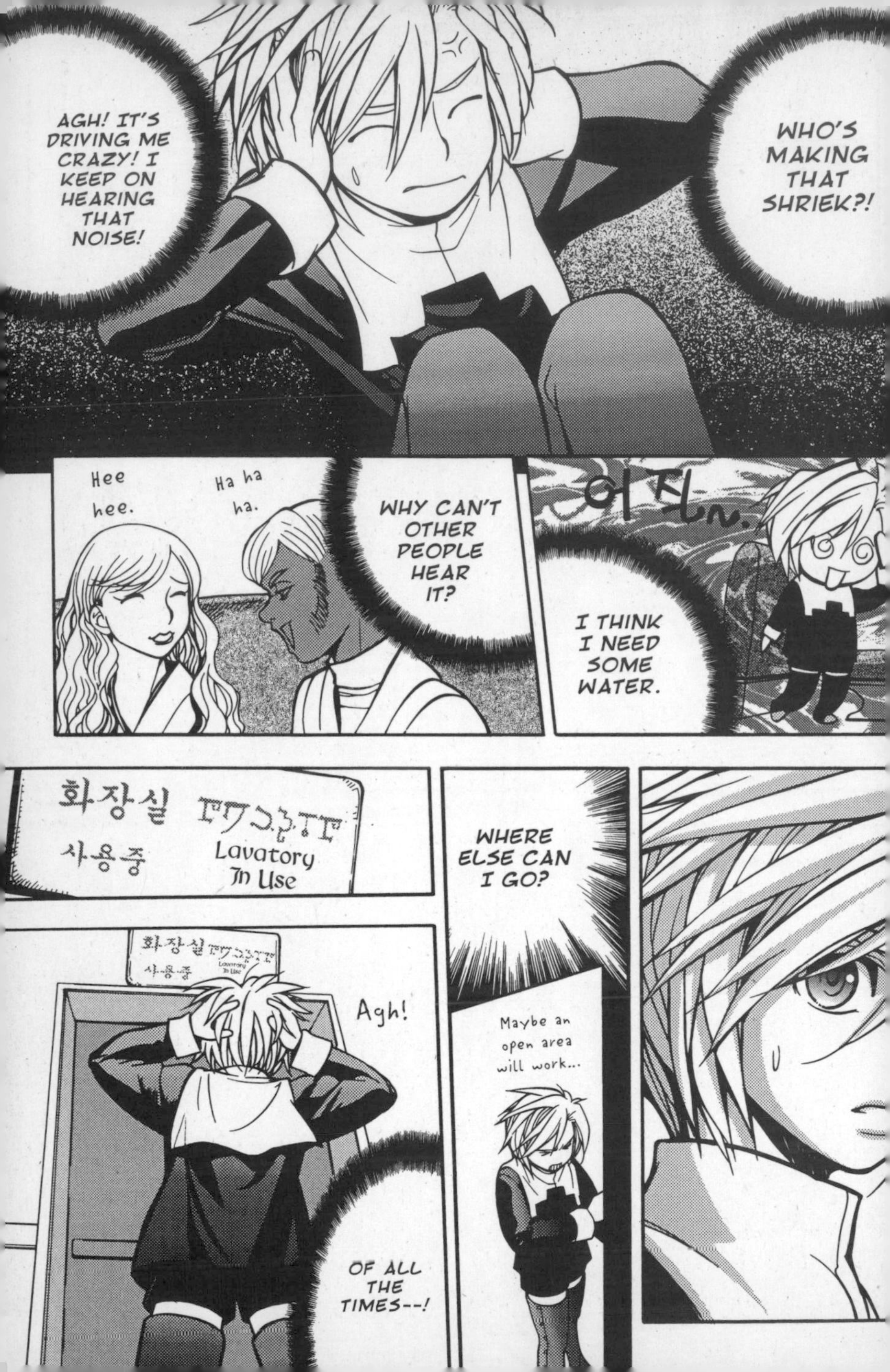
AGH! IT'S DRIVING ME CRAZY! I KEEP ON HEARING THAT NOISE!
WHO'S MAKING THAT SHRIEK?!
Hee hee.
Ha ha ha.
WHY CAN'T OTHER PEOPLE HEAR IT?
I THINK I NEED SOME WATER.
화장실
사용중
Lavatory
In Use
화장실
사용중
Lavatory
In Use
Agh!
OF ALL THE TIMES--!
WHERE ELSE CAN I GO?
Maybe an open area will work...

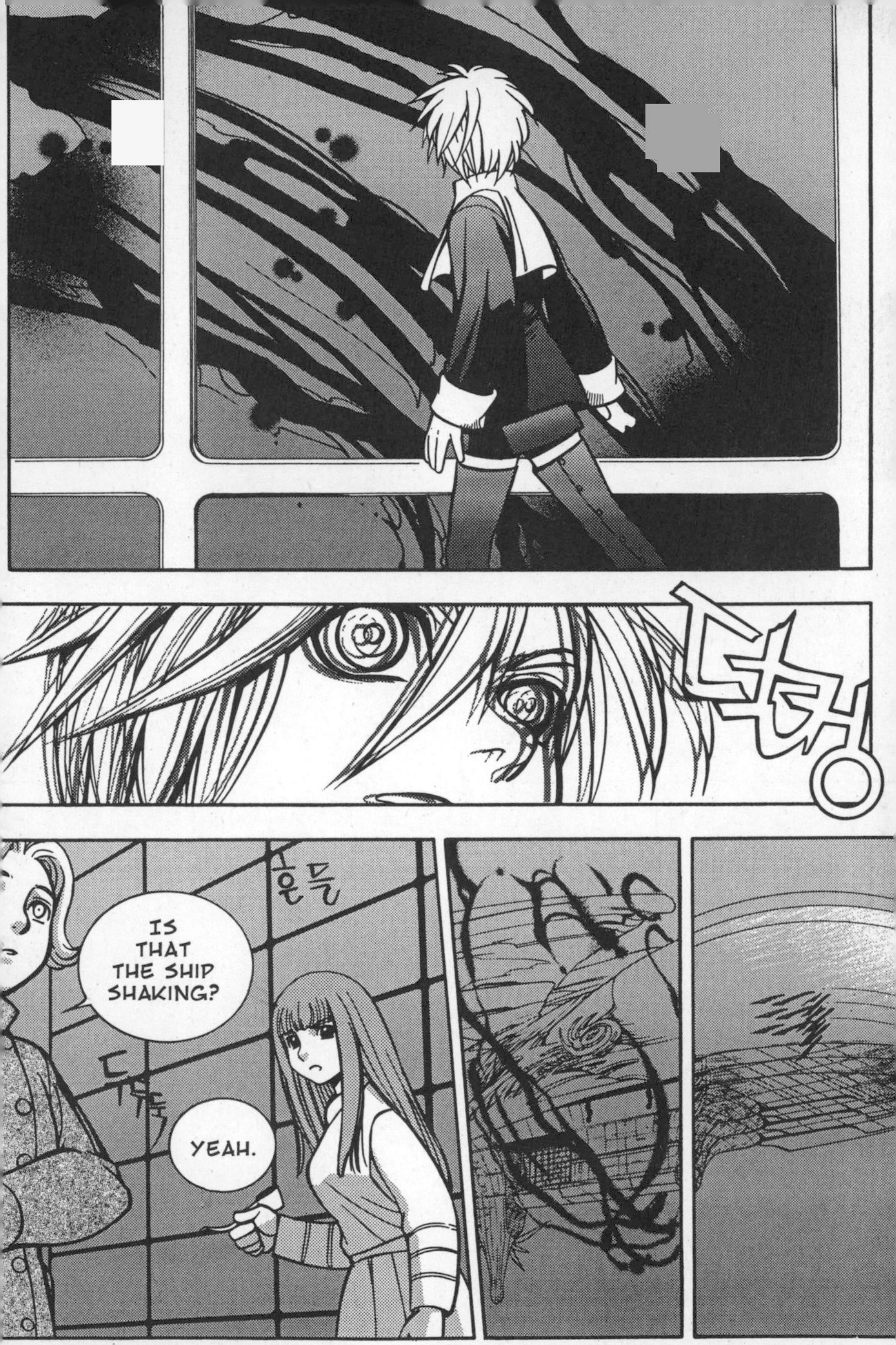
IS THAT THE SHIP SHAKING?
YEAH.

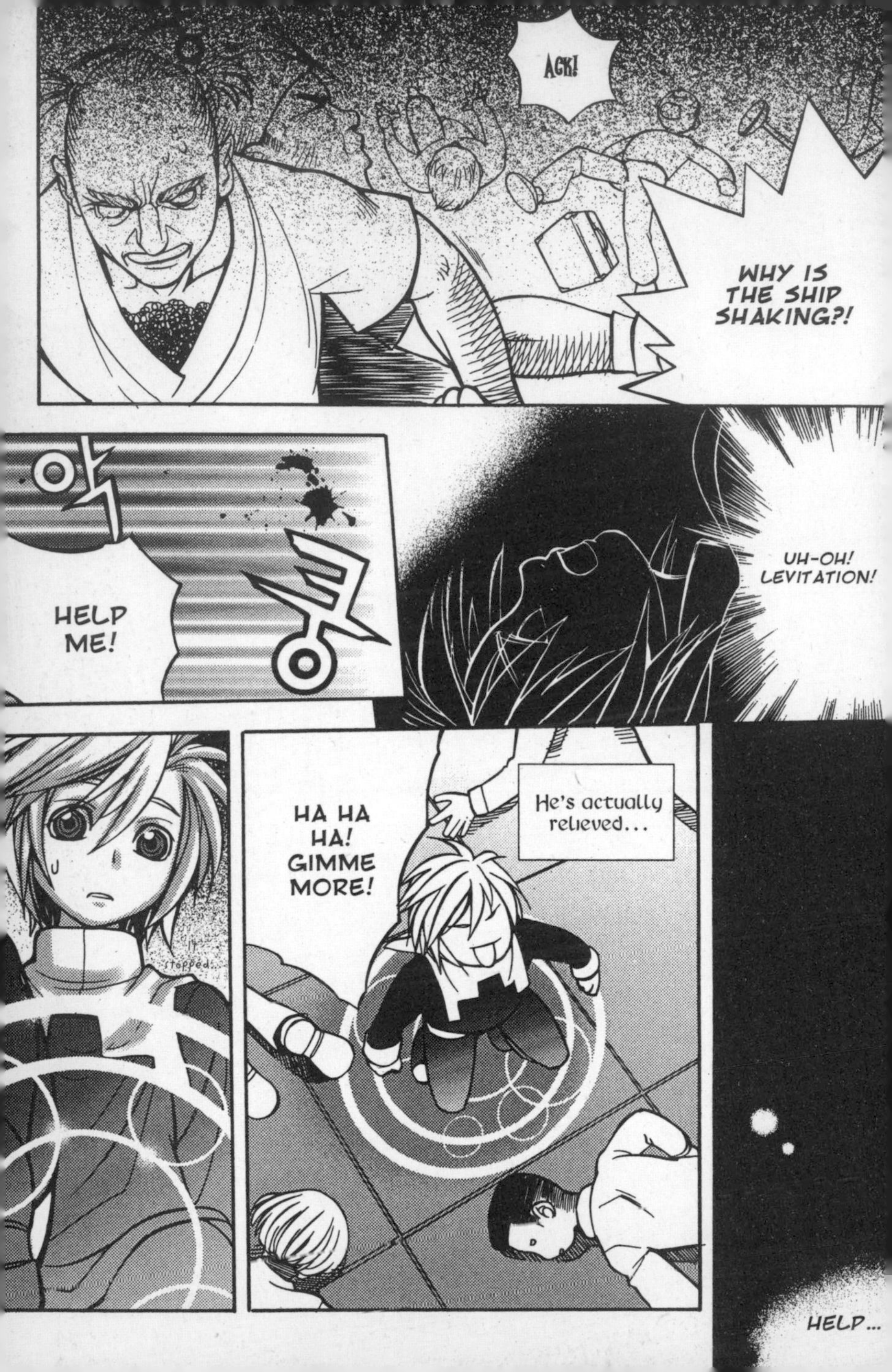
ACK!
WHY IS THE SHIP SHAKING?!
HELP ME!
UH-OH! LEVITATION!
It stopped.
HA HA HA! GIMME MORE!
He's actually relieved...
HELP...

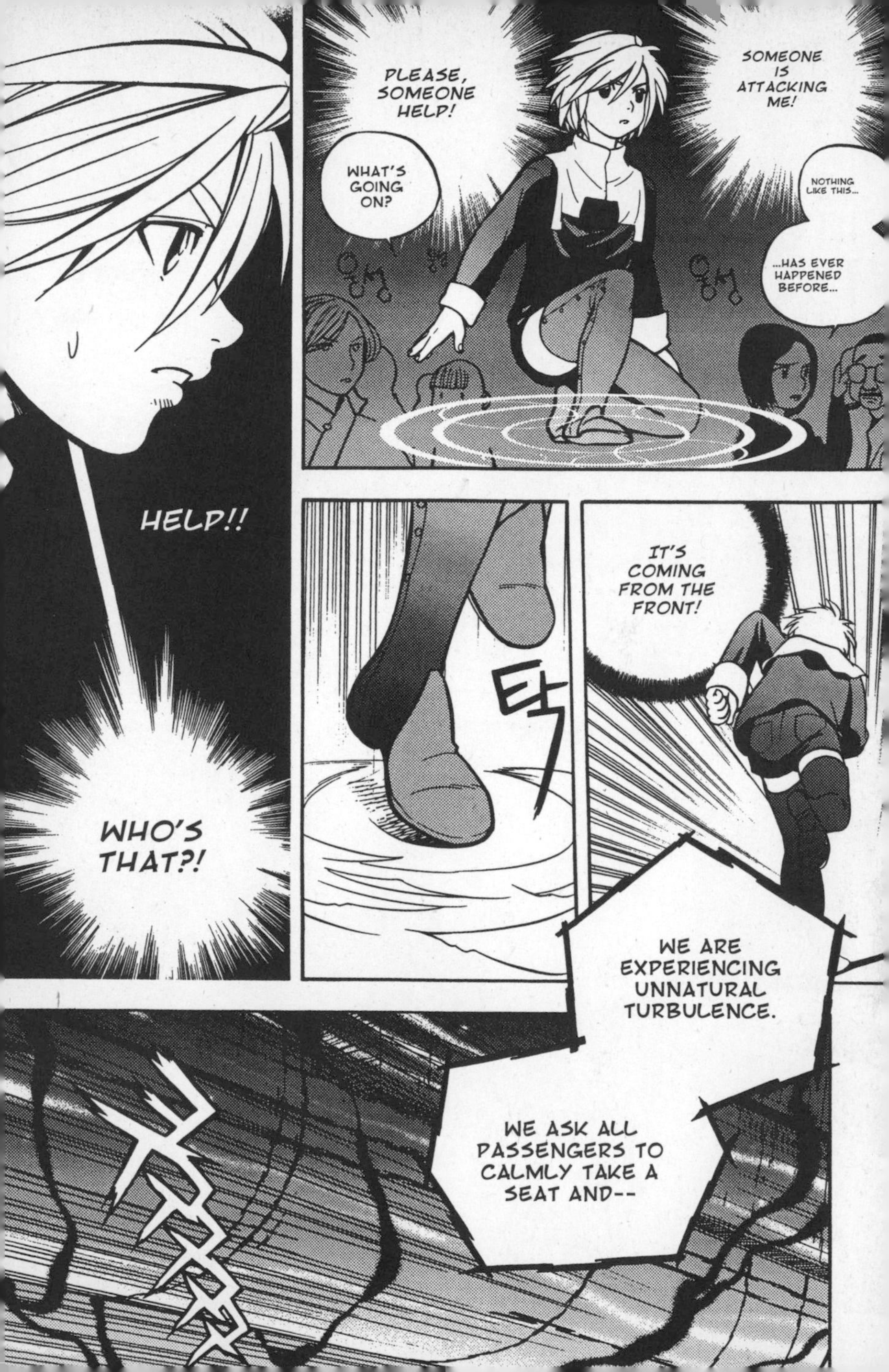
HELP!!
WHO'S THAT?!
PLEASE, SOMEONE HELP!
WHAT'S GOING ON?
SOMEONE IS ATTACKING ME!
NOTHING LIKE THIS...
...HAS EVER HAPPENED BEFORE...
IT'S COMING FROM THE FRONT!
WE ARE EXPERIENCING UNNATURAL TURBULENCE.
WE ASK ALL PASSENGERS TO CALMLY TAKE A SEAT AND--

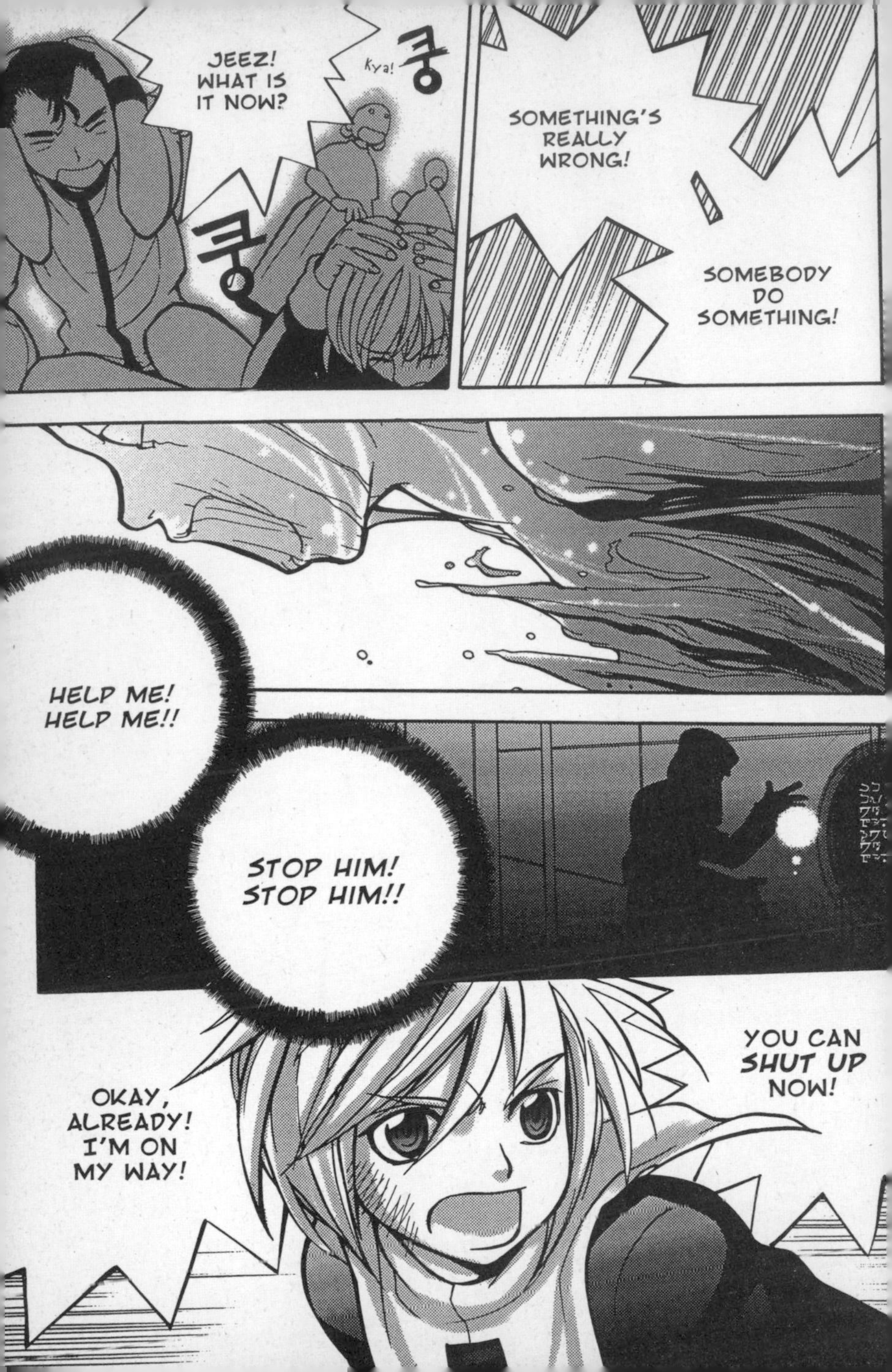
JEEZ! WHAT IS IT NOW?
Kya!
쿵
쿵
SOMETHING'S REALLY WRONG!
SOMEBODY DO SOMETHING!
HELP ME! HELP ME!!
STOP HIM! STOP HIM!!
OKAY, ALREADY! I'M ON MY WAY!
YOU CAN SHUT UP NOW!

LUPUS THE WEREWOLF

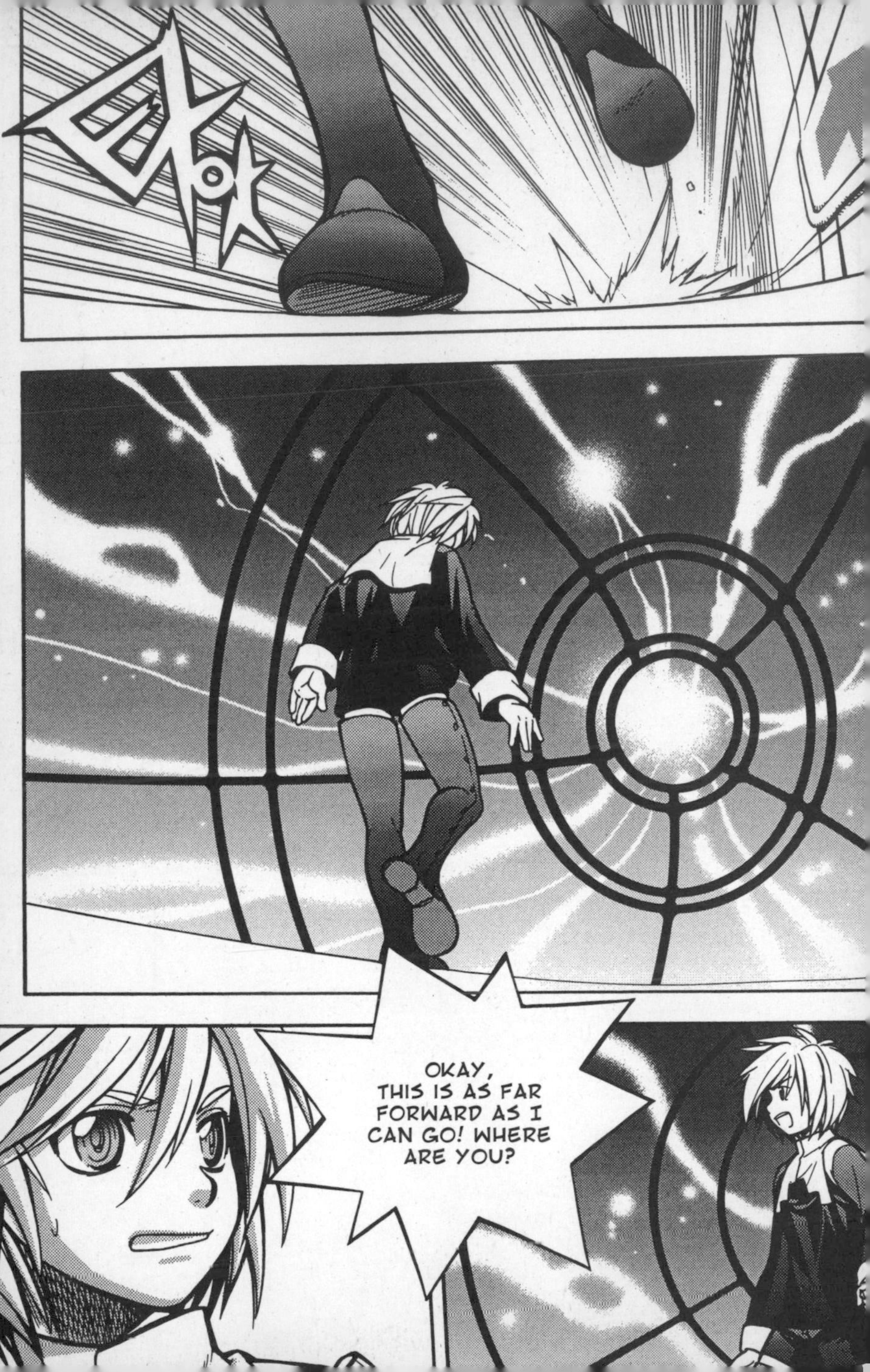
OKAY, THIS IS AS FAR FORWARD AS I CAN GO! WHERE ARE YOU?

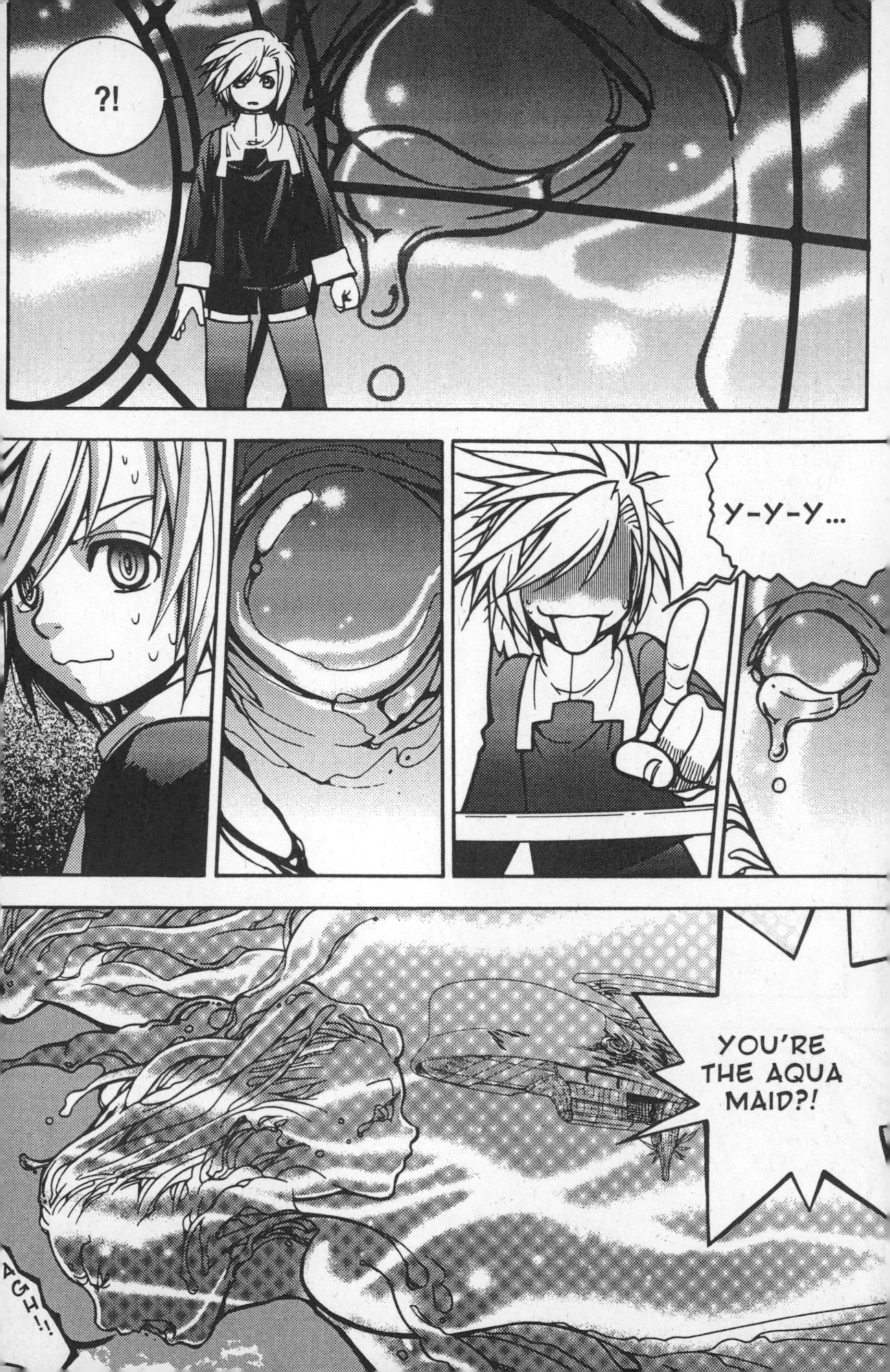
?!
Y-Y-Y...
YOU'RE THE AQUA MAID?!
AGH!!

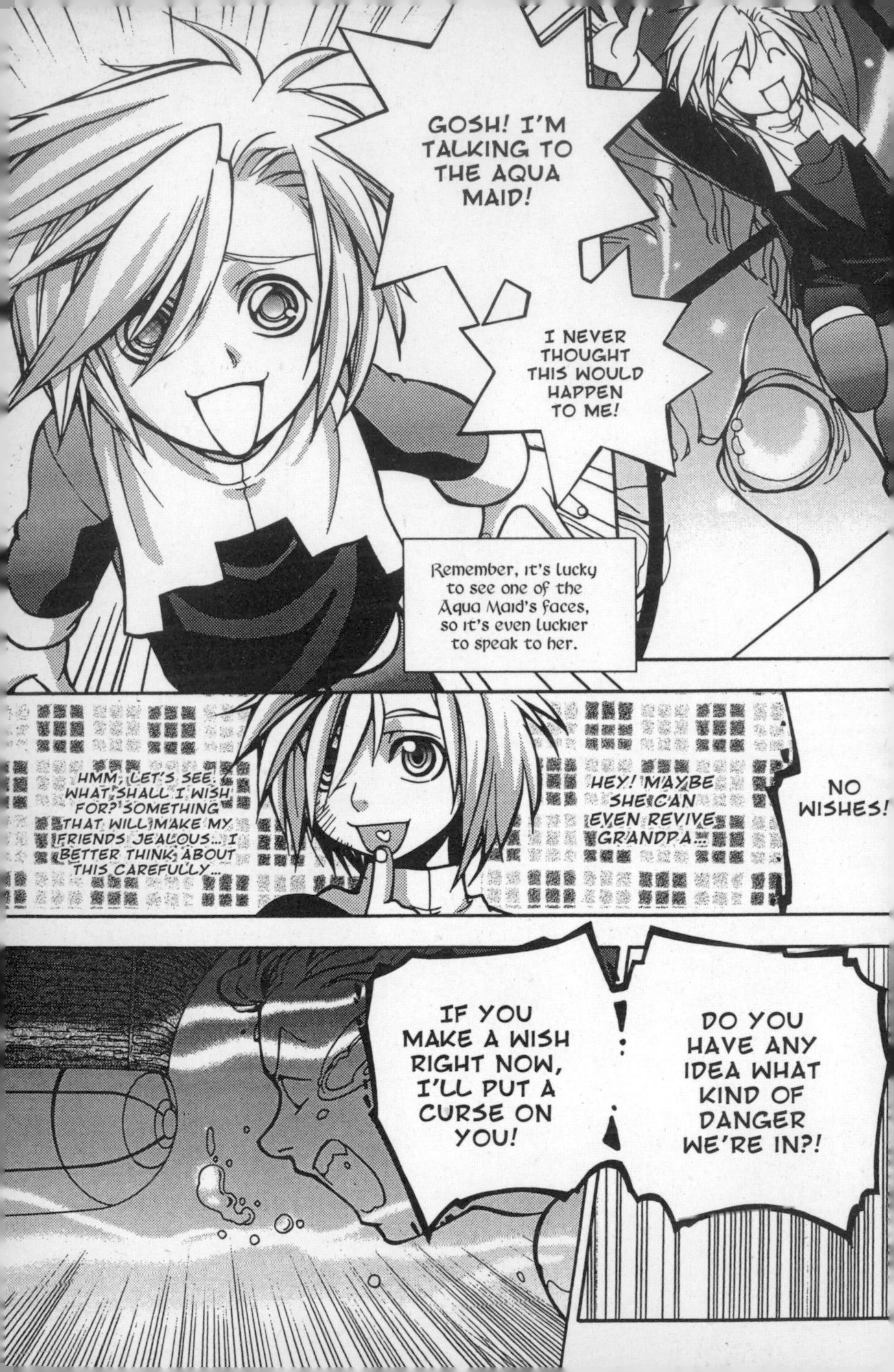
GOSH! I'M TALKING TO THE AQUA MAID!
I NEVER THOUGHT THIS WOULD HAPPEN TO ME!
Remember, it's lucky to see one of the Aqua Maid's faces, so it's even luckier to speak to her.
HMM, LET'S SEE. WHAT SHALL I WISH FOR? SOMETHING THAT WILL MAKE MY FRIENDS JEALOUS... I BETTER THINK ABOUT THIS CAREFULLY...
HEY! MAYBE SHE CAN EVEN REVIVE GRANDPA...
NO WISHES!
IF YOU MAKE A WISH RIGHT NOW, I'LL PUT A CURSE ON YOU!
DO YOU HAVE ANY IDEA WHAT KIND OF DANGER WE'RE IN?!

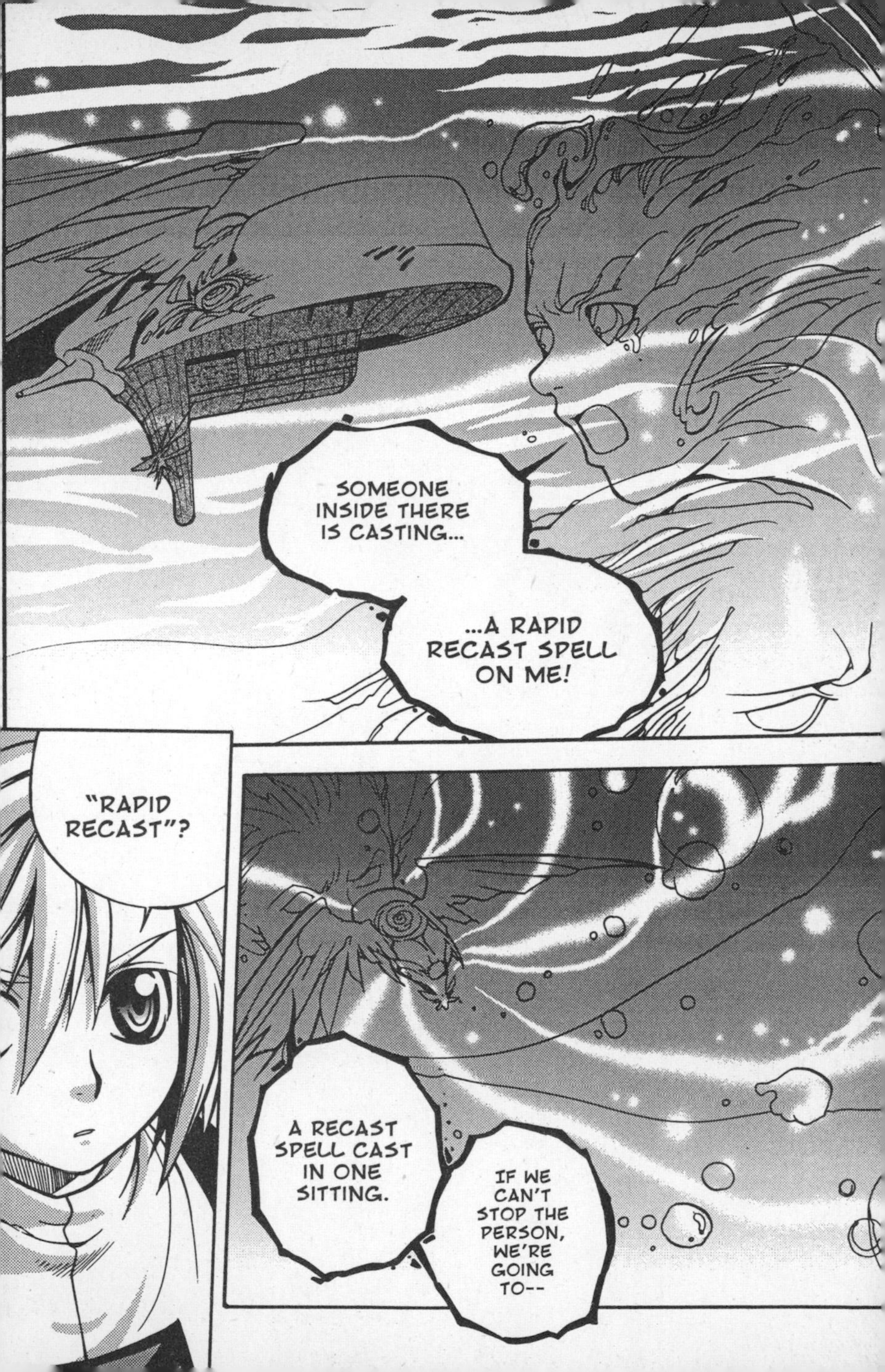
SOMEONE INSIDE THERE IS CASTING...
...A RAPID RECAST SPELL ON ME!
"RAPID RECAST"?
A RECAST SPELL CAST IN ONE SITTING.
IF WE CAN'T STOP THE PERSON, WE'RE GOING TO--

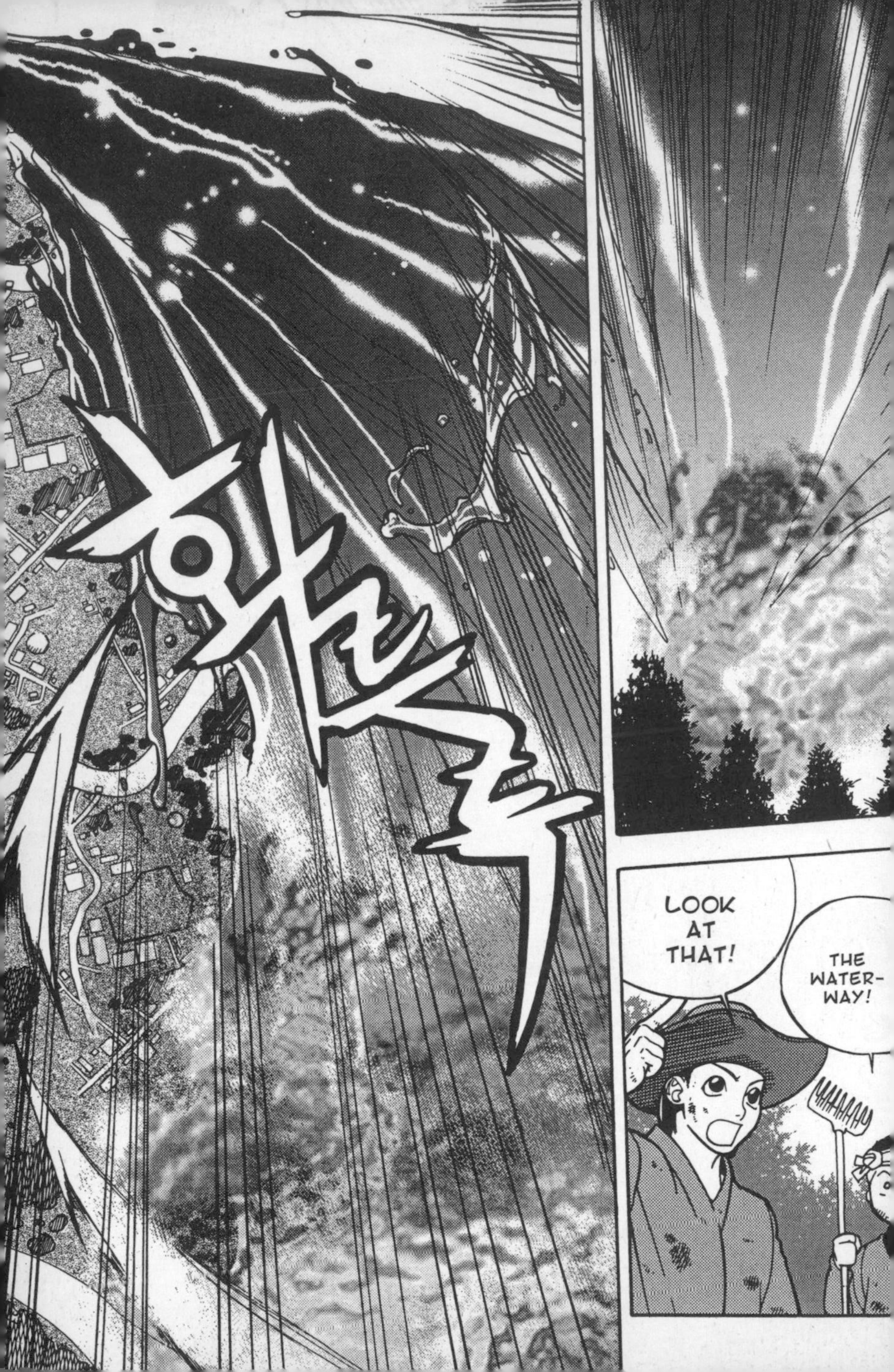
LOOK AT THAT!
THE WATER-WAY!

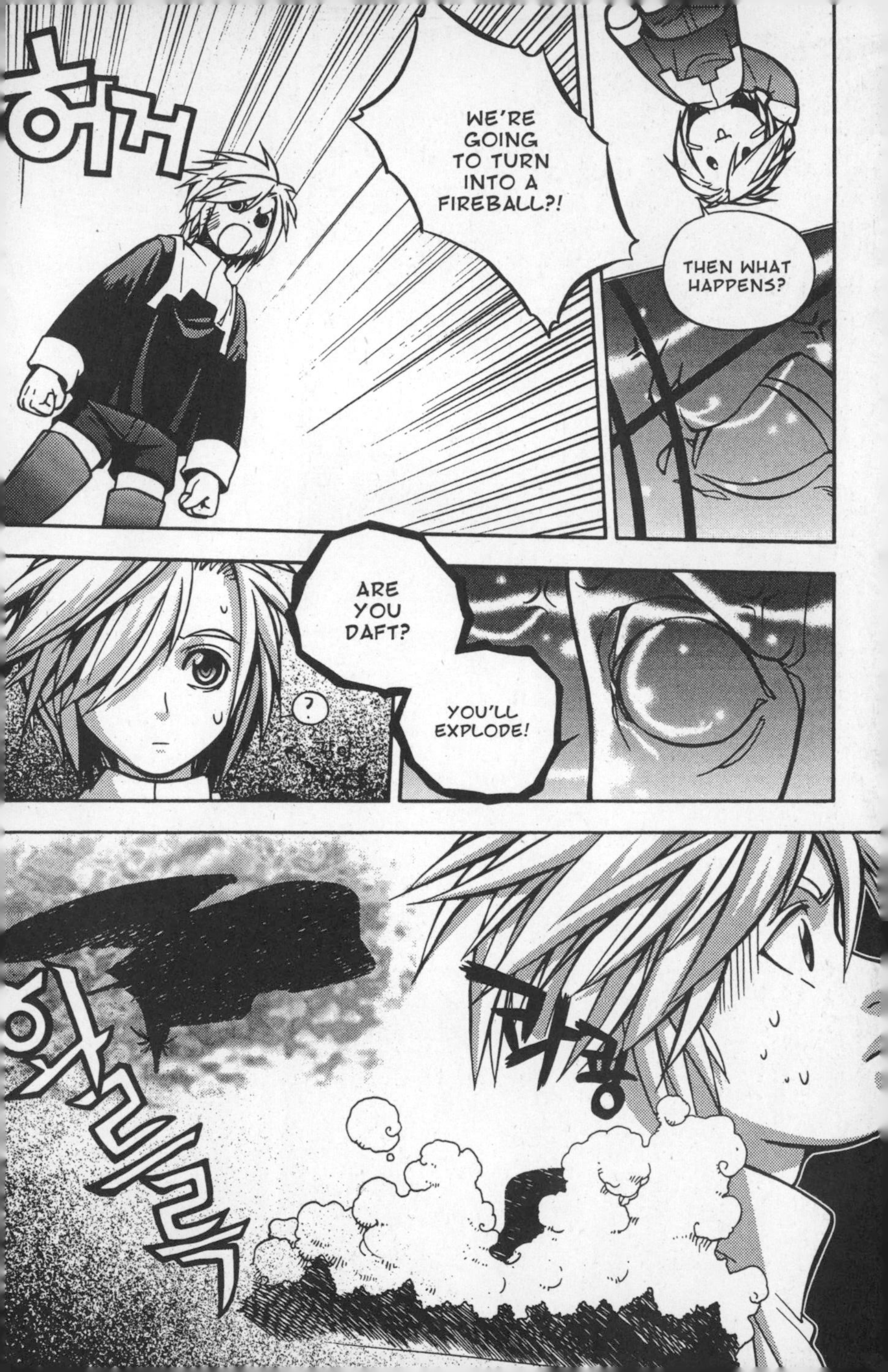
WE'RE GOING TO TURN INTO A FIREBALL?!
THEN WHAT HAPPENS?
?
ARE YOU DAFT?
YOU'LL EXPLODE!

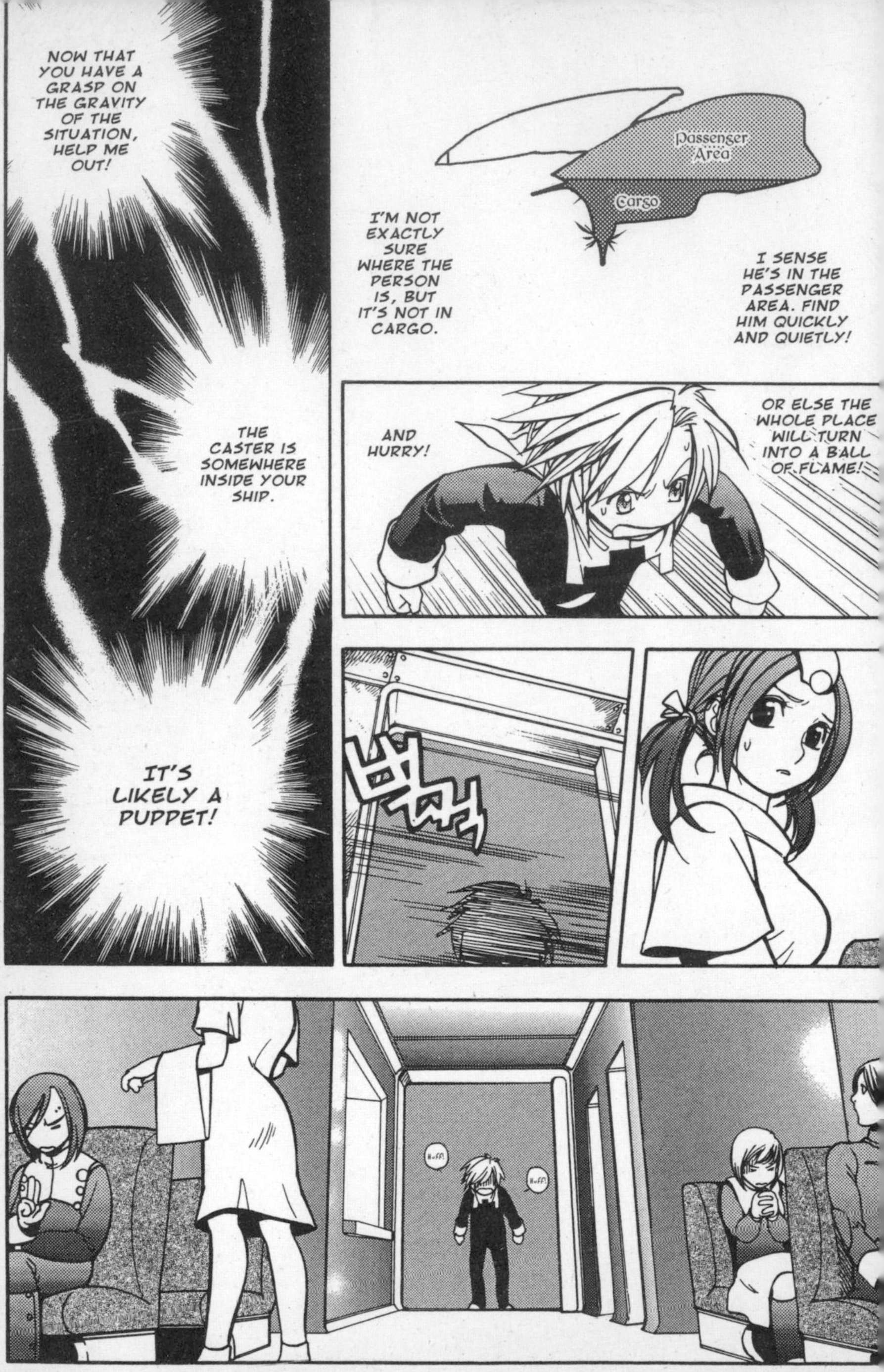
NOW THAT YOU HAVE A GRASP ON THE GRAVITY OF THE SITUATION, HELP ME OUT!
THE CASTER IS SOMEWHERE INSIDE YOUR SHIP.
IT'S LIKELY A PUPPET!
Passenger Area
Cargo
I'M NOT EXACTLY SURE WHERE THE PERSON IS, BUT IT'S NOT IN CARGO.
I SENSE HE'S IN THE PASSENGER AREA. FIND HIM QUICKLY AND QUIETLY!
AND HURRY!
OR ELSE THE WHOLE PLACE WILL TURN INTO A BALL OF FLAME!
Huff!
Huff!

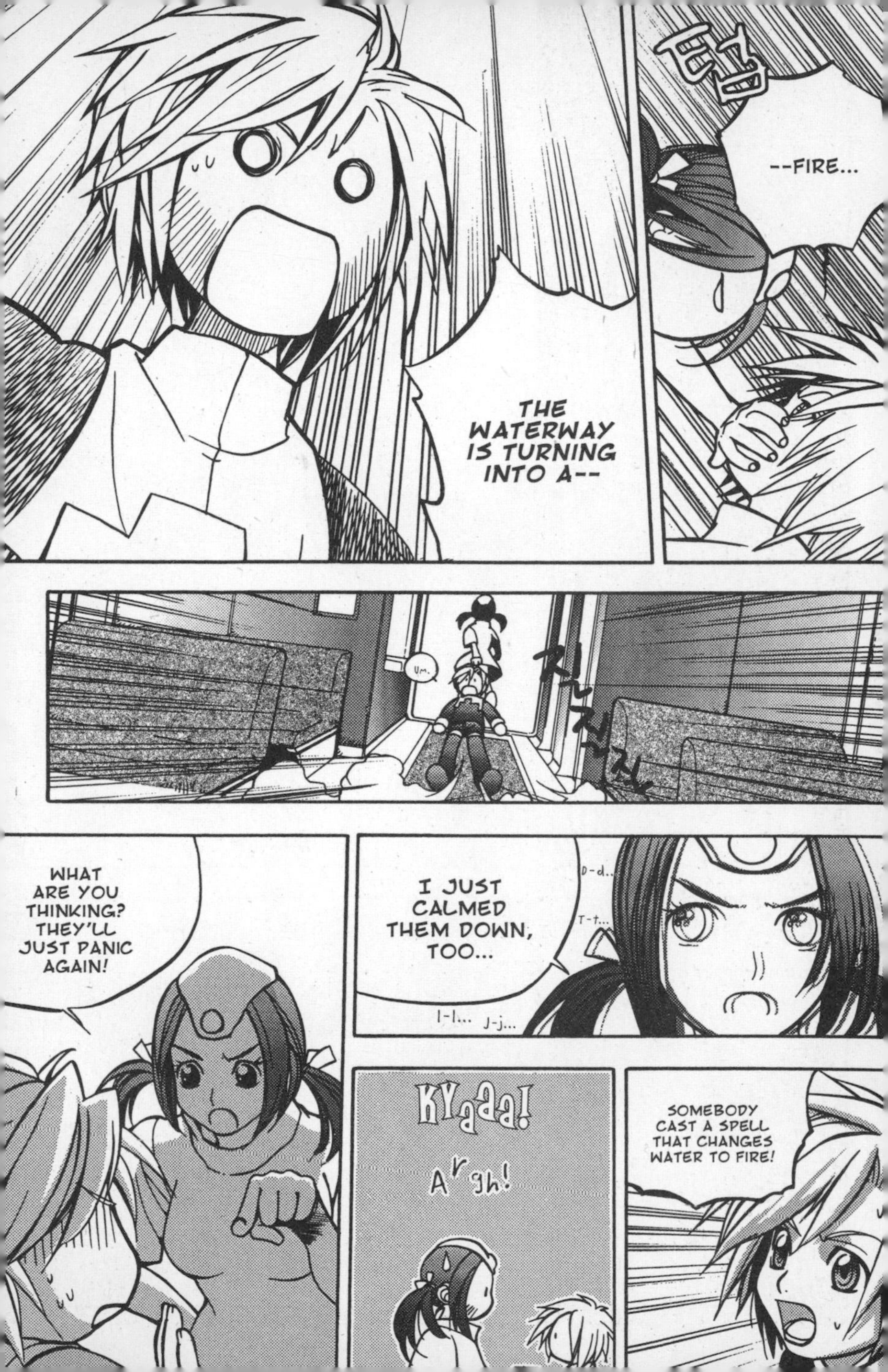
THE WATERWAY IS TURNING INTO A--
--FIRE...
UM.
WHAT ARE YOU THINKING? THEY'LL JUST PANIC AGAIN!
I JUST CALMED THEM DOWN, TOO...
D-d...
T-t...
I-I... J-j...
KYaaa!
Argh!
SOMEBODY CAST A SPELL THAT CHANGES WATER TO FIRE!

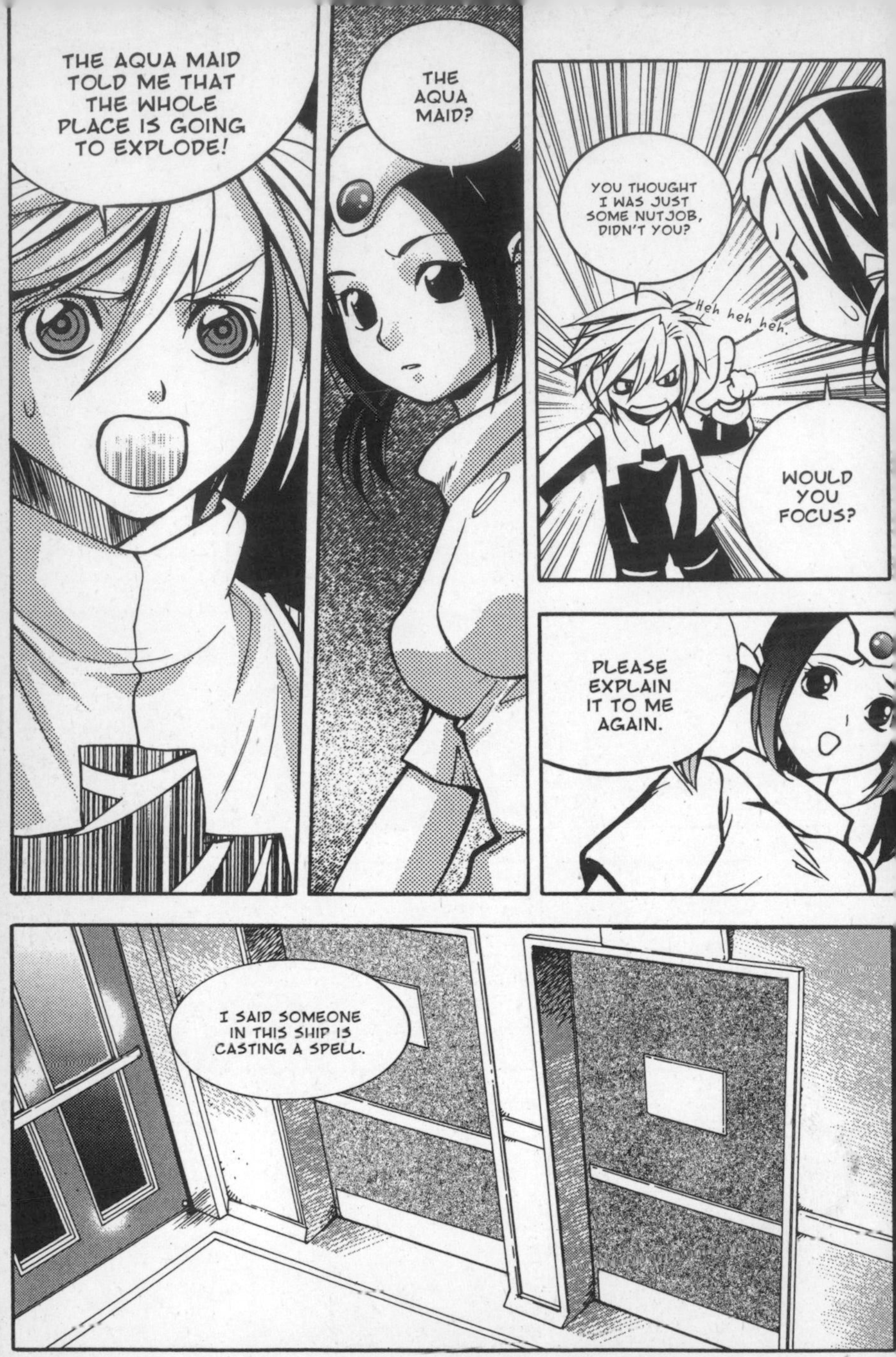
THE AQUA MAID TOLD ME THAT THE WHOLE PLACE IS GOING TO EXPLODE!
THE AQUA MAID?
YOU THOUGHT I WAS JUST SOME NUTJOB, DIDN'T YOU?
Heh heh heh.
WOULD YOU FOCUS?
PLEASE EXPLAIN IT TO ME AGAIN.
I SAID SOMEONE IN THIS SHIP IS CASTING A SPELL.

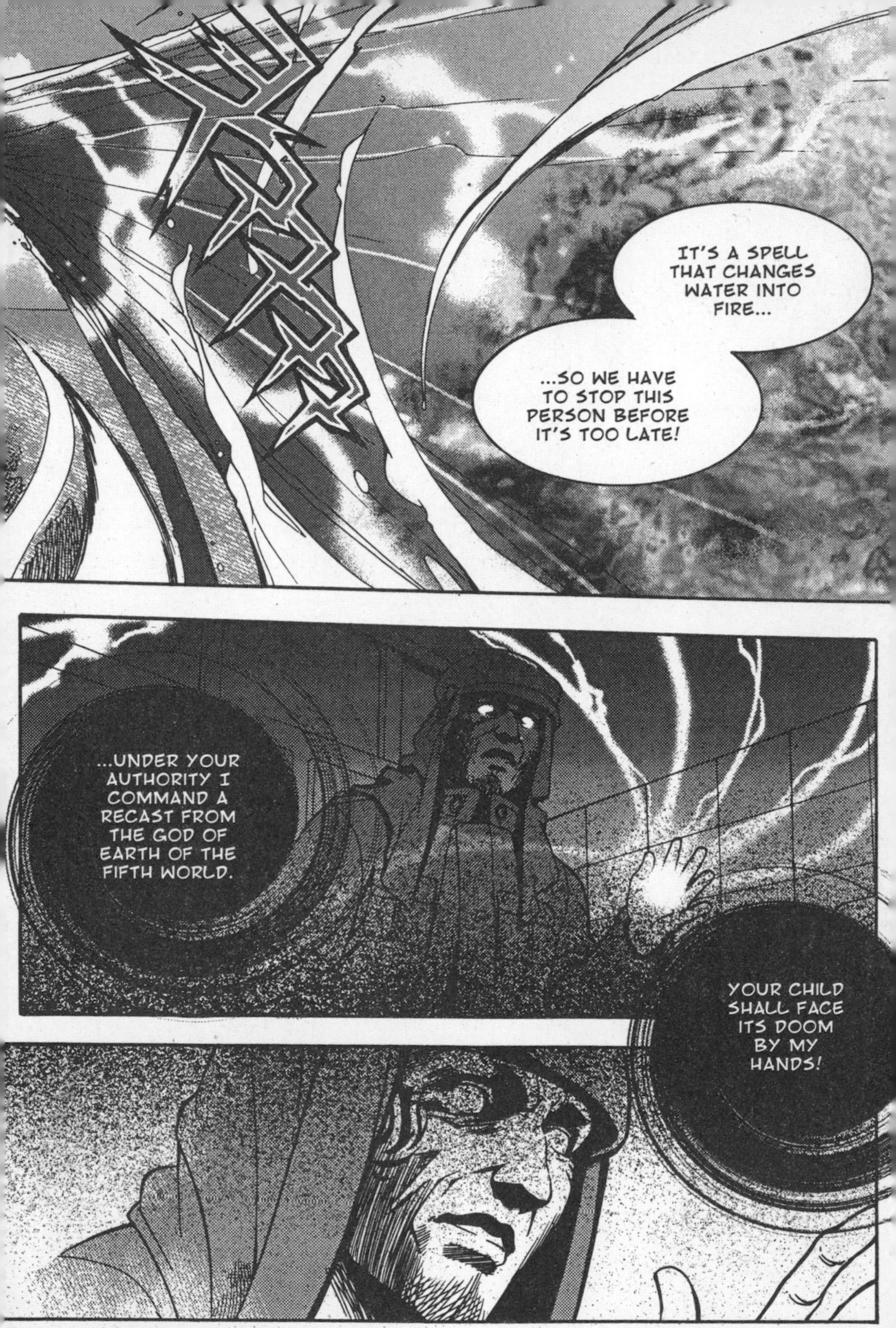
IT'S A SPELL THAT CHANGES WATER INTO FIRE...
...SO WE HAVE TO STOP THIS PERSON BEFORE IT'S TOO LATE!
...UNDER YOUR AUTHORITY I COMMAND A RECAST FROM THE GOD OF EARTH OF THE FIFTH WORLD.
YOUR CHILD SHALL FACE ITS DOOM BY MY HANDS!

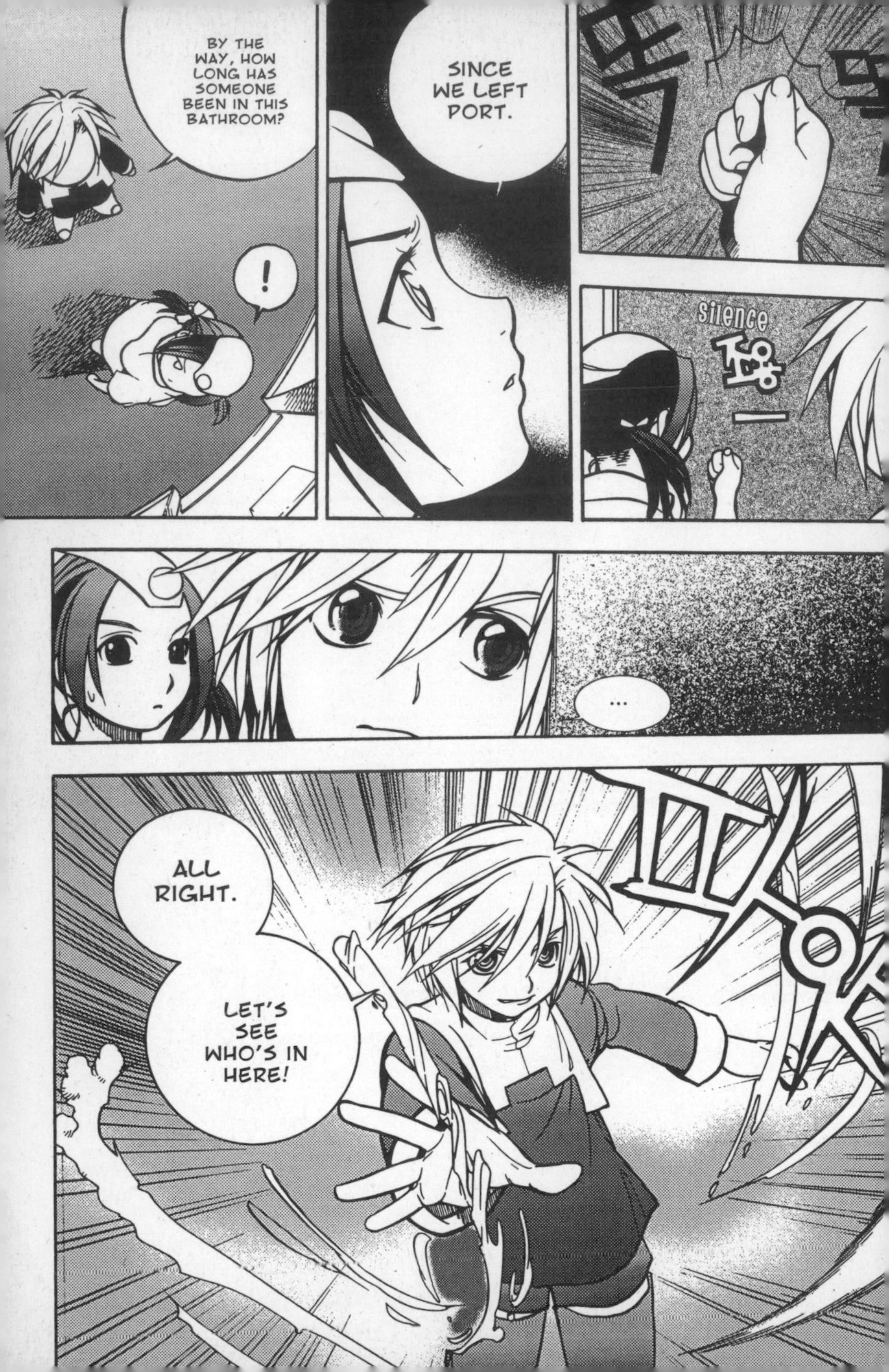
BY THE WAY, HOW LONG HAS SOMEONE BEEN IN THIS BATHROOM?
!
SINCE WE LEFT PORT.
silence
...
ALL RIGHT.
LET'S SEE WHO'S IN HERE!

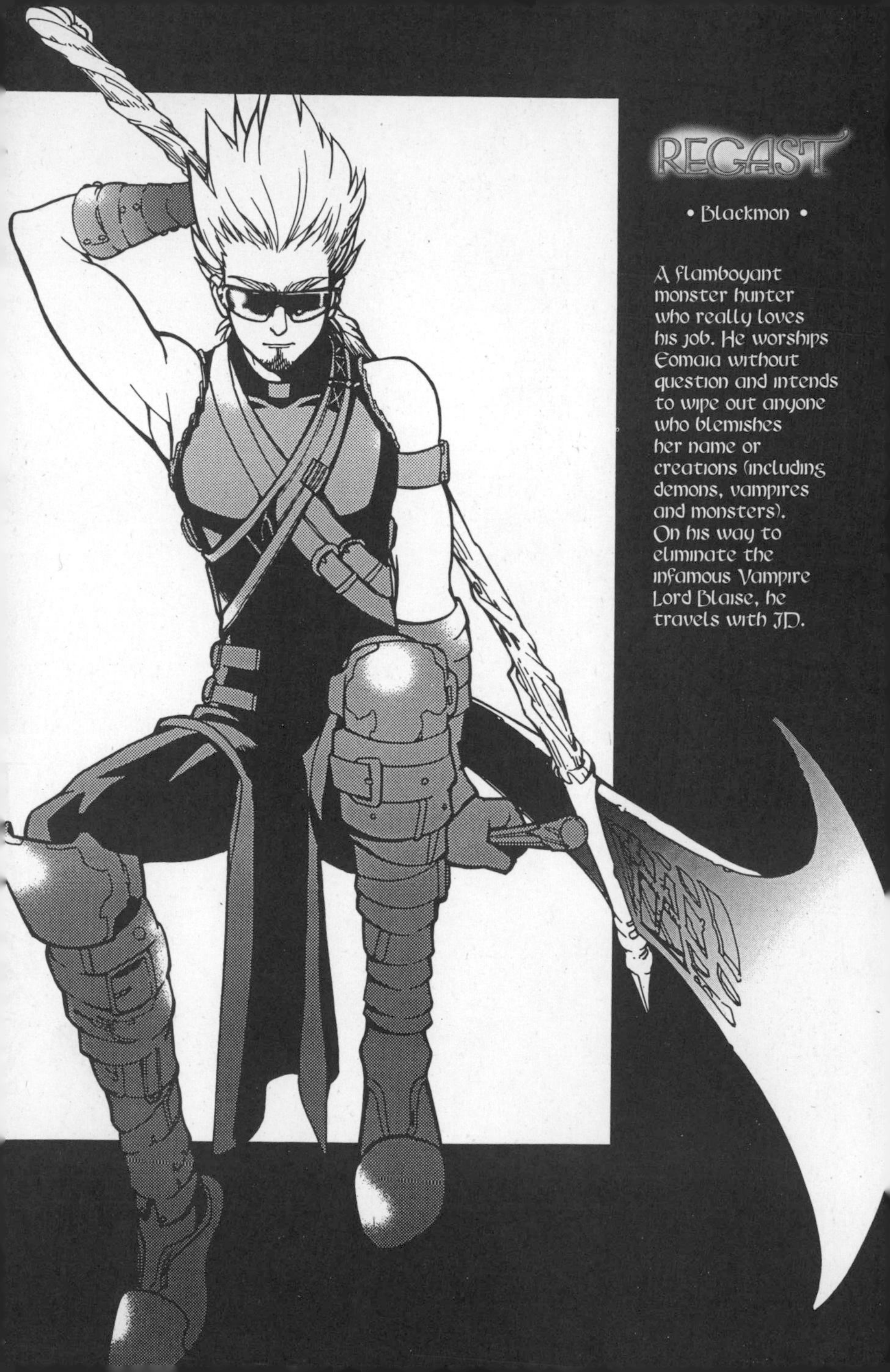

REGAST

• Blackmon •

A flamboyant monster hunter who really loves his job. He worships Eomaia without question and intends to wipe out anyone who blemishes her name or creations (including demons, vampires and monsters). On his way to eliminate the infamous Vampire Lord Blaise, he travels with JD.

REGAST

• Carmen •

Blaise's younger sister. She's intelligent, cruel and greedy. Though Blaise constantly yearns for adventure, she manages to keep him at home by bringing up the tragic incident in their past. A future nemesis for JD?

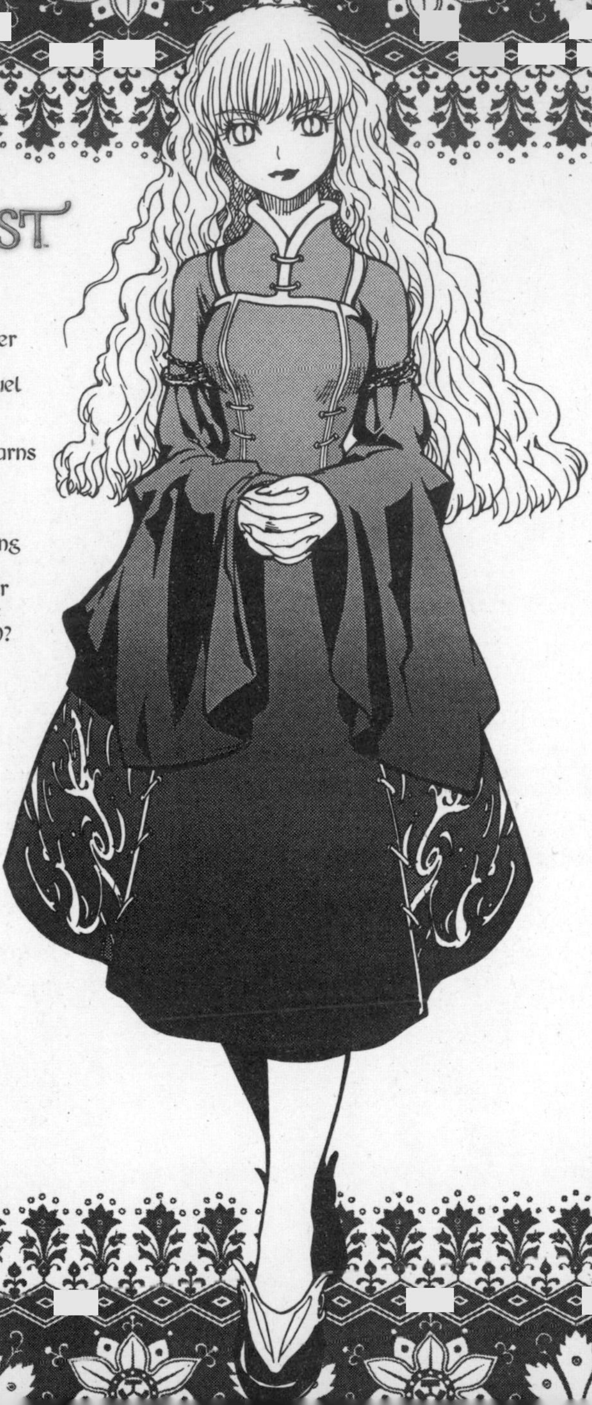

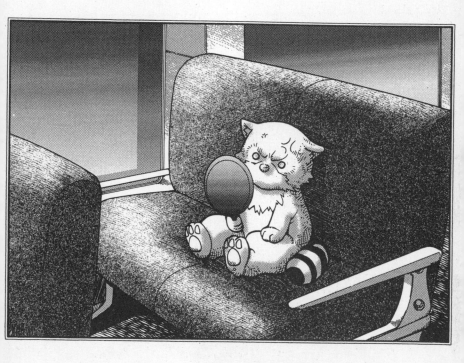

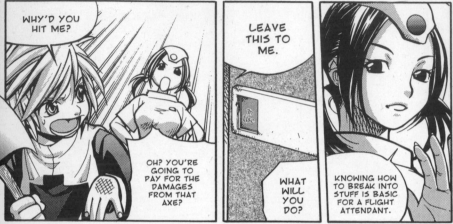

WHY'D YOU HIT ME?

OH? YOU'RE GOING TO PAY FOR THE DAMAGES FROM THAT AXE?

LEAVE THIS TO ME.

WHAT WILL YOU DO?

KNOWING HOW TO BREAK INTO STUFF IS BASIC FOR A FLIGHT ATTENDANT.

SPIRIT IN CHAINS...

...I ALLOW THEE FREEDOM.

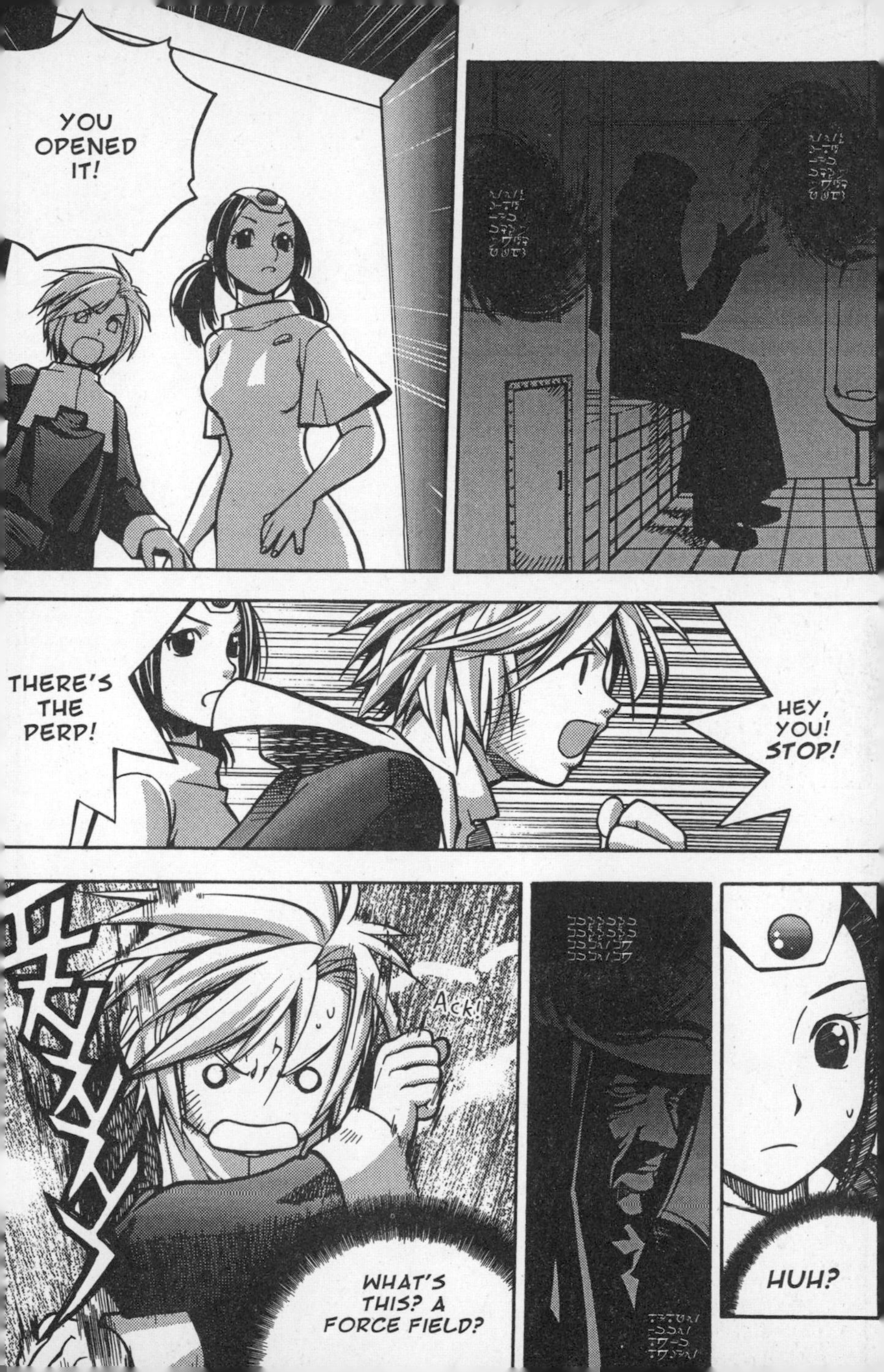
YOU OPENED IT!
THERE'S THE PERP!
HEY, YOU! STOP!
Ack!
WHAT'S THIS? A FORCE FIELD?
HUH?

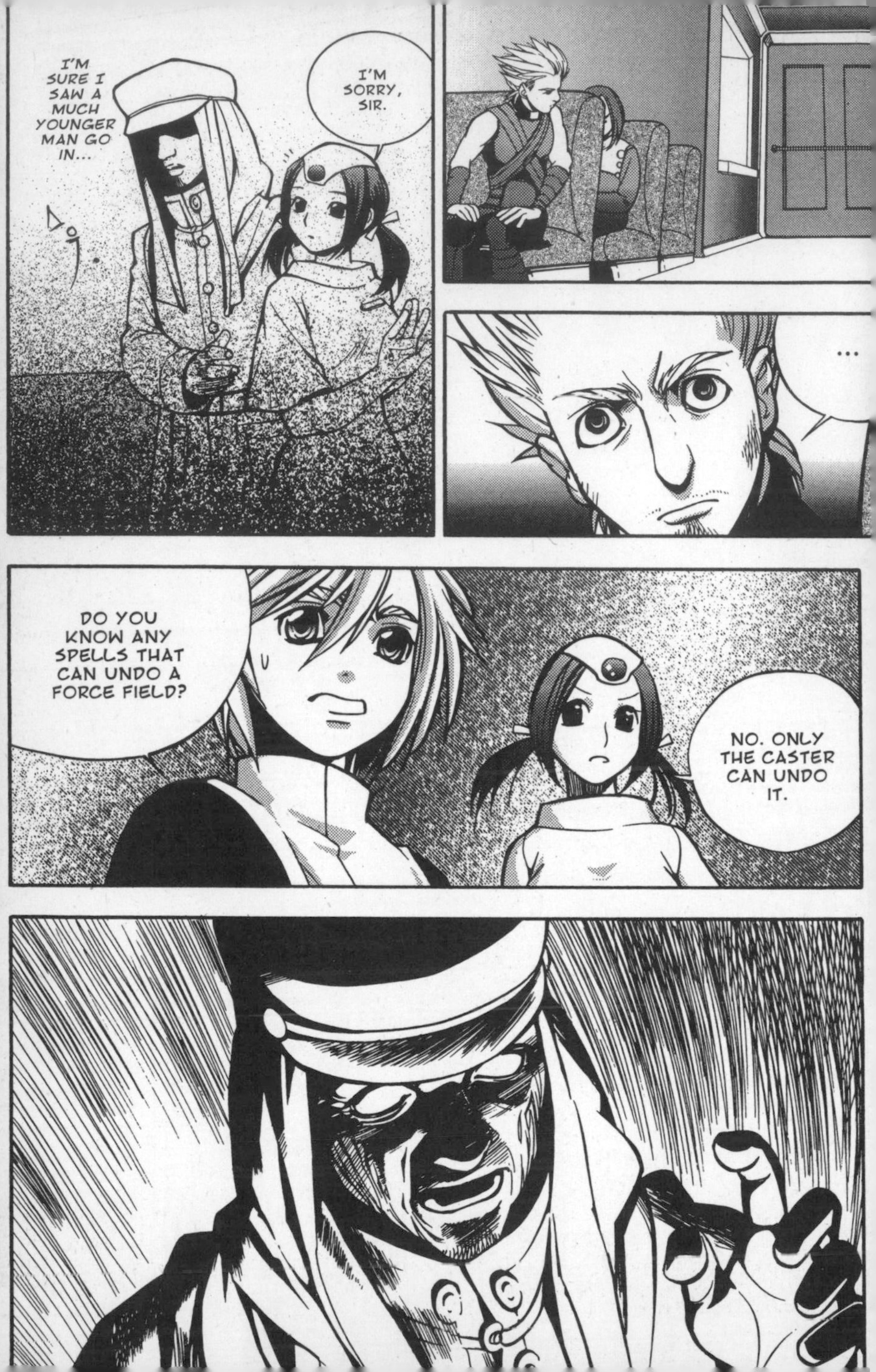
I'M SURE I SAW A MUCH YOUNGER MAN GO IN...
I'M SORRY, SIR.
...
DO YOU KNOW ANY SPELLS THAT CAN UNDO A FORCE FIELD?
NO. ONLY THE CASTER CAN UNDO IT.

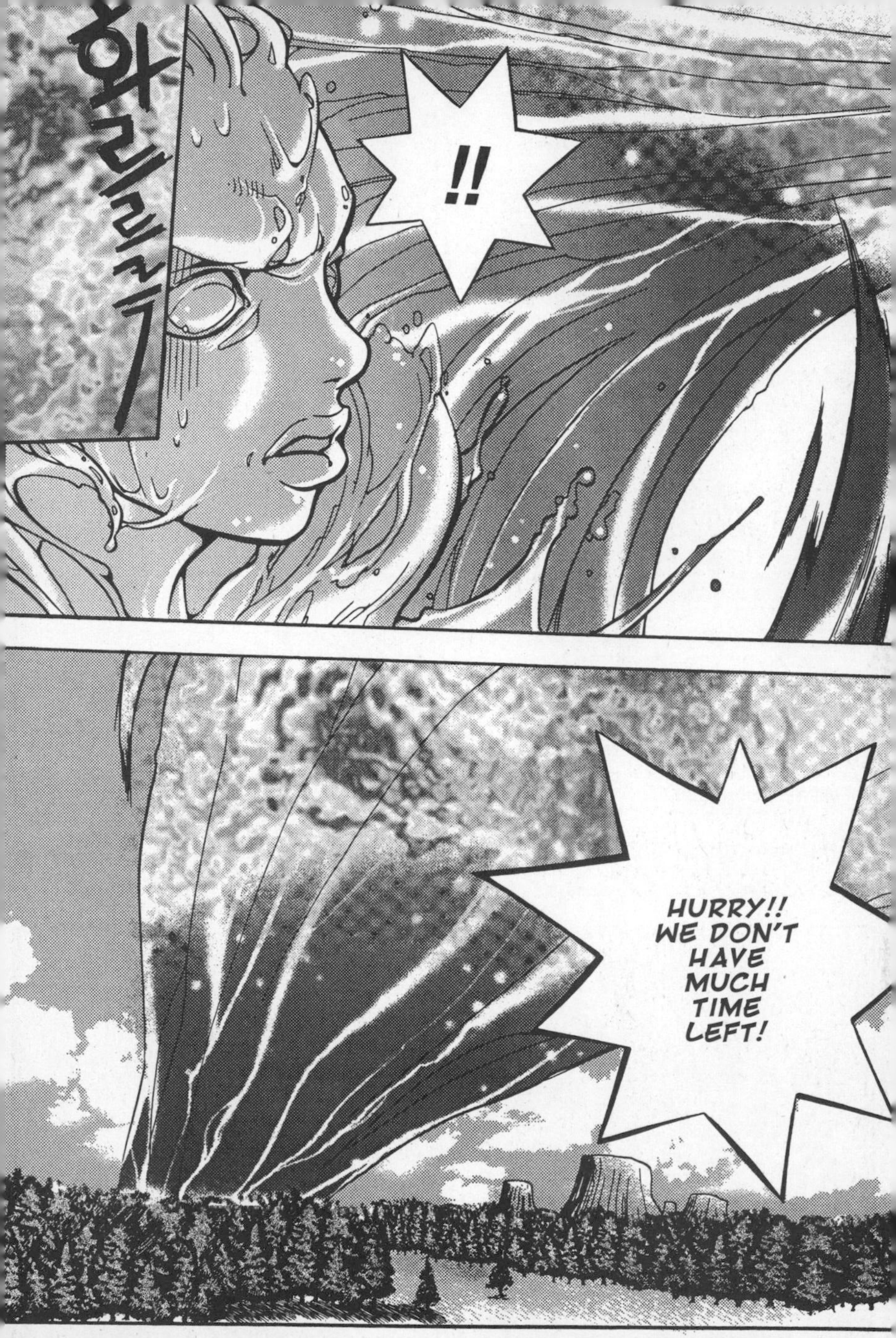
화르르르륵
!!
HURRY!! WE DON'T HAVE MUCH TIME LEFT!

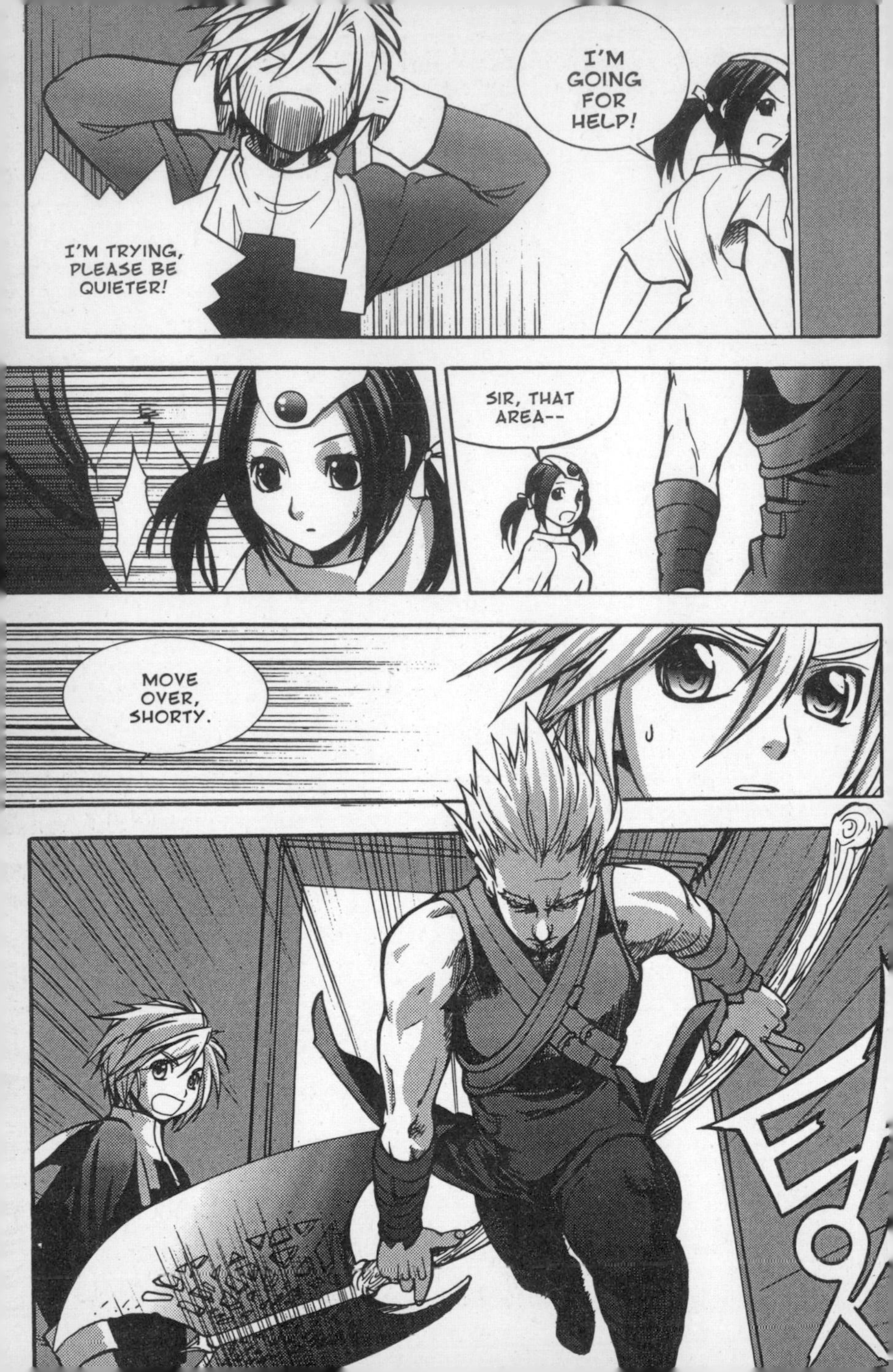
I'M GOING FOR HELP!
I'M TRYING, PLEASE BE QUIETER!
SIR, THAT AREA--
MOVE OVER, SHORTY.

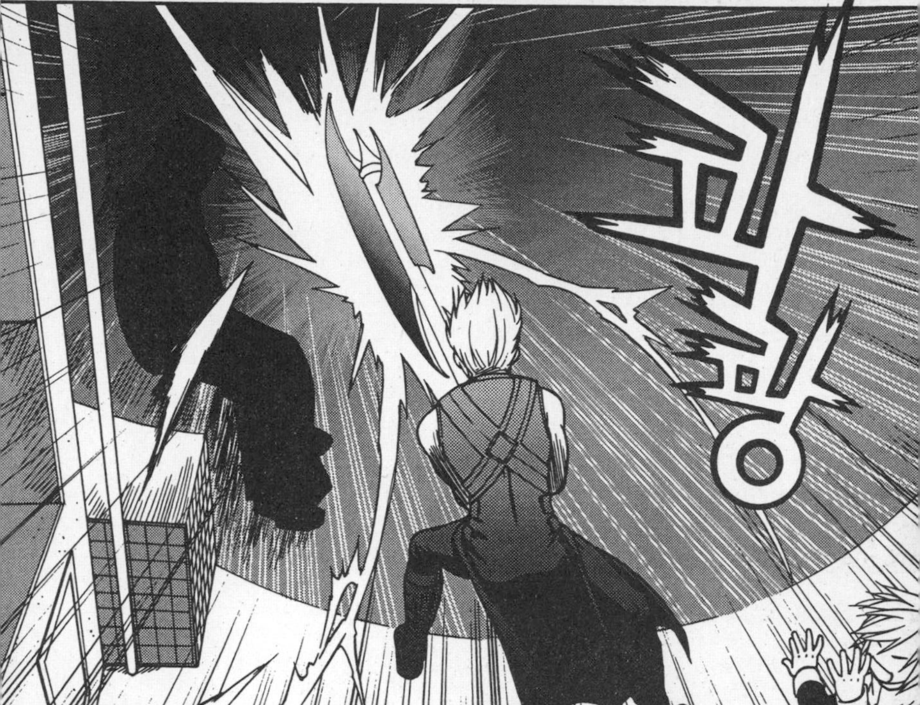

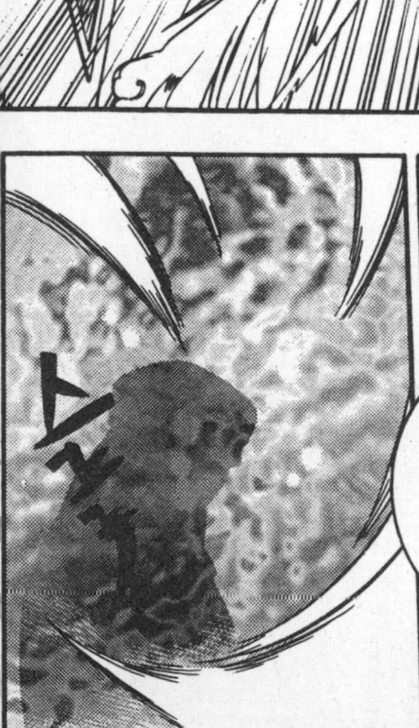

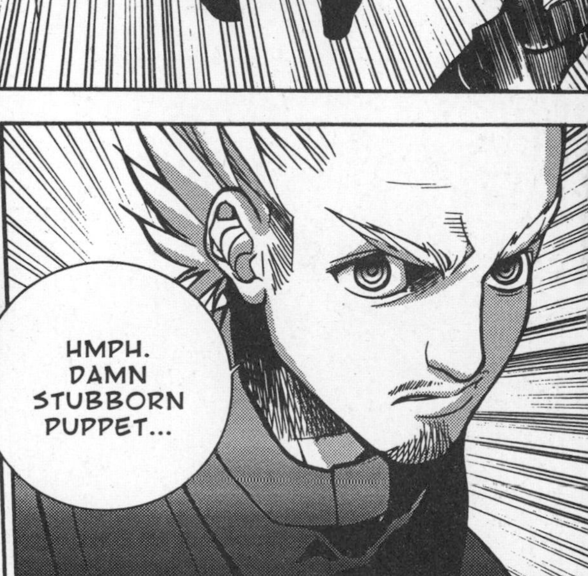
HMPH. DAMN STUBBORN PUPPET...

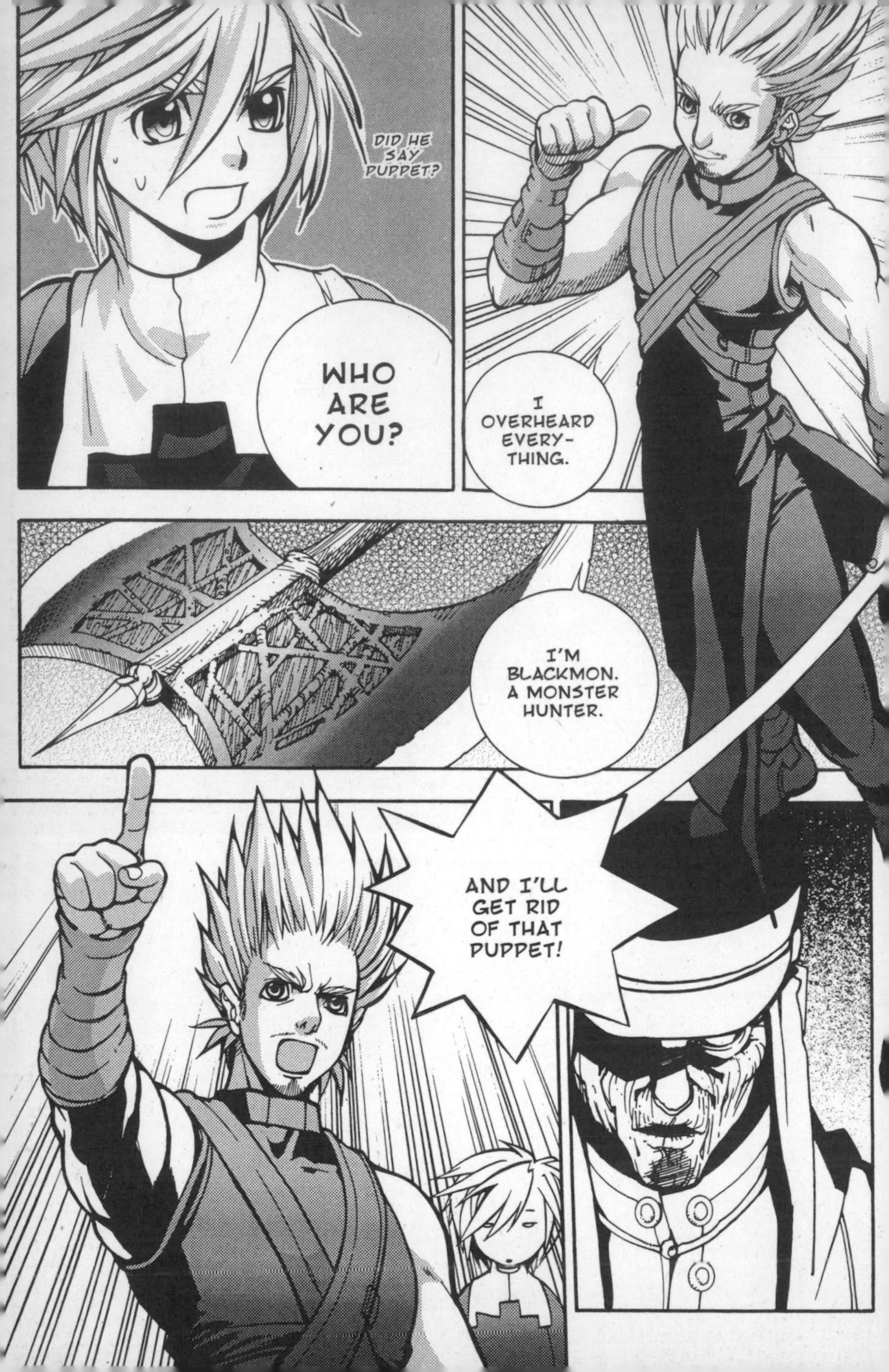
DID HE SAY PUPPET?
WHO ARE YOU?
I OVERHEARD EVERY-THING.
I'M BLACKMON. A MONSTER HUNTER.
AND I'LL GET RID OF THAT PUPPET!

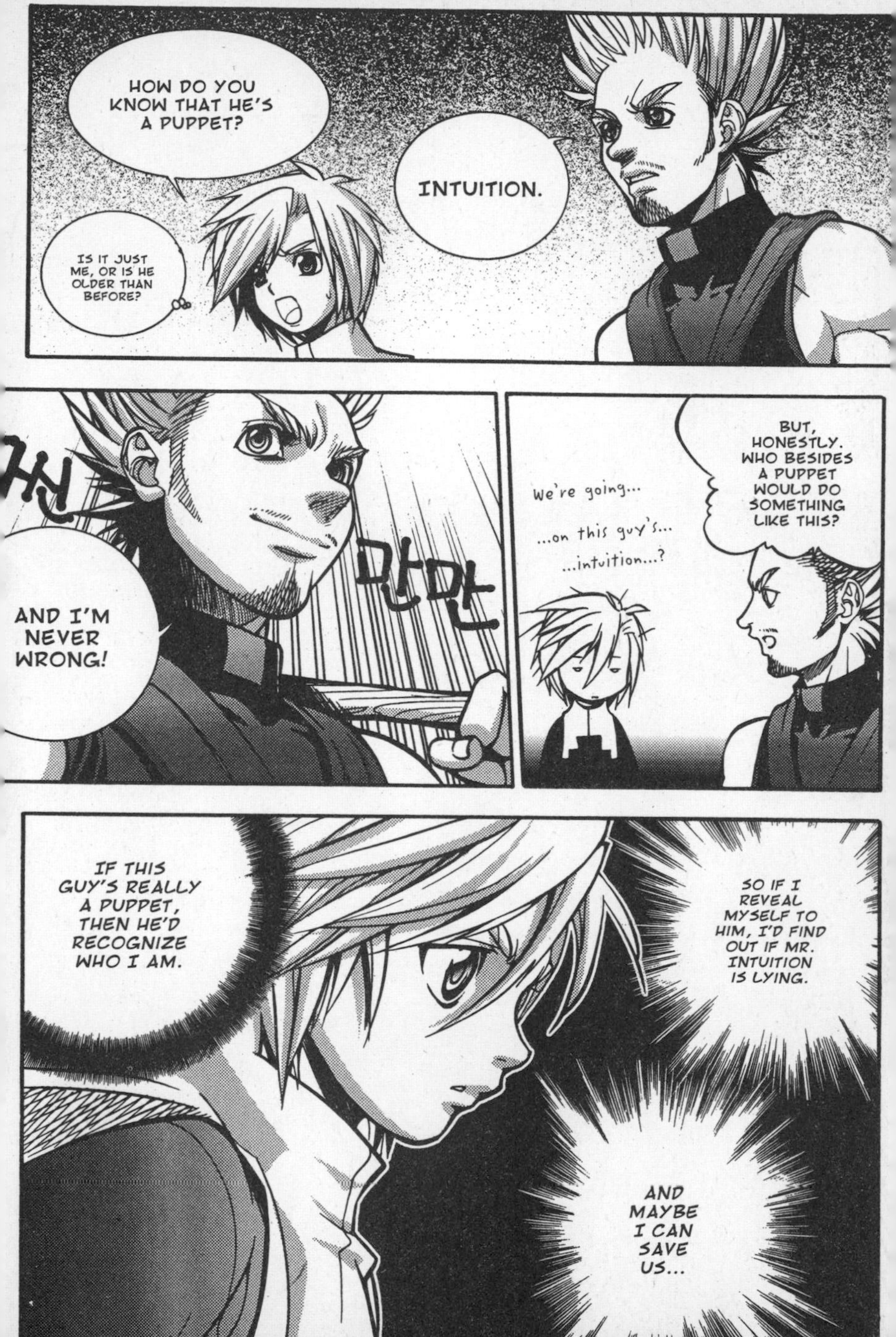

HOW DO YOU KNOW THAT HE'S A PUPPET?
IS IT JUST ME, OR IS HE OLDER THAN BEFORE?
INTUITION.
AND I'M NEVER WRONG!
BUT, HONESTLY. WHO BESIDES A PUPPET WOULD DO SOMETHING LIKE THIS?
We're going...
...on this guy's...
...intuition...?
IF THIS GUY'S REALLY A PUPPET, THEN HE'D RECOGNIZE WHO I AM.
SO IF I REVEAL MYSELF TO HIM, I'D FIND OUT IF MR. INTUITION IS LYING.
AND MAYBE I CAN SAVE US...

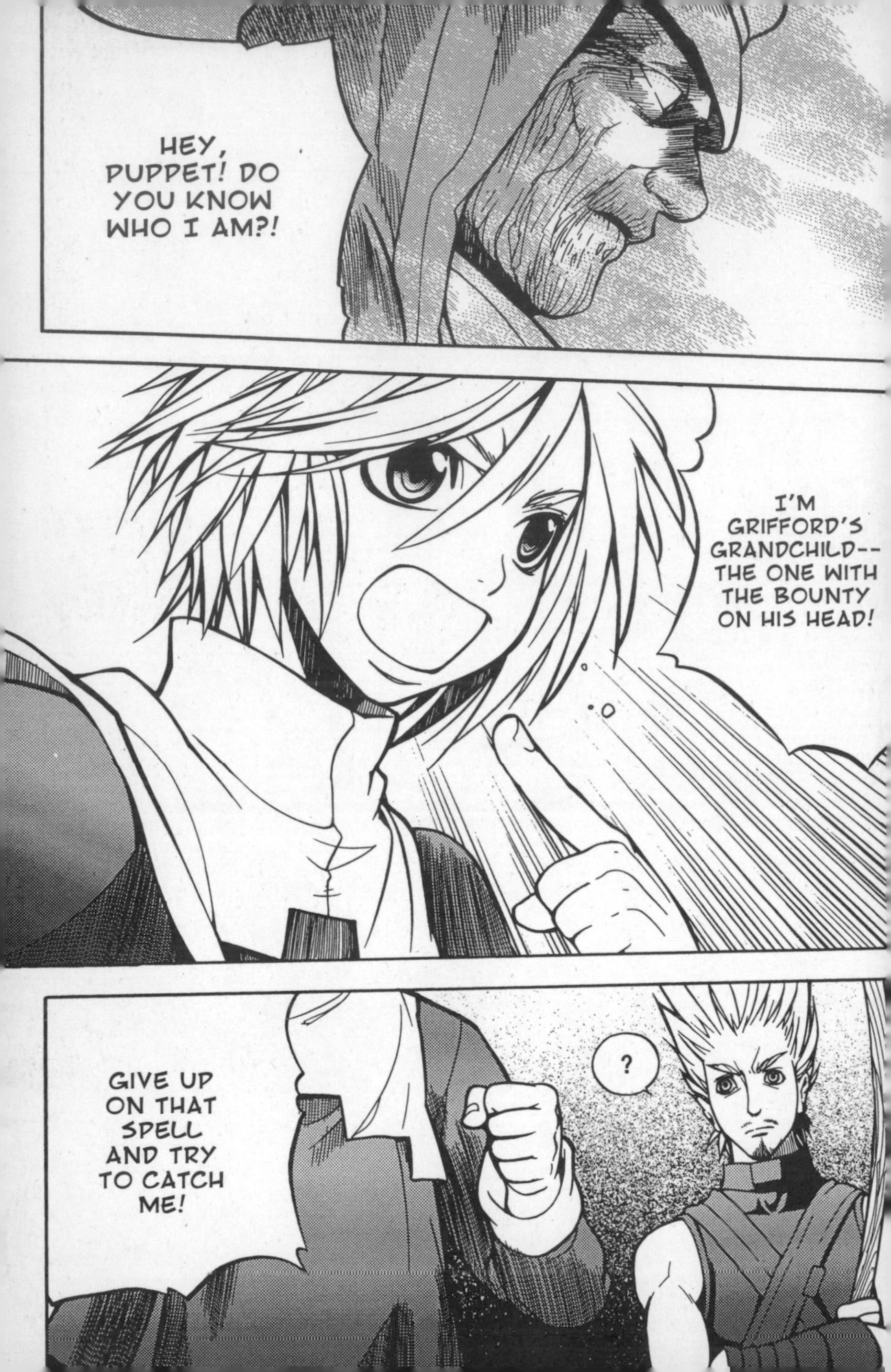
HEY, PUPPET! DO YOU KNOW WHO I AM?!
I'M GRIFFORD'S GRANDCHILD-- THE ONE WITH THE BOUNTY ON HIS HEAD!
GIVE UP ON THAT SPELL AND TRY TO CATCH ME!
?

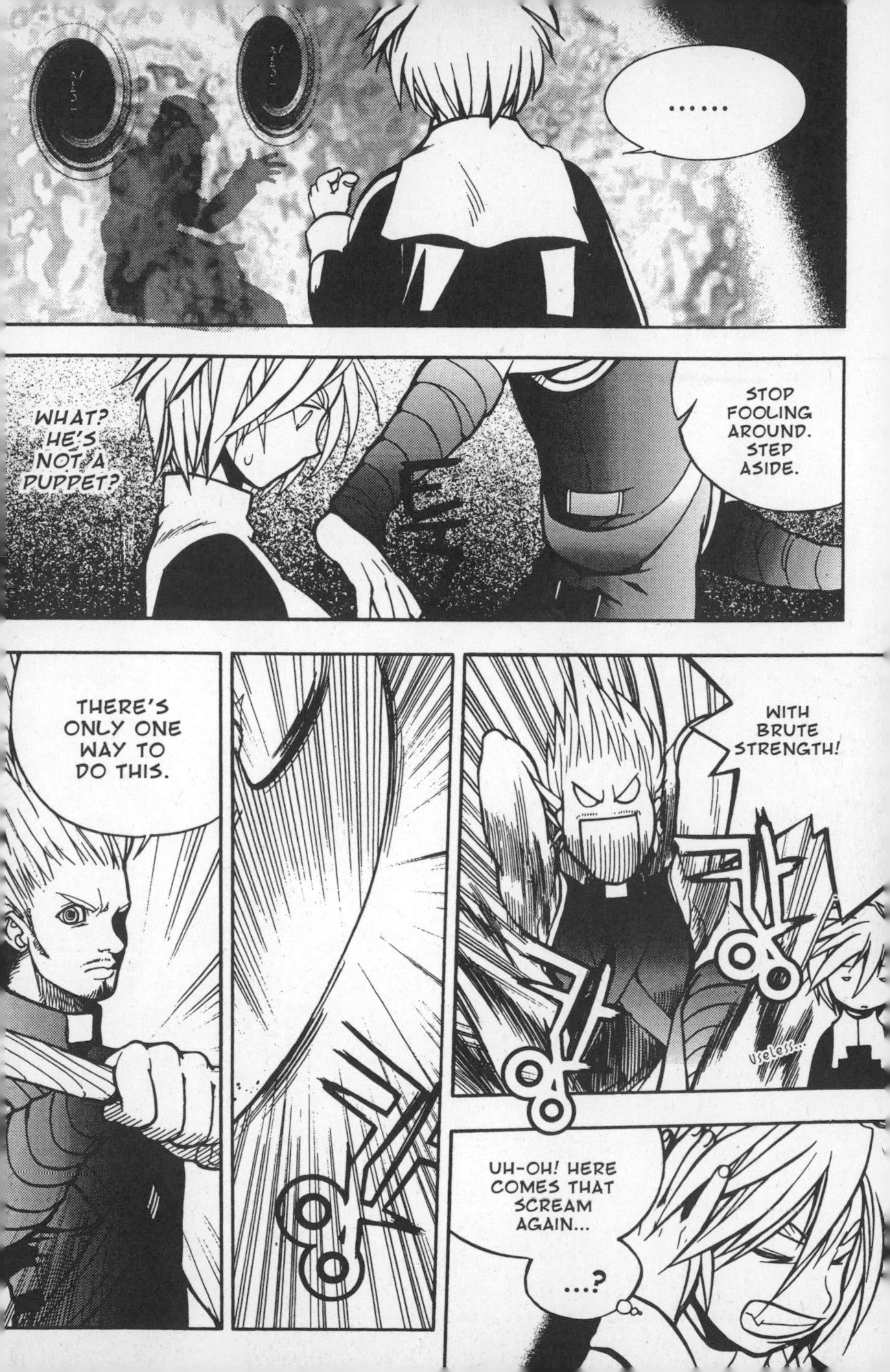
......
WHAT? HE'S NOT A PUPPET?
STOP FOOLING AROUND. STEP ASIDE.
THERE'S ONLY ONE WAY TO DO THIS.
WITH BRUTE STRENGTH!
Useless...
UH-OH! HERE COMES THAT SCREAM AGAIN...
...?

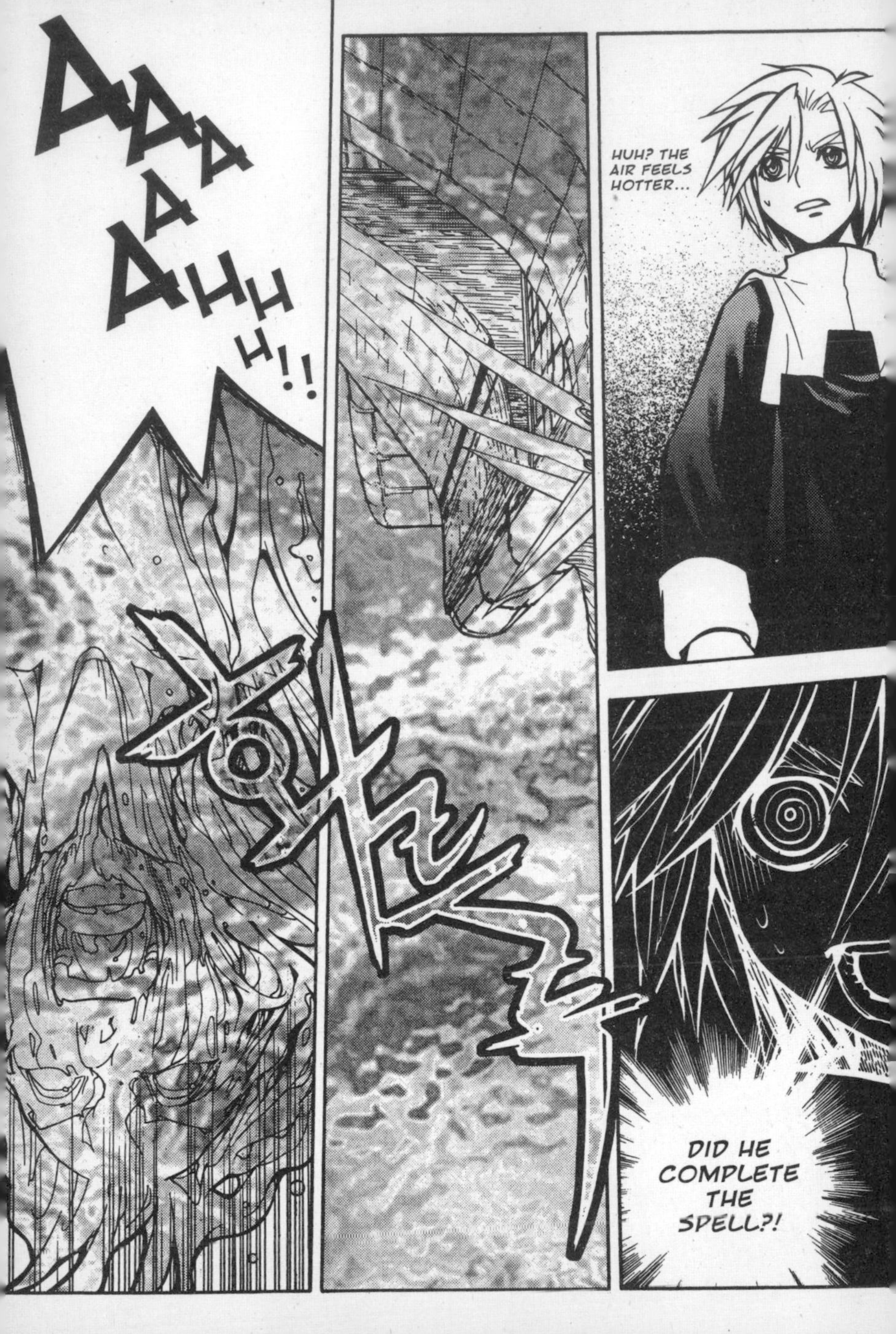
AAAAAHHHH!!
HUH? THE AIR FEELS HOTTER...
DID HE COMPLETE THE SPELL?!

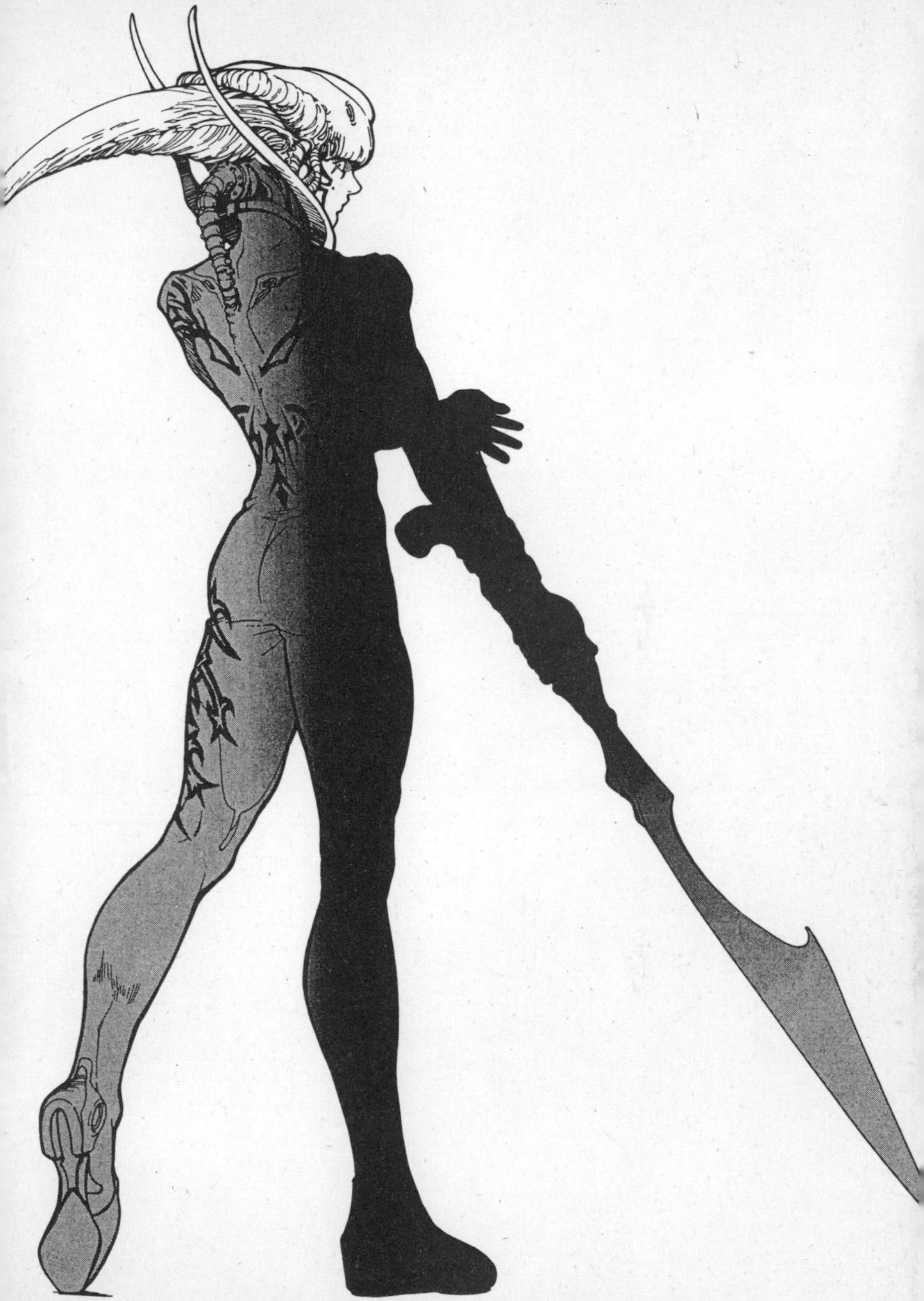

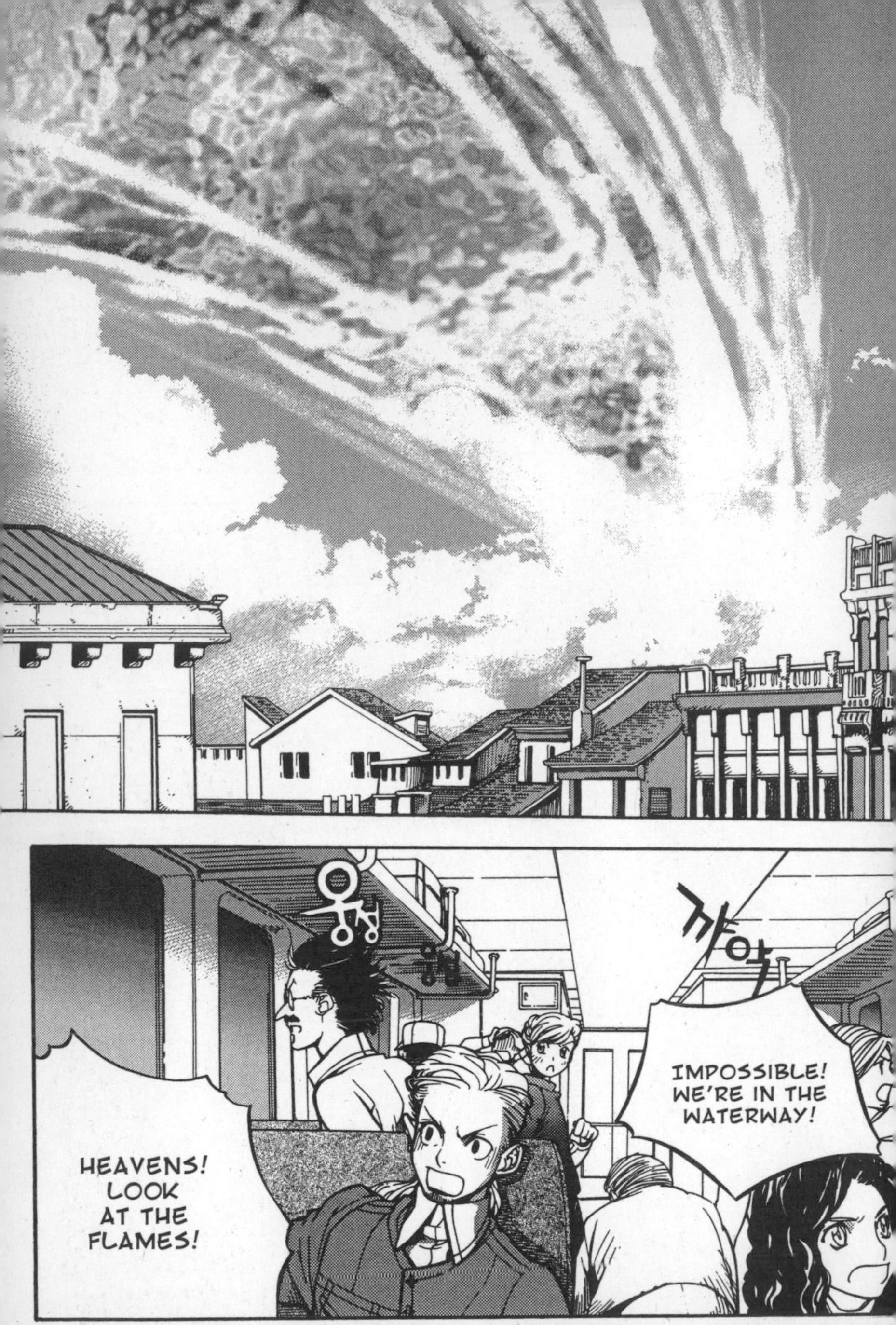
HEAVENS! LOOK AT THE FLAMES!
IMPOSSIBLE! WE'RE IN THE WATERWAY!

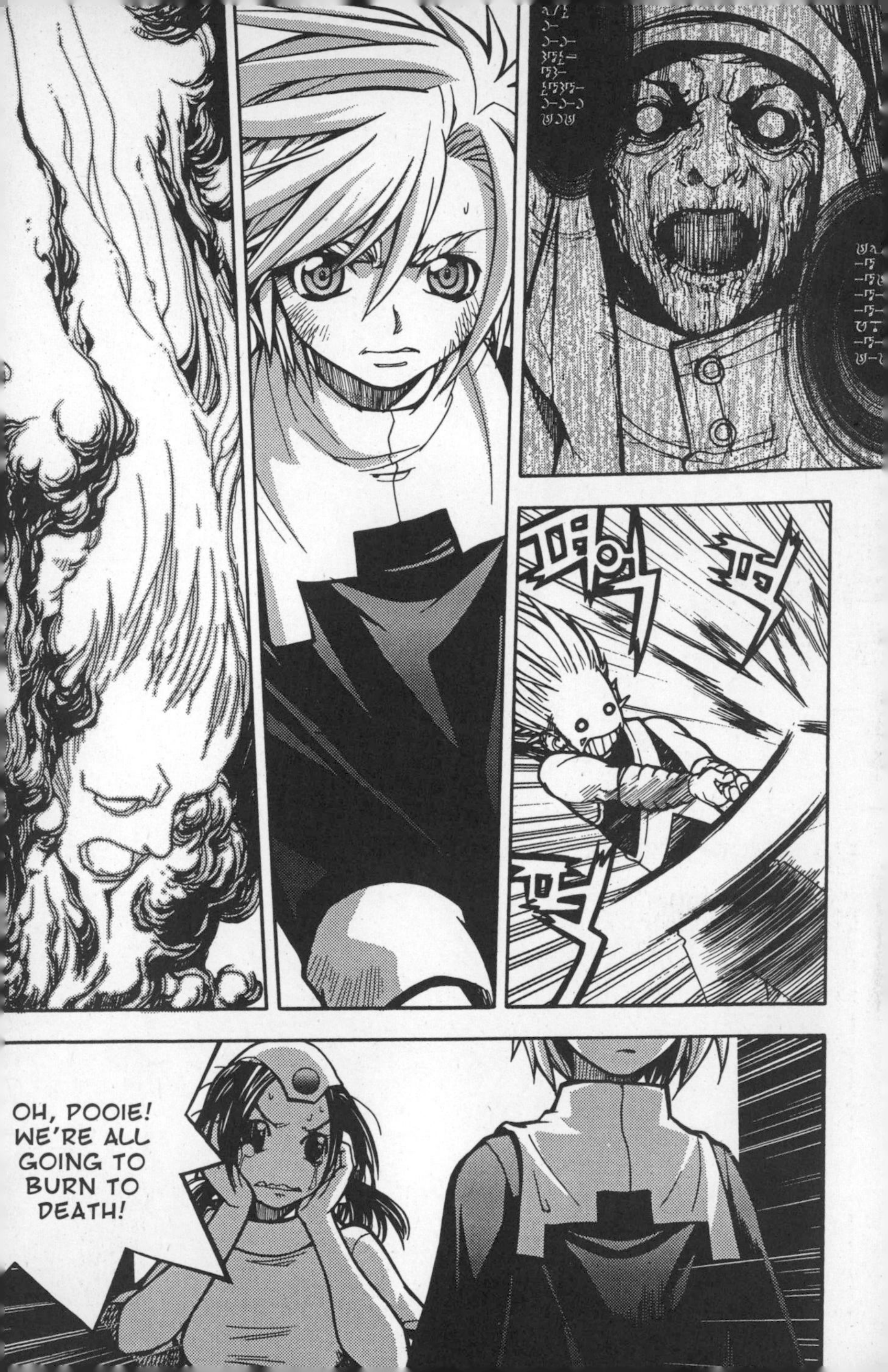
OH, POOIE! WE'RE ALL GOING TO BURN TO DEATH!

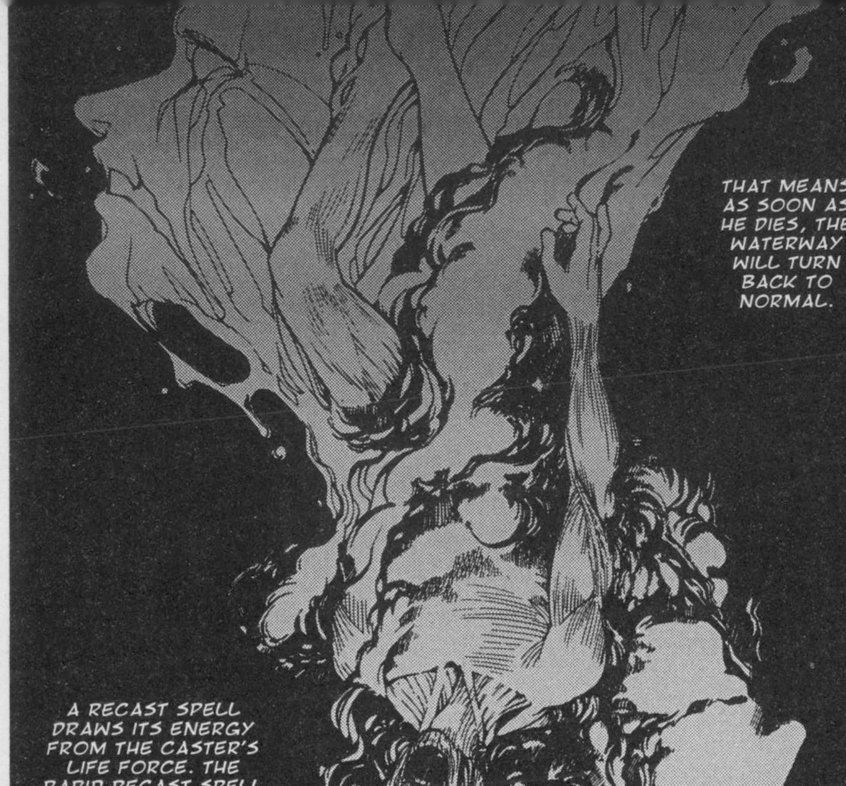
THAT MEANS AS SOON AS HE DIES, THE WATERWAY WILL TURN BACK TO NORMAL.
A RECAST SPELL DRAWS ITS ENERGY FROM THE CASTER'S LIFE FORCE. THE RAPID RECAST SPELL IS EATING AWAY AT THIS CASTER'S LIFE AT AN INCREDIBLY FAST RATE.
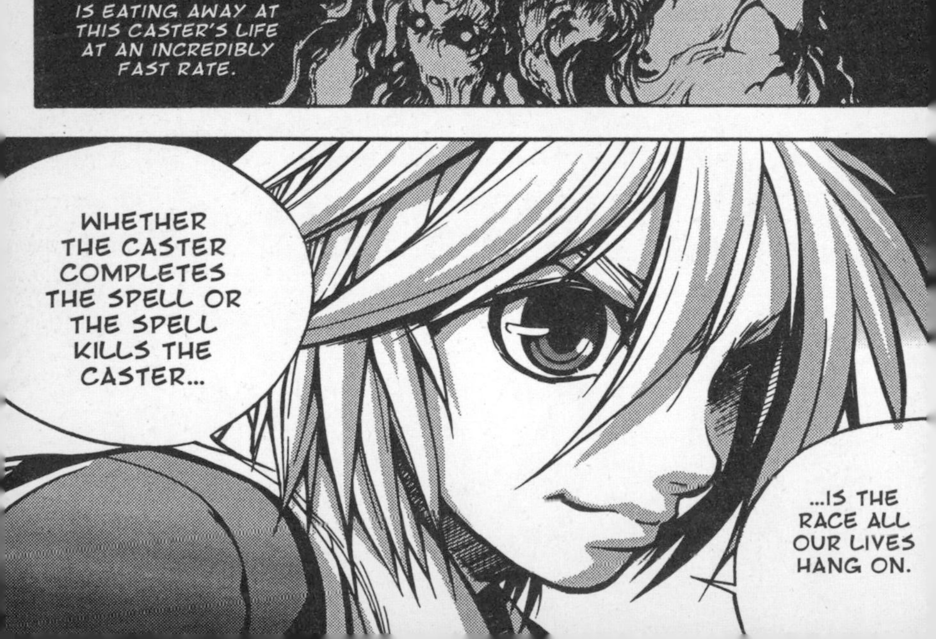
WHETHER THE CASTER COMPLETES THE SPELL OR THE SPELL KILLS THE CASTER...
...IS THE RACE ALL OUR LIVES HANG ON.

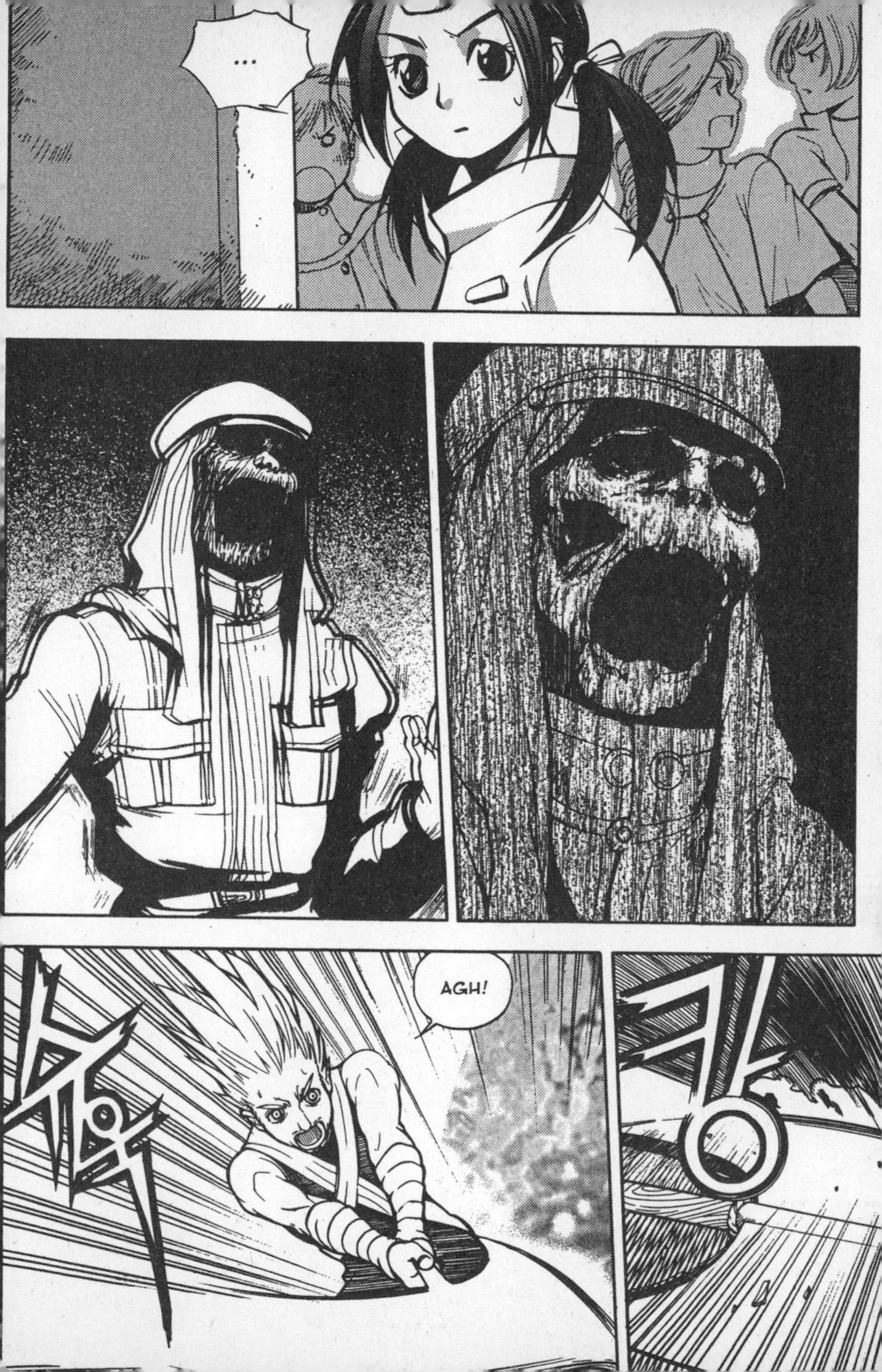
...
AGH!

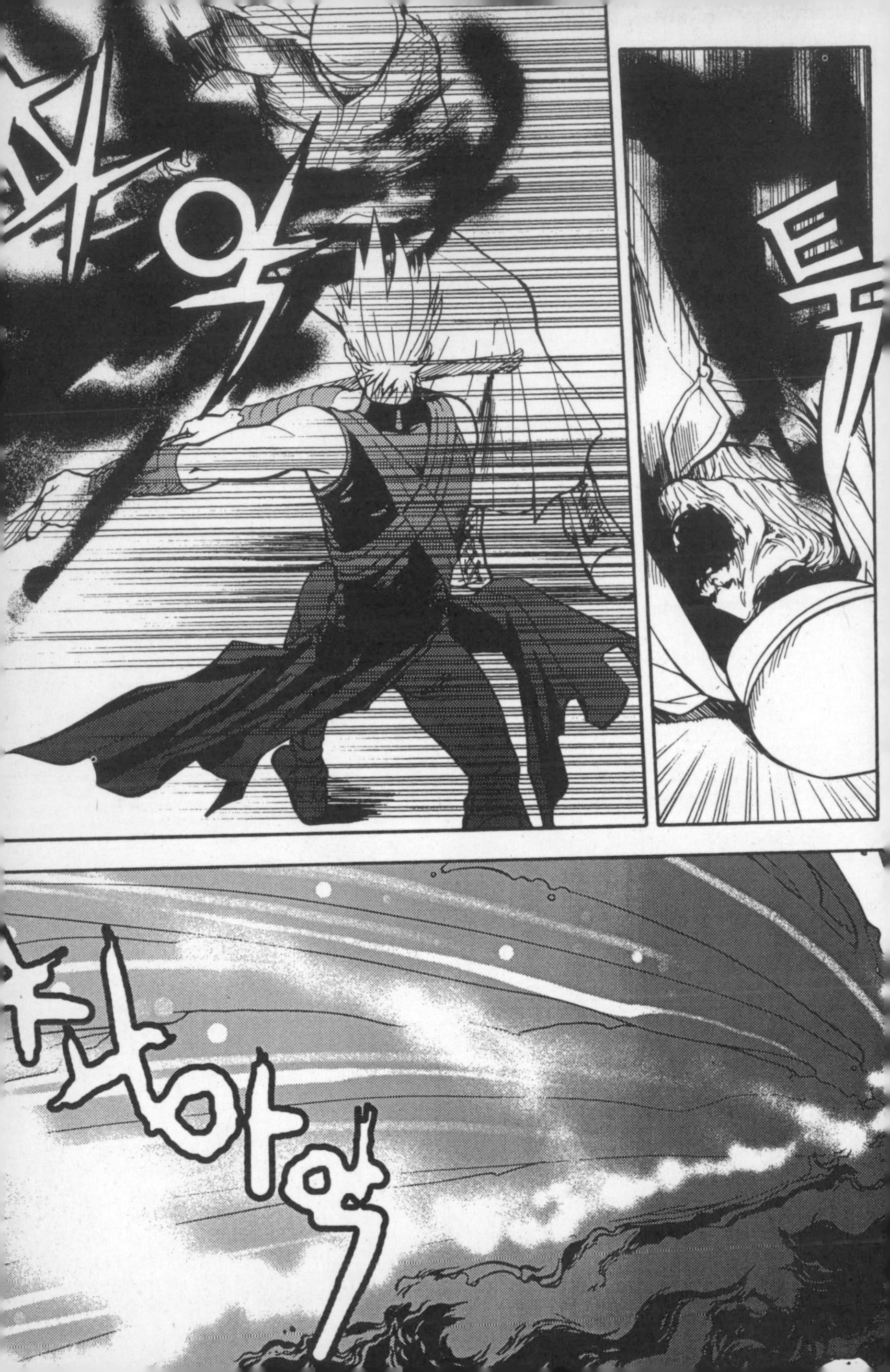

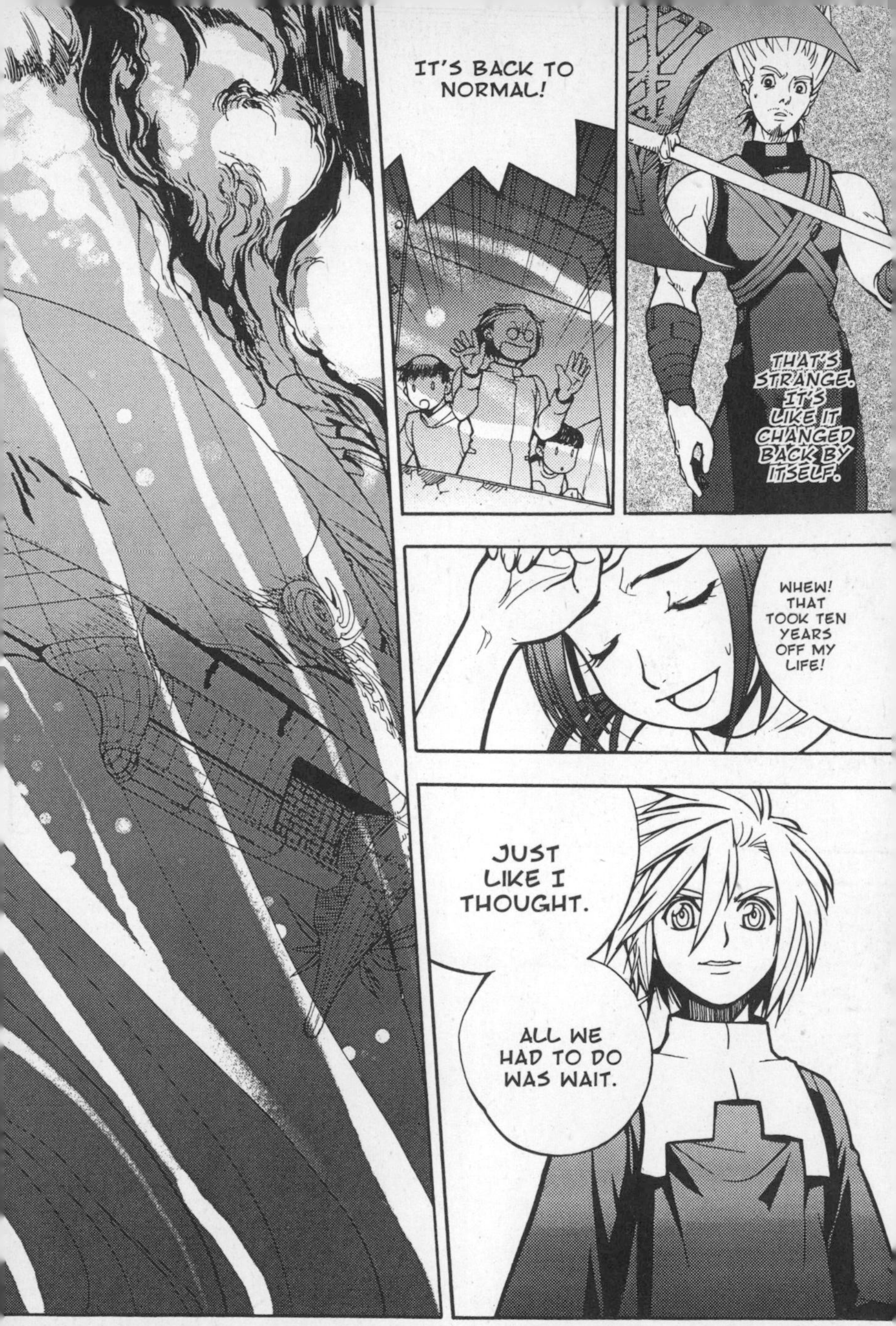
IT'S BACK TO NORMAL!
THAT'S STRANGE. IT'S LIKE IT CHANGED BACK BY ITSELF.
WHEW! THAT TOOK TEN YEARS OFF MY LIFE!
JUST LIKE I THOUGHT.
ALL WE HAD TO DO WAS WAIT.

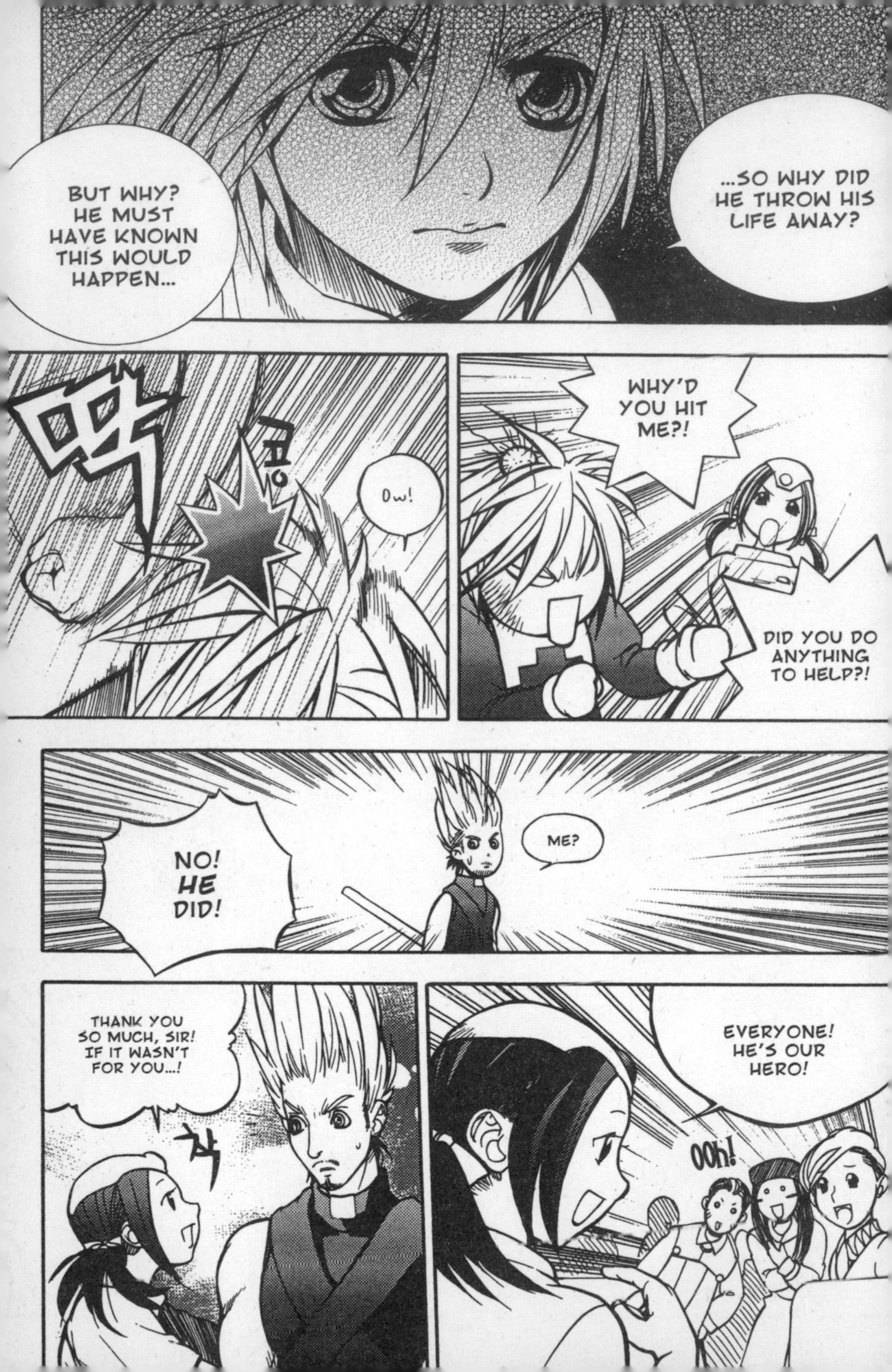
BUT WHY? HE MUST HAVE KNOWN THIS WOULD HAPPEN...
...SO WHY DID HE THROW HIS LIFE AWAY?
Ow!
WHY'D YOU HIT ME?!
DID YOU DO ANYTHING TO HELP?!
NO! HE DID!
ME?
THANK YOU SO MUCH, SIR! IF IT WASN'T FOR YOU...!
EVERYONE! HE'S OUR HERO!
OOh!

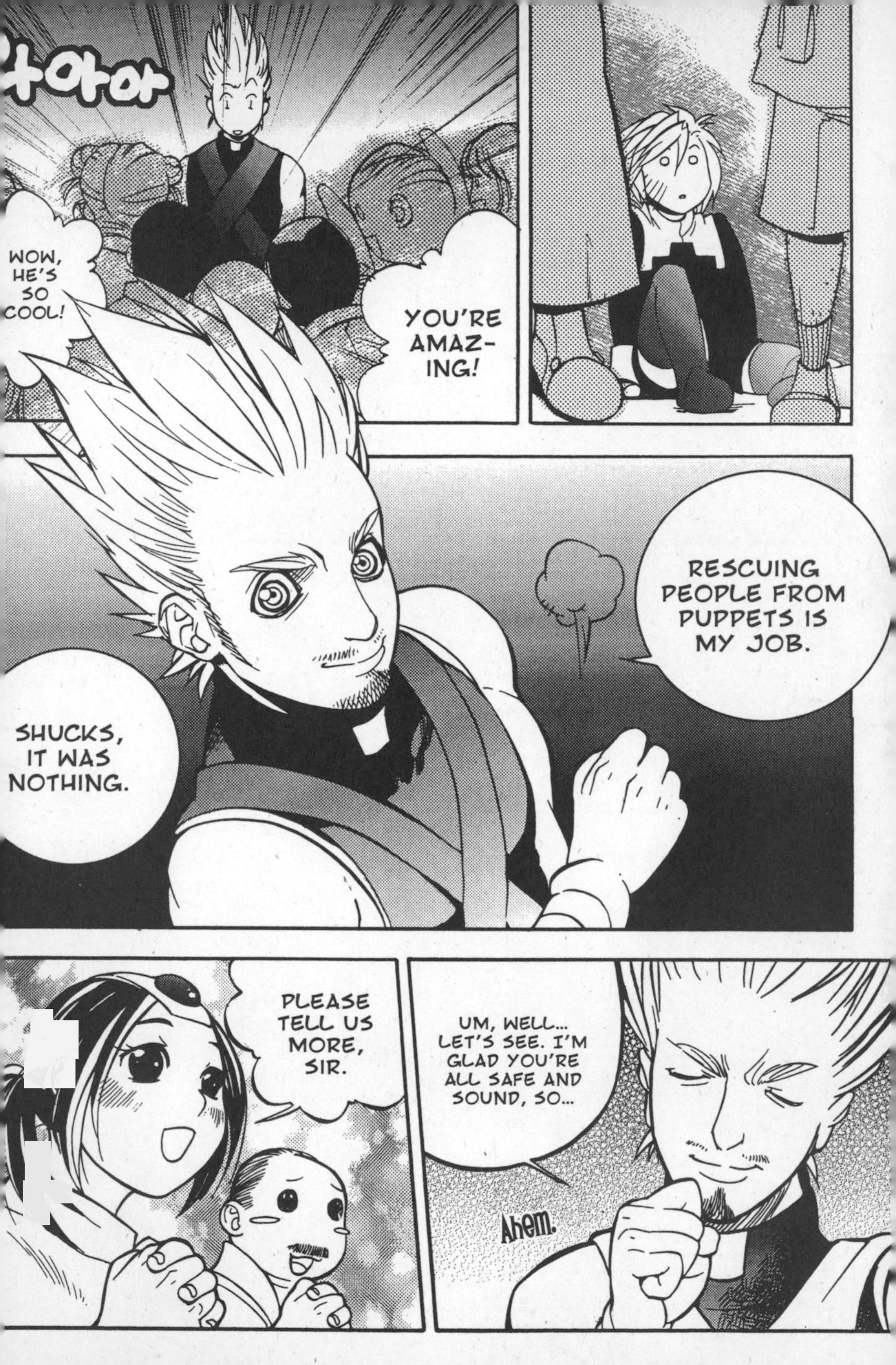
WOW, HE'S SO COOL!
YOU'RE AMAZ-ING!
SHUCKS, IT WAS NOTHING.
RESCUING PEOPLE FROM PUPPETS IS MY JOB.
PLEASE TELL US MORE, SIR.
UM, WELL... LET'S SEE. I'M GLAD YOU'RE ALL SAFE AND SOUND, SO...
Ahem.

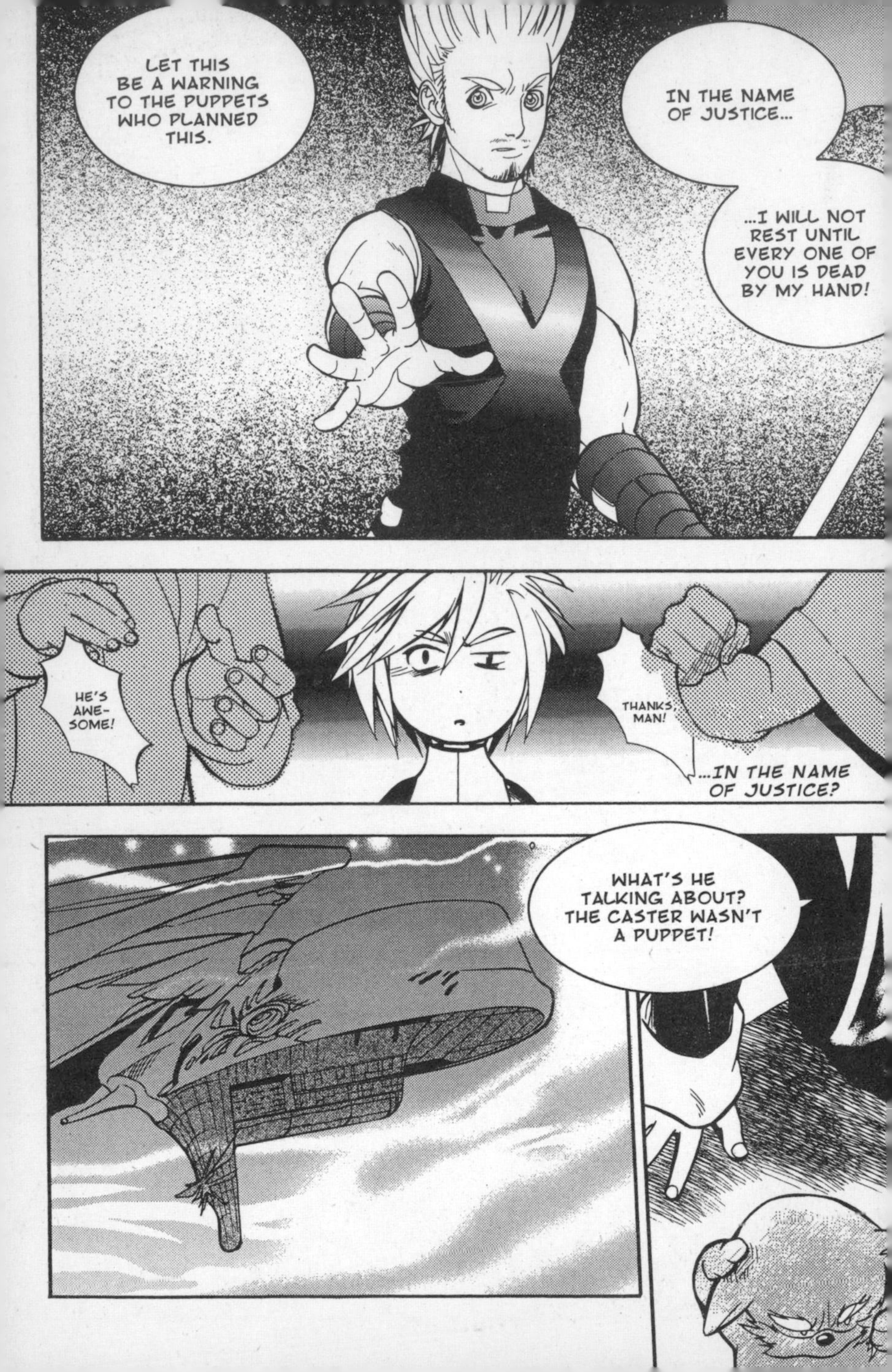
LET THIS BE A WARNING TO THE PUPPETS WHO PLANNED THIS.
IN THE NAME OF JUSTICE...
...I WILL NOT REST UNTIL EVERY ONE OF YOU IS DEAD BY MY HAND!
HE'S AWE-SOME!
THANKS, MAN!
...IN THE NAME OF JUSTICE?
WHAT'S HE TALKING ABOUT? THE CASTER WASN'T A PUPPET!

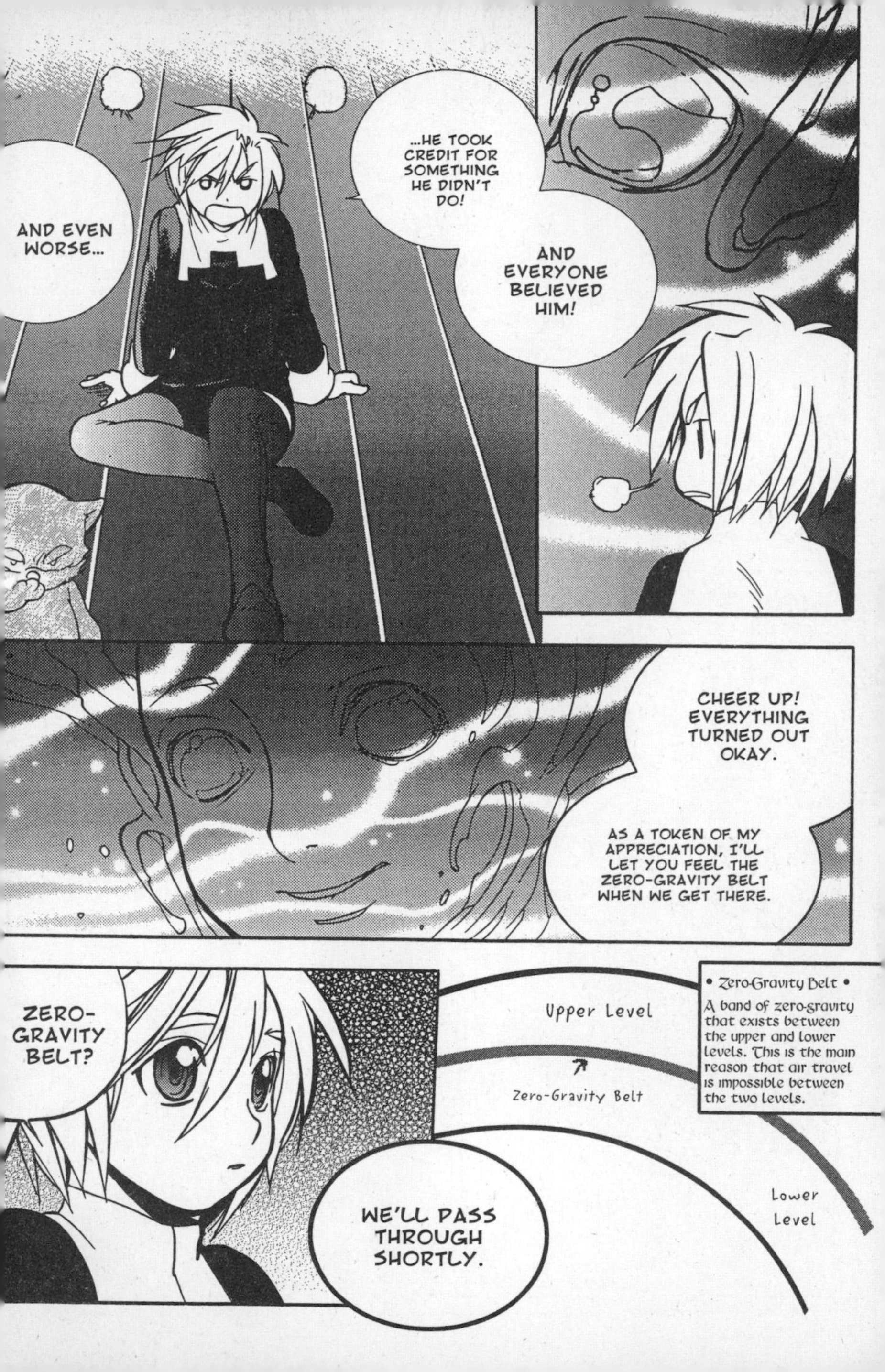
AND EVEN WORSE...
...HE TOOK CREDIT FOR SOMETHING HE DIDN'T DO!
AND EVERYONE BELIEVED HIM!
CHEER UP! EVERYTHING TURNED OUT OKAY.
AS A TOKEN OF MY APPRECIATION, I'LL LET YOU FEEL THE ZERO-GRAVITY BELT WHEN WE GET THERE.
ZERO-GRAVITY BELT?
Upper Level
Zero-Gravity Belt
Lower Level
• Zero-Gravity Belt •
A band of zero-gravity that exists between the upper and lower levels. This is the main reason that air travel is impossible between the two levels.
WE'LL PASS THROUGH SHORTLY.

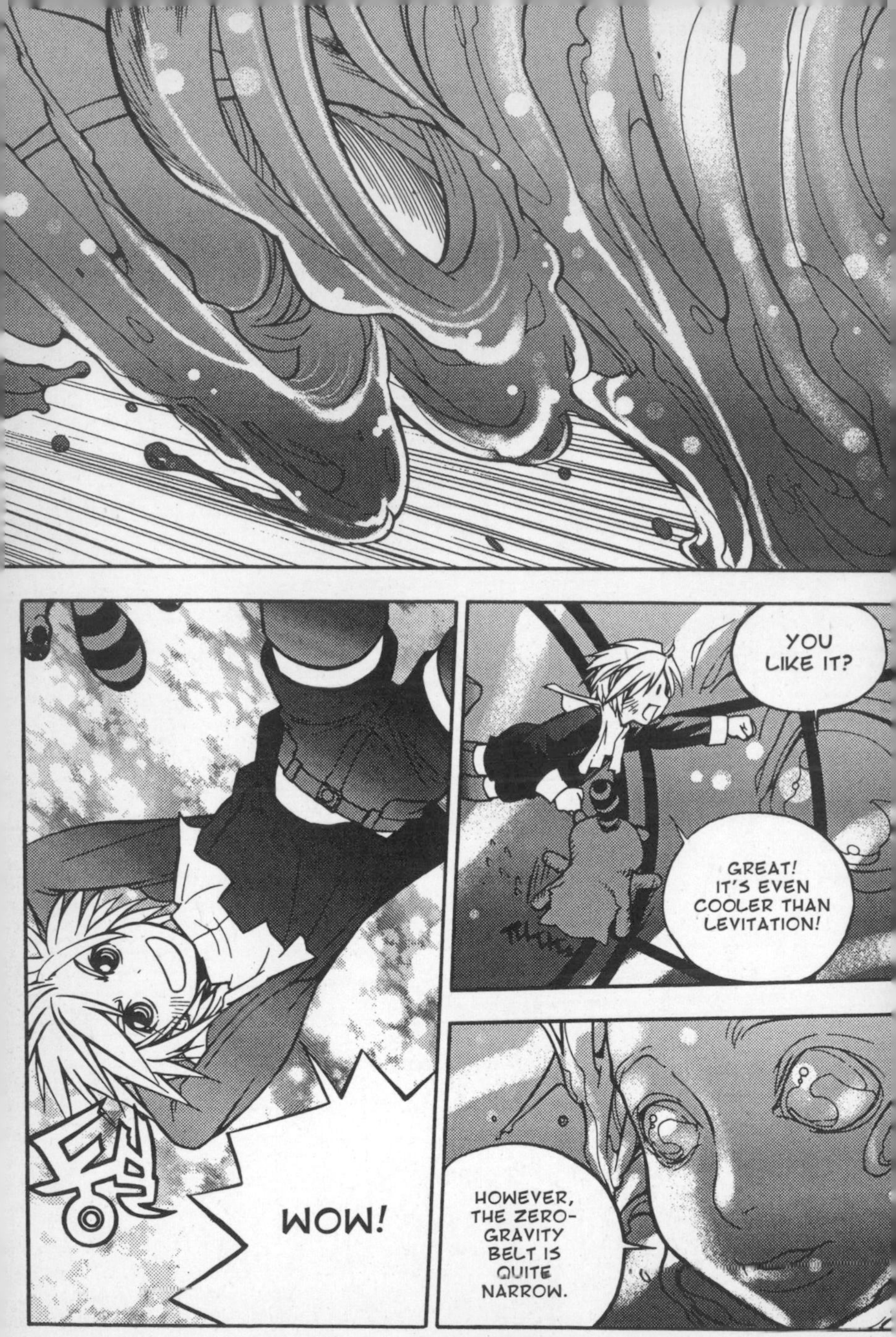
WOW!
YOU LIKE IT?
GREAT! IT'S EVEN COOLER THAN LEVITATION!
HOWEVER, THE ZERO-GRAVITY BELT IS QUITE NARROW.

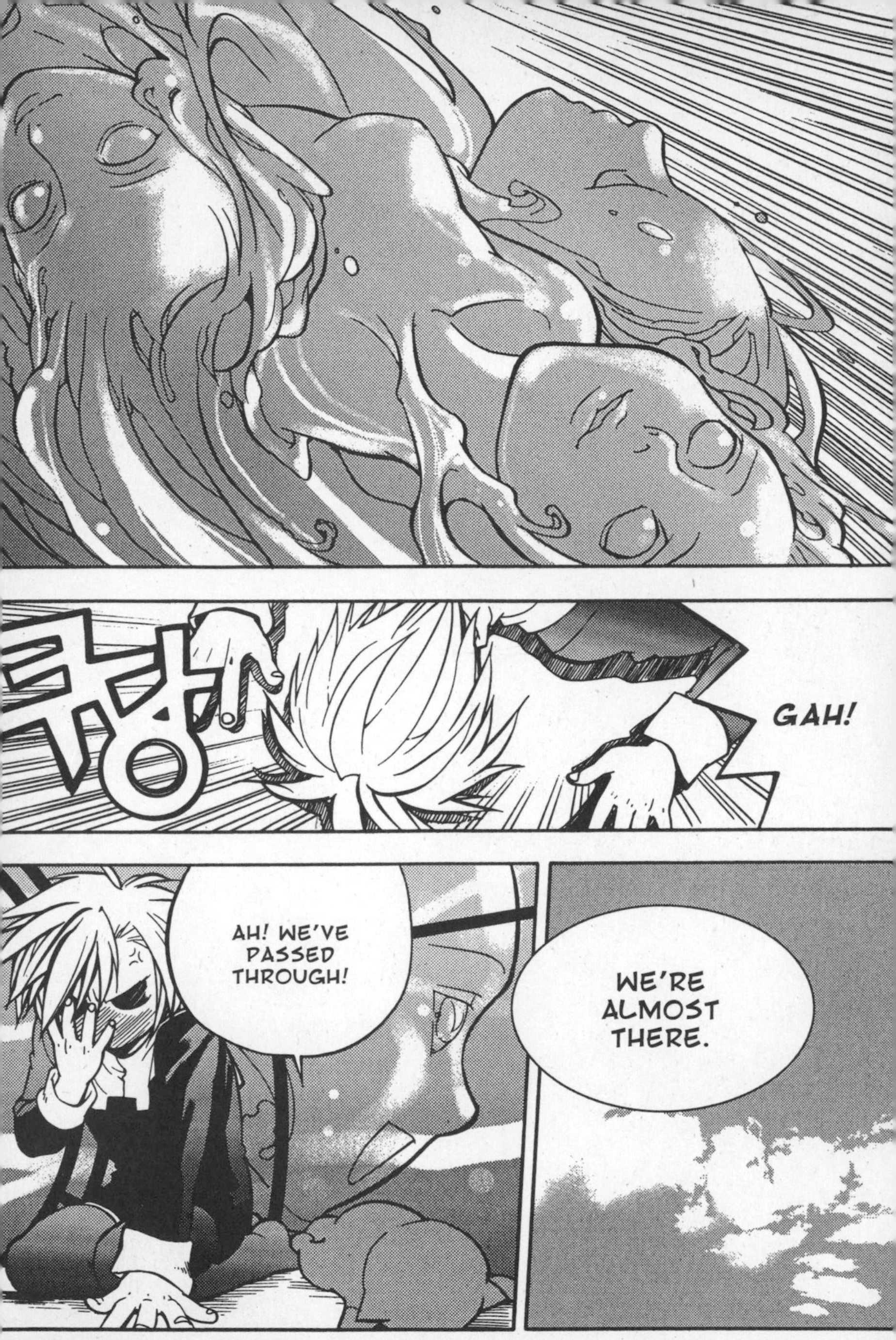
GAH!
AH! WE'VE PASSED THROUGH!
WE'RE ALMOST THERE.

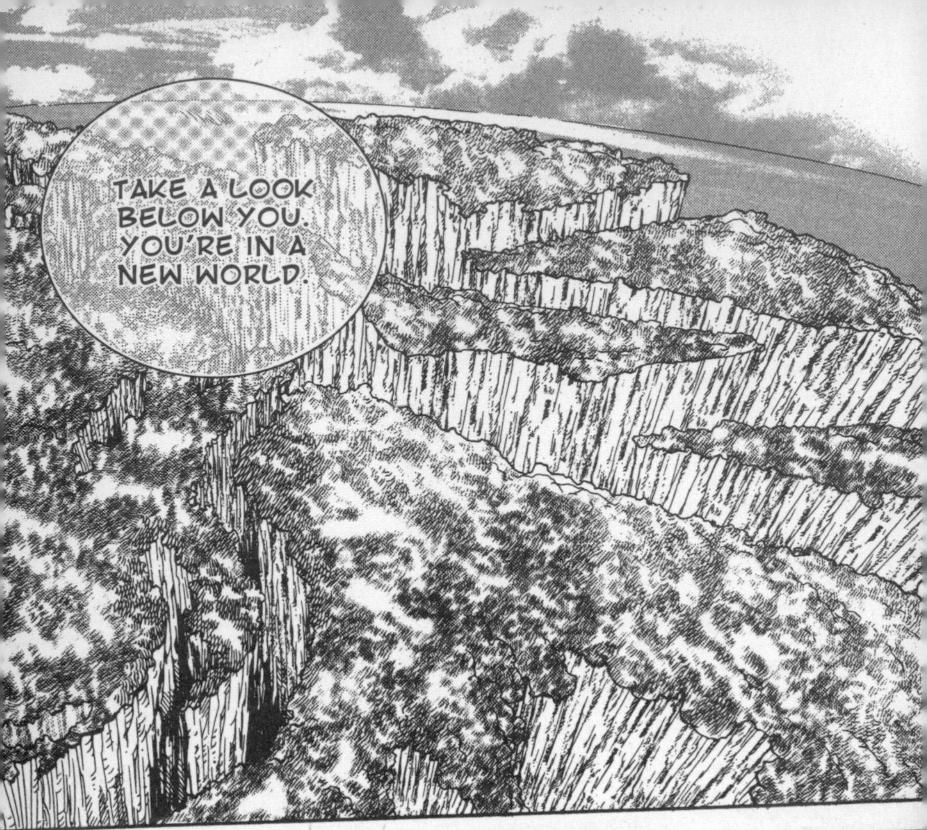
TAKE A LOOK BELOW YOU. YOU'RE IN A NEW WORLD.
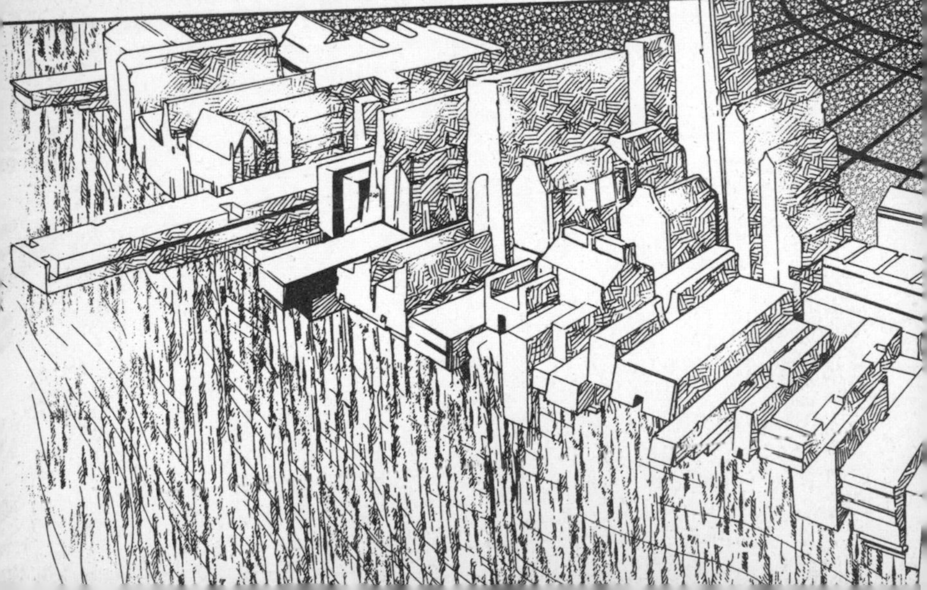

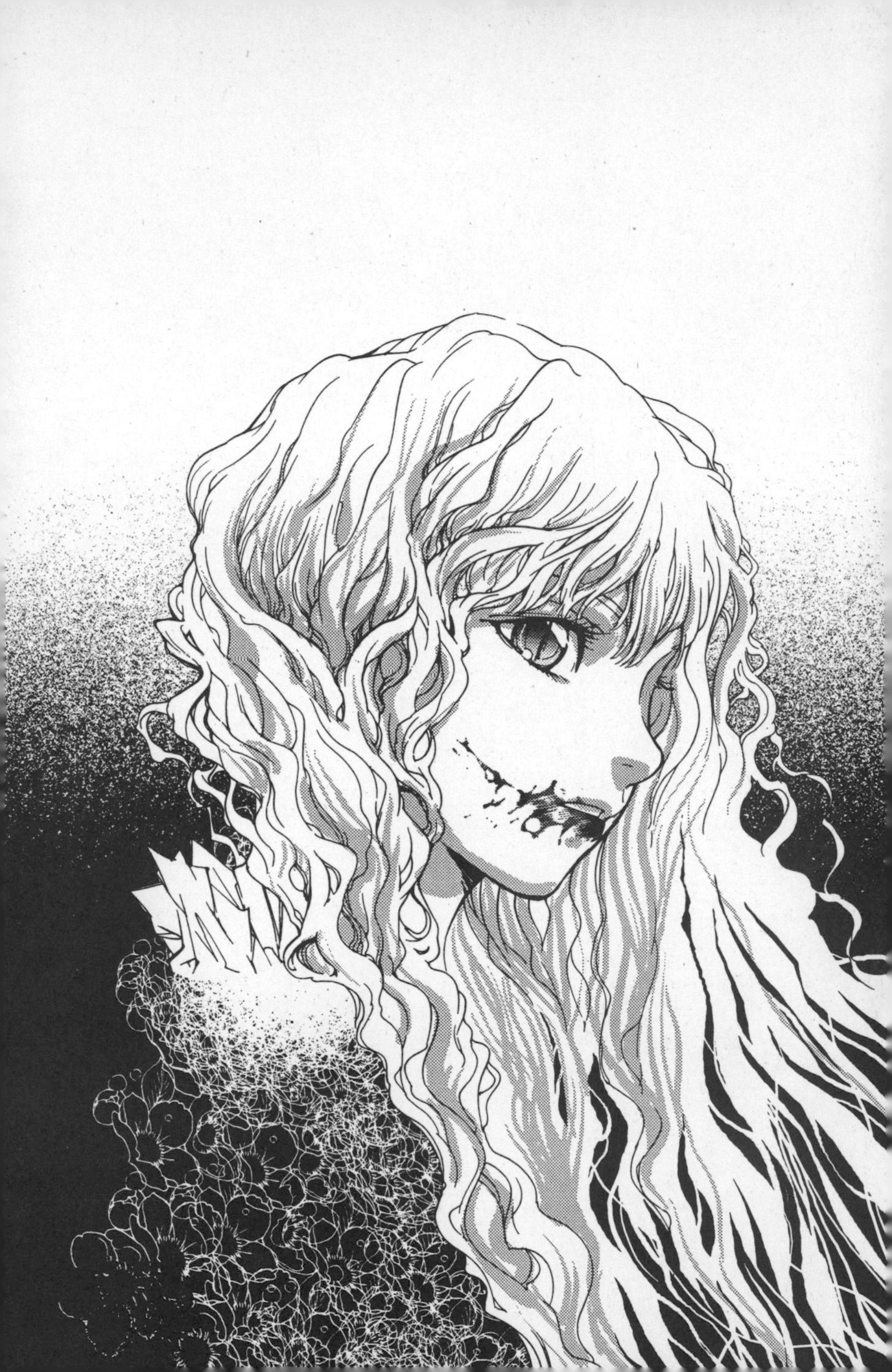

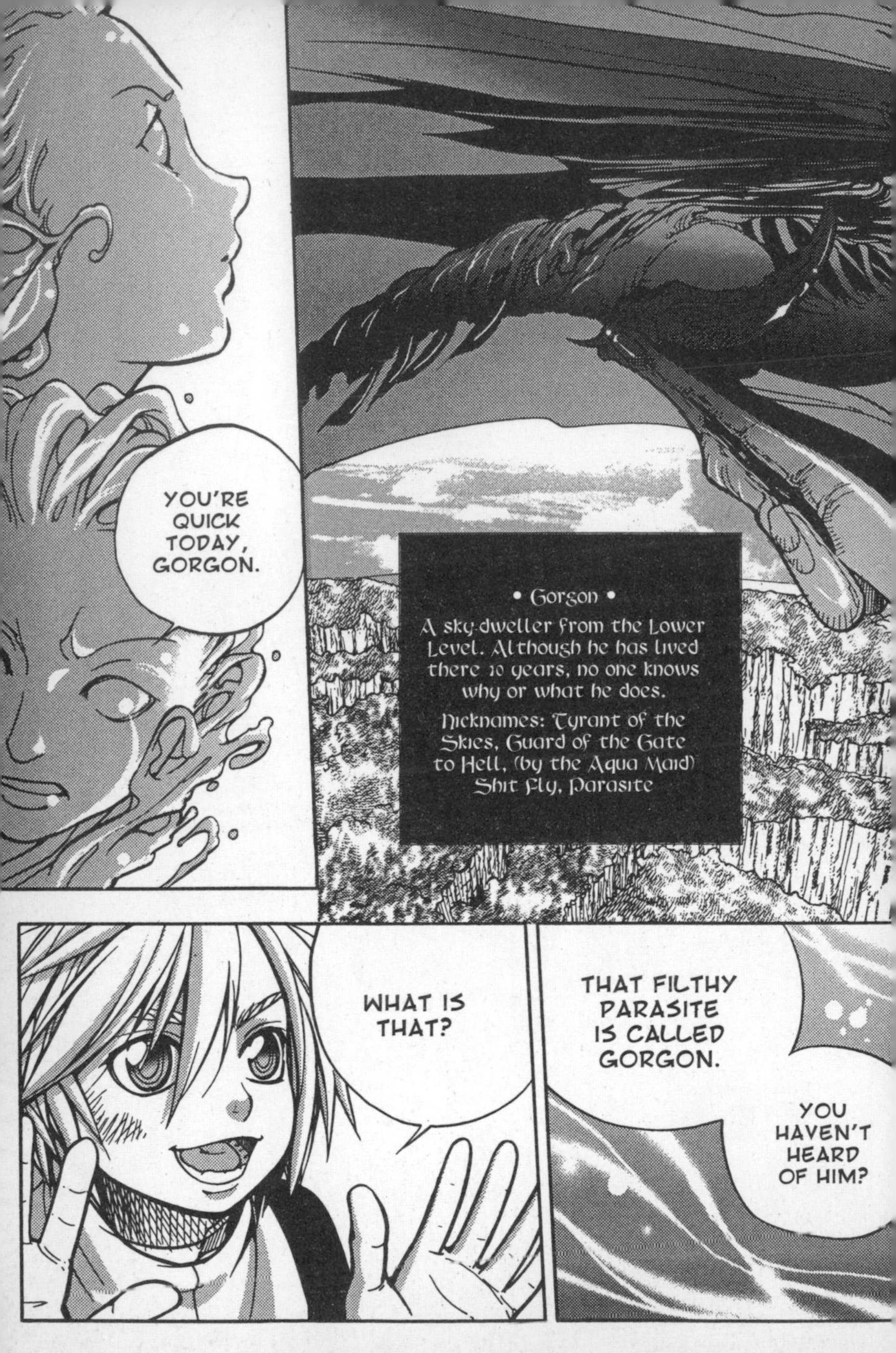
YOU'RE QUICK TODAY, GORGON.
• Gorgon •
A sky-dweller from the Lower Level. Although he has lived there 10 years, no one knows why or what he does.
Nicknames: Tyrant of the Skies, Guard of the Gate to Hell, (by the Aqua Maid) Shit Fly, Parasite
WHAT IS THAT?
THAT FILTHY PARASITE IS CALLED GORGON.
YOU HAVEN'T HEARD OF HIM?

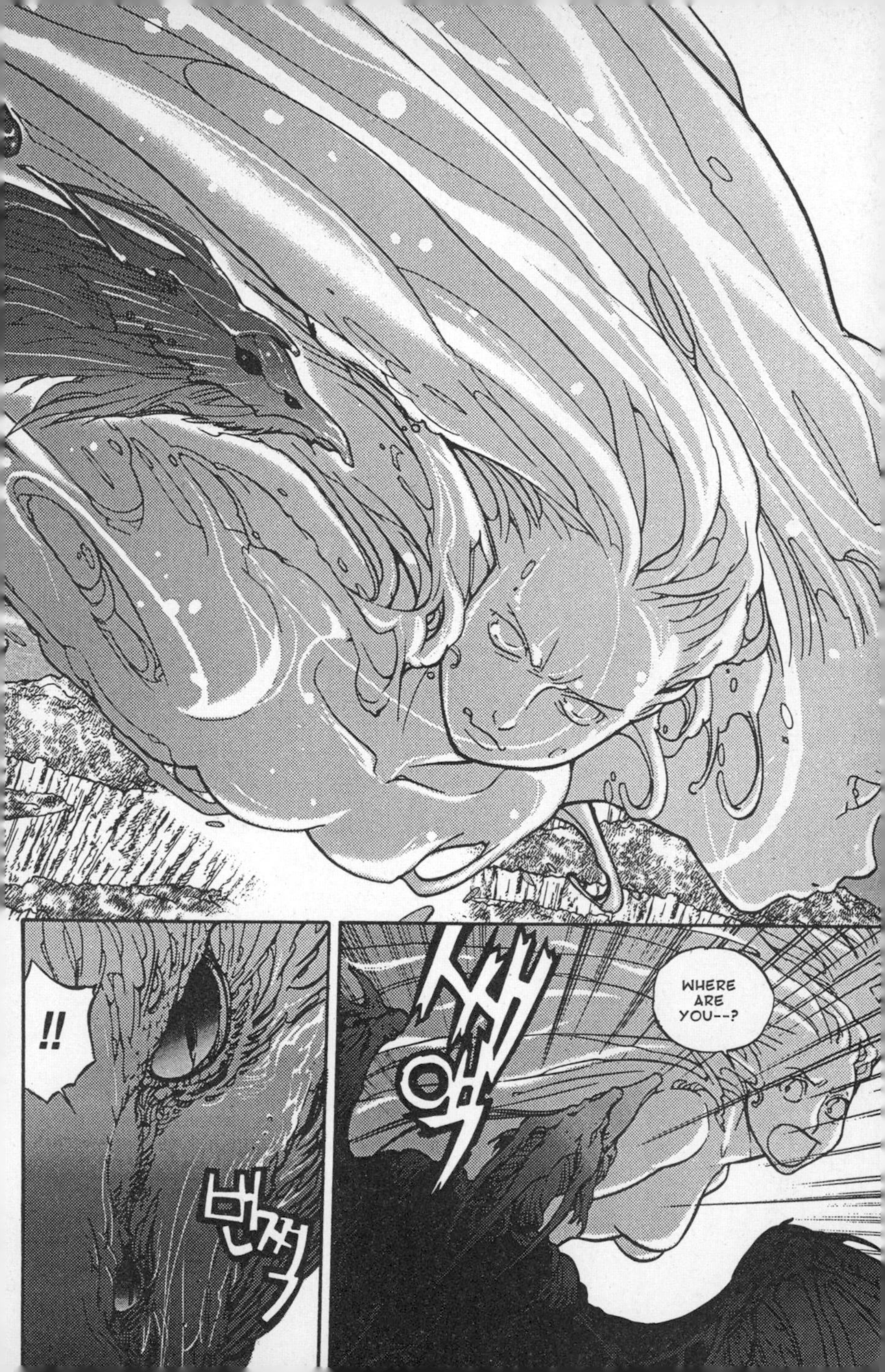
!!
WHERE ARE YOU--?

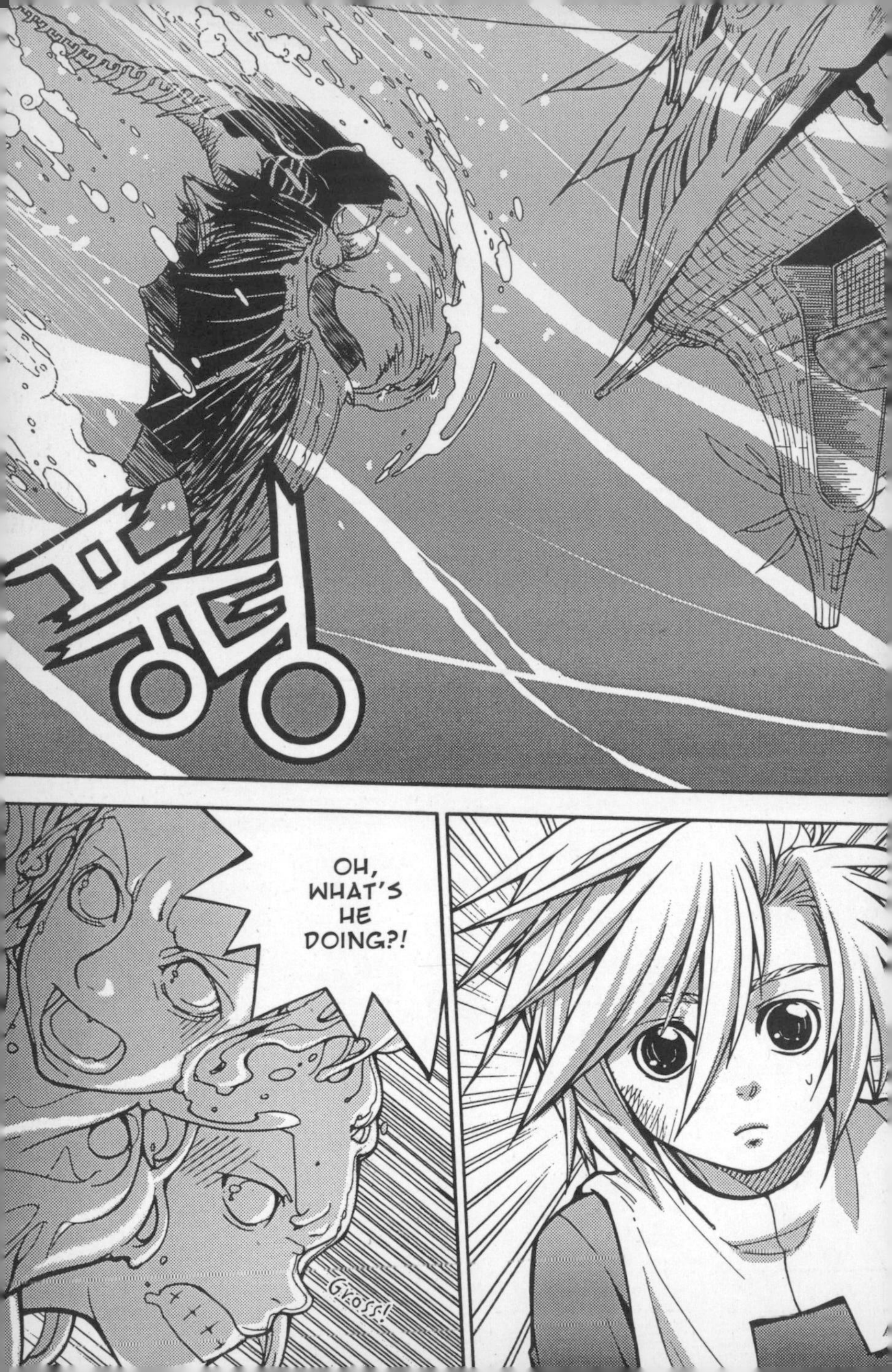
OH, WHAT'S HE DOING?!
Gross!

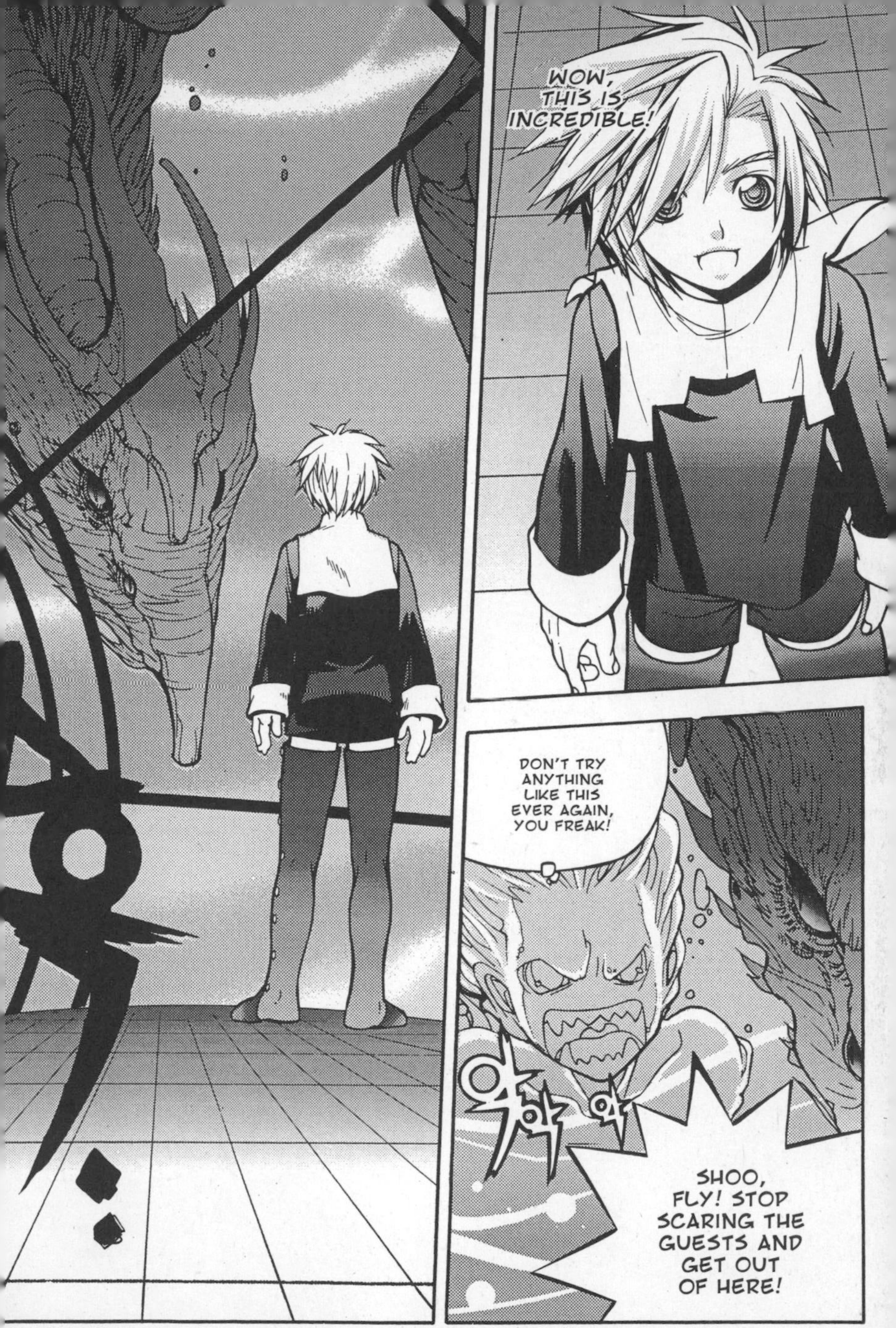
WOW, THIS IS INCREDIBLE!
DON'T TRY ANYTHING LIKE THIS EVER AGAIN, YOU FREAK!
SHOO, FLY! STOP SCARING THE GUESTS AND GET OUT OF HERE!

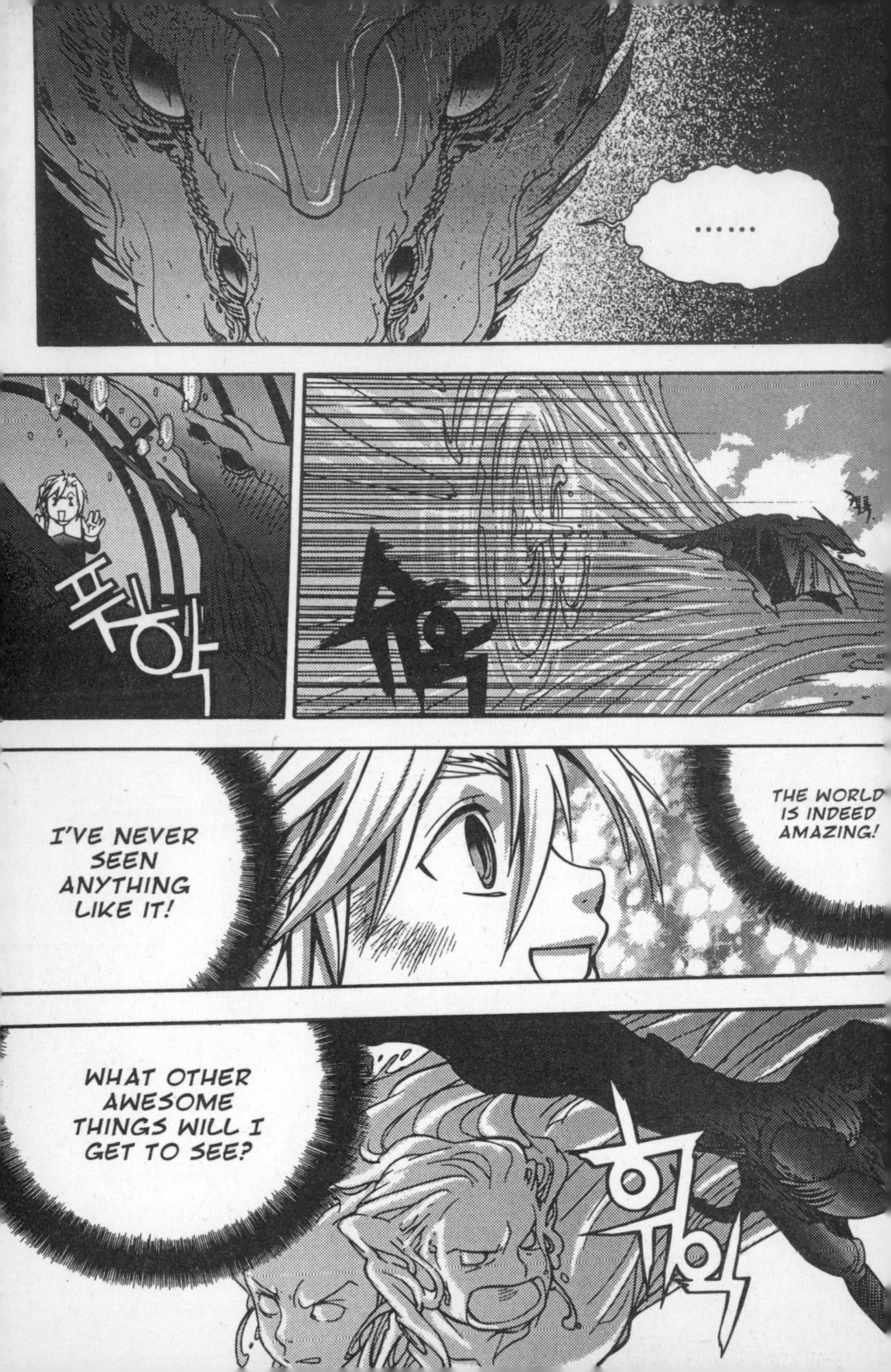
......
I'VE NEVER SEEN ANYTHING LIKE IT!
THE WORLD IS INDEED AMAZING!
WHAT OTHER AWESOME THINGS WILL I GET TO SEE?

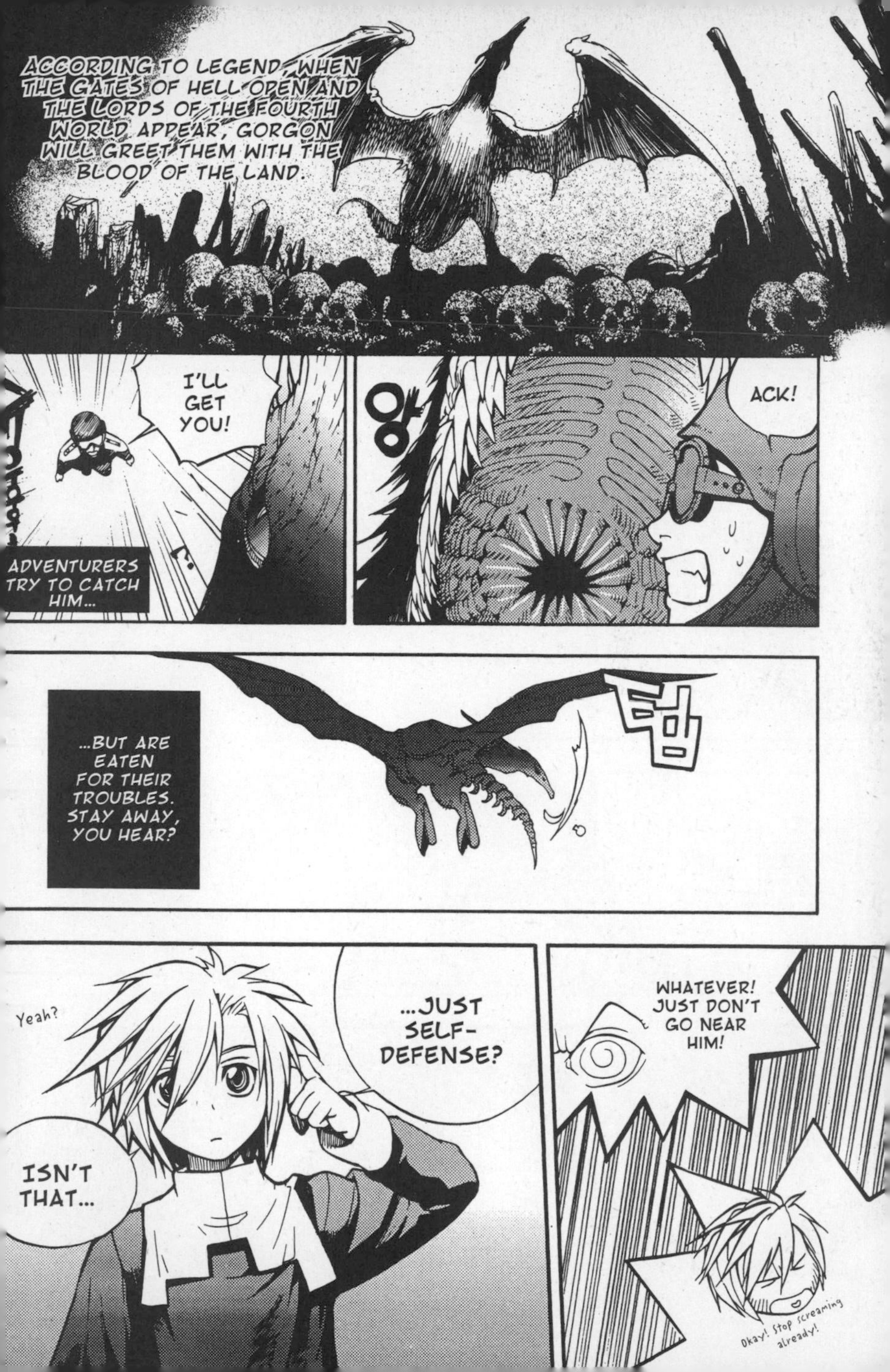
ACCORDING TO LEGEND, WHEN THE GATES OF HELL OPEN AND THE LORDS OF THE FOURTH WORLD APPEAR, GORGON WILL GREET THEM WITH THE BLOOD OF THE LAND.
I'LL GET YOU!
ADVENTURERS TRY TO CATCH HIM...
ACK!
...BUT ARE EATEN FOR THEIR TROUBLES. STAY AWAY, YOU HEAR?
Yeah?
ISN'T THAT...
...JUST SELF-DEFENSE?
WHATEVER! JUST DON'T GO NEAR HIM!
Okay! Stop screaming already!

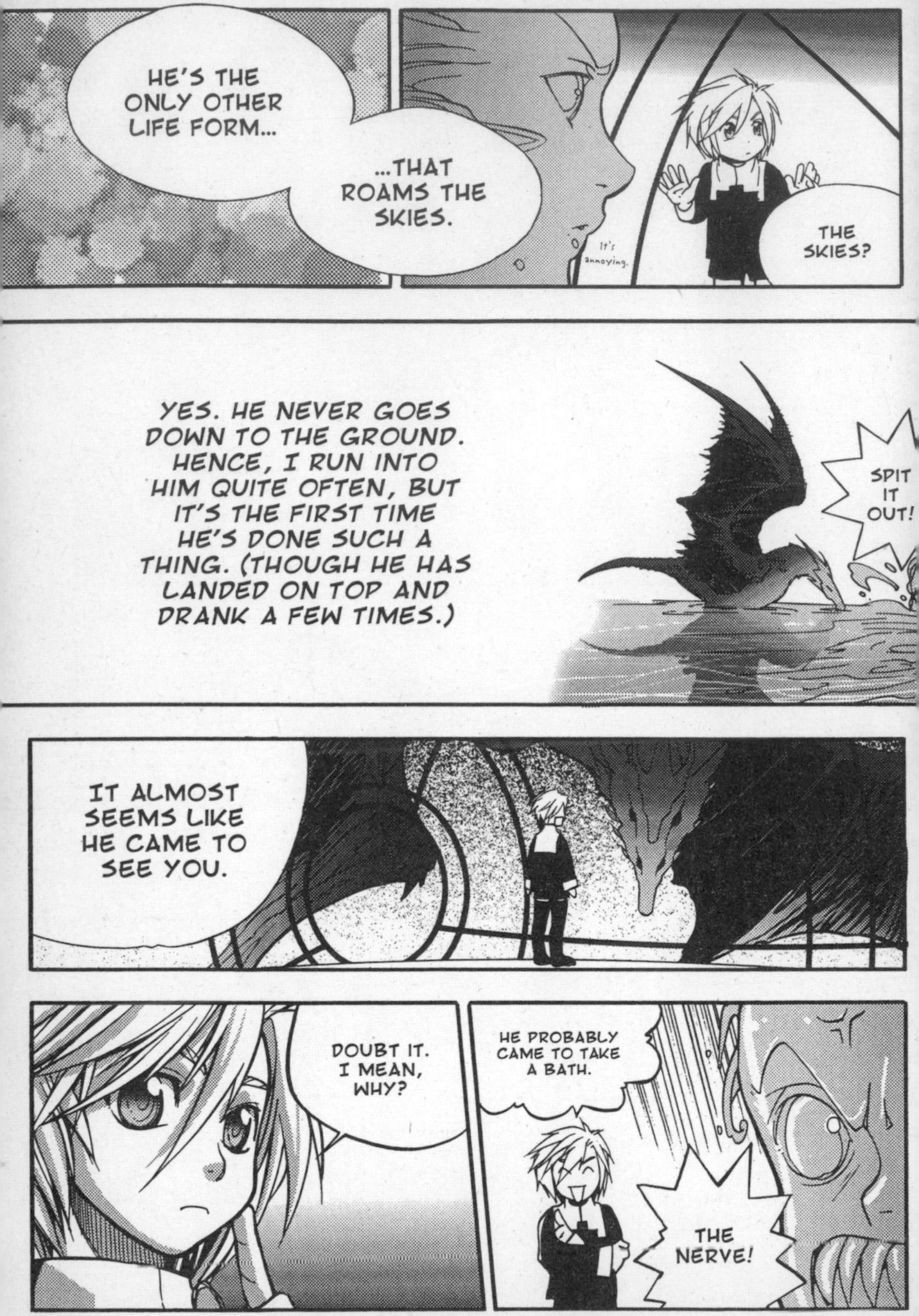
HE'S THE ONLY OTHER LIFE FORM...
...THAT ROAMS THE SKIES.
It's annoying.
THE SKIES?
YES. HE NEVER GOES DOWN TO THE GROUND. HENCE, I RUN INTO HIM QUITE OFTEN, BUT IT'S THE FIRST TIME HE'S DONE SUCH A THING. (THOUGH HE HAS LANDED ON TOP AND DRANK A FEW TIMES.)
SPIT IT OUT!
IT ALMOST SEEMS LIKE HE CAME TO SEE YOU.
DOUBT IT. I MEAN, WHY?
HE PROBABLY CAME TO TAKE A BATH.
THE NERVE!

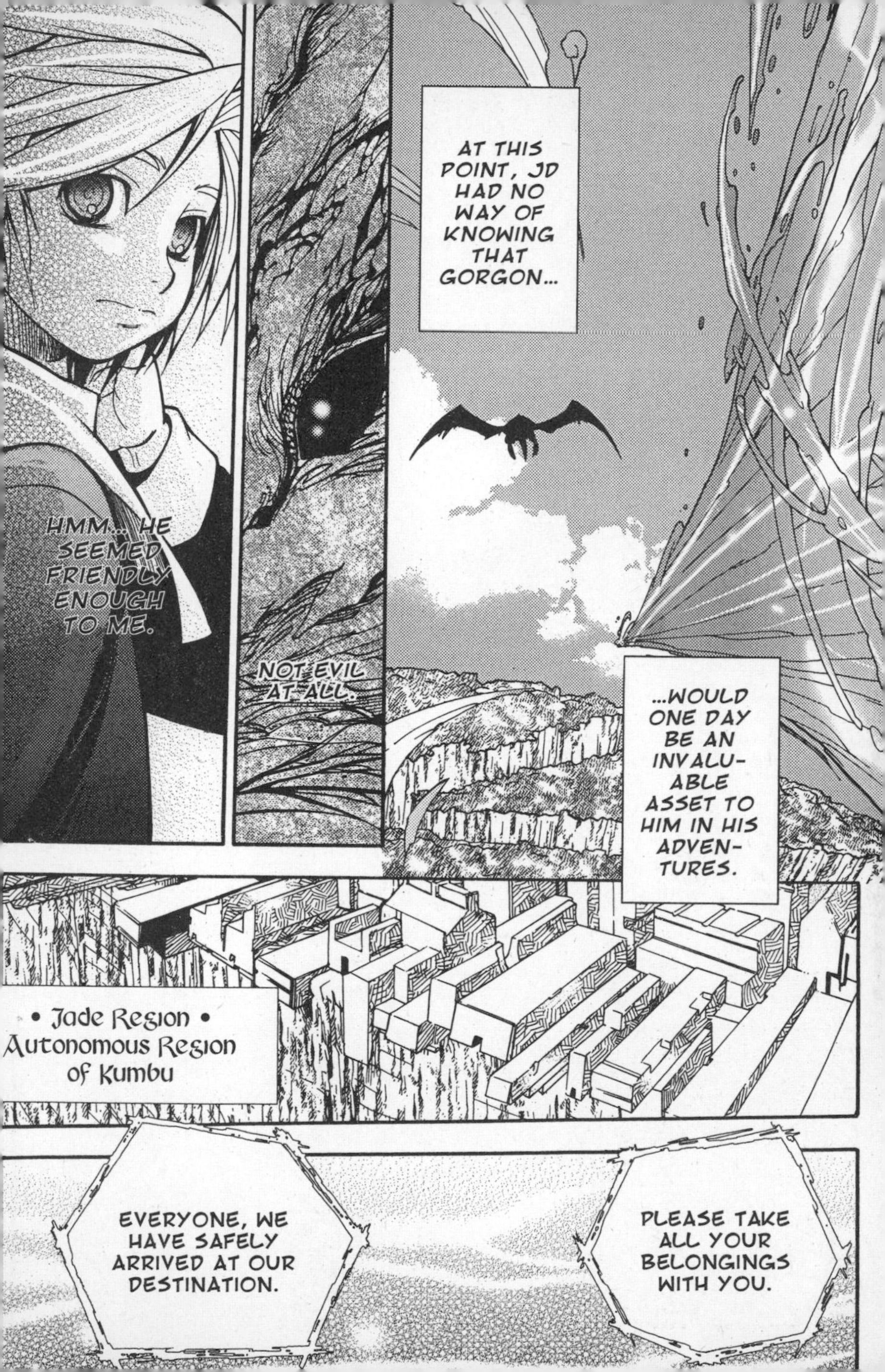
HMM... HE SEEMED FRIENDLY ENOUGH TO ME.
NOT EVIL AT ALL.
AT THIS POINT, JD HAD NO WAY OF KNOWING THAT GORGON...
...WOULD ONE DAY BE AN INVALU-ABLE ASSET TO HIM IN HIS ADVEN-TURES.
• Jade Region • Autonomous Region of Kumbu
EVERYONE, WE HAVE SAFELY ARRIVED AT OUR DESTINATION.
PLEASE TAKE ALL YOUR BELONGINGS WITH YOU.

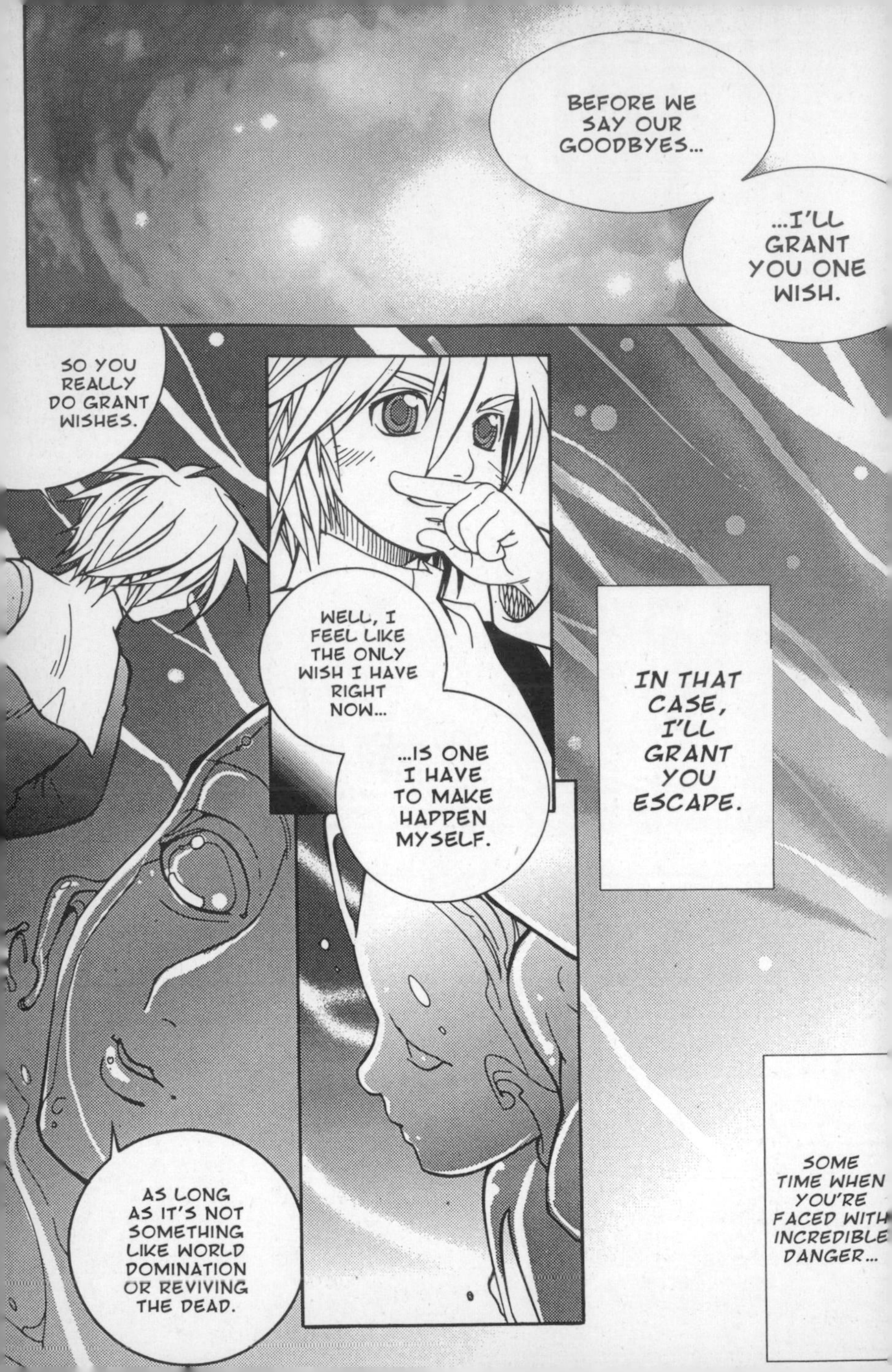

BEFORE WE SAY OUR GOODBYES...
...I'LL GRANT YOU ONE WISH.
SO YOU REALLY DO GRANT WISHES.
WELL, I FEEL LIKE THE ONLY WISH I HAVE RIGHT NOW...
...IS ONE I HAVE TO MAKE HAPPEN MYSELF.
IN THAT CASE, I'LL GRANT YOU ESCAPE.
AS LONG AS IT'S NOT SOMETHING LIKE WORLD DOMINATION OR REVIVING THE DEAD.
SOME TIME WHEN YOU'RE FACED WITH INCREDIBLE DANGER...

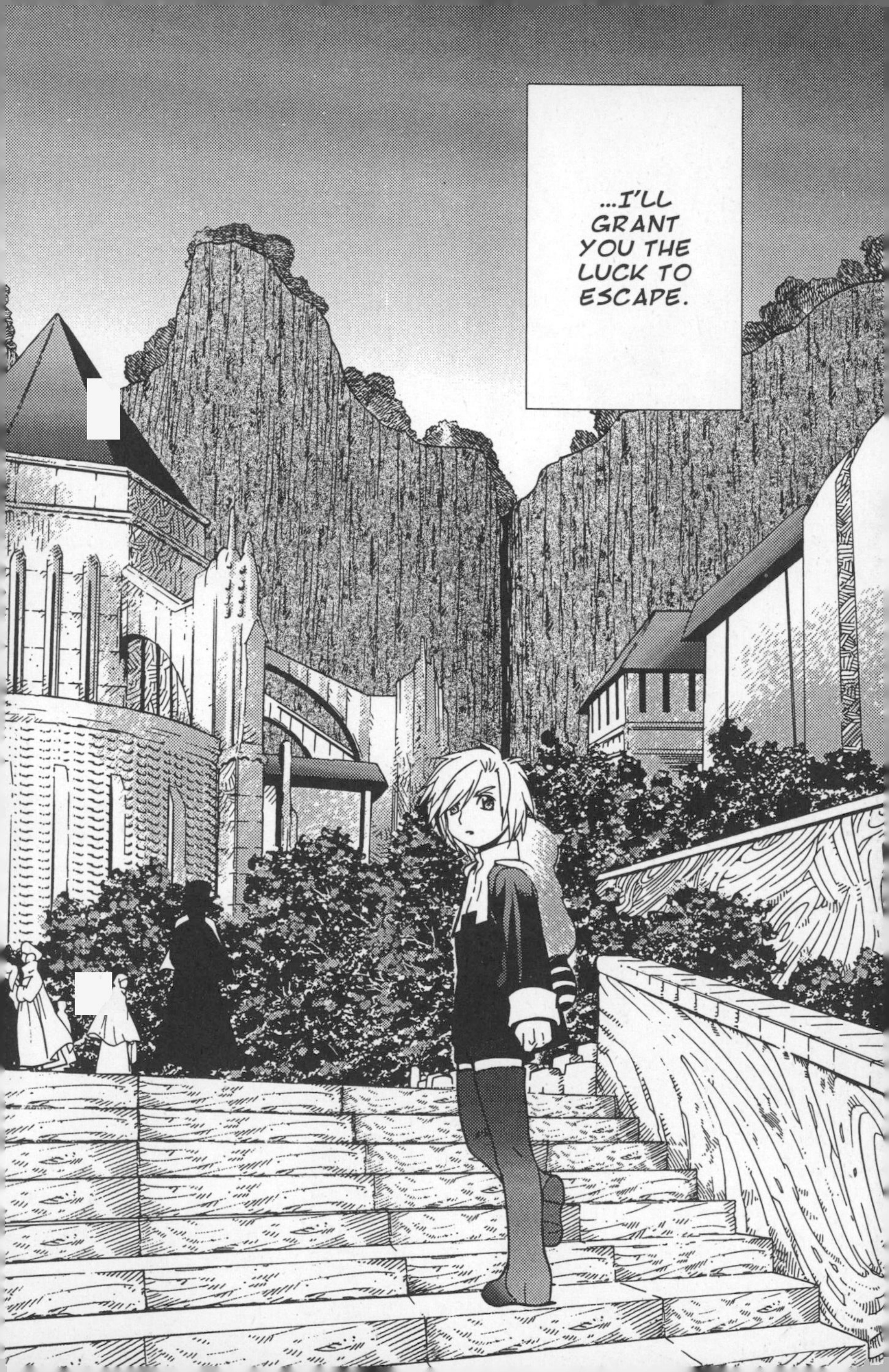
...I'LL GRANT YOU THE LUCK TO ESCAPE.

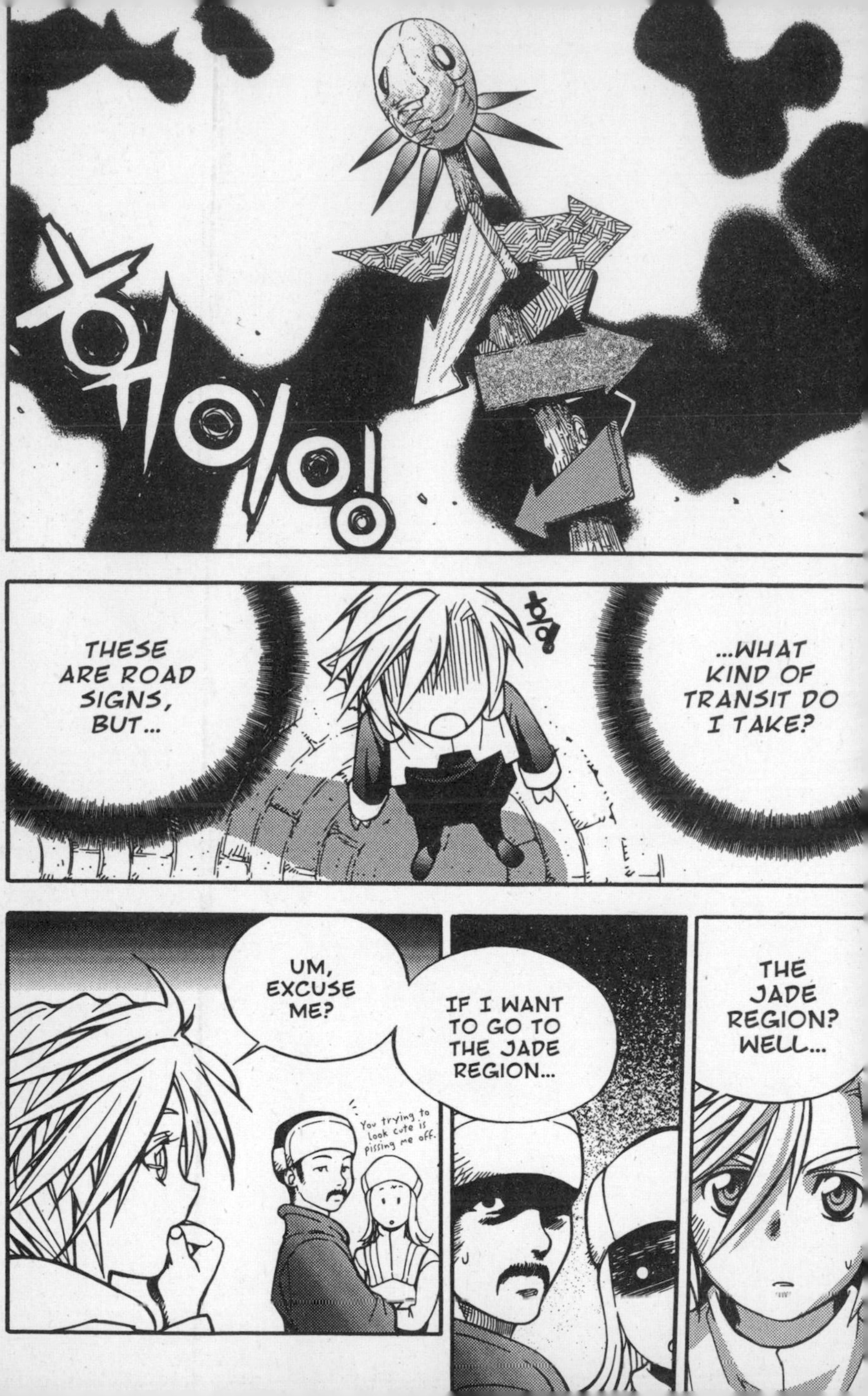
THESE ARE ROAD SIGNS, BUT...
...WHAT KIND OF TRANSIT DO I TAKE?
UM, EXCUSE ME?
You trying to look cute is pissing me off.
IF I WANT TO GO TO THE JADE REGION...
THE JADE REGION? WELL...

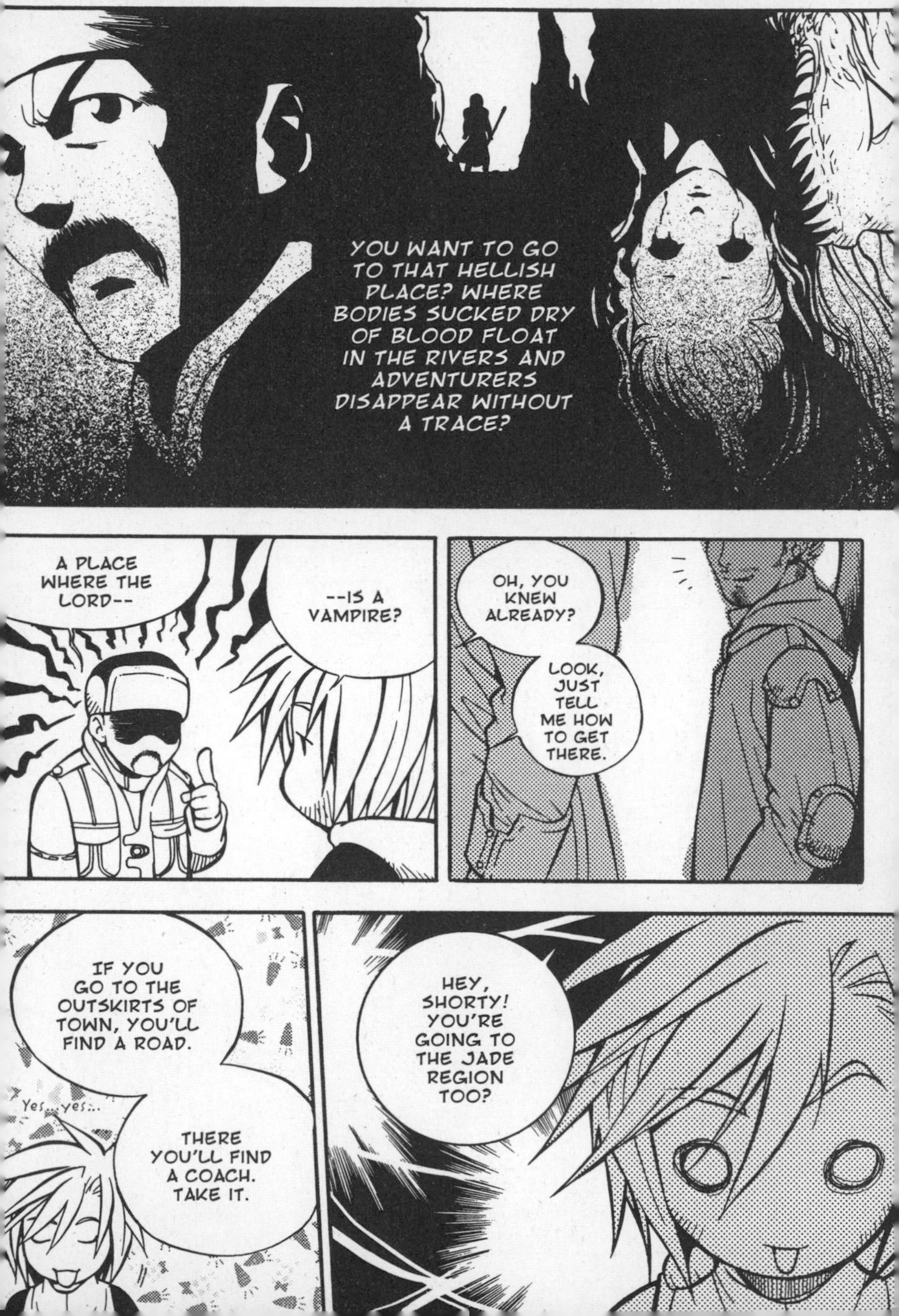
YOU WANT TO GO TO THAT HELLISH PLACE? WHERE BODIES SUCKED DRY OF BLOOD FLOAT IN THE RIVERS AND ADVENTURERS DISAPPEAR WITHOUT A TRACE?
A PLACE WHERE THE LORD--
--IS A VAMPIRE?
OH, YOU KNEW ALREADY?
LOOK, JUST TELL ME HOW TO GET THERE.
IF YOU GO TO THE OUTSKIRTS OF TOWN, YOU'LL FIND A ROAD.
Yes... yes...
THERE YOU'LL FIND A COACH. TAKE IT.
HEY, SHORTY! YOU'RE GOING TO THE JADE REGION TOO?

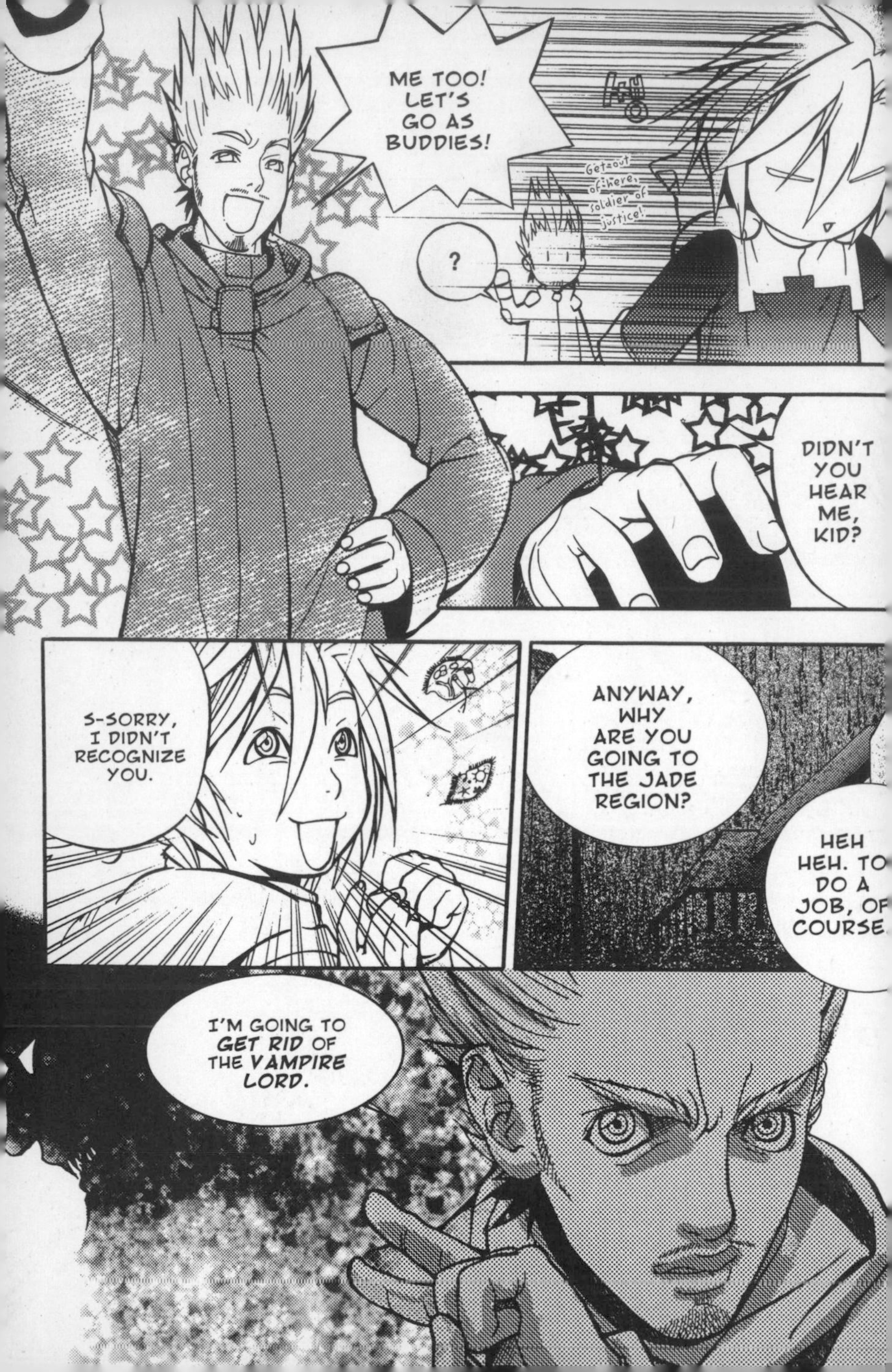
ME TOO! LET'S GO AS BUDDIES!
?
Get out of here, soldier of justice!
DIDN'T YOU HEAR ME, KID?
S-SORRY, I DIDN'T RECOGNIZE YOU.
ANYWAY, WHY ARE YOU GOING TO THE JADE REGION?
HEH HEH. TO DO A JOB, OF COURSE.
I'M GOING TO *GET RID* OF THE *VAMPIRE LORD*.

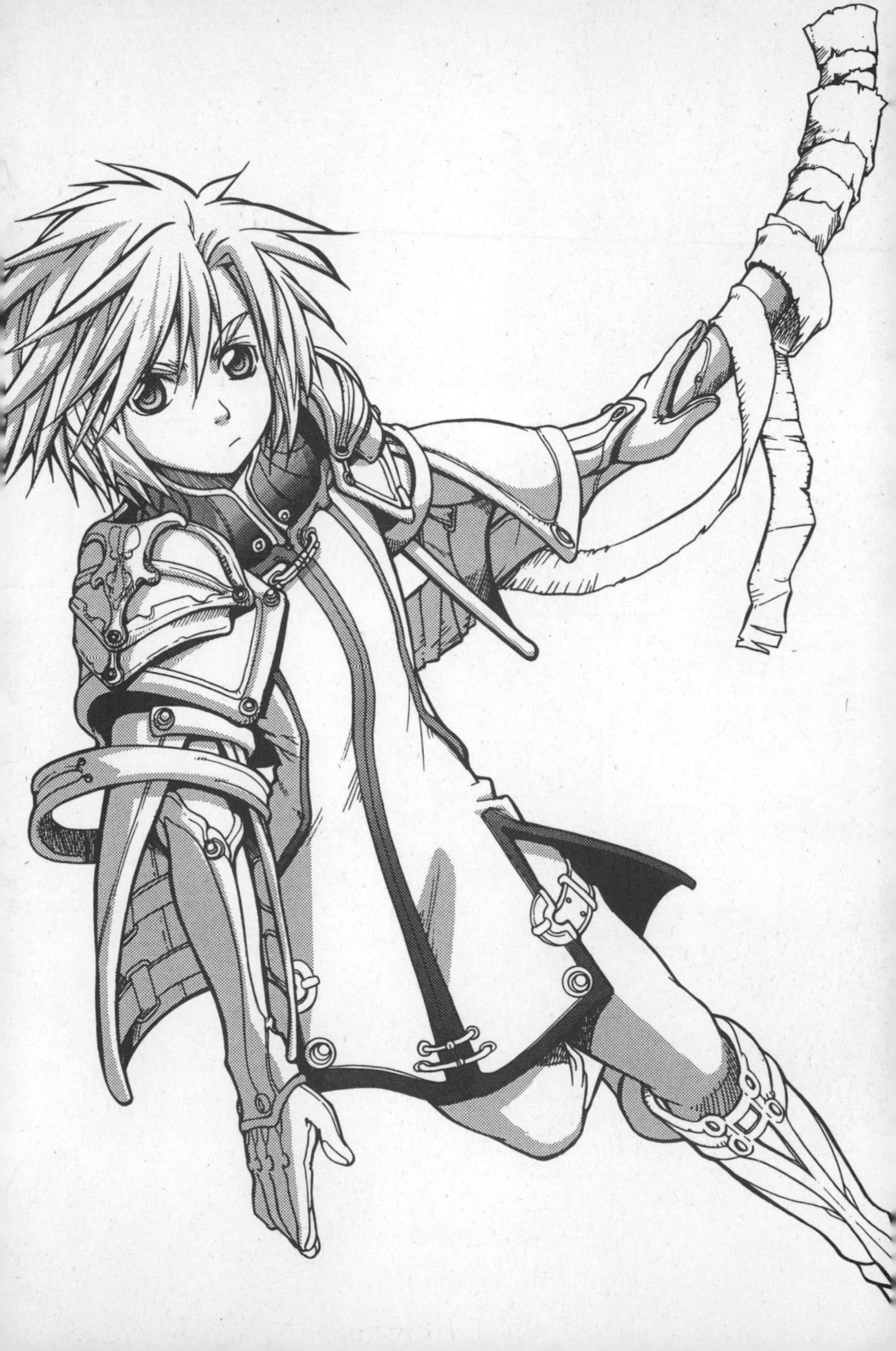

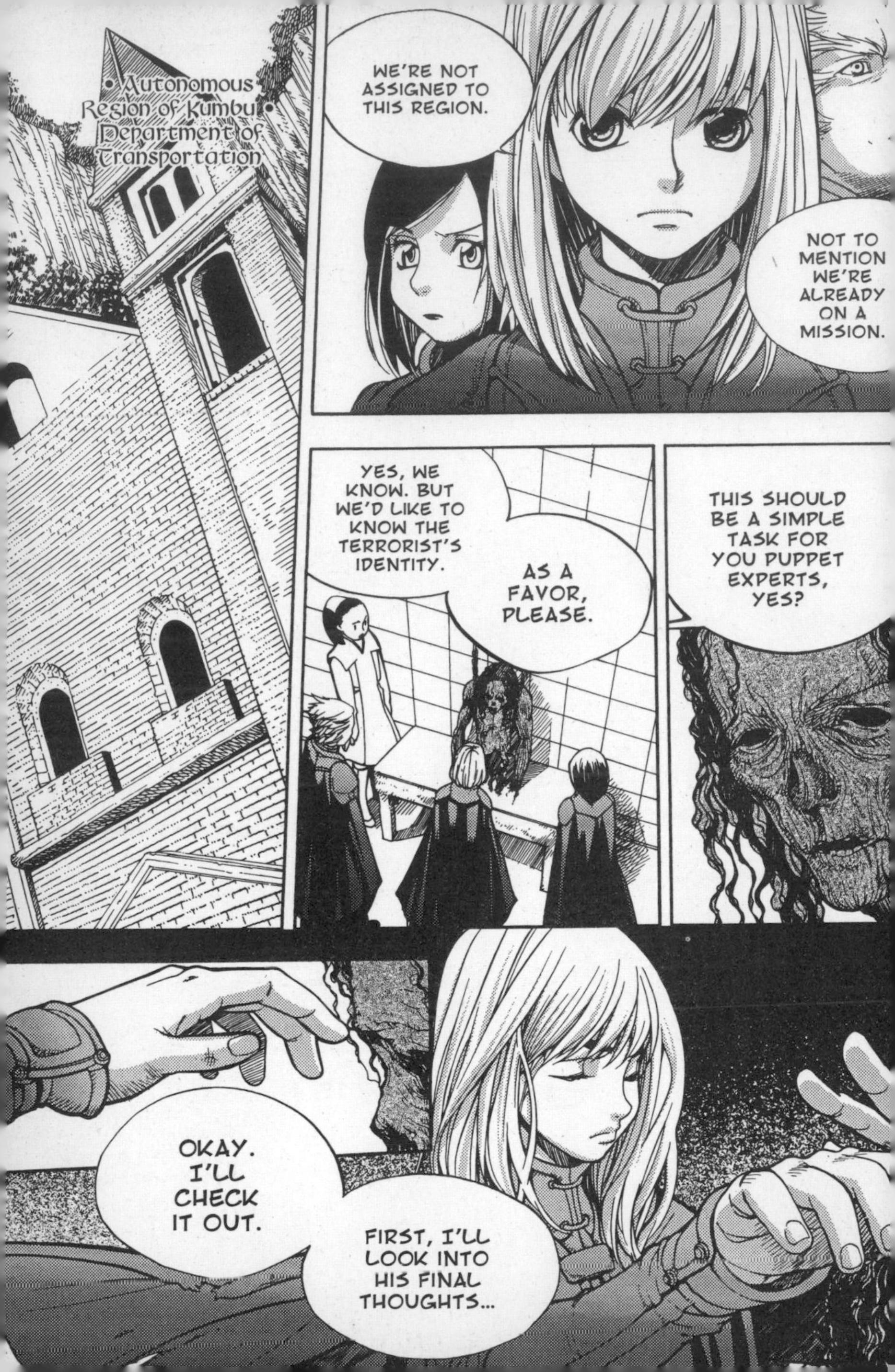
• Autonomous Region of Kumbu • Department of Transportation
WE'RE NOT ASSIGNED TO THIS REGION.
NOT TO MENTION WE'RE ALREADY ON A MISSION.
YES, WE KNOW. BUT WE'D LIKE TO KNOW THE TERRORIST'S IDENTITY.
AS A FAVOR, PLEASE.
THIS SHOULD BE A SIMPLE TASK FOR YOU PUPPET EXPERTS, YES?
OKAY. I'LL CHECK IT OUT.
FIRST, I'LL LOOK INTO HIS FINAL THOUGHTS...

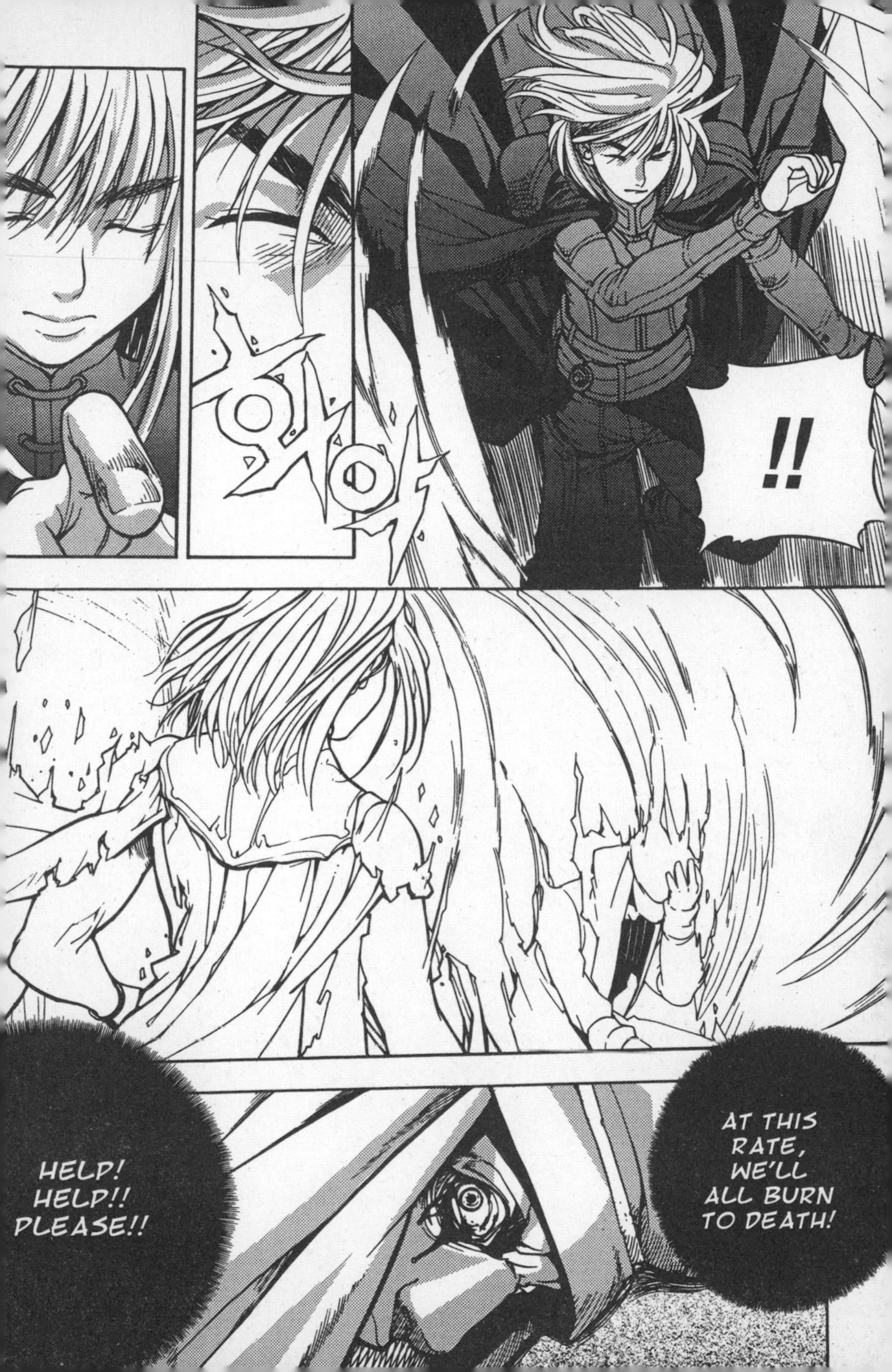
!!
HELP!
HELP!!
PLEASE!!
AT THIS
RATE,
WE'LL
ALL BURN
TO DEATH!

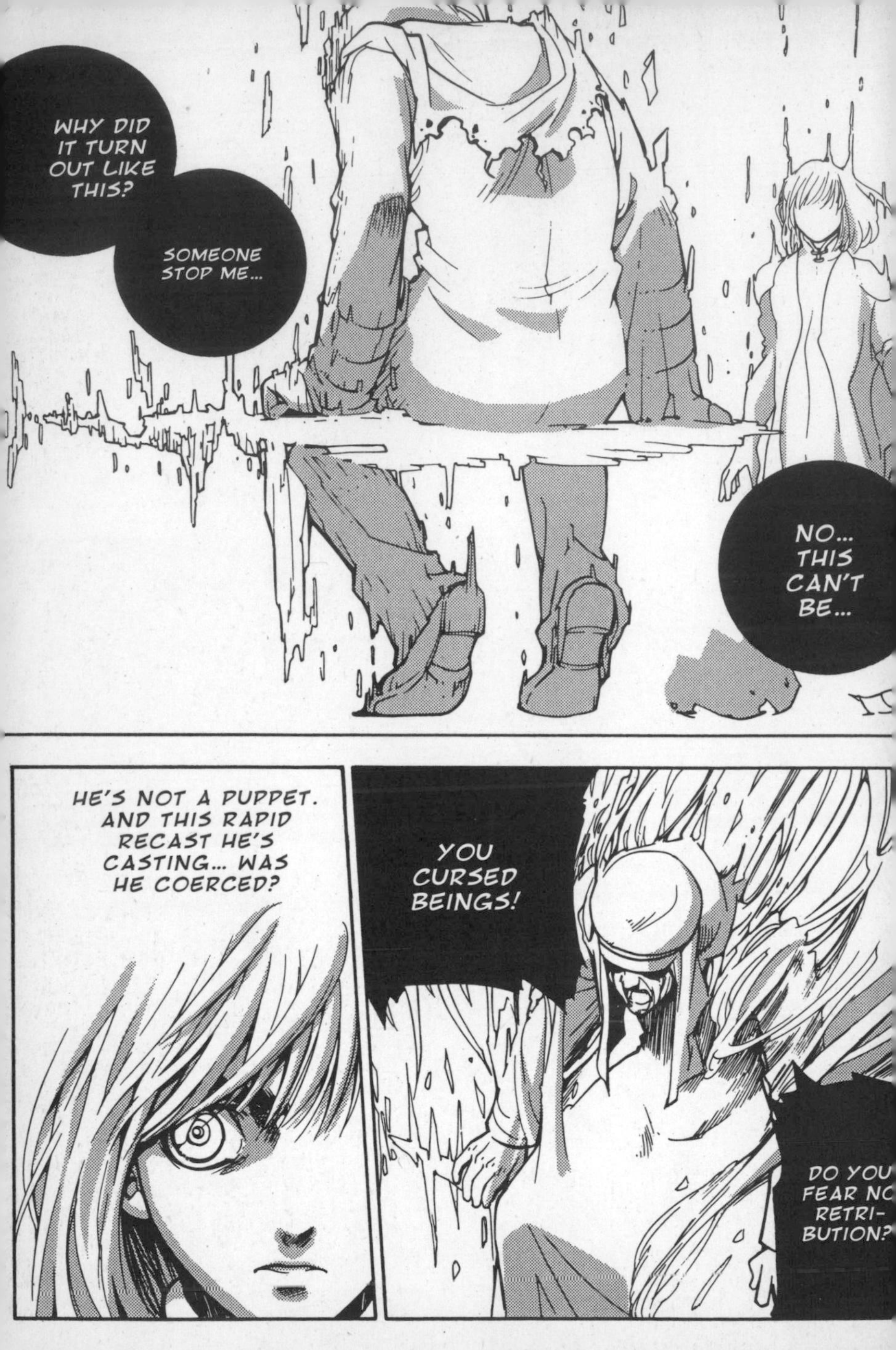
WHY DID IT TURN OUT LIKE THIS?
SOMEONE STOP ME...
NO... THIS CAN'T BE...
HE'S NOT A PUPPET. AND THIS RAPID RECAST HE'S CASTING... WAS HE COERCED?
YOU CURSED BEINGS!
DO YOU FEAR NO RETRI-BUTION?

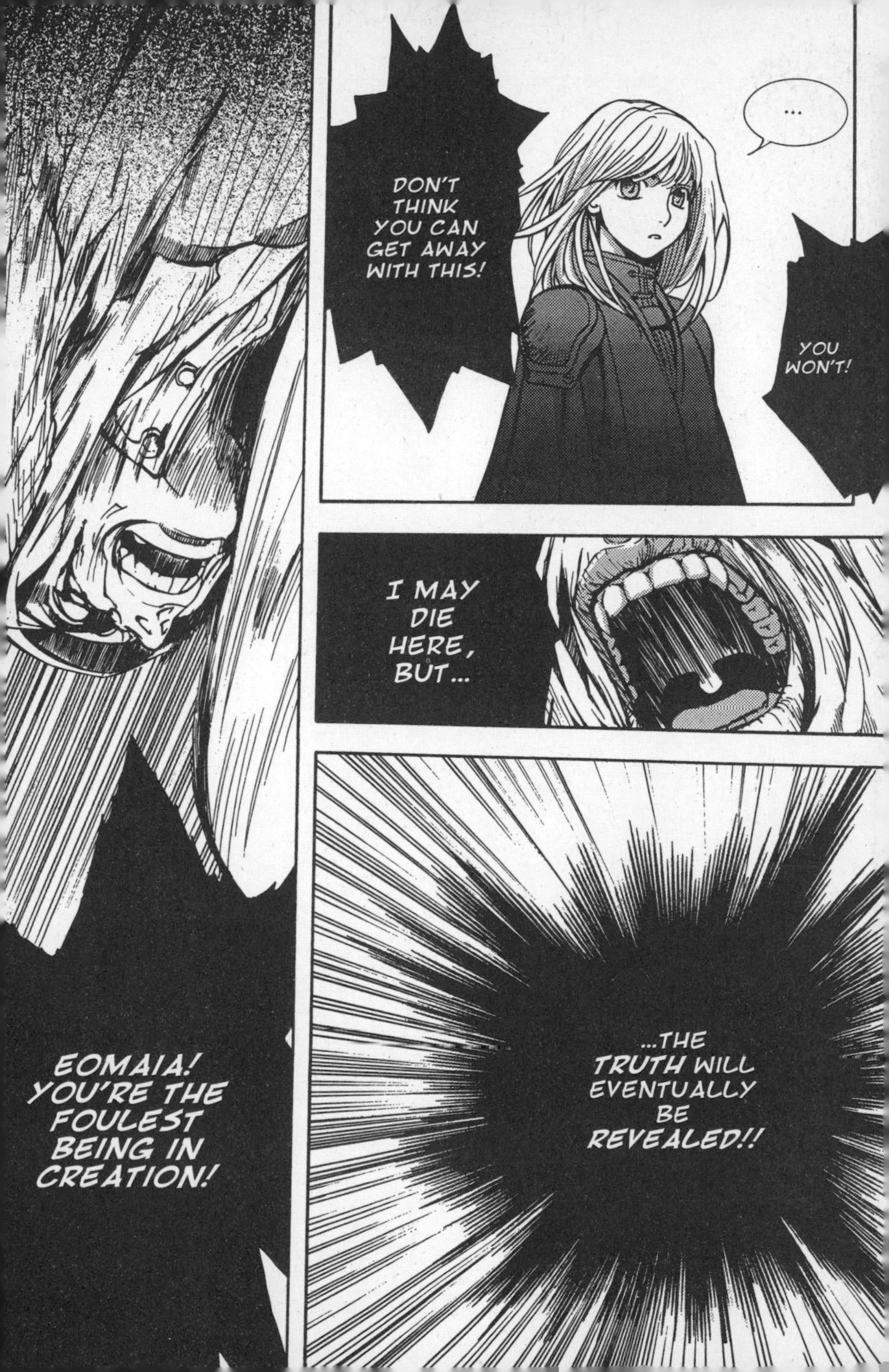
EOMAIA! YOU'RE THE FOULEST BEING IN CREATION!
...
DON'T THINK YOU CAN GET AWAY WITH THIS!
YOU WON'T!
I MAY DIE HERE, BUT...
...THE TRUTH WILL EVENTUALLY BE REVEALED!!

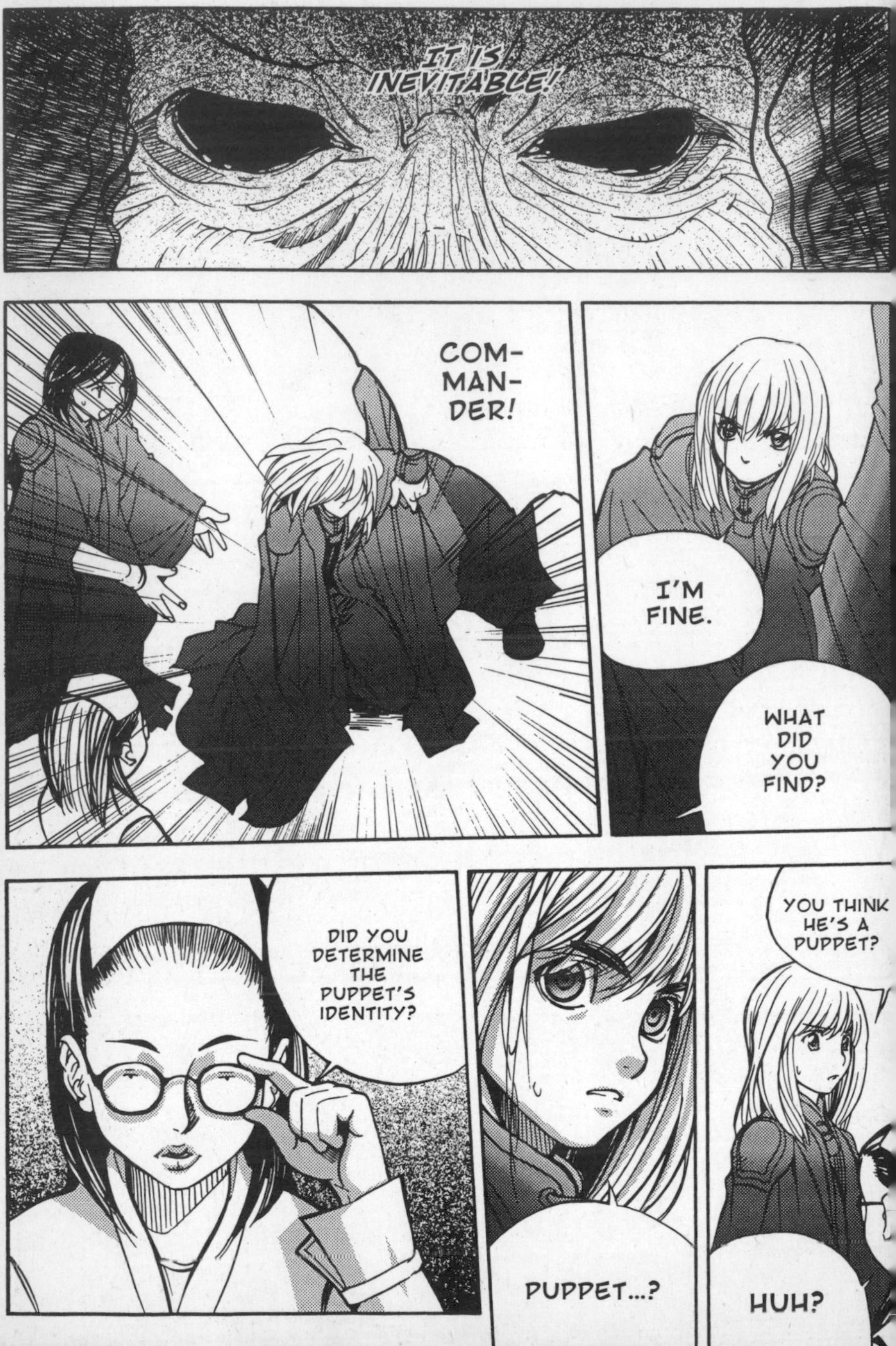
IT IS INEVITABLE!
COM-MAN-DER!
I'M FINE.
WHAT DID YOU FIND?
DID YOU DETERMINE THE PUPPET'S IDENTITY?
PUPPET...?
YOU THINK HE'S A PUPPET?
HUH?

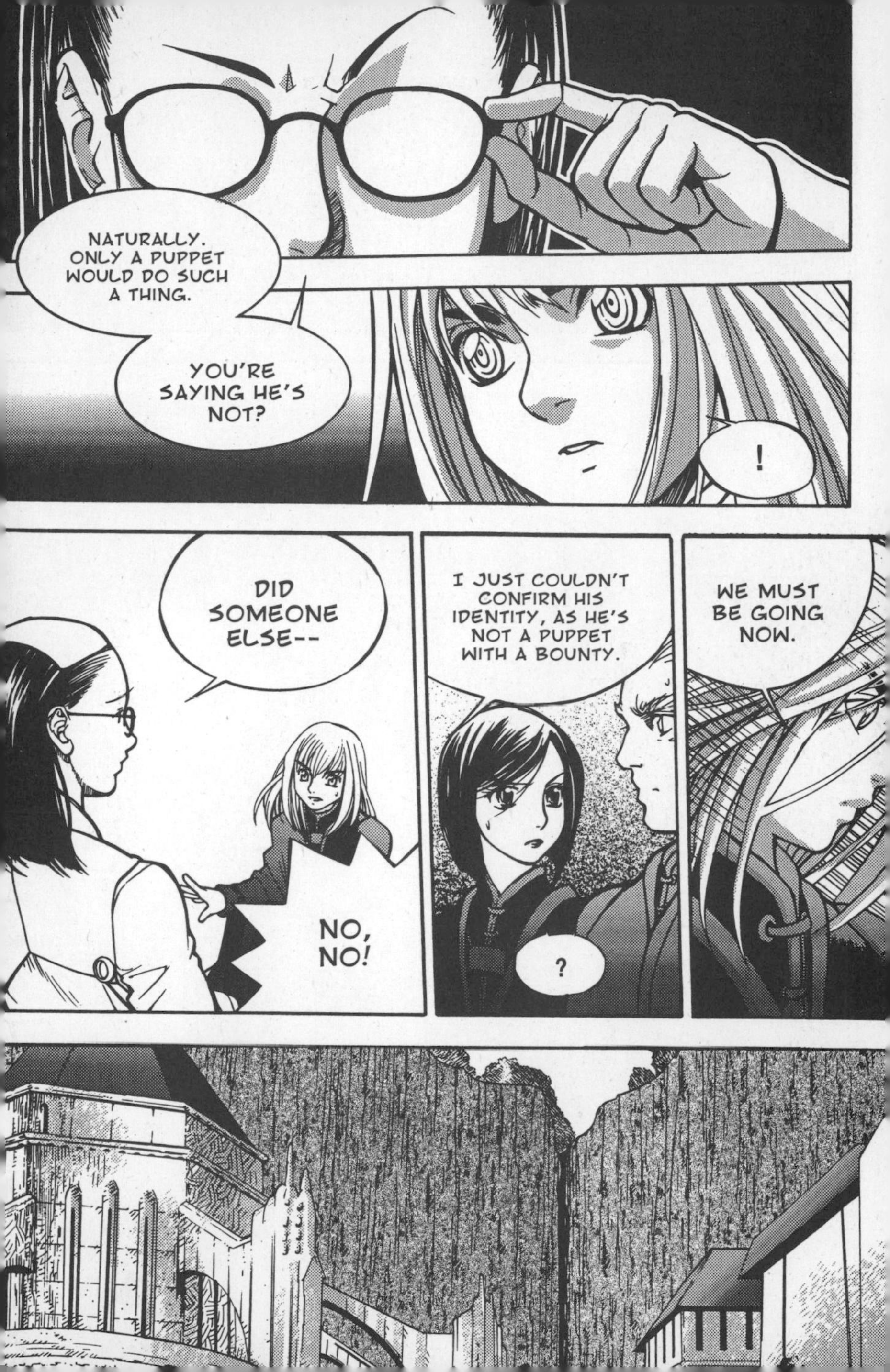
NATURALLY. ONLY A PUPPET WOULD DO SUCH A THING.
YOU'RE SAYING HE'S NOT?
!
DID SOMEONE ELSE--
NO, NO!
I JUST COULDN'T CONFIRM HIS IDENTITY, AS HE'S NOT A PUPPET WITH A BOUNTY.
?
WE MUST BE GOING NOW.

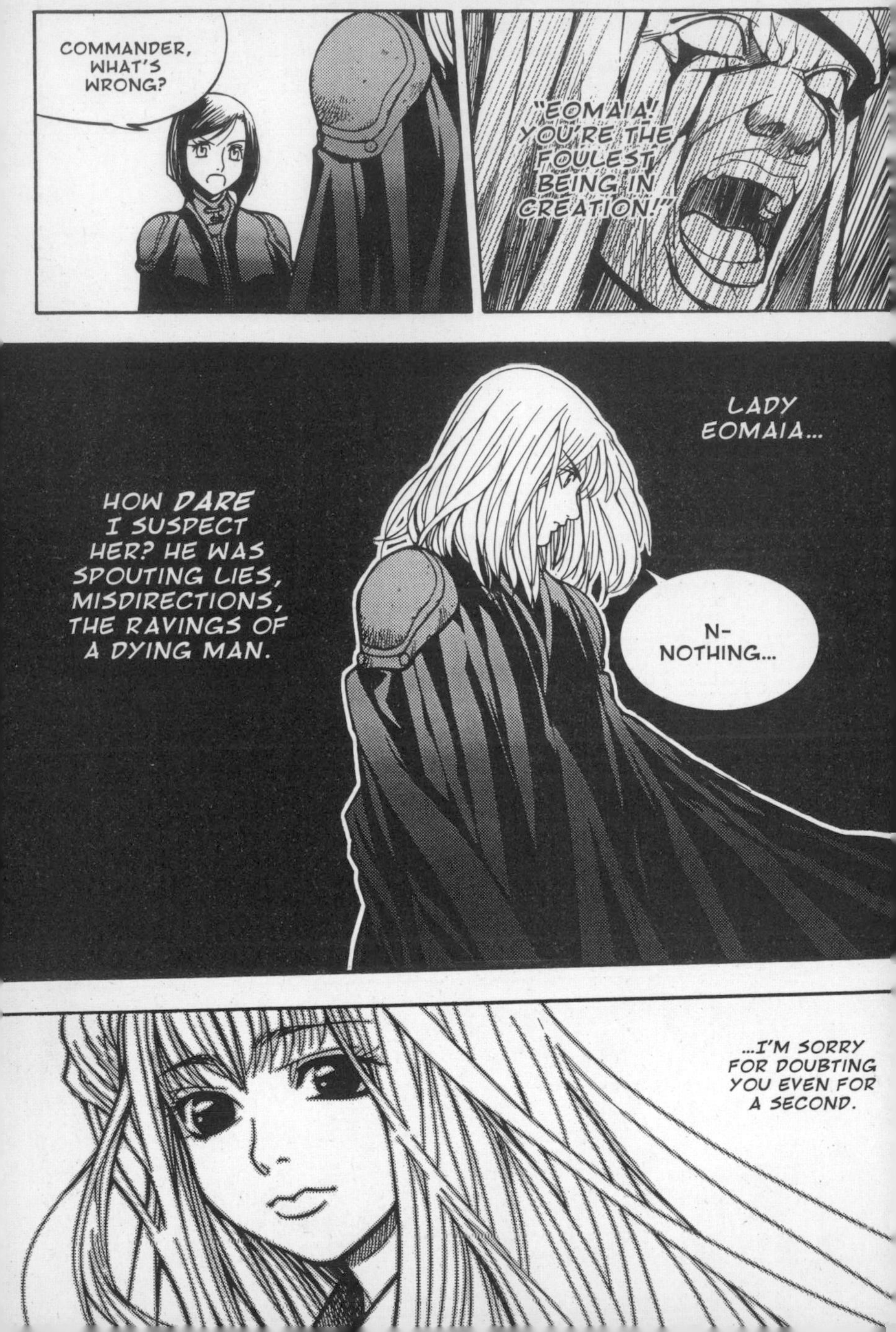
COMMANDER, WHAT'S WRONG?
"EOMAIA! YOU'RE THE FOULEST BEING IN CREATION!"
HOW DARE I SUSPECT HER? HE WAS SPOUTING LIES, MISDIRECTIONS, THE RAVINGS OF A DYING MAN.
LADY EOMAIA...
N- NOTHING...
...I'M SORRY FOR DOUBTING YOU EVEN FOR A SECOND.

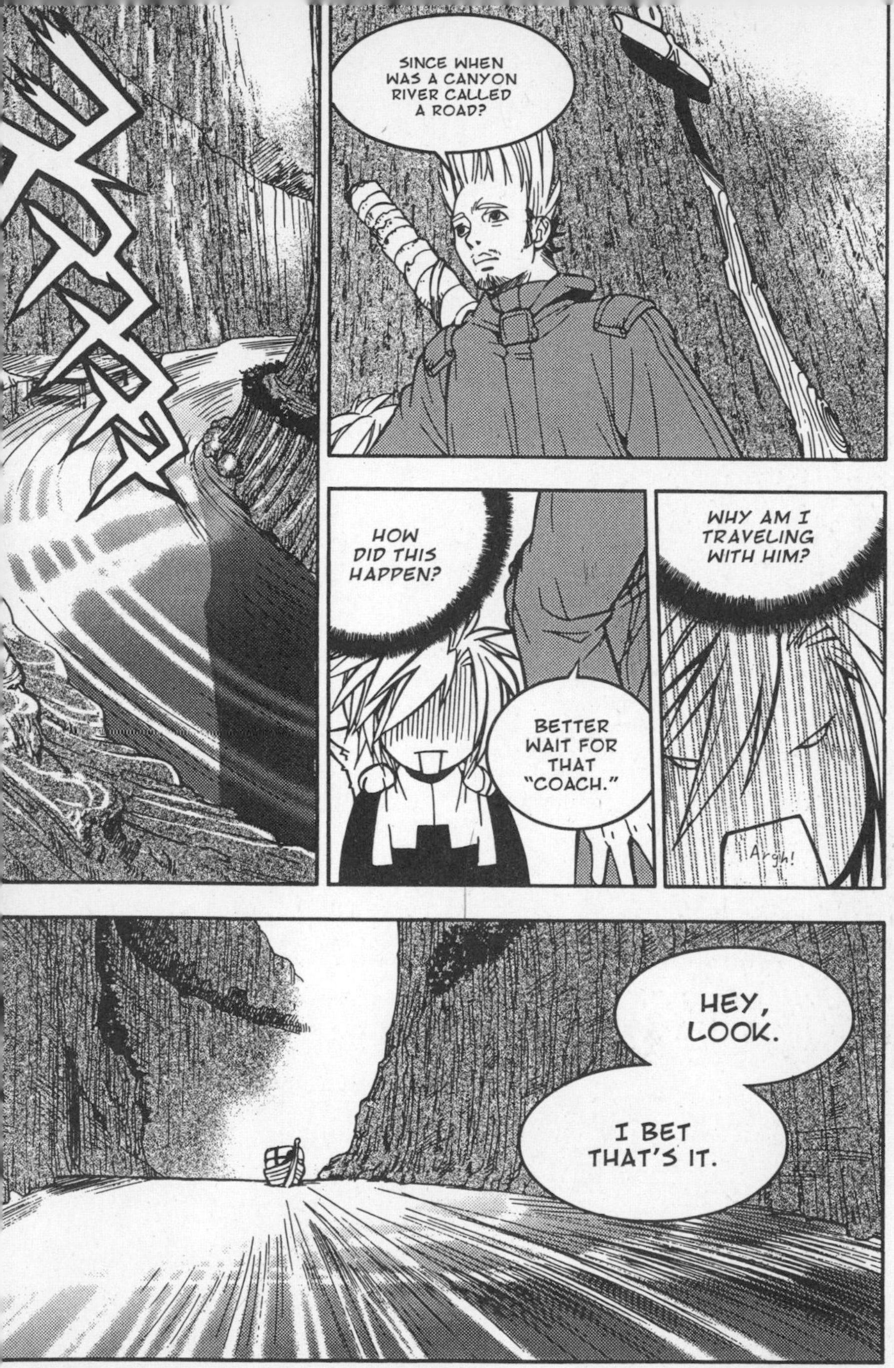
SINCE WHEN WAS A CANYON RIVER CALLED A ROAD?
HOW DID THIS HAPPEN?
BETTER WAIT FOR THAT "COACH."
WHY AM I TRAVELING WITH HIM?
Argh!
HEY, LOOK.
I BET THAT'S IT.

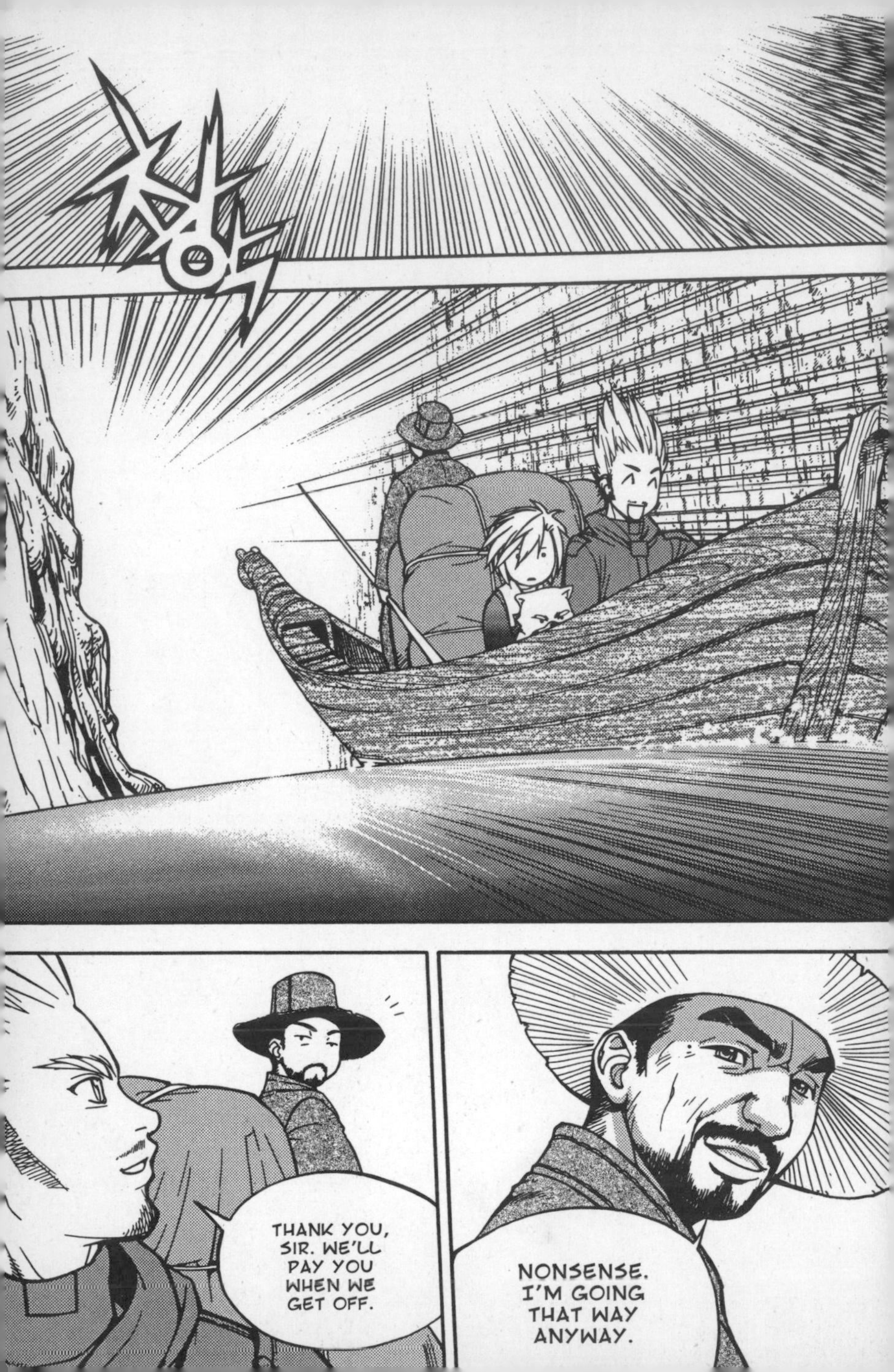
THANK YOU, SIR. WE'LL PAY YOU WHEN WE GET OFF.
NONSENSE. I'M GOING THAT WAY ANYWAY.

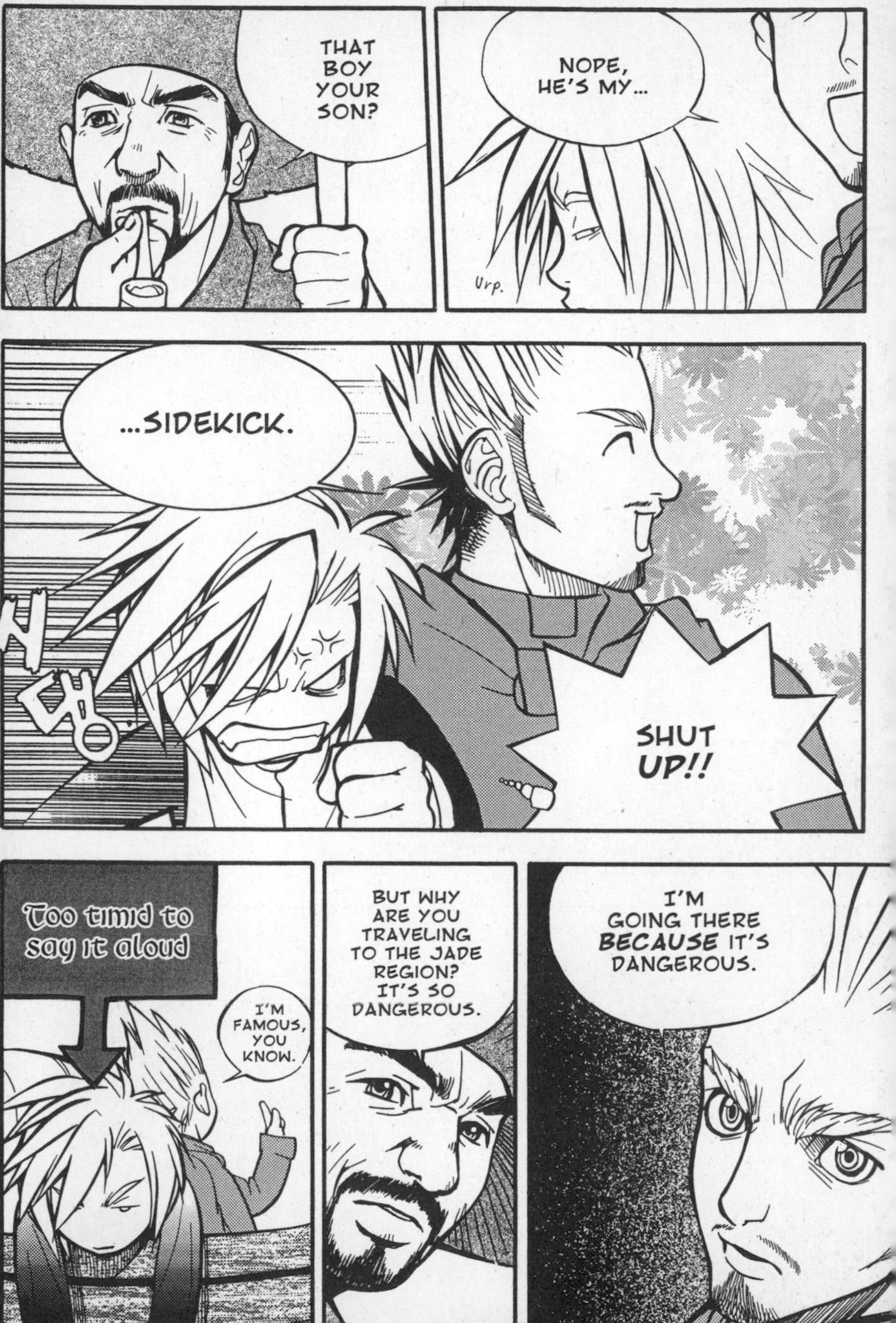
THAT BOY YOUR SON?
NOPE, HE'S MY...
Urp.
...SIDEKICK.
SHUT UP!!
Too timid to say it aloud
I'M FAMOUS, YOU KNOW.
BUT WHY ARE YOU TRAVELING TO THE JADE REGION? IT'S SO DANGEROUS.
I'M GOING THERE BECAUSE IT'S DANGEROUS.

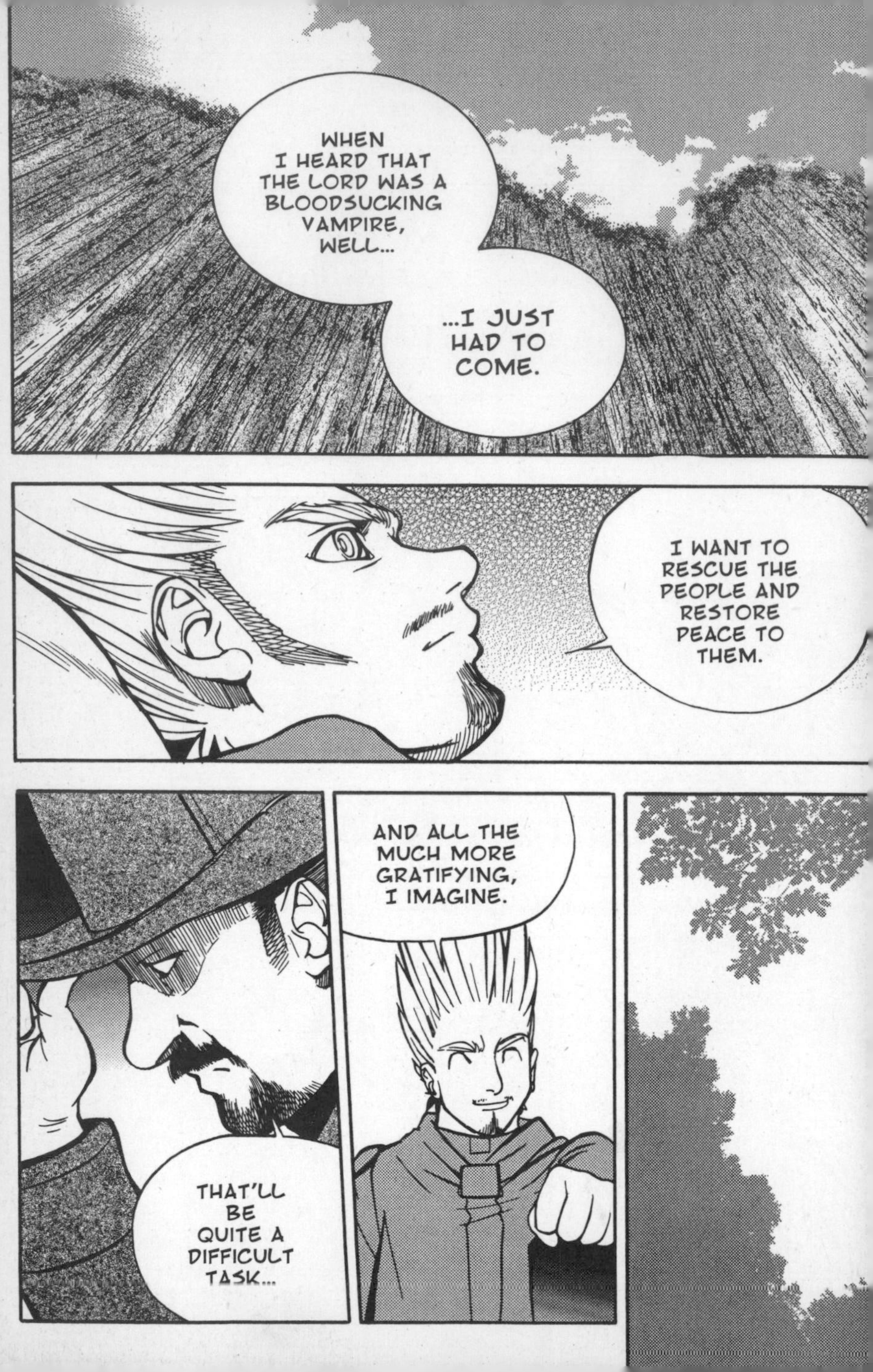
WHEN I HEARD THAT THE LORD WAS A BLOODSUCKING VAMPIRE, WELL...
...I JUST HAD TO COME.
I WANT TO RESCUE THE PEOPLE AND RESTORE PEACE TO THEM.
THAT'LL BE QUITE A DIFFICULT TASK...
AND ALL THE MUCH MORE GRATIFYING, I IMAGINE.

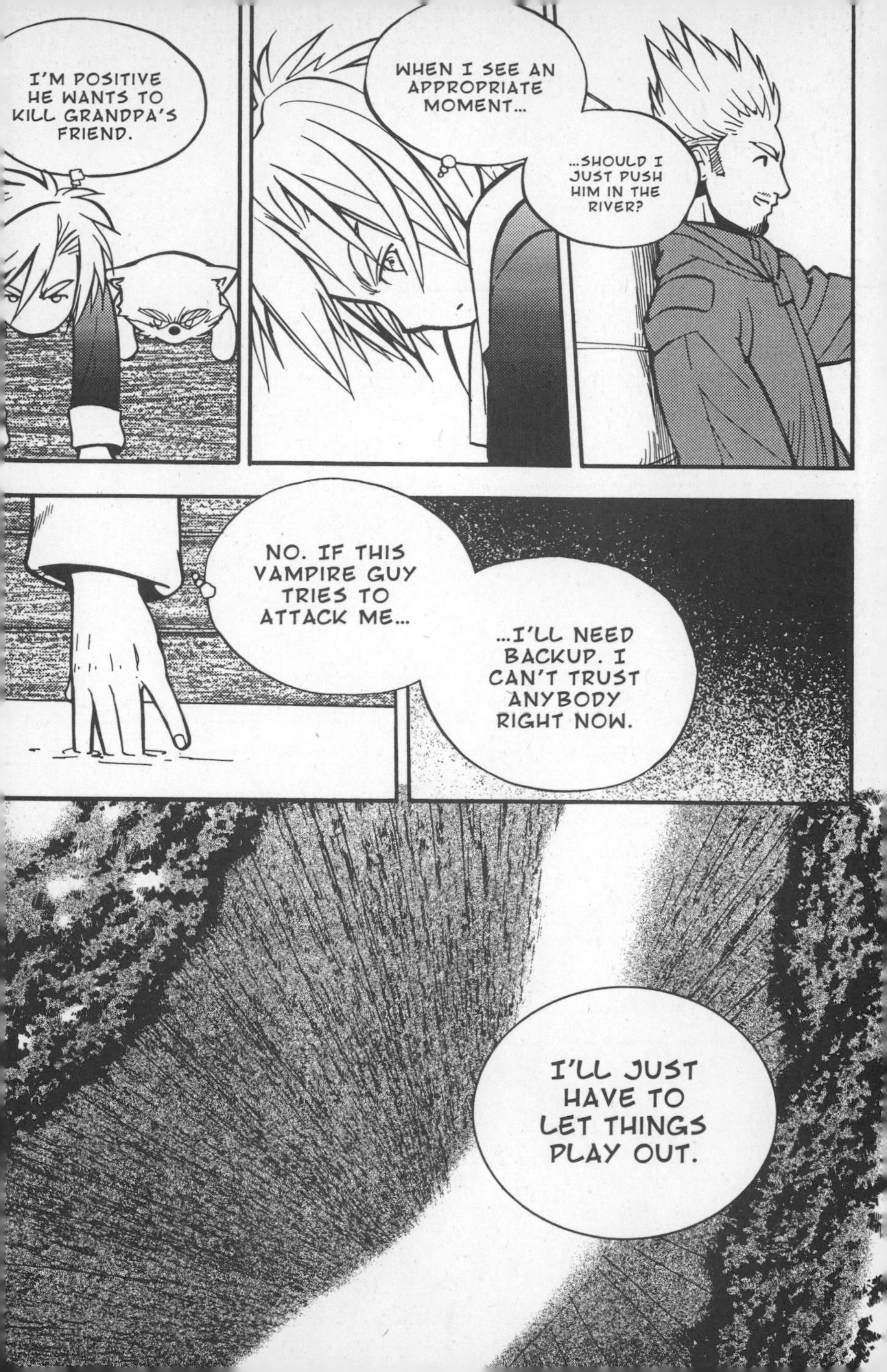
I'M POSITIVE HE WANTS TO KILL GRANDPA'S FRIEND.
WHEN I SEE AN APPROPRIATE MOMENT...
...SHOULD I JUST PUSH HIM IN THE RIVER?
NO. IF THIS VAMPIRE GUY TRIES TO ATTACK ME...
...I'LL NEED BACKUP. I CAN'T TRUST ANYBODY RIGHT NOW.
I'LL JUST HAVE TO LET THINGS PLAY OUT.

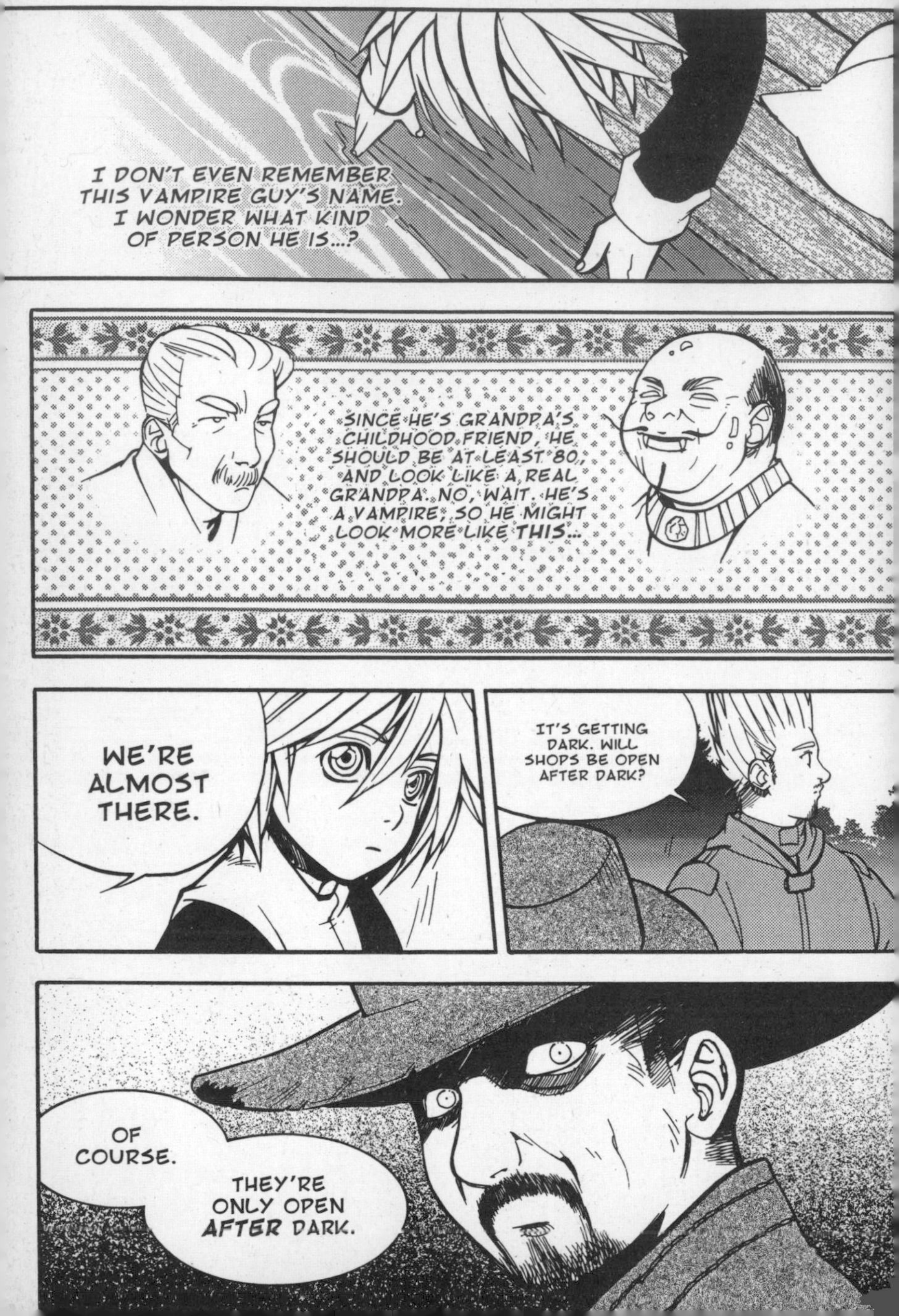
I DON'T EVEN REMEMBER THIS VAMPIRE GUY'S NAME. I WONDER WHAT KIND OF PERSON HE IS...?
SINCE HE'S GRANDPA'S CHILDHOOD FRIEND, HE SHOULD BE AT LEAST 80, AND LOOK LIKE A REAL GRANDPA. NO, WAIT. HE'S A VAMPIRE, SO HE MIGHT LOOK MORE LIKE THIS...
WE'RE ALMOST THERE.
IT'S GETTING DARK. WILL SHOPS BE OPEN AFTER DARK?
OF COURSE.
THEY'RE ONLY OPEN AFTER DARK.

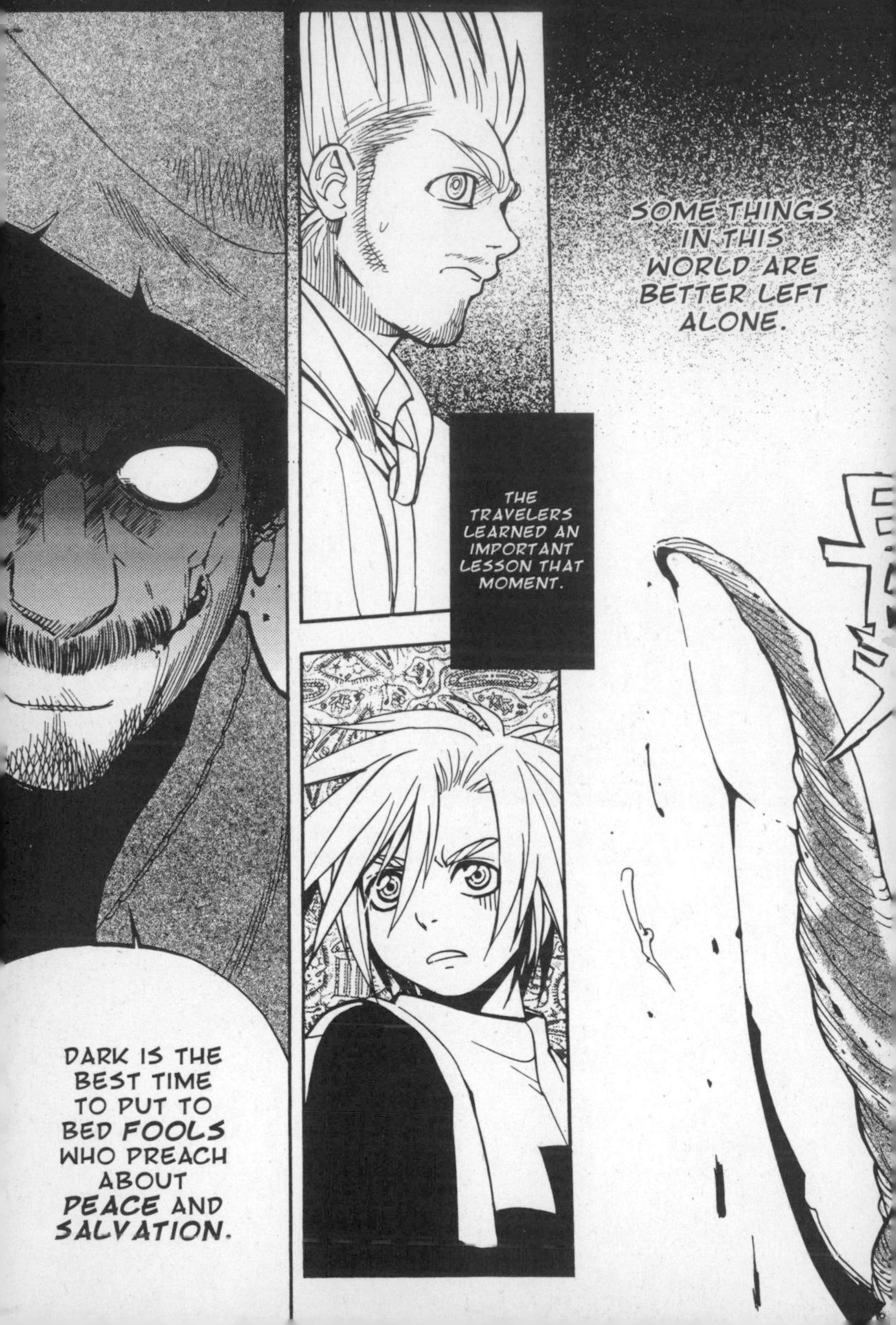
DARK IS THE BEST TIME TO PUT TO BED FOOLS WHO PREACH ABOUT PEACE AND SALVATION.
THE TRAVELERS LEARNED AN IMPORTANT LESSON THAT MOMENT.
SOME THINGS IN THIS WORLD ARE BETTER LEFT ALONE.

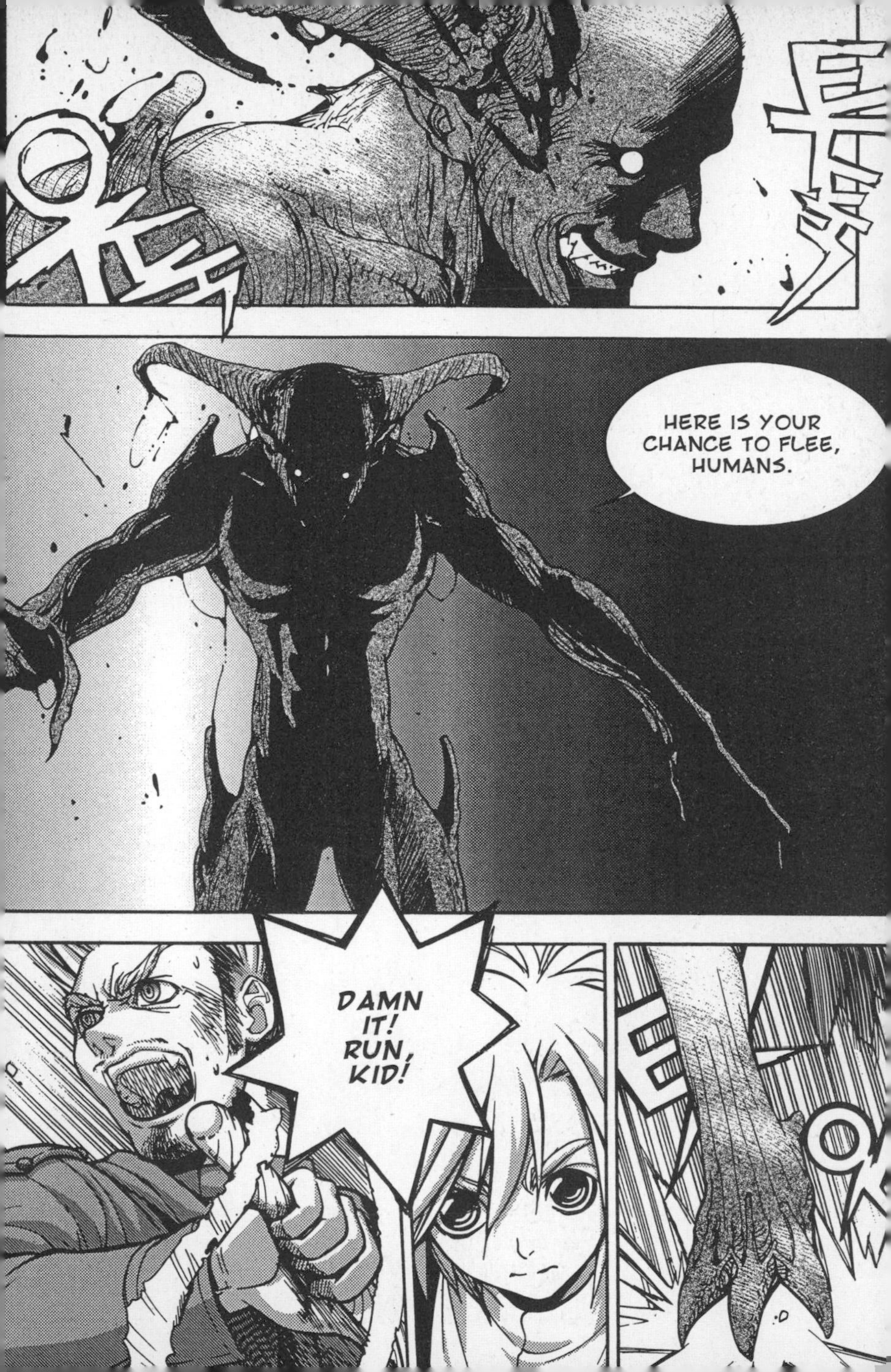
HERE IS YOUR CHANCE TO FLEE, HUMANS.
DAMN IT! RUN, KID!

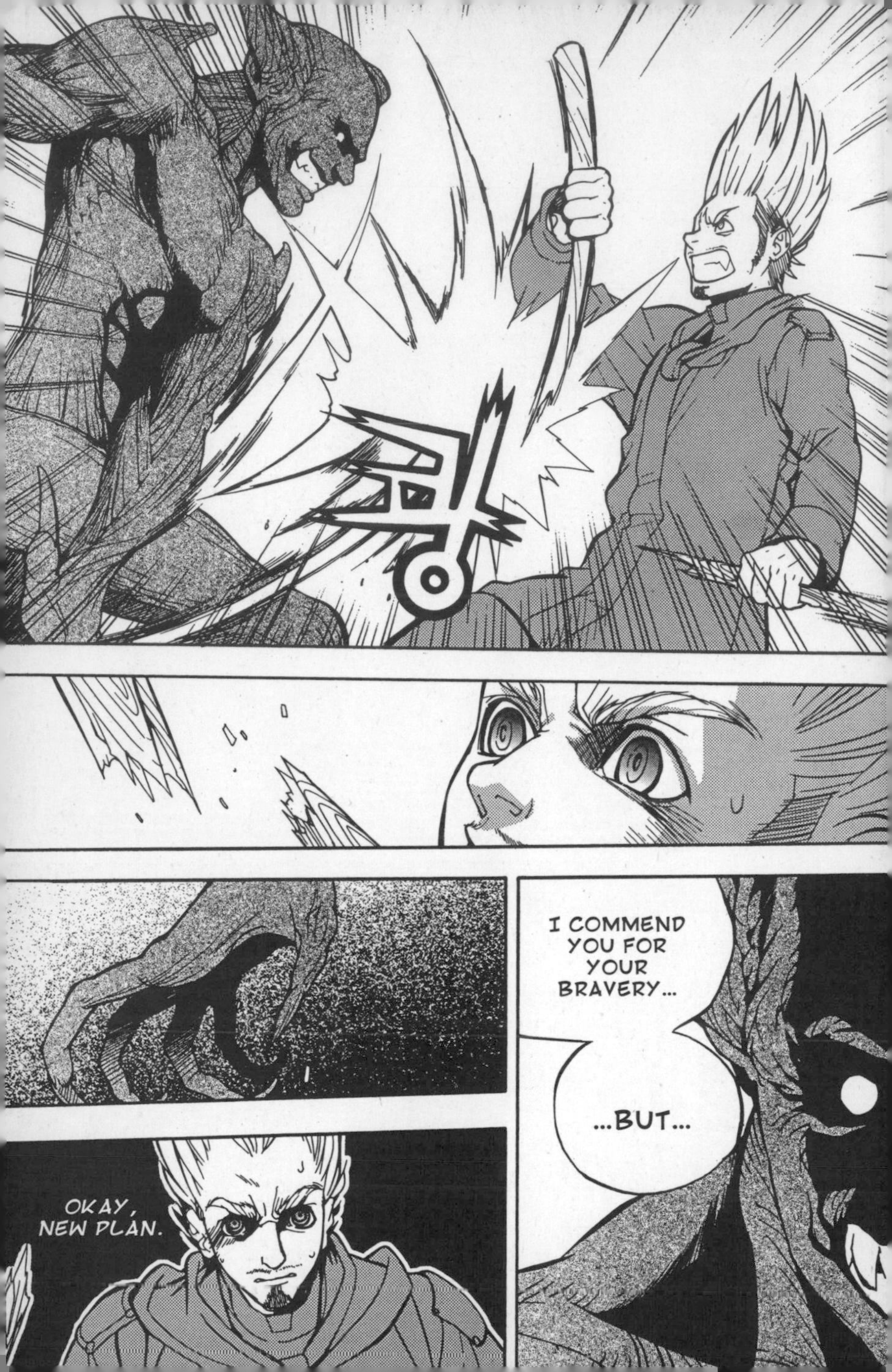
I COMMEND YOU FOR YOUR BRAVERY...
...BUT...
OKAY, NEW PLAN.

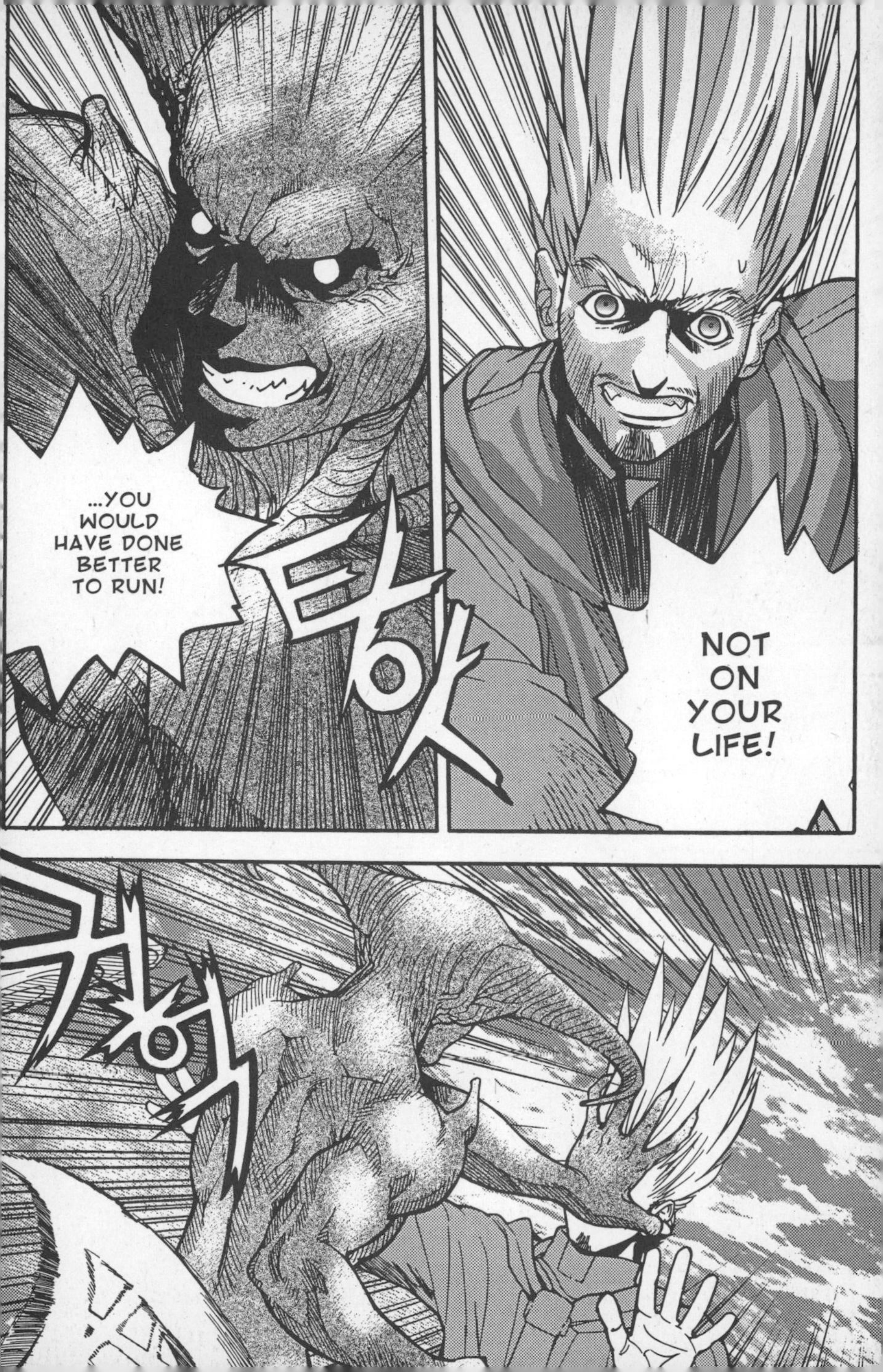
...YOU WOULD HAVE DONE BETTER TO RUN!
NOT ON YOUR LIFE!

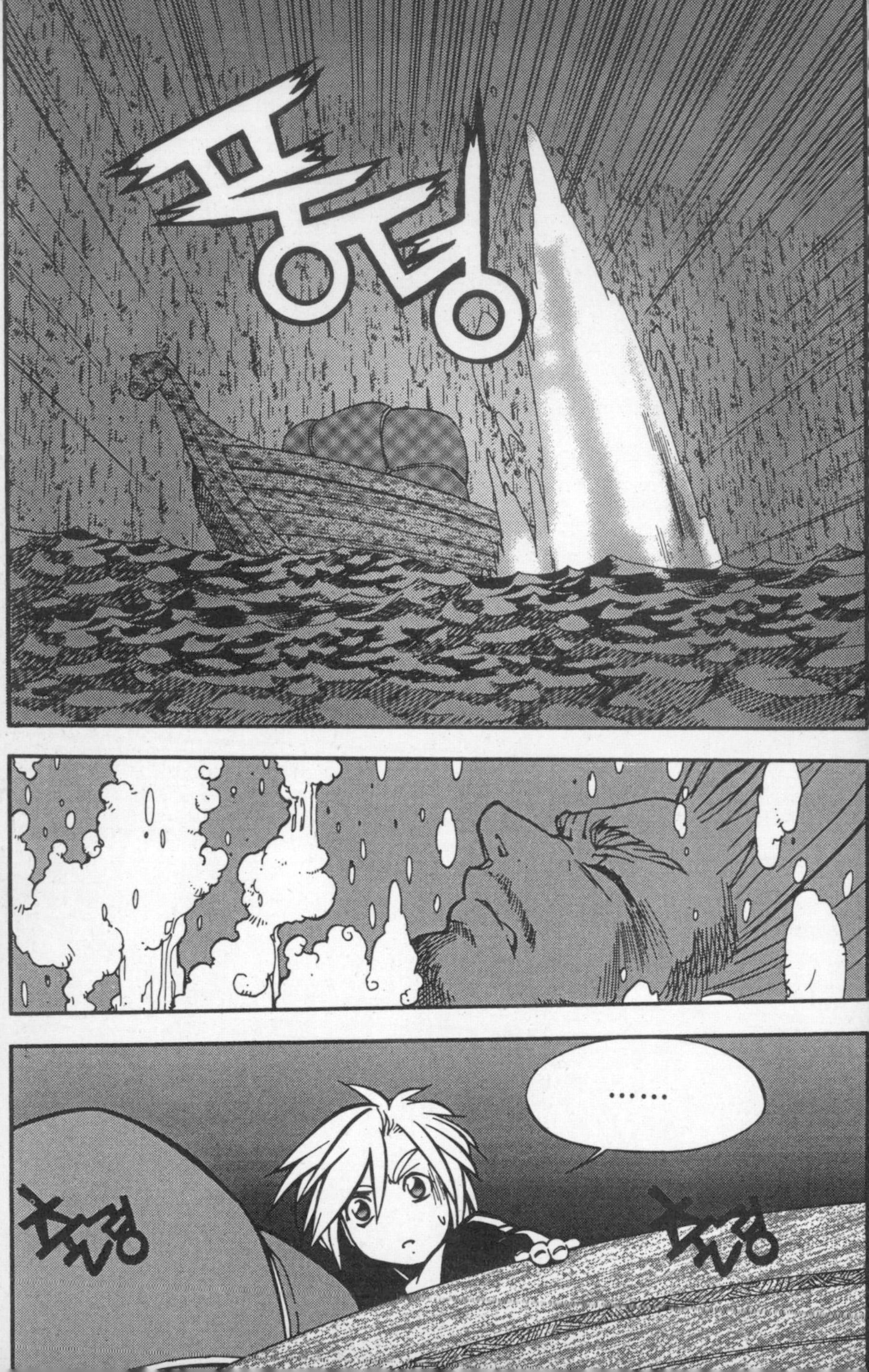
풍덩
......
찰랑
찰랑

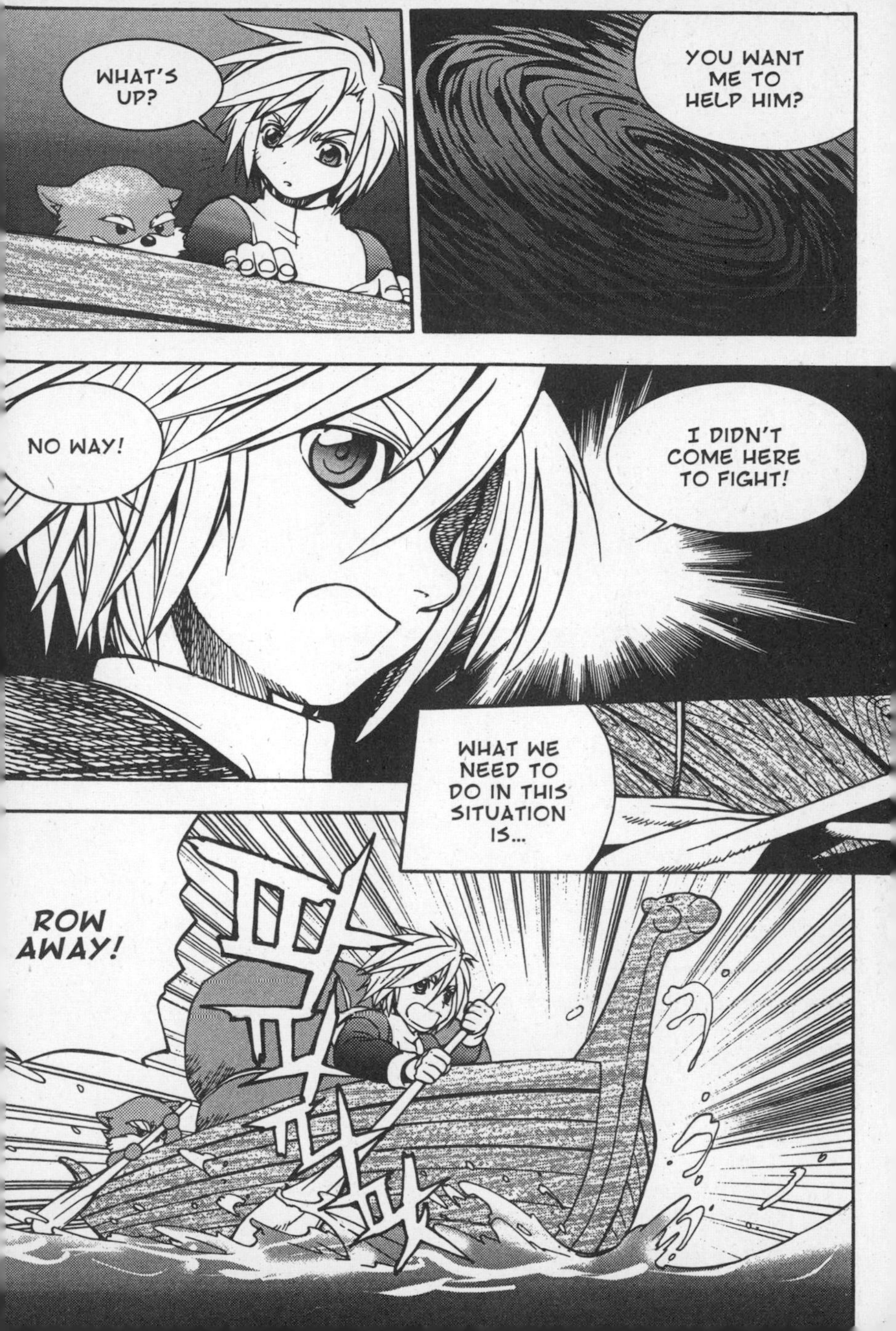
WHAT'S UP?
YOU WANT ME TO HELP HIM?
NO WAY!
I DIDN'T COME HERE TO FIGHT!
WHAT WE NEED TO DO IN THIS SITUATION IS...
ROW AWAY!

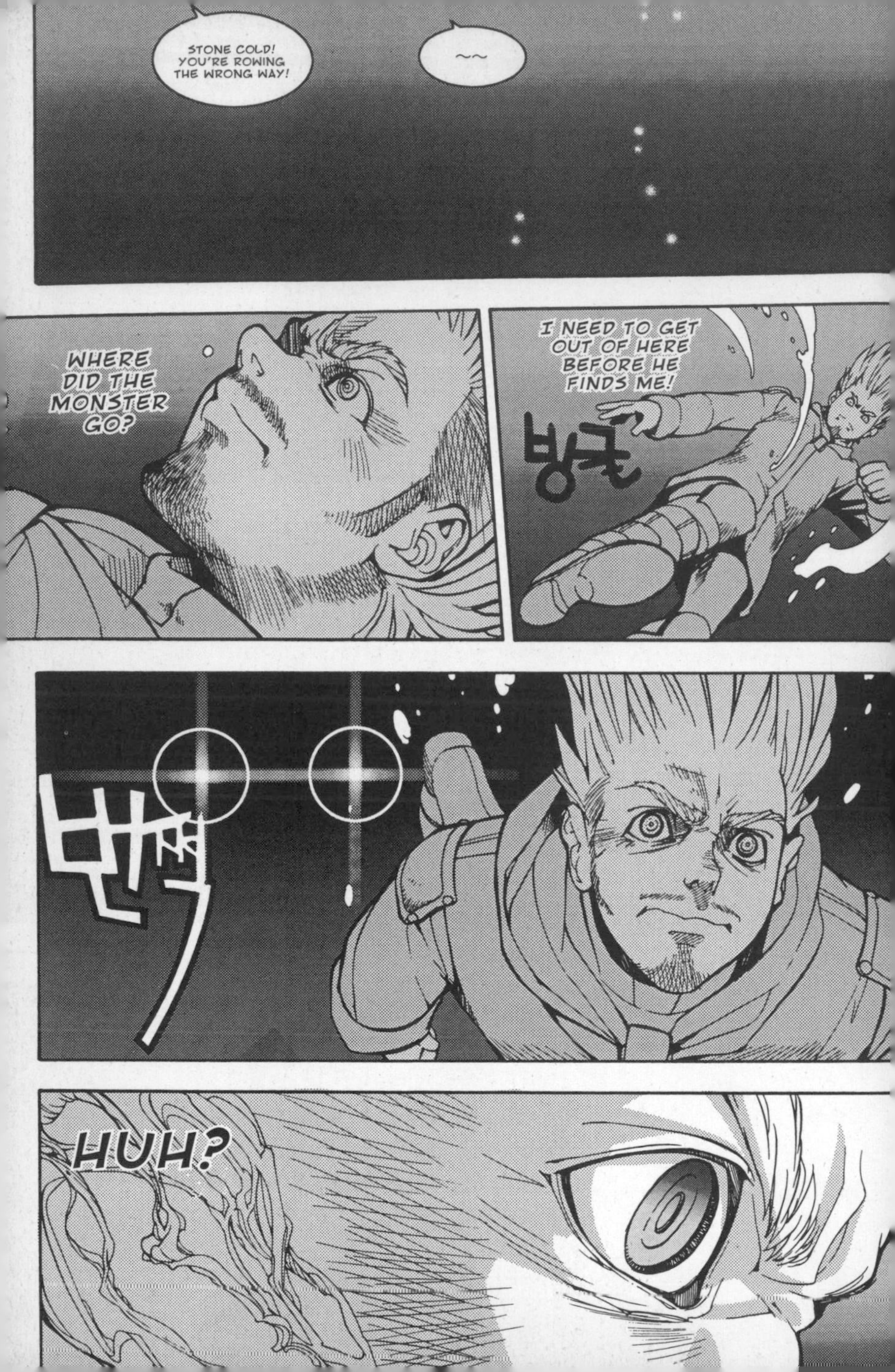
STONE COLD! YOU'RE ROWING THE WRONG WAY!
~~
WHERE DID THE MONSTER GO?
I NEED TO GET OUT OF HERE BEFORE HE FINDS ME!
HUH?

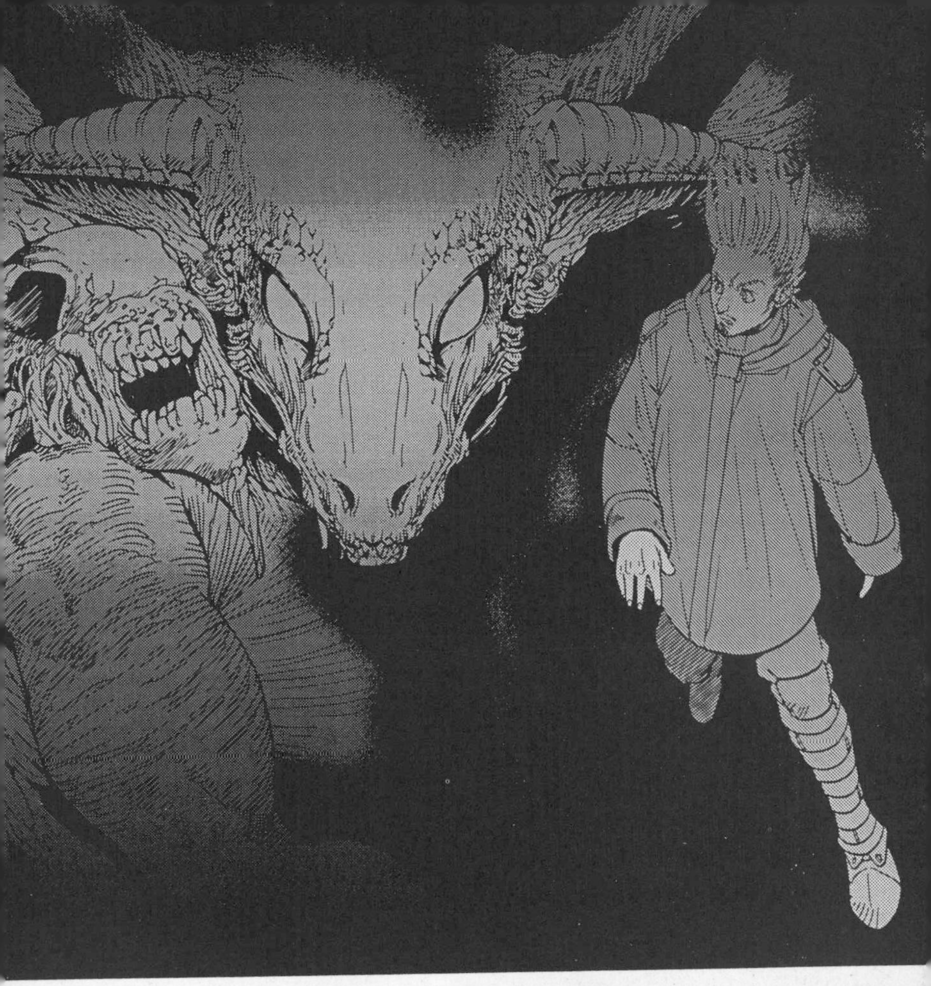
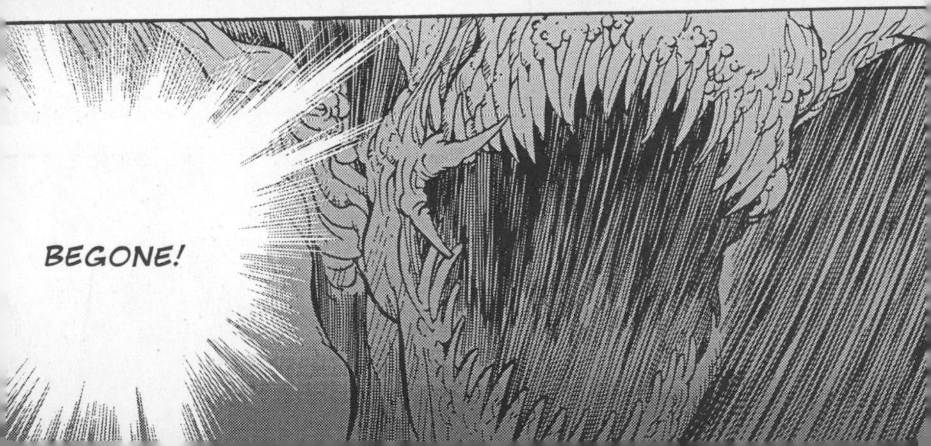
BEGONE!

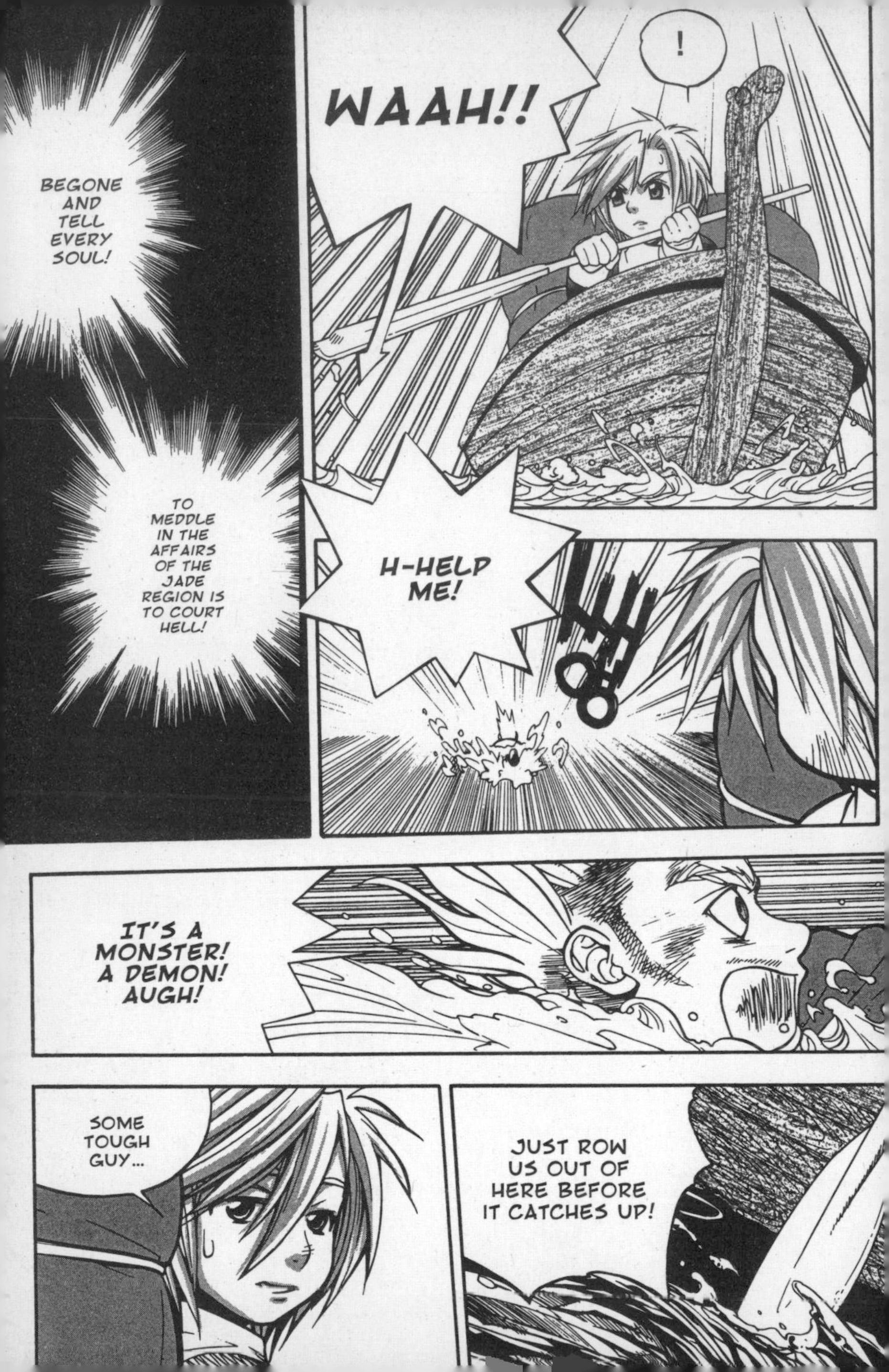
BEGONE AND TELL EVERY SOUL!
TO MEDDLE IN THE AFFAIRS OF THE JADE REGION IS TO COURT HELL!
!
WAAH!!
H-HELP ME!
IT'S A MONSTER! A DEMON! AUGH!
SOME TOUGH GUY...
JUST ROW US OUT OF HERE BEFORE IT CATCHES UP!

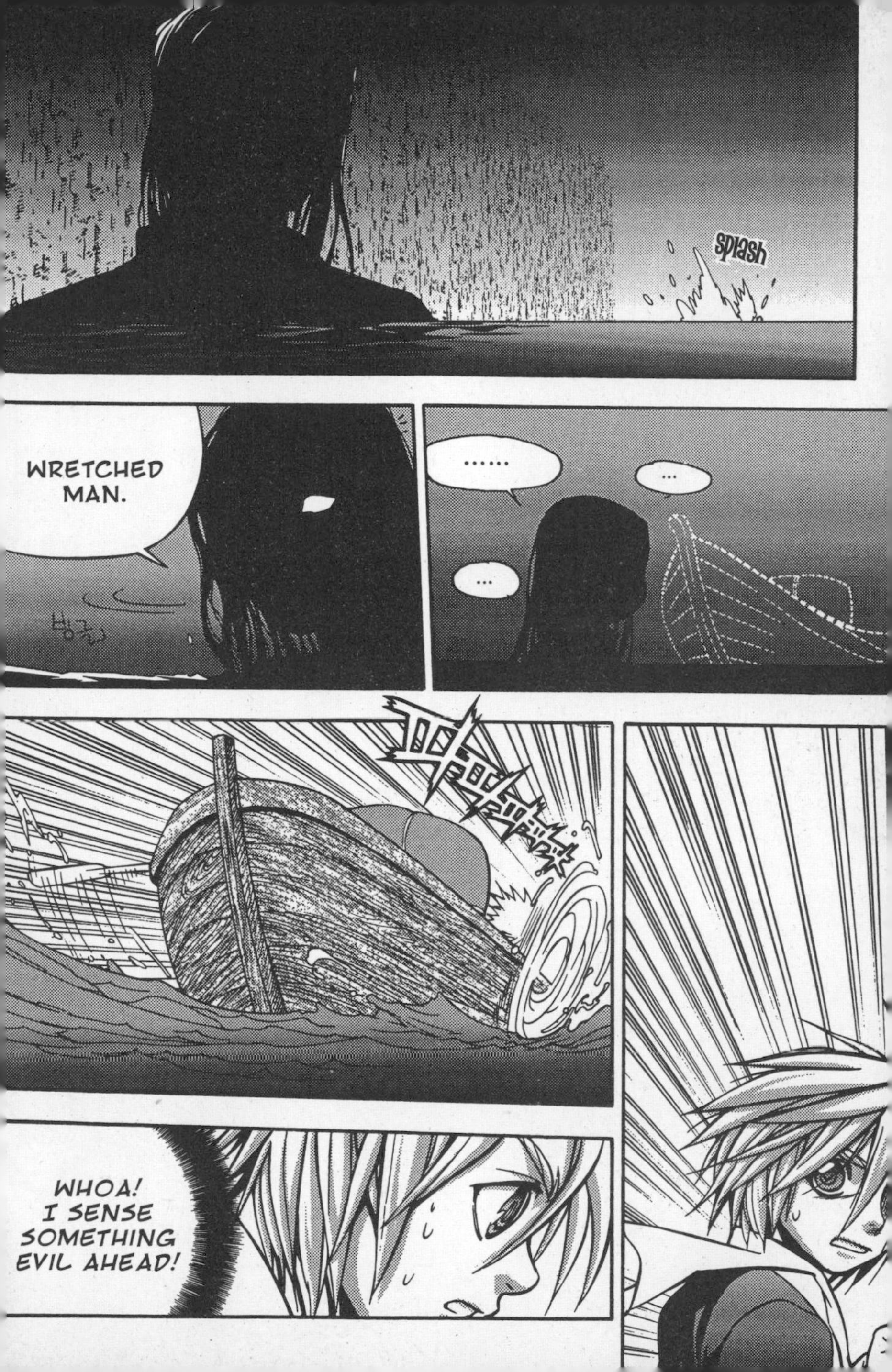
SPLASH
WRETCHED MAN.
....
...
...
WHOA! I SENSE SOMETHING EVIL AHEAD!

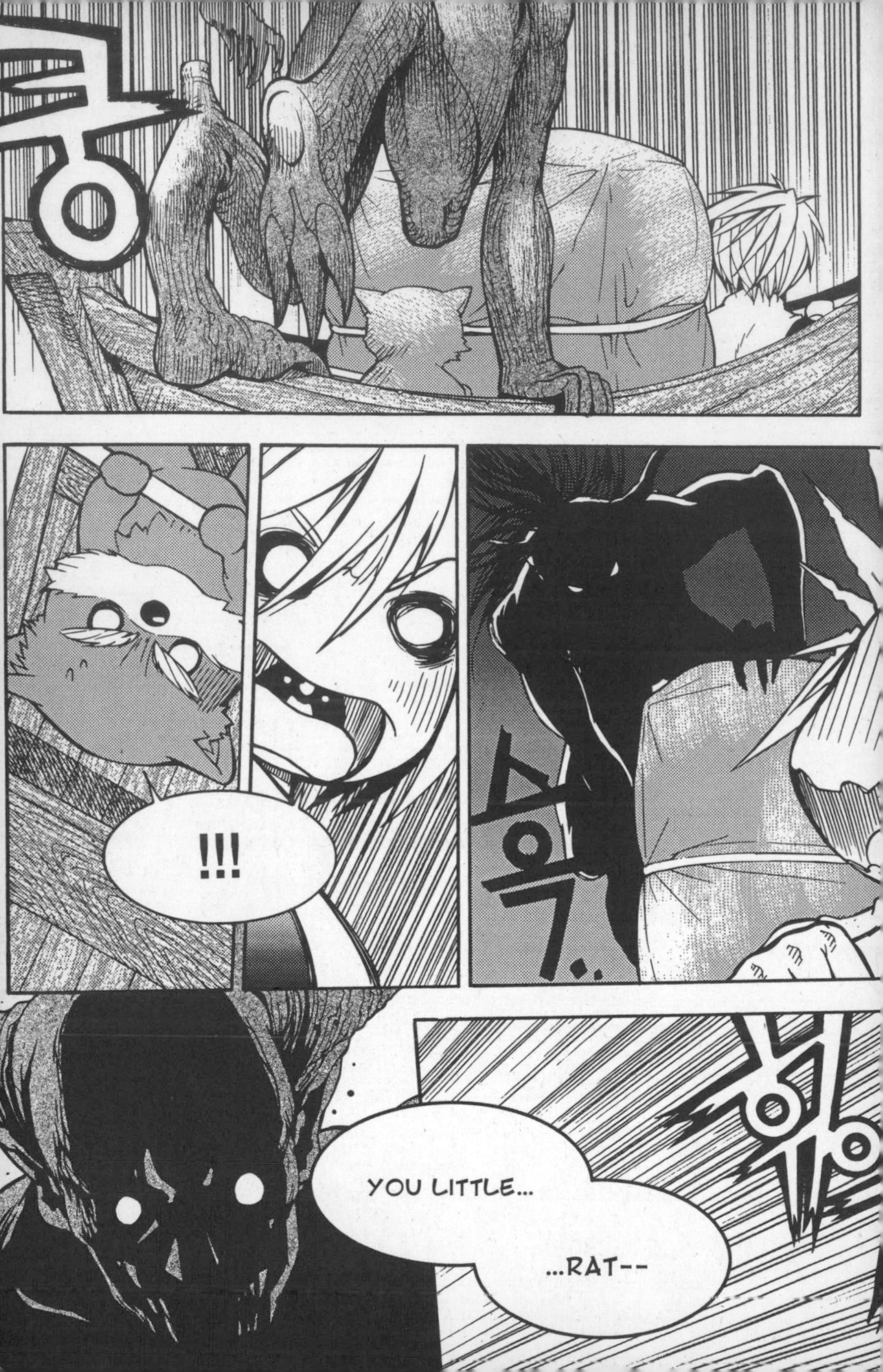
쿵
!!!
스윽
YOU LITTLE...
...RAT--

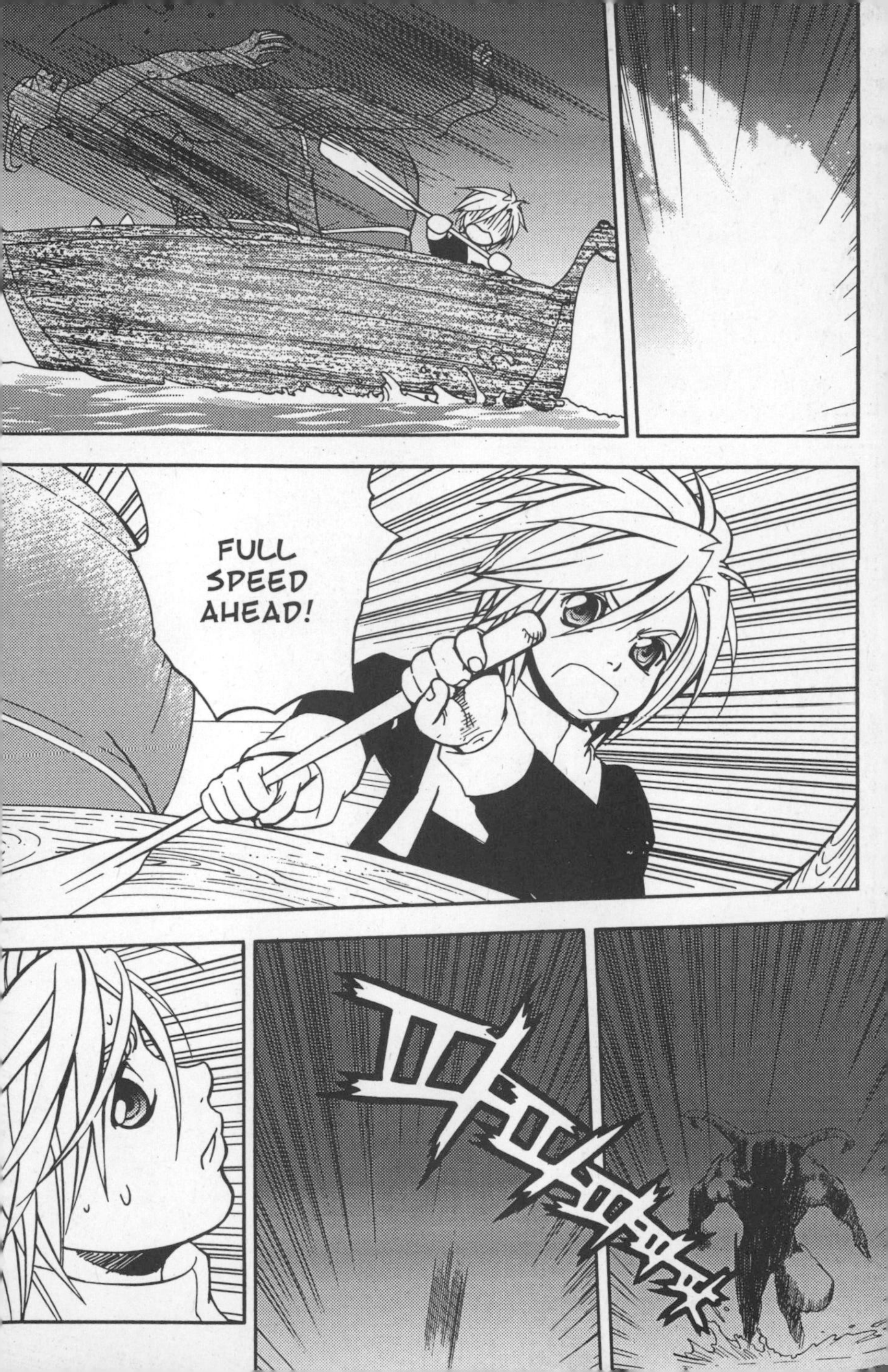
FULL SPEED AHEAD!

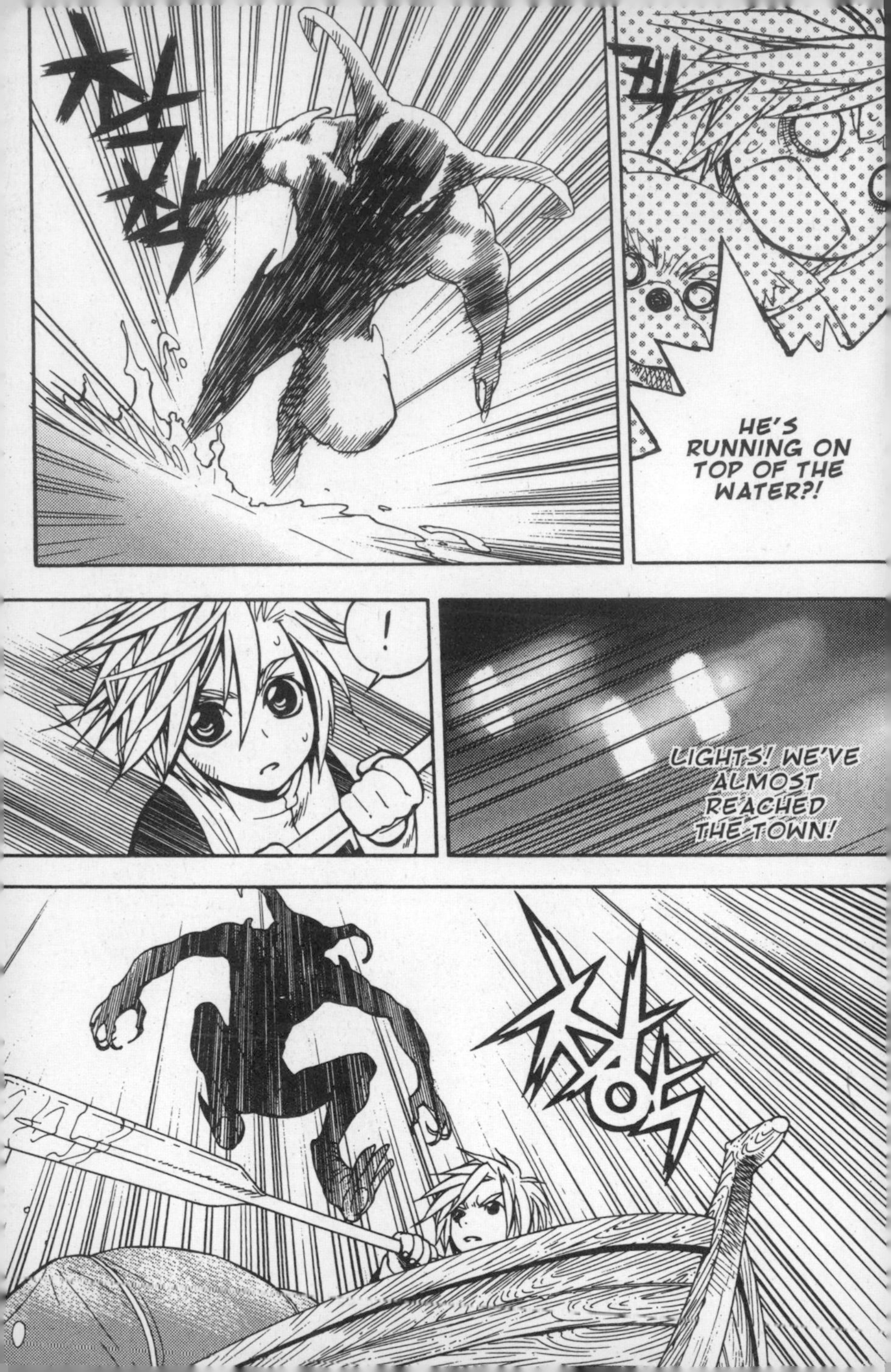
HE'S RUNNING ON TOP OF THE WATER?!
!
LIGHTS! WE'VE ALMOST REACHED THE TOWN!

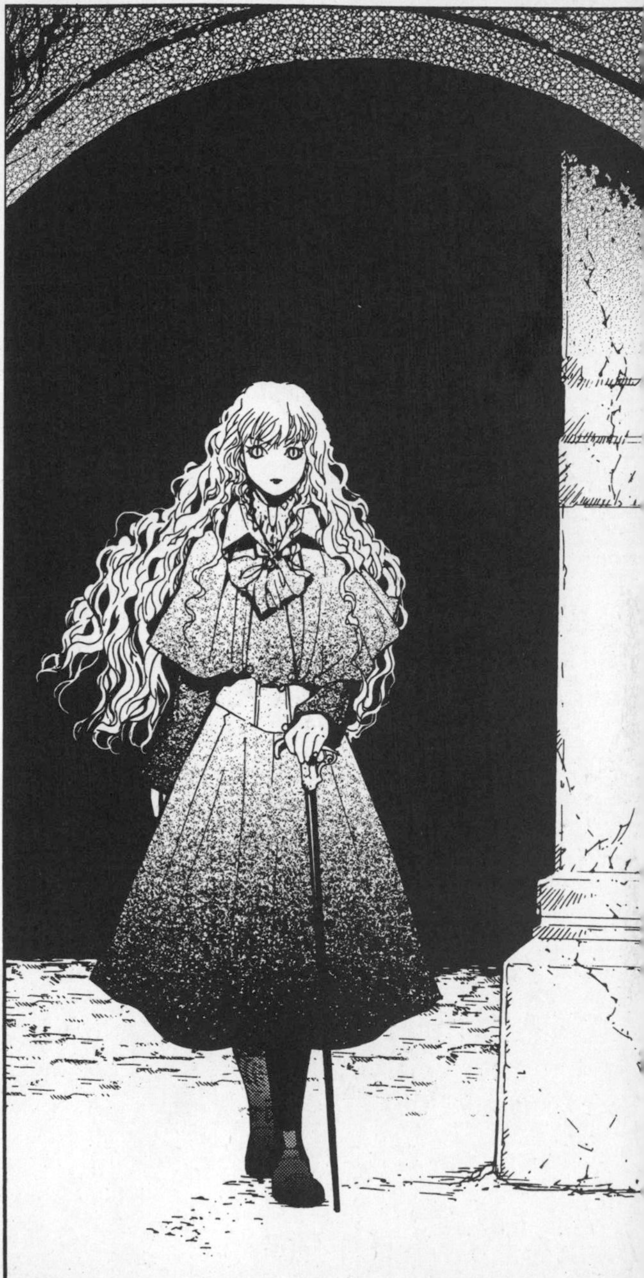

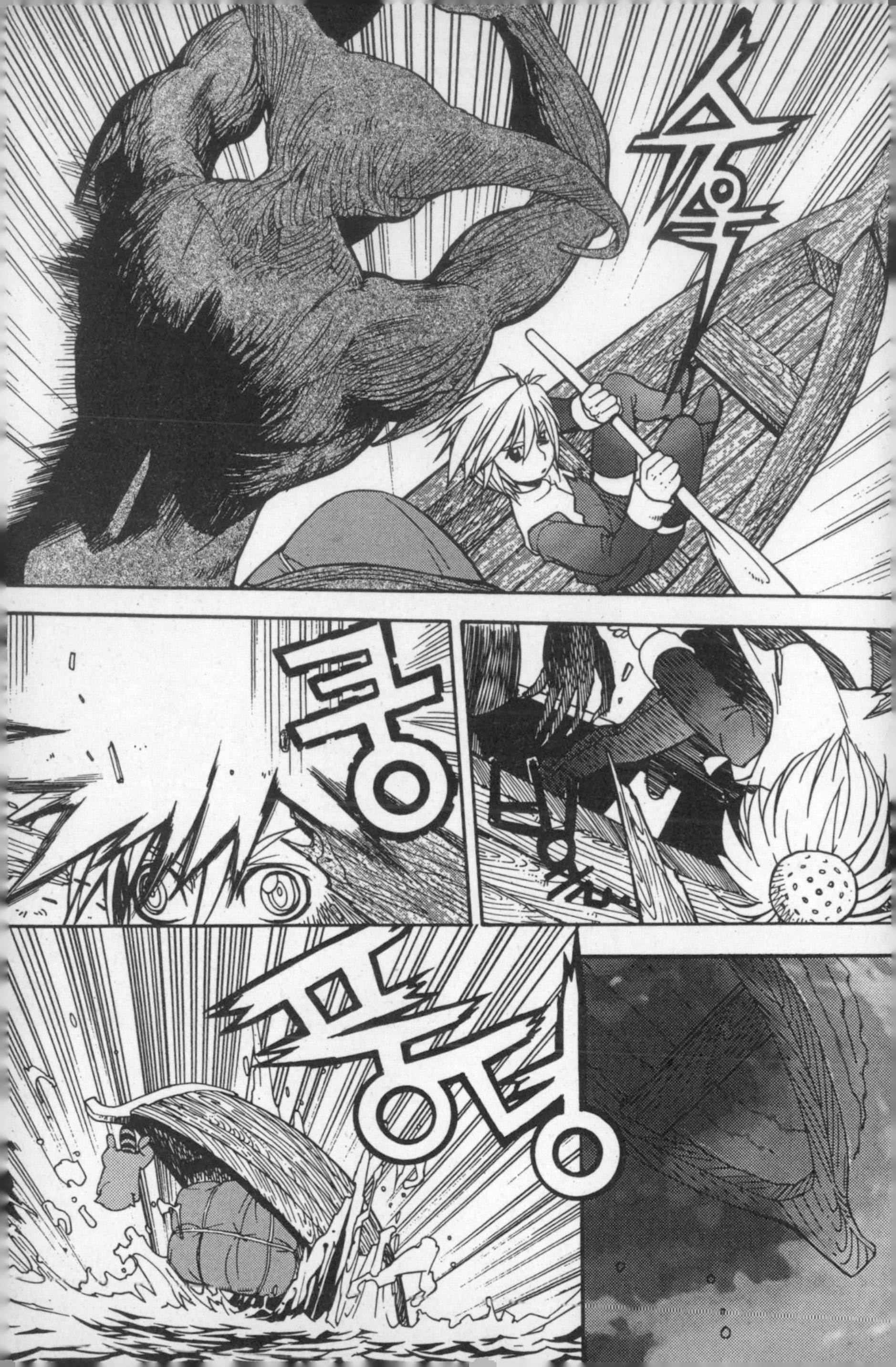
스윽
쿵
빙
풍덩

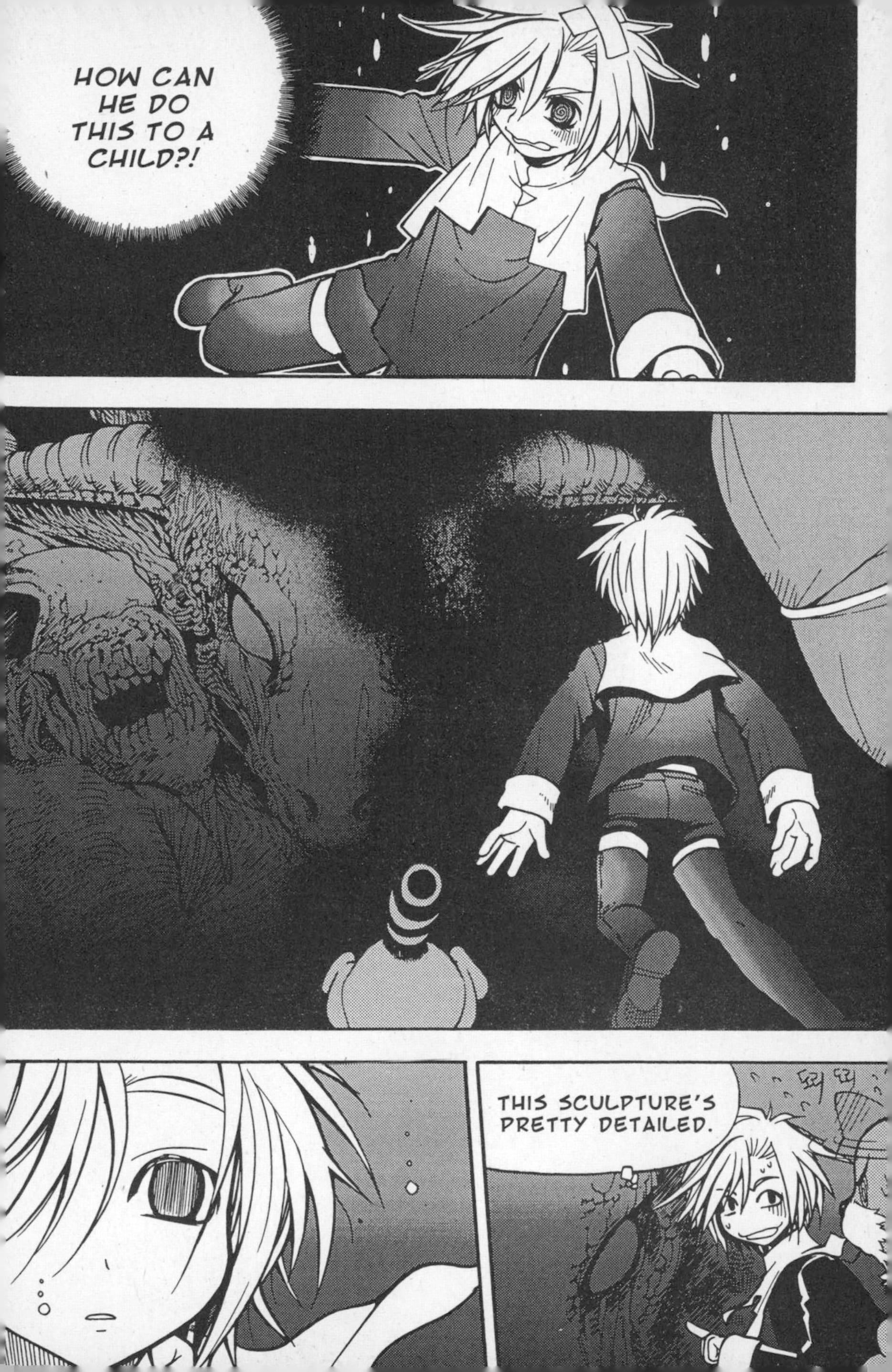
HOW CAN HE DO THIS TO A CHILD?!
THIS SCULPTURE'S PRETTY DETAILED.

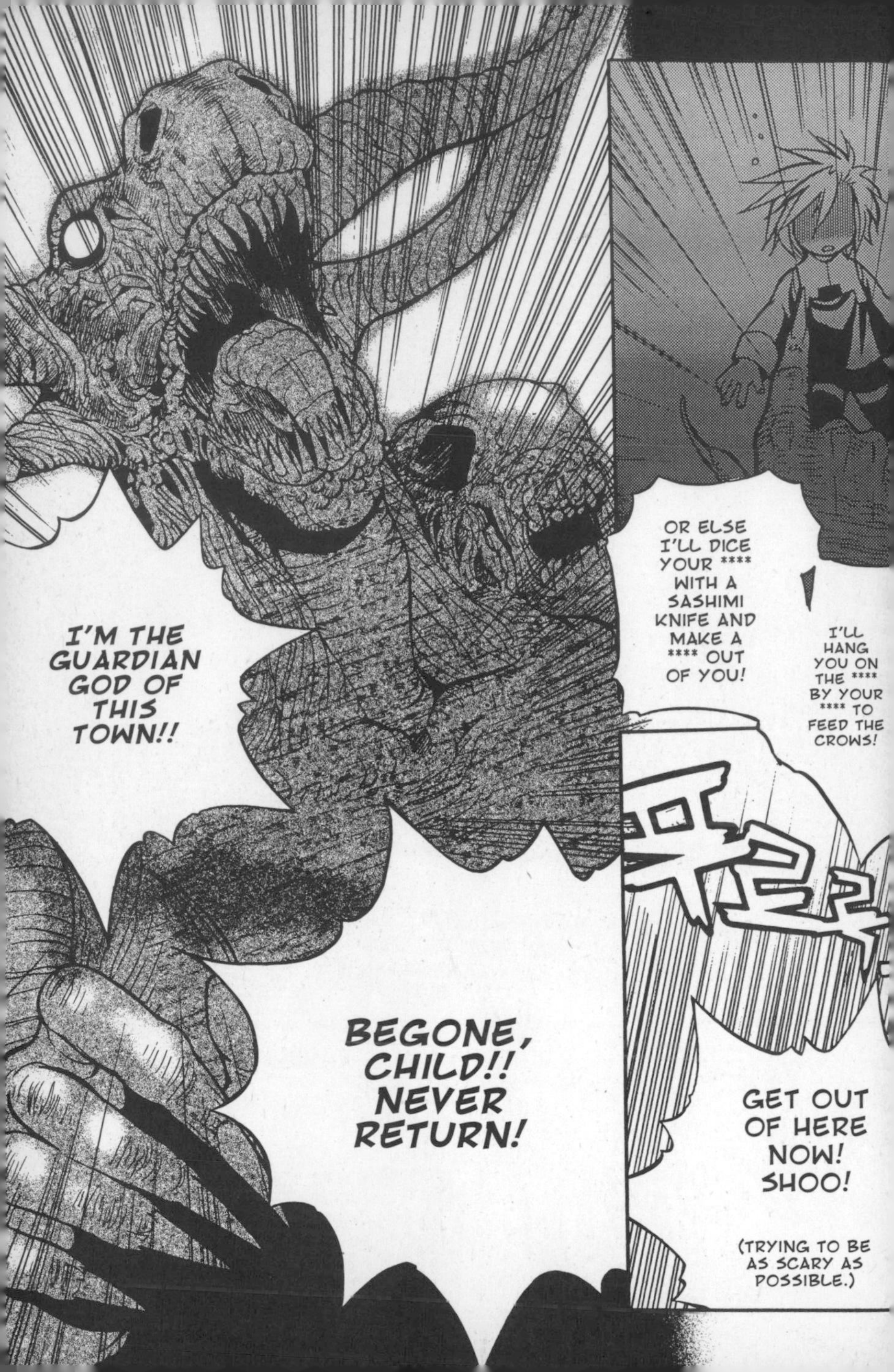
I'M THE GUARDIAN GOD OF THIS TOWN!!
BEGONE, CHILD!! NEVER RETURN!
OR ELSE I'LL DICE YOUR **** WITH A SASHIMI KNIFE AND MAKE A **** OUT OF YOU!
I'LL HANG YOU ON THE **** BY YOUR **** TO FEED THE CROWS!
GET OUT OF HERE NOW! SHOO!
(TRYING TO BE AS SCARY AS POSSIBLE.)

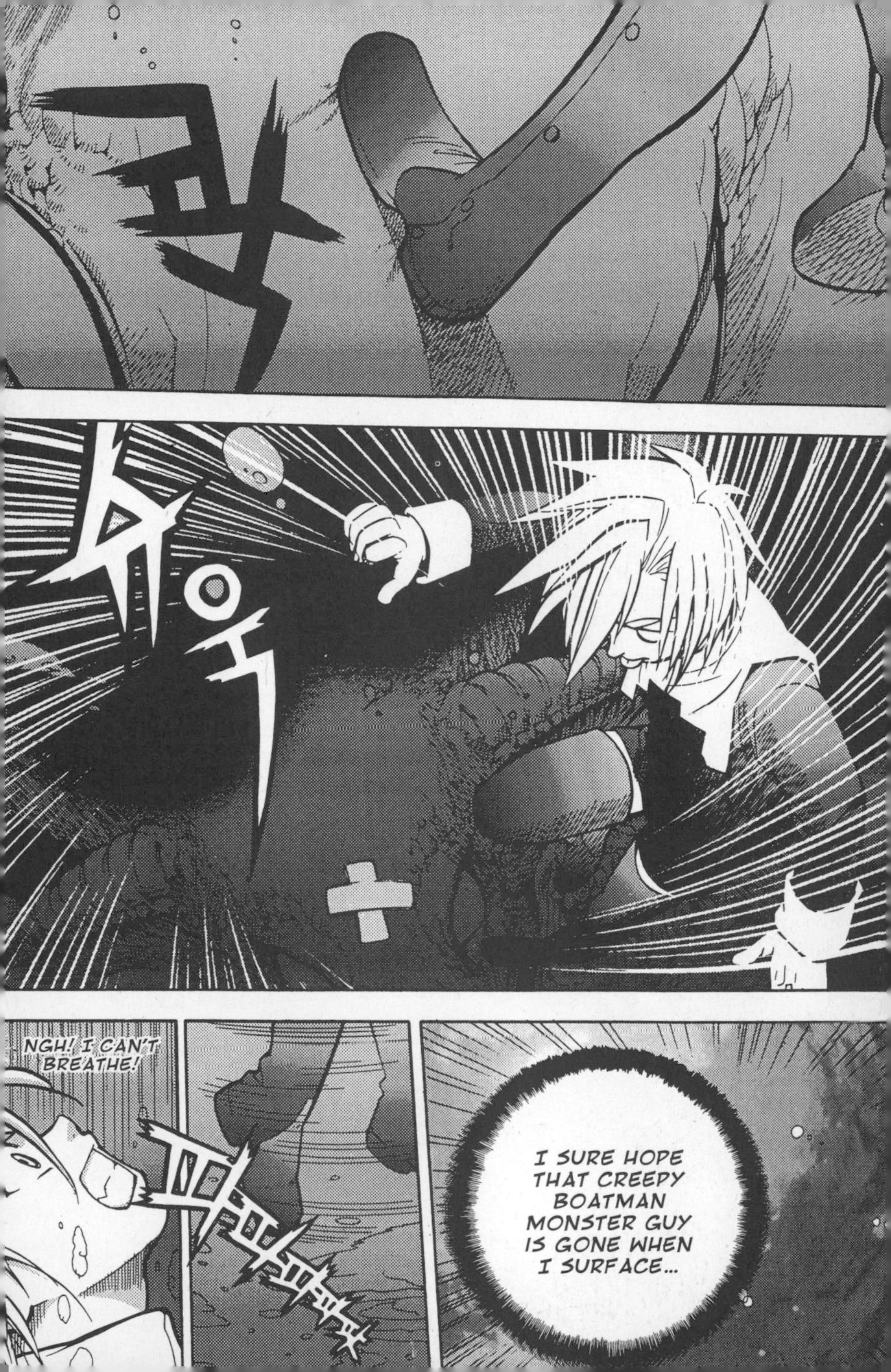
NGH! I CAN'T BREATHE!
I SURE HOPE THAT CREEPY BOATMAN MONSTER GUY IS GONE WHEN I SURFACE...

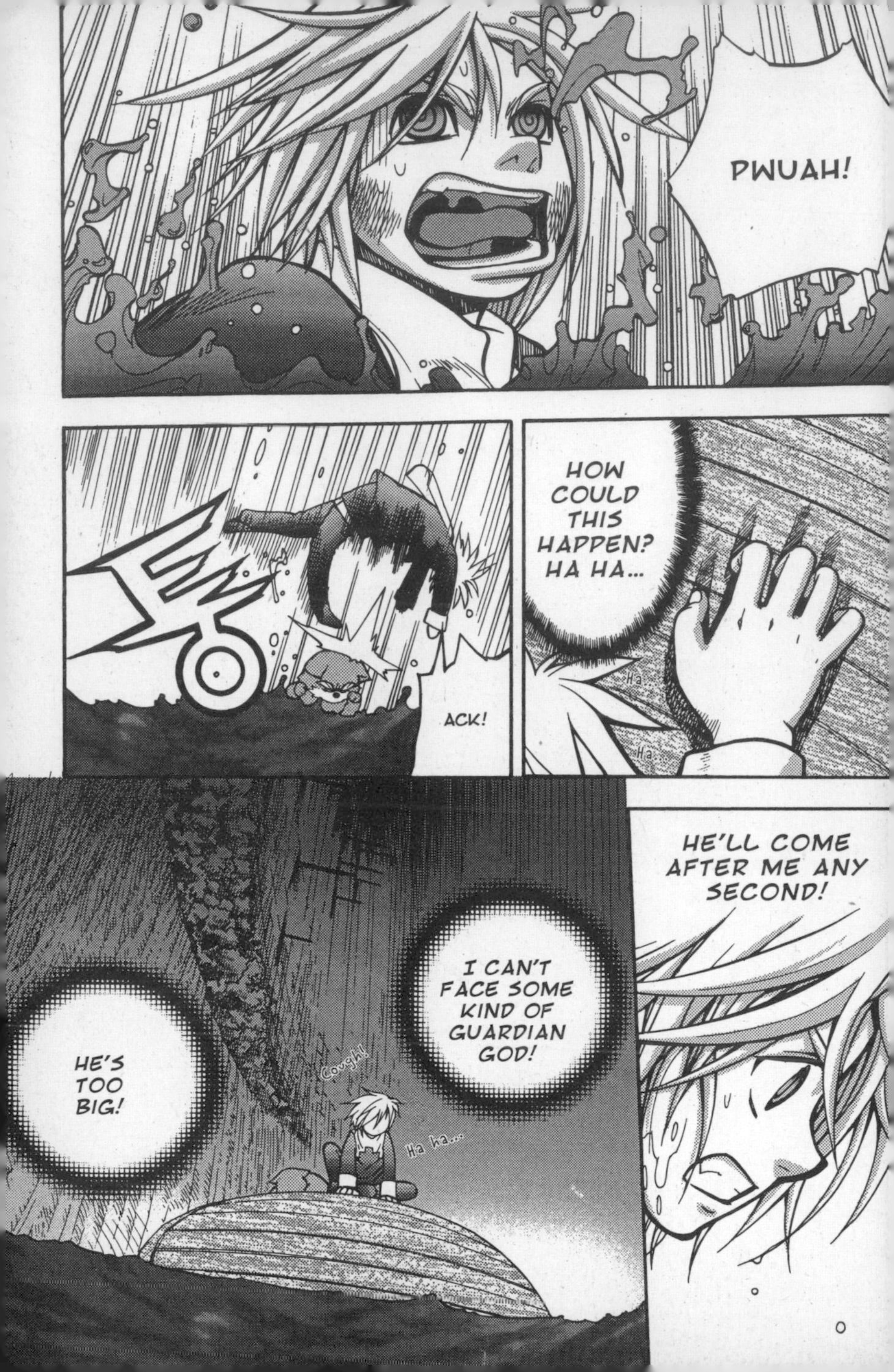
PWUAH!
ACK!
HOW COULD THIS HAPPEN? HA HA...
Ha
Ha
HE'S TOO BIG!
Cough!
Ha ha...
I CAN'T FACE SOME KIND OF GUARDIAN GOD!
HE'LL COME AFTER ME ANY SECOND!

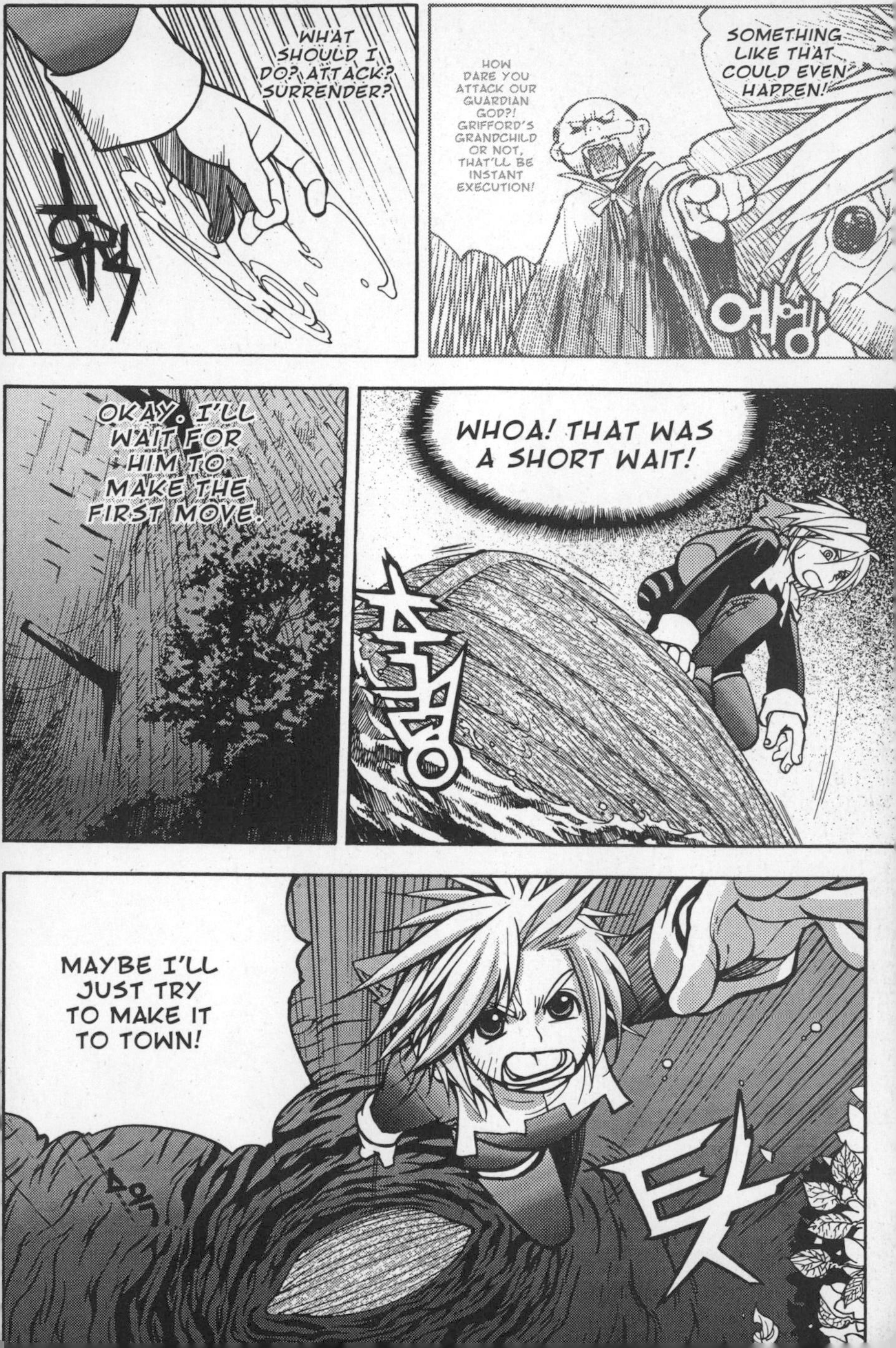
WHAT SHOULD I DO? ATTACK? SURRENDER?
HOW DARE YOU ATTACK OUR GUARDIAN GOD?! GRIFFORD'S GRANDCHILD OR NOT, THAT'LL BE INSTANT EXECUTION!
SOMETHING LIKE THAT COULD EVEN HAPPEN!
OKAY. I'LL WAIT FOR HIM TO MAKE THE FIRST MOVE.
WHOA! THAT WAS A SHORT WAIT!
MAYBE I'LL JUST TRY TO MAKE IT TO TOWN!

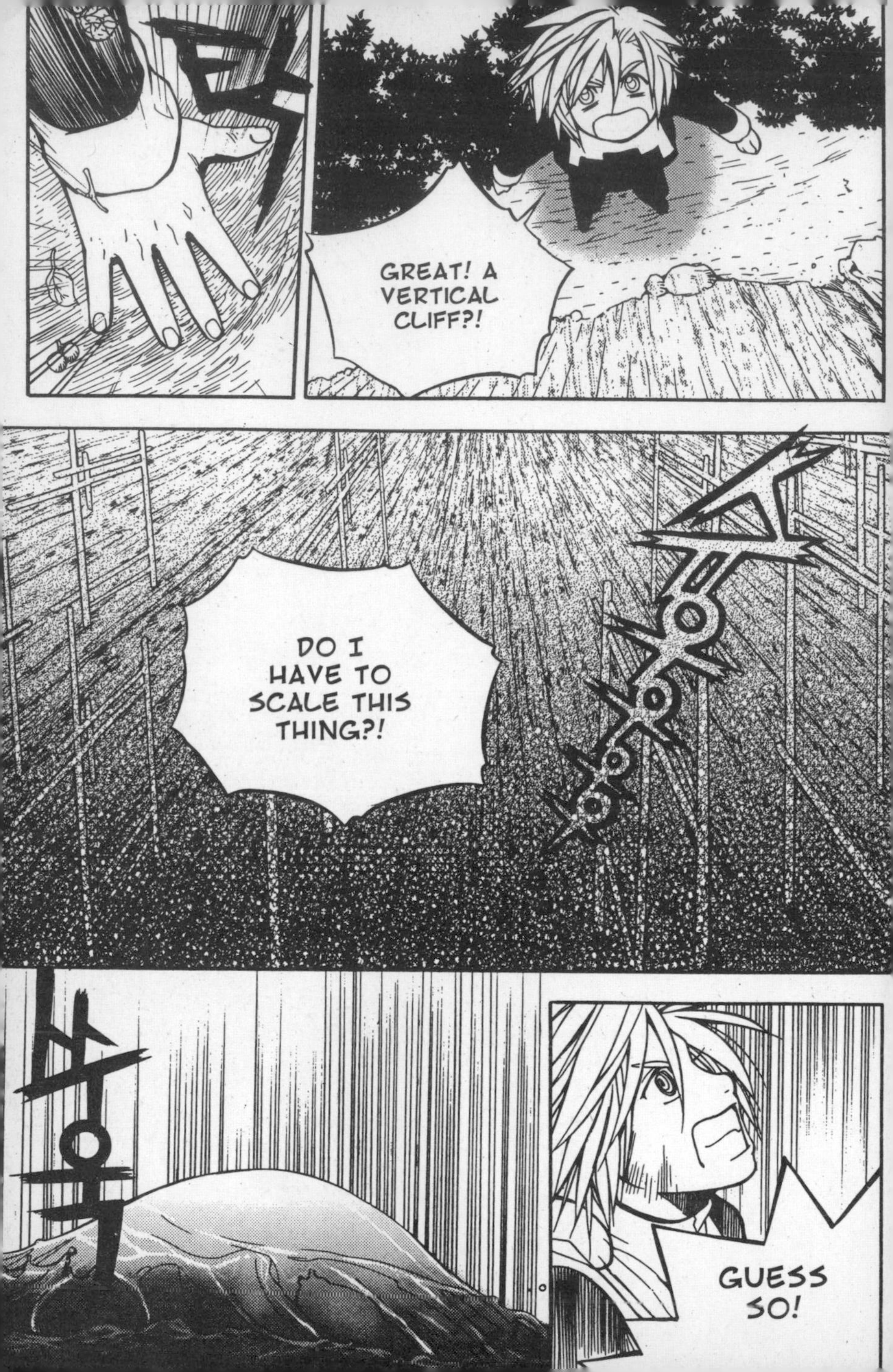
GREAT! A VERTICAL CLIFF?!
DO I HAVE TO SCALE THIS THING?!
GUESS SO!

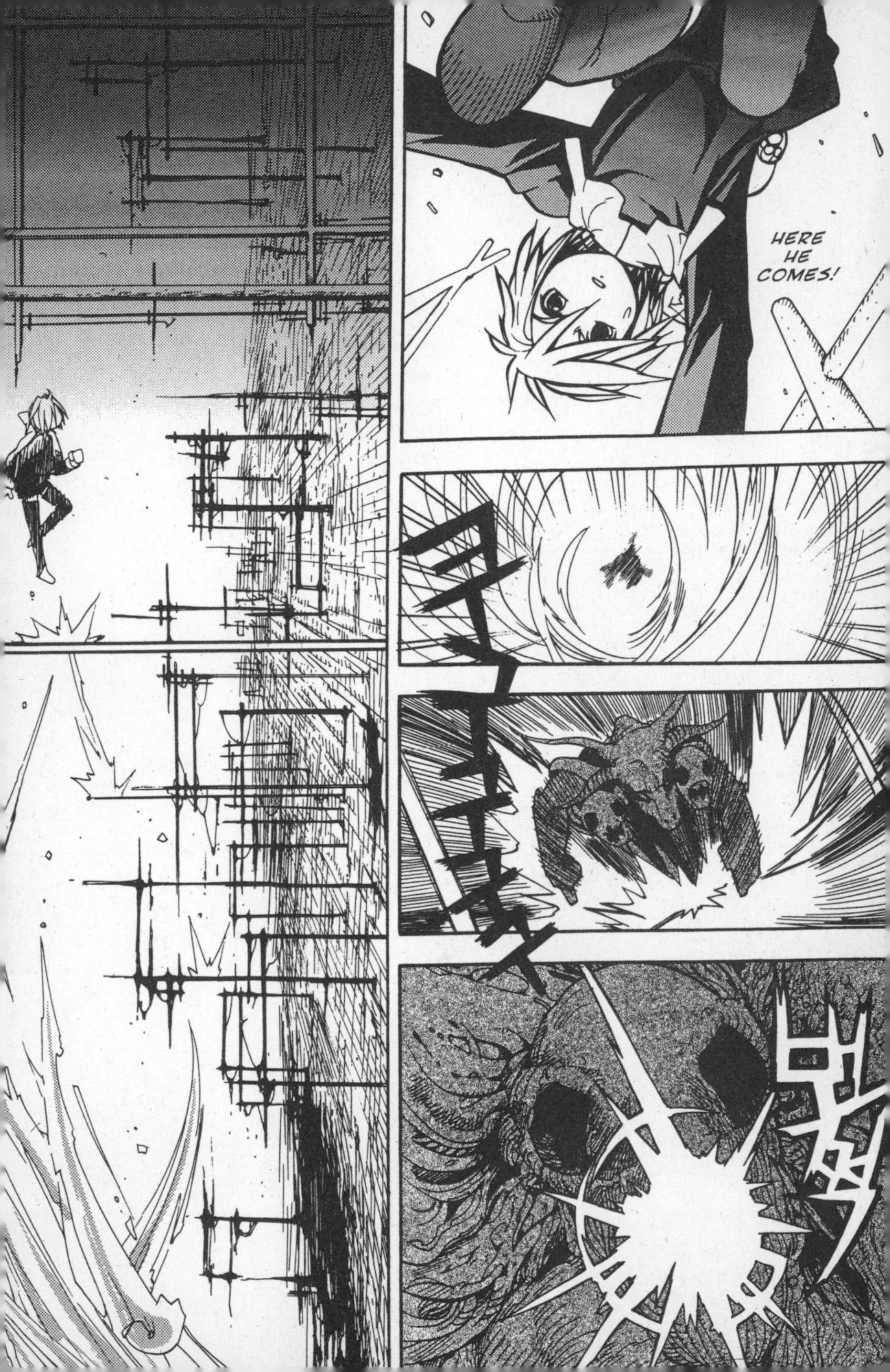
HERE HE COMES!

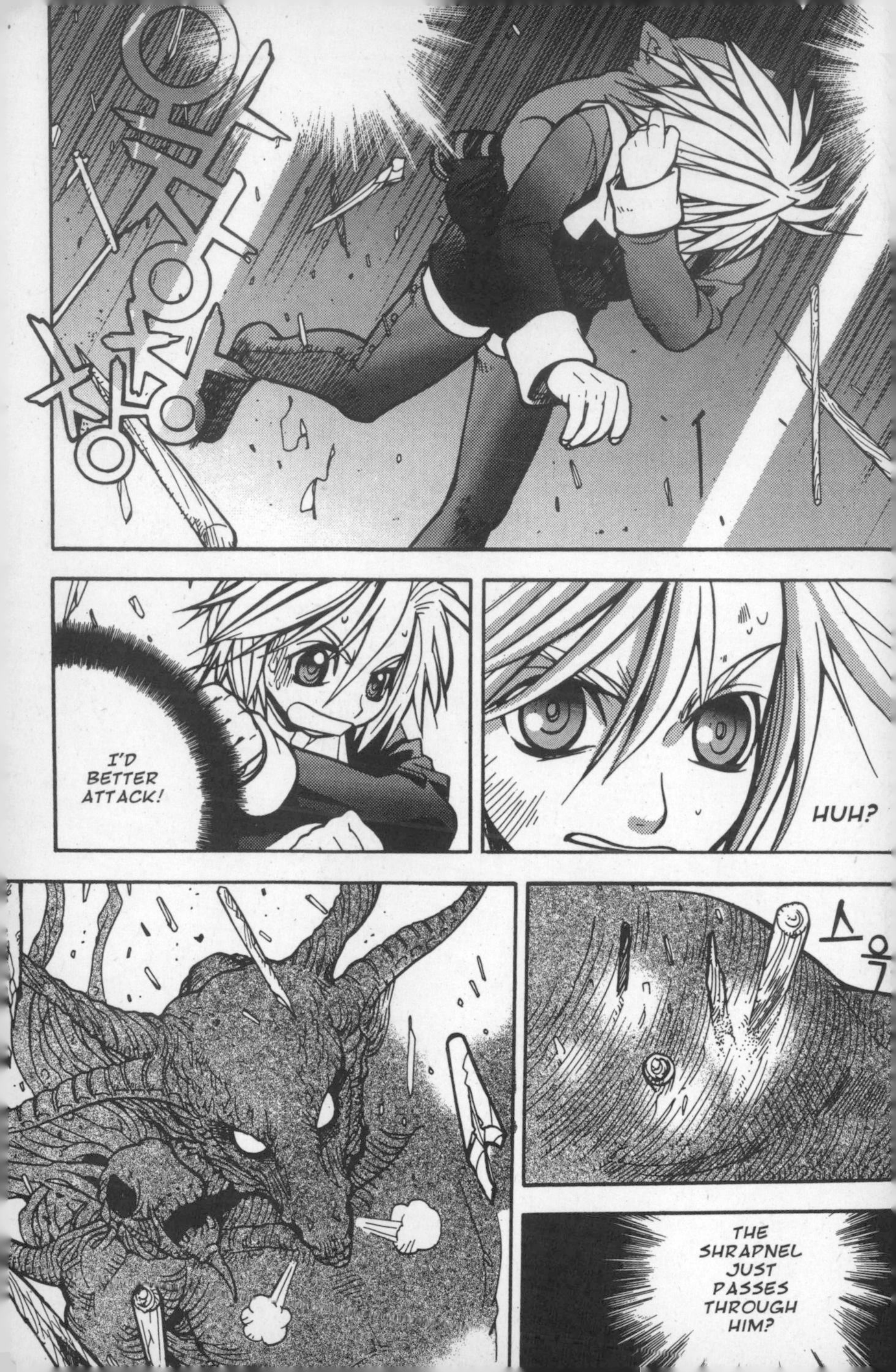
I'D BETTER ATTACK!
HUH?
THE SHRAPNEL JUST PASSES THROUGH HIM?

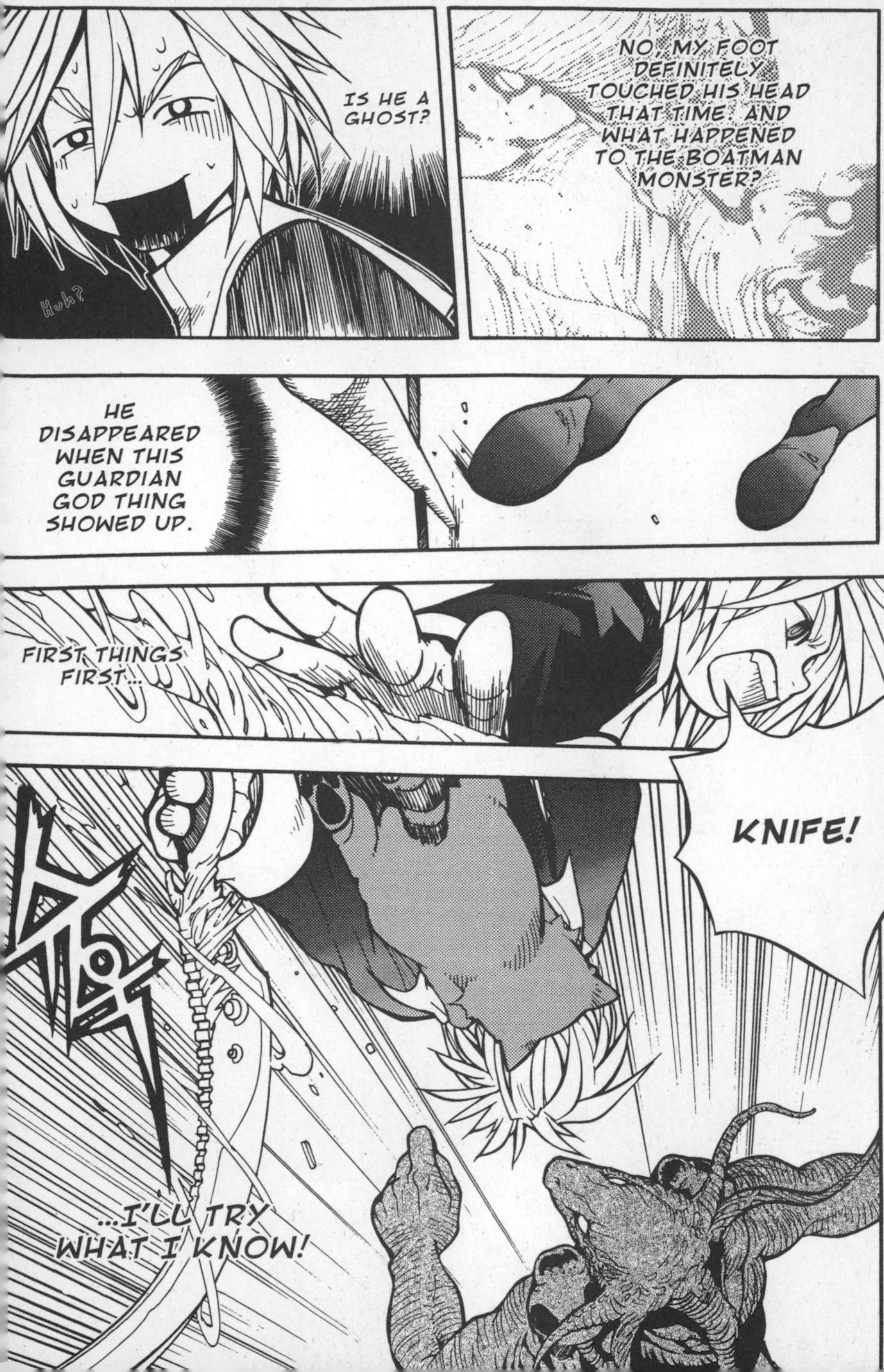
IS HE A GHOST?
Huh?
NO, MY FOOT DEFINITELY TOUCHED HIS HEAD THAT TIME. AND WHAT HAPPENED TO THE BOATMAN MONSTER?
HE DISAPPEARED WHEN THIS GUARDIAN GOD THING SHOWED UP.
FIRST THINGS FIRST...
KNIFE!
...I'LL TRY WHAT I KNOW!

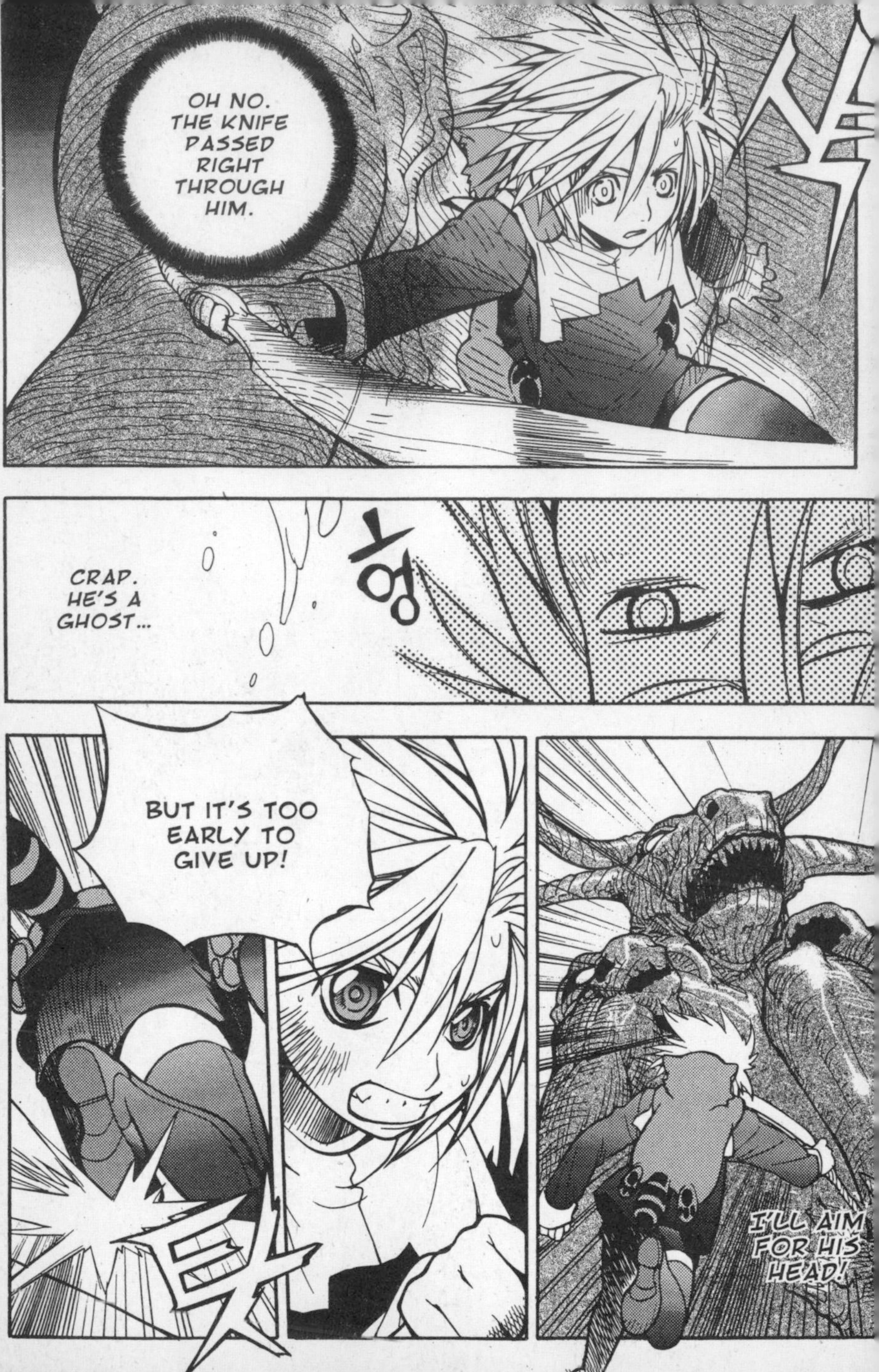
OH NO. THE KNIFE PASSED RIGHT THROUGH HIM.
CRAP. HE'S A GHOST...
BUT IT'S TOO EARLY TO GIVE UP!
I'LL AIM FOR HIS HEAD!

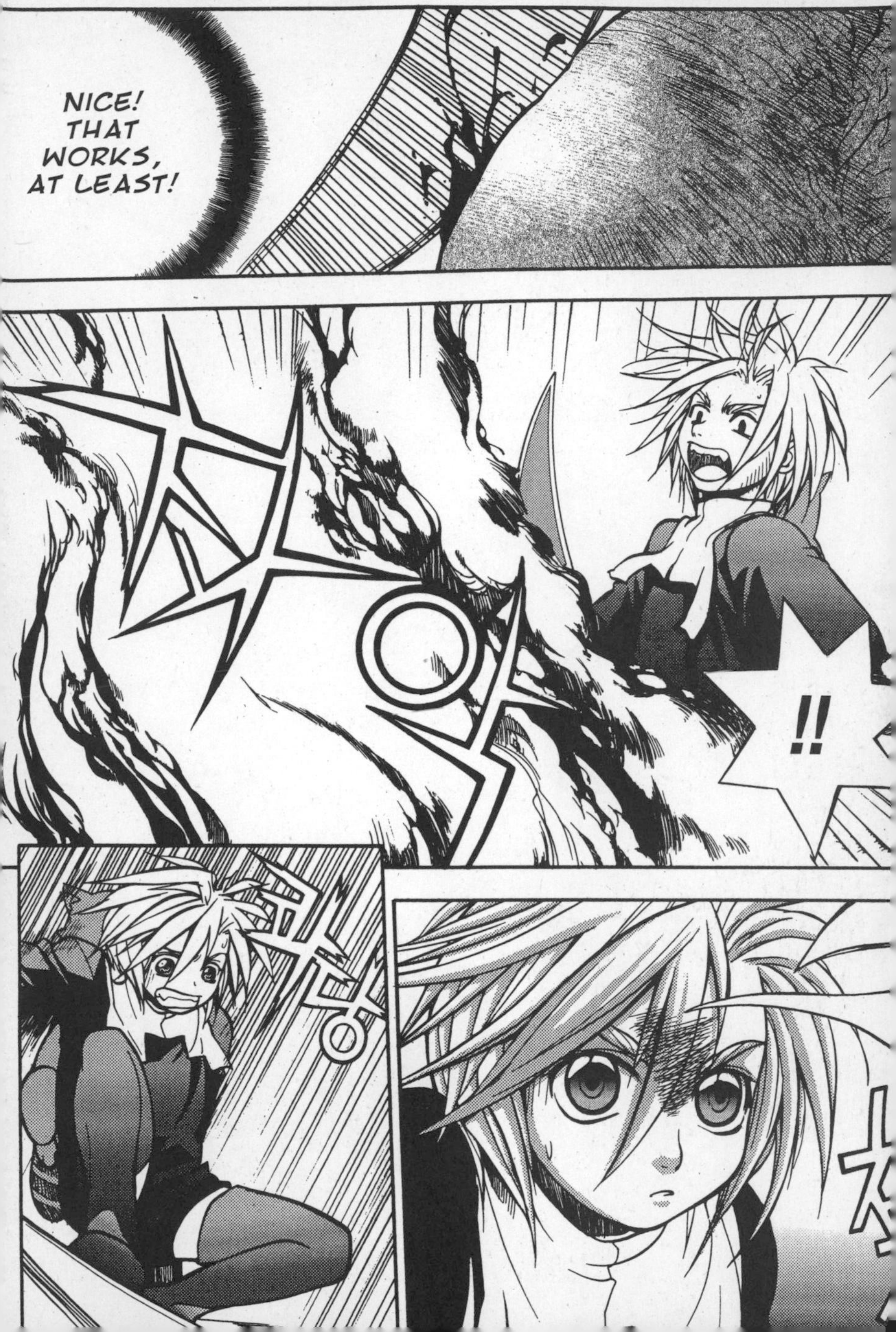
NICE! THAT WORKS, AT LEAST!
!!

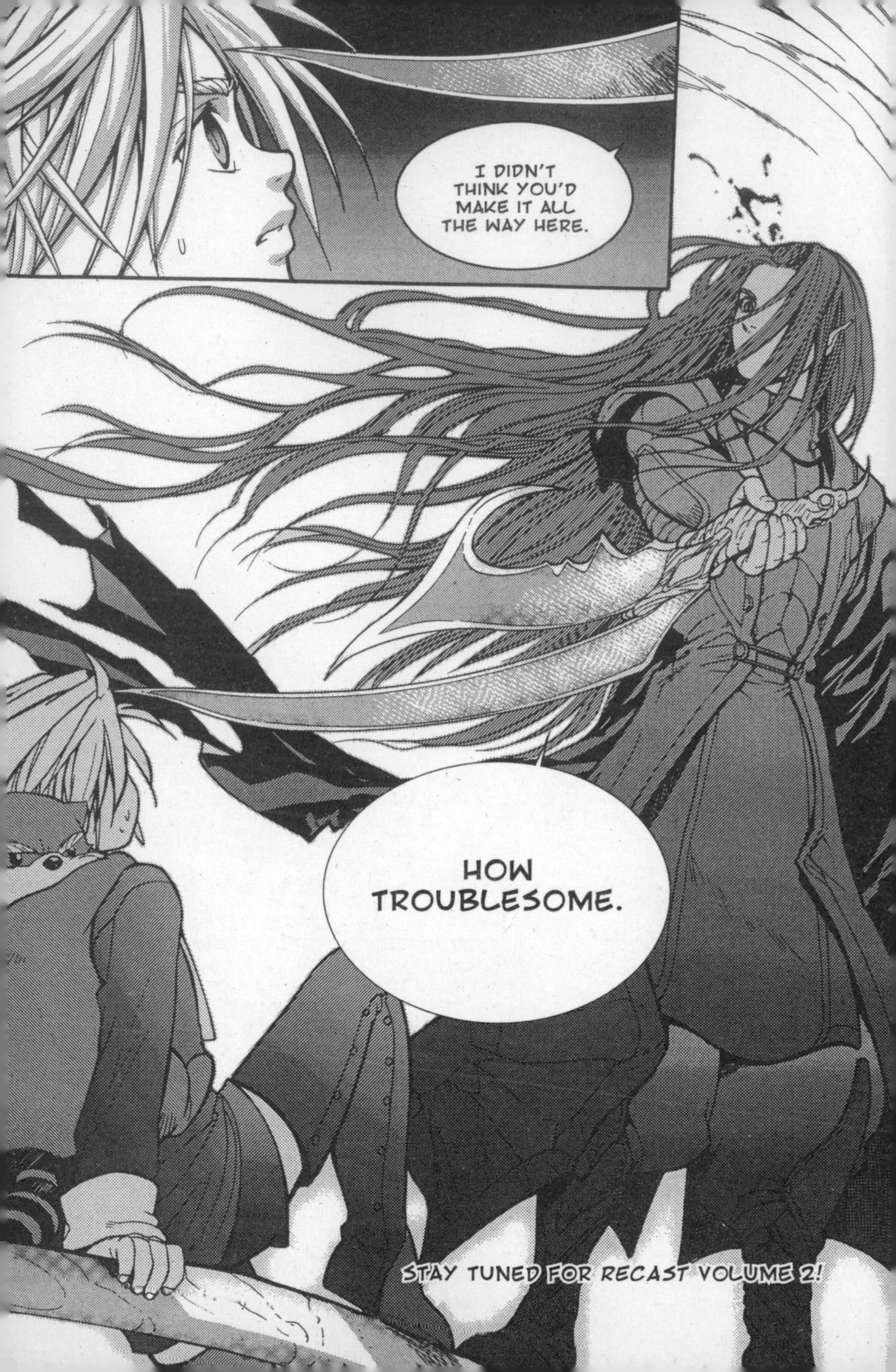
I DIDN'T THINK YOU'D MAKE IT ALL THE WAY HERE.
HOW TROUBLESOME.
STAY TUNED FOR RECAST VOLUME 2!

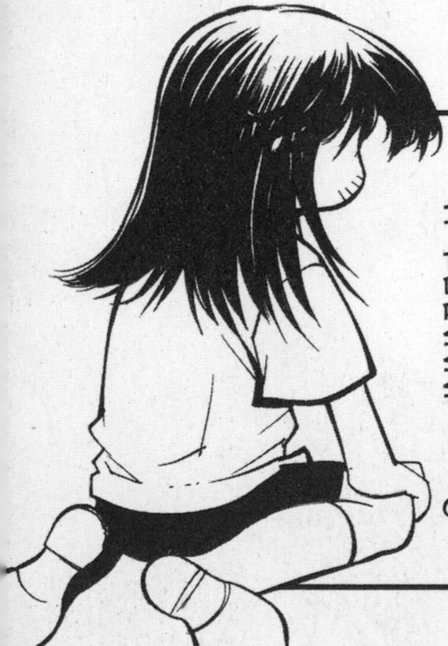

IT'S ALREADY BEEN A YEAR...

TIMES PASSES SO QUICKLY. I DIDN'T REALLY UNDERSTAND THE PASSAGE OF TIME WHEN I WAS A STUDENT. IT'S TRUE WHAT THEY SAY: "TIME FLIES AFTER YOUR SOPHOMORE YEAR IN COLLEGE."

OCTOBER 2003

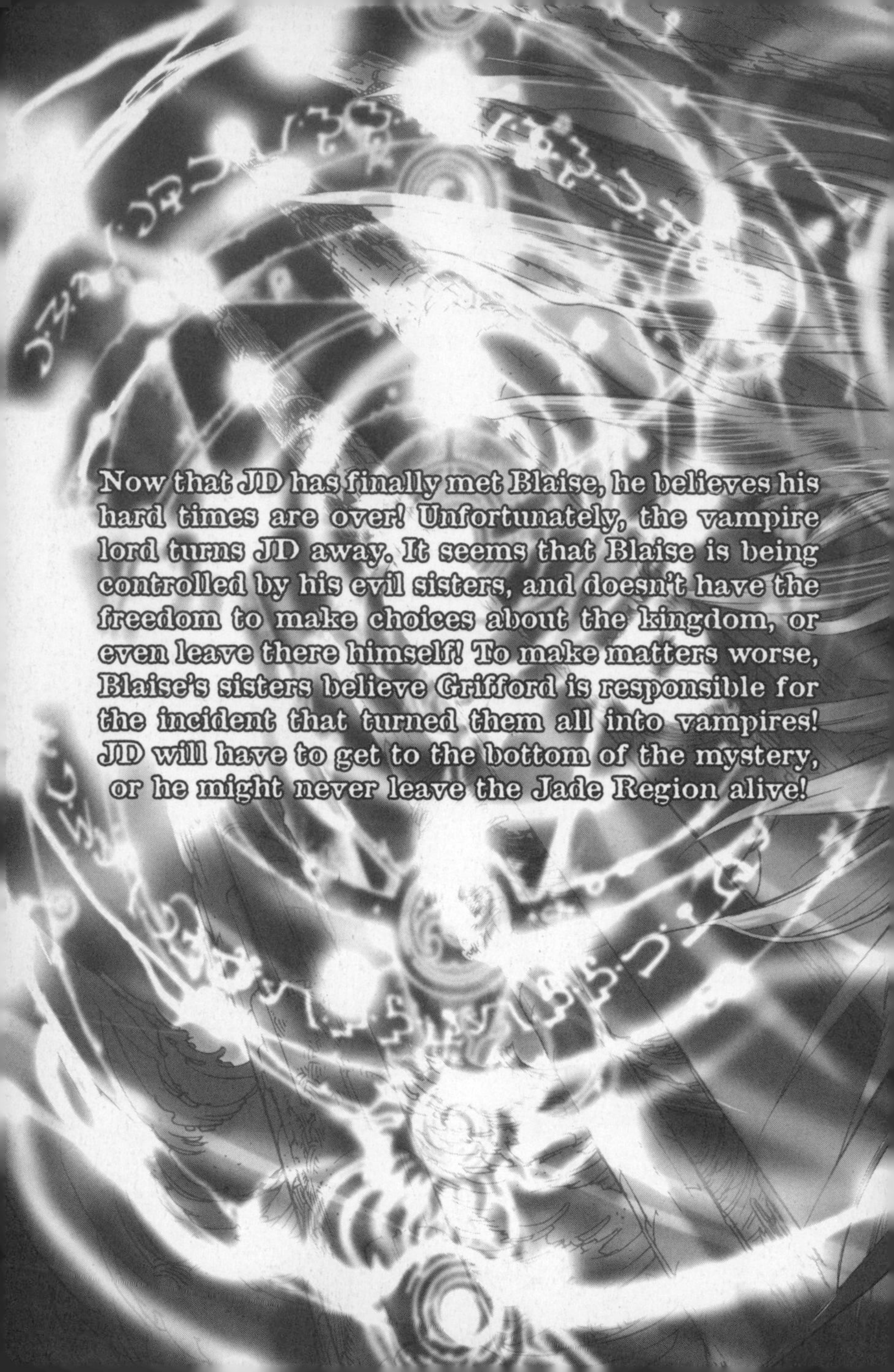

Now that JD has finally met Blaise, he believes his hard times are over! Unfortunately, the vampire lord turns JD away. It seems that Blaise is being controlled by his evil sisters, and doesn't have the freedom to make choices about the kingdom, or even leave there himself! To make matters worse, Blaise's sisters believe Grifford is responsible for the incident that turned them all into vampires! JD will have to get to the bottom of the mystery, or he might never leave the Jade Region alive!

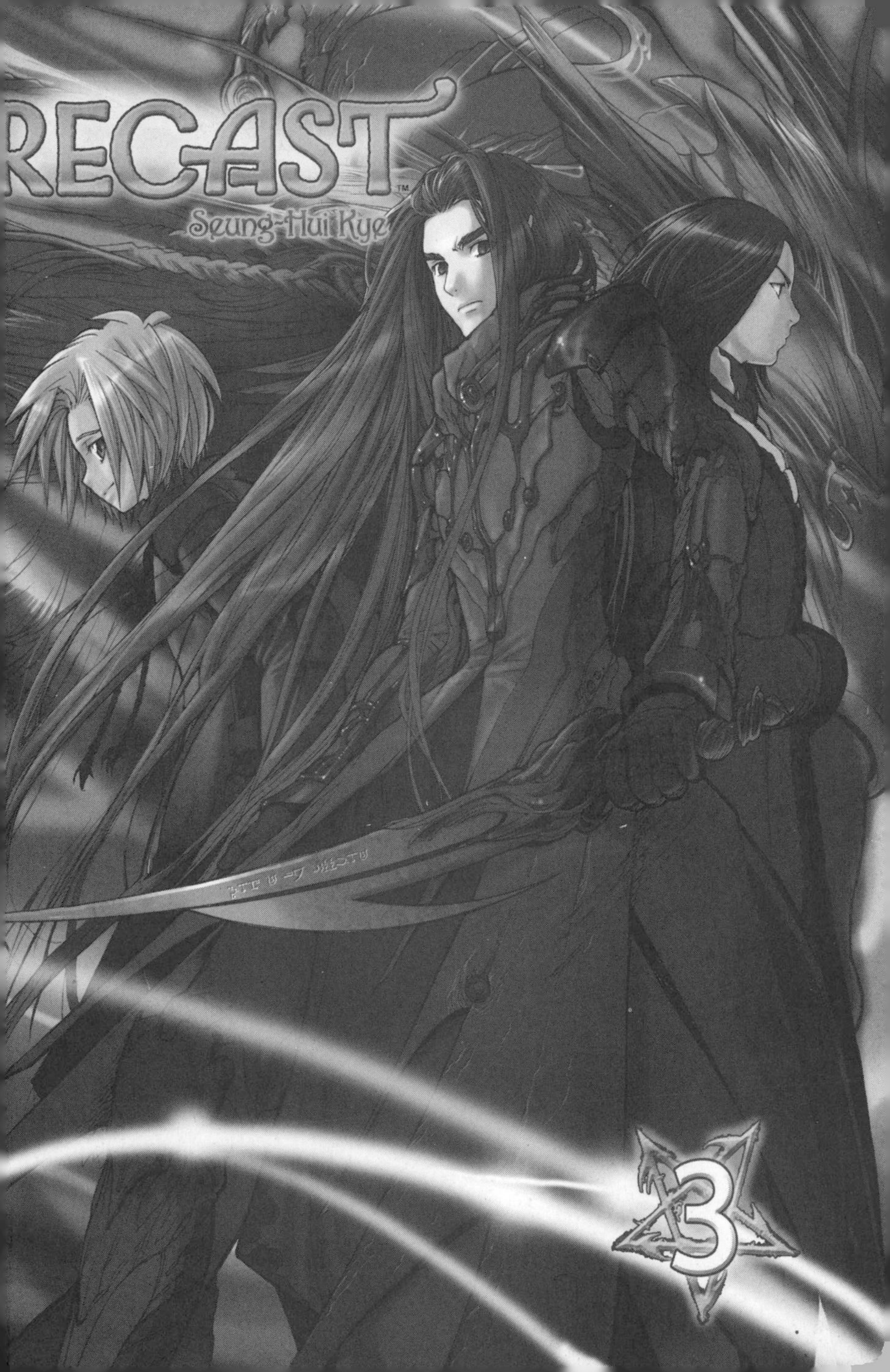
RECAST™
Seung-Hui Kye
3

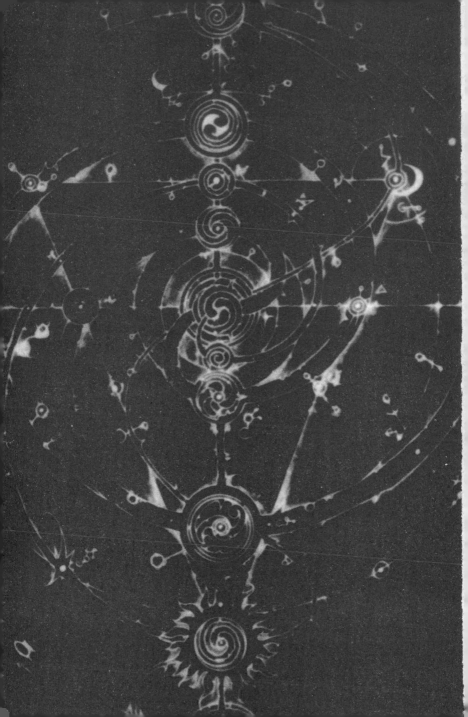